Journey of No Return

Journey of No Return

FIVE GERMAN–SPEAKING
LITERARY EXILES IN BRITAIN,
1933–1945

Richard Dove

Libris

First published 2000

Copyright © Richard Dove, 2000

Libris
10 Burghley Road
London NW5 1UE

A catalogue record for this book is available from the British Library

ISBN 1 870352 36 X

Designed and produced by Kitzinger, London
Printed and bound by Biddles Ltd, Guildford

Contents

List of Illustrations   vii
Acknowledgements   viii
Note on Sources   ix

INTRODUCTION   I

PART ONE: The Flight of Intellectuals
Departure . . .   15
   Alfred Kerr. The King of Critics   17
   Max Herrmann-Neiße. The Poet as Outsider   20
   Karl Otten. A Writer of Conviction   23
   Robert Neumann. With the Pens of Others   27
   Stefan Zweig. The World's Most Translated Living Author   31
. . . and Arrival   35

PART TWO: The Waiting Room (1933–1936)
   The Cultural Context   38
   Stefan Zweig: 'Miles away from Politics'   43
   Robert Neumann: Lost in Translation   63
   Max Herrmann-Neiße: 'My Life is ever Emptier'   74
   Alfred Kerr: 'An Irreproachable and Harmless Young
      Man of 67 Years'   88

PART THREE: Isolation or Integration (1936–1939)
Aspects of Appeasement   97
   Karl Otten: The Shadow of Spain   102
   Alfred Kerr: Living 'from Miracle to Miracle'   118
   Max Herrmann-Neiße: 'Monologue on a Foreign Stage'   126

The End of Austria   139

  Stefan Zweig: The Burden of Success   142

  Robert Neumann: An Expert in Survival   151

Peace in Our Time   159

PART FOUR: Enemy Aliens (1939–41)

The Phoney War and Internment   168

  'Concentration Camp, English Style':
    Robert Neumann's Internment Diary   174

  The World of Yesterday   184

  'Quietly and Inconspicuously'   189

'Doing Their Bit' – German Writers at the BBC   195

  'Marching On': Karl Otten as Scriptwriter   197

  'Serving the Cause': Alfred Kerr and the BBC   203

PART FIVE: No Man's Land (1941–45)

Writers without Language   207

  Death of a European   209

  Metamorphosis: The Making of an 'English' Author   216

  Alfred Kerr: The Limits of Cultural Mobility   223

'After the War is Over. . .'   229

  Thoughts on Germany   231

  Free Austria   247

PART SIX: Return Journey

'Once an Emigré, Always an Emigré':
    the Reception of Exile Literature in Post-War Germany   255

NOTES   267

BIBLIOGRAPHY   290

INDEX   301

List of Illustrations

Following page 148

1   Stefan Zweig in Alexandra Palace television studio, London 1937 (photo. Eduard Fitbauer)

2   Stefan Zweig in the garden of his house in Bath, 1940 (photo. G. Altmann, reproduced from Newman Flower's *Just as it Happened*)

3   Alfred Kerr in 1941 (Stiftung Akademie der Künste, Berlin)

4   Alfred Kerr, his daughter Judith and his wife Julia *c.* 1941 (Stiftung Akademie der Künste, Berlin)

5   Max Herrmann-Neiße, drawing by Martin Bloch, 1936 (private collection)

6   Max Herrmann-Neiße in Hyde Park, 1935 (Universitäts- und Landesbibliothek, Münster)

7   Karl Otten, drawing by Egon Schiele, 1914 (Historisches Museum der Stadt Wien)

8   Karl Otten in the garden of 58 Hampstead Way, Golders Green, 1939 (Otten Estate)

9   Robert Neumann in 1936 (private collection)

10 Robert Neumann in the garden of the 'Plague House', Cranbrook, Kent, after 1948 (reproduced from Robert Neumann, *Stimmen der Freunde*, Kurt Desch Verlag)

Acknowledgements

Writing a book is often a lonely activity but one which also depends crucially on the cooperation of others. I should like to thank the staff at the following libraries and archives for their help and advice in locating the appropriate sources: the Deutsches Literaturarchiv, Marbach am Neckar (particularly Frau Ingrid Kussmaul and Dr Ingrid Belke); the Österreichische Nationalbibliothek, Handschriftensammlung, Vienna (particularly Dr Eva Irblich); the Dokumentationsarchiv des Öster-reichischen Widerstandes, Vienna (particularly Dr Siegwart Gangl-mair); the Theatermuseum, Vienna; the Stiftung Archiv der Akademie der Künste, Berlin; the Bundesarchiv, Koblenz; the Deutsches Exil-archiv 1933–45, Deutsche Bibliothek, Frankfurt am Main (particularly Marie-Luise Hahn); the British Library, London; the Newspaper Library, Colindale; the Public Record Office, Kew; the Library of the Religious Society of Friends, London; the University of Reading Library (particularly Michael Bott); the Institute of Germanic Studies, London (particularly Bill Abbey); the BBC Written Archives Centre, Caversham; the BBC Sound Archive; and the Gollancz Archive (Livia Gollancz).

I am also grateful to a number of individuals: to Ellen Otten, whose copious memory (usually confirmed by an appropriate document) was a source of constant surprise and inspiration; Hermann Ruch, who generously supplied information on several points; Martin Esslin, for information on the BBC German Service; Louise Haworth and Edith Crossman for their memories of Karl Otten; Elisabeth Vear, for her lively reminiscences of Robert Neumann; Judith Kneale-Kerr, for talking to me about her father, the late Desmond Flower, for his memories of Stefan Zweig and for his ready fund of information about Cassells. My publisher offered sensible advice; Charmian Brinson and Iris Dove read parts of the manuscript and made various useful suggestions; Christine Shuttleworth compiled the index.

I am also grateful to the following for permission to quote from published or unpublished material: Michael Neumann, Zollikon and

Liepmann AG, Zurich, for Robert Neumann; Ellen Otten, Minusio/ Locarno, for Karl Otten; Atrium Verlag for Stefan Zweig; Sir Michael Kerr and Judith Kneale-Kerr for Alfred Kerr; Verlag Zweitausendeins for Max Herrmann-Neiße. Finally, I am indebted to the British Academy and the Leverhulme Trust for financial support to pursue research for parts of this book.

NOTE ON SOURCES

My research for this book has naturally included reading the published works of the five authors concerned; some of these were never published in English or, if they were, are long out of print. Some works are available only in German. The translations from any such German texts are my own. Inevitably, I have also made extensive use of unpublished sources held in the following libraries, archives and private collections:

BBC SA	BBC Sound Archive, London
BBC WAC	BBC Written Archives Centre, Caversham
BL MS	British Library, London (Department of Manuscripts)
DEA	Deutsche Bibliothek, Deutsches Exilarchiv 1933–45 (German Library, German Exile Archive 1933–45), Frankfurt am Main
DLA	Deutsches Literaturarchiv (German Literary Archive), Marbach am Neckar
DÖW	Dokumentationsstelle des Österreichischen Widerstandes (Documentation Centre of the Austrian Resistance), Vienna
ÖNB	Österreichische Nationalbibliothek, Handschriftensammlung (Austrian National Library, Manuscripts Department), Vienna
Otten Estate	Unpublished papers and manuscripts by Karl Otten, held by Ellen Otten, Minusio/Locarno
PRO	Public Record Office, Kew
Reading	University of Reading Library
St.Bib	Stadtbibliothek (City Library), Vienna
SAdK	Alfred-Kerr-Archiv, Stiftung Akademie der Künste (Academy of Arts), Berlin

Going into exile is 'the journey of no return'. Anyone who sets out on it dreaming of coming home is lost. He may return – but the place he will find is no longer the one he left. He may return to people he missed, to places he loved and did not forget, to the region where his own language is spoken. But he never returns home.

Carl Zuckmayer, A Part of Myself, *translated by Richard and Clara Winston (1970); first published as* Als wär's ein Stück von mir *(1966).*

Introduction

History is highly selective, imposing a present perspective on past events, so that whatever is perceived as inappropriate, unimportant or uncomfortable from a contemporary viewpoint can be marginalised or even ignored. This book is an attempt to rescue a piece of cultural history which has been widely neglected and which is in danger of vanishing from view: the story of German-speaking writers fleeing Nazi persecution who found refuge in Britain between 1933 and 1945. It seeks to trace the interaction of historical events and personal experience – and their literary construction in fiction and autobiography.

Hans-Albert Walter, the doyen of German exile studies, once remarked that German-speaking exile in Britain was 'a very sparsely worked field'. That situation has changed greatly and in recent years the topic has received considerable, if belated, scholarly attention in both Germany and Britain. The pioneering work in exile studies concentrated on 'basic research', i.e. on the historical and political framework of exile.[1] Equally, the earliest studies of exile in Britain were historical studies, focusing on aspects of government policy such as immigration practice or internment, or the activities of political groups in exile.[2] These were followed by general historical studies or collections of historical documents.[3] Other publications adopted a sociological perspective, seeking to illuminate 'the ambiguities of assimilation' or to document the contribution of German-speaking Jews to British society.[4] There has also been a growing number of biographical accounts, often based on oral history, which attempt to make the everyday experience of exile comprehensible to the outsider.

Contributions to the field of culture in British exile have been less common, but there have been important volumes focusing on specific aspects, such as film and theatre or the visual arts.[5] There have been relatively few studies of exile literature in Britain. Sylvia Patsch's pioneering study of Austrian writers in exile in Britain, including chapters on the English-language novels of Hans Flesch-Brunningen, Robert Neumann and Hermynia zur Mühlen, has been followed up only sporadically.[6] There have been isolated studies of individual authors, such as Stefan Zweig, Erich Fried, Hermynia zur Mühlen or Paul Frischauer, but these have understandably sought to portray a complete life, in which the exile period sometimes played only a subsidiary role. In recent years several collections of essays have appeared but so far no single book has dealt with the unique parameters of literary exile in Britain and their effect on German-speaking authors.

The very definition of exile is fluid. It was, for example, an administrative measure used by the Bolshevik regime in Russia or the fascist government in Italy to banish political opponents to isolated and inaccessible places. The Nazis chose to imprison their opponents in concentration camps. Those who had fled the country to escape this fate were, in the official jargon of the Nazi regime, 'Emigranten' (émigrés), a term rejected by most of those it designated. In his poem 'Über die Bezeichnung Emigranten' ('Concerning the Term Emigrant'), Brecht remarked that an émigré was someone who had left voluntarily, which he and his like had not. They considered themselves 'Exilanten' – exiles. To the countries which received them, however, they were neither émigrés nor exiles, but 'refugees'. Much of the history of the thirties might be written in the semantic spaces between these three words.

The main influx of exiles into Britain did not begin until 1938–39, following the annexation of Austria and the Sudetenland, and the horrors of the 'Kristallnacht' pogrom. Studies of exile in Britain have consequently focused almost exclusively on the years after 1938. The present study seeks to redress this imbalance by assigning equal weight to the earlier years, some aspects of which are dealt with here for the first time. It does not pretend to be a history of German literature in exile in Britain, but rather an essay in collective biography, following the lives in exile of five prominent literary figures who found refuge in London after 1933: three Germans – the doyen of Berlin theatre critics, Alfred Kerr, the poet Max Herrmann-Neiße and the novelist and journalist Karl Otten, as well as two Austrians – the novelist Robert Neumann and Stefan Zweig, who had gained international fame with a series of historical biographies. With the notable exception of Zweig, the exile biographies of these writers remain largely unwritten, their literary work in exile virtually forgotten.

The choice of these five authors requires brief comment. They have been chosen because of obvious biographical parallels – and divergencies. Firstly, they were among only a handful of writers who sought sanctuary in Britain during the first years of exile. (Neumann, Herrmann-Neiße and Zweig all came to London in 1933, Kerr in 1935, Otten in 1936.) With the exception of the celebrated dramatist Ernst Toller (whose story I have told elsewhere)[7] they were virtually the only established writers to do so; before their enforced emigration, they had all published a substantial body of work.

Some will object that the five writers include not a single woman. Among the younger émigrés who arrived in Britain during these early years were young women with literary aspirations, such as Ruth Feiner, Lilo Linke or Hilde Spiel, who actually published her first novel shortly before leaving her native Vienna to join the young writer Peter de Mendelssohn in London, where they married. However, they inevitably came with much less cultural baggage – and less emotional investment in the past. Though their names will reappear in these pages, this study is essentially concerned with the impact of exile on the *mature* writer. The only famous woman writer to reach Britain before the war was the Austrian novelist Hermynia zur Mühlen who, unlike the authors chosen, did not arrive until June 1939. Unlike them, she came with an excellent knowledge of English, having translated authors as diverse as Jerome K. Jerome and Upton Sinclair. Despite this, she came to Britain reluctantly and only after her failure to secure an entry visa to the United States.

Though the five authors selected show many biographical parallels, there are also divergencies. They did not belong to the same literary generation, four being in mid-career, while the fifth, Alfred Kerr, was already in his late sixties; nor did they represent a coherent literary group, indeed in some cases they had never even met. Moreover, the conditions of exile ensured that there were often only perfunctory contacts between them. Alfred Kerr and Max Herrmann-Neiße, who had been united in mutual regard for many years in Berlin, met infrequently in London; Karl Otten and Robert Neumann shared exile in Britain for twenty years, but met only once, their acquaintance blossoming only when they became neighbours during their second (voluntary) exile in Switzerland. Furthermore, they offer virtually no examples of literary collaboration: even the film treatment of *Manon Lescaut*, on which Zweig and Neumann collaborated, was never filmed.

The most striking common feature of these five lives is the involuntary conjuncture of the personal and the political. The exiles were, however unwillingly, figures in a political landscape. Even those who considered themselves totally unpolitical, like Stefan Zweig, found that politics increasingly intruded on their lives. Careers which had flowed along very different channels before 1933 suddenly began to converge, forced into confluence by the sheer pressure of external events. The primary aim of this book is therefore implicit in its method: while tracing the course of individual biographies, it will also consider them as a collective paradigm of literary exile in Britain.

The State of Exile

'Exile is death,' wrote the Roman poet Ovid, banished to the very edge of the Empire on the Black Sea. 'Exile is life,' proclaimed the French writer Victor Hugo in the defiant inscription he placed over the door of his house in exile in Guernsey.[8] Both statements are of course rhetorical: the day-to-day reality of exile is both more fantastical and more mundane.

There is no doubt that many of the intellectuals who fled Hitler's Germany had already, in the final years of the Weimar Republic, drifted into a state of alienation amounting to 'intellectual exile'. But this was immeasurably different from the effects of the physical exile which ensued after January 1933.

In the early phases of exile it was the material problems which predominated, the need to find some immediate means of subsistence, a problem exacerbated by the abrupt loss or relativization of professional skills. The lawyer loses his power of advocacy in a foreign language, the scholar may feel his knowledge diminished, the doctor finds his skills not even recognised. For the professional classes, to which German-speaking émigrés predominantly belonged, exile therefore meant a rapid impoverishment.

But exile is not simply a material predicament, it is also a state of mind, a sense of estrangement. It means an almost complete dislocation of the normal patterns of life: the physical separation from friends and even family, the abrupt loss of job and income, the disruption of daily routines, the disappearance of familiar landmarks, the sudden absence of the social and cultural certainties which previously buttressed existence.

Exile is above all a sense of dispossession. For most of the refugees from Hitler's Third Reich, life in exile was a shadow existence, a mere semblance of the 'real' life they had led in Frankfurt or Munich, Berlin or Vienna. The exile's sense of displacement is vividly evoked in a short anecdote by the Austrian writer Alfred Polgar. It concerns an émigré who is finally offered a job in Australia, and hastens to tell a friend the good news. 'Australia?' the friend asks, 'Isn't that a bit far away?' – only to receive the reply: 'Far? Far from where?' The lapidary answer came to encapsulate the loss of roots, the disorientation of those whose universe has lost its centre.

The twentieth century did not invent the phenomenon of exile, but it did add a new dimension to it, which often heightened the despair of the victims. To survive, twentieth-century exiles must master the black arts of bureaucracy, learning how to acquire the passports and visas which are the sole evidence that they exist, and to obtain the affidavits, letters of recommendation and work permits which alone will enable them to prolong that existence.

The Loss of Language

For many German-speaking refugees, and certainly for those who arrived in Britain, exile entailed the loss not only of their homeland but also of their native language – and for none more so than the writer, for whom language is the very tool of his trade. Virtually all the authors who fled Hitler's Germany in 1933 had already seen their work proscribed by the regime, a measure entailing severance from their publishing outlets and the abrupt loss of royalty income from German sales. Most crucially, it meant the loss of a reading public with whom they shared a common language and cultural heritage. They were confronted with the challenge of adapting to an alien culture, a challenge which was

perhaps greater in Britain than in any other country of refuge. Since
there was no reading public for German books, the exiled writer was – to
a greater extent than in Paris, Prague or Amsterdam – dependent on
access to the British market, that is, on the mediation of the translator.
This dependence became more acute in the course of the decade, as
Nazism spread across Central Europe, eliminating the residual market
for German books outside the Third Reich.

The economic prospects for German writers in the British market,
and the difficulties they encountered, varied greatly with what they
wrote. A journalist cannot really practice his or her craft through translation, but may find the transition to a new language easier than a
creative writer. Several journalists were eventually able to make a career
in British journalism, notable examples being Stefan Lorant, Sebastian
Haffner and Willi Frischauer. The creative writer perhaps has more
chance of being translated, but being more concerned with linguistic
connotation and association, has greater difficulty in adopting the
language of the host country, though, as we shall see, several younger
writers did make the transition to writing in English.

The material and artistic problems of exile were even greater for the
dramatist, whose work depends crucially on the mediation of actor and
director. To be staged, a play must not only be translated, but also
adapted to the requirements of local taste and convention. Plays by
exiled dramatists were rarely staged in Britain and even when they were,
the author often found himself eclipsed by the adaptor. Bruno Frank's
comedy *Storm in a Teacup* (*Sturm im Wasserglas*) achieved great success
in London in an 'Anglo-Scottish' version by J. M. Bridie. British critics
named it 'the best comedy of 1936', but gave the credit largely to the
adaptor: 'Bridie has never given us anything funnier' declared the *Daily
Mail*. Ernst Toller's play *Die blinde Göttin* was adapted for the London
stage as *Blind Man's Buff* by Denis Johnston. Though Toller insisted on
the play being billed as a work of joint authorship, only the opening
scene was actually taken from his original play.

The poet, drawing on cultural and linguistic allusions which often
fail to cross frontiers, is even more vulnerable to the vagaries of exile.
Poetry is always a minority taste, its publication subject to acknowledged commercial constraints. In exile, these limitations are com-

pounded by the intrinsic problems of translation, which will rarely convey more than an approximation of the author's original meaning. By the same token, the poet is hardly likely to countenance writing in a second language, which, as the Austrian poet Theodor Kramer recognised, is merely a means of practical communication:

Die Sprache lern' ich nicht um zu gestalten;
es ist für mich genug, sie zu verstehen,
des fremden Landes Sitten einzuhalten.
Es drängt mich nicht, in ihnen aufzugehen.

I do not learn the language in order to compose / it is enough for me to understand it / and to keep the customs of a foreign country. / I have no urge to assimilate to them.[9]

Anglo-German relations

The history of Anglo-German literary relations is a chequered one, which in the twentieth century has often amounted to little more than mutual incomprehension; 'literary' judgements have all too often been determined by the prevailing political constellation.

One of the most significant differences between British writers and their German-speaking counterparts lay in the tradition of the political writer in Germany, which can be traced back to Börne, Heine, Büchner and Freiligrath. It was a tradition which, despite such examples as Swift or Defoe, lacked any direct equivalent in English literature. The interaction of writing and politics, elaborated by Heinrich Mann in his influential essay 'Geist und Tat' of 1910, reached its peak in Germany and Austria in the inter-war years. This was not merely exemplified in personal commitment and involvement – though an unusually high proportion of writers were politically active – but can be traced in the subject-matter of literary works and their critical reception. Such a political focus was particularly conspicuous in the theatre where the plays of Toller, Brecht, Horvath and others enacted and interpreted the tumultuous political reality of the Weimar Republic.

However, there were also numerous novels with political subject-matter, among them Ernst Ottwalt's *Ruhe und Ordnung* ('Law and

Order') (1929), Theodor Plievier's *Des Kaisers Kulis* ('The Kaiser's Coolies') (1930), Klaus Neukranz's *Barrikaden am Wedding* ('Barricades in Wedding') (1930), and Erik Reger's *Union der festen Hand* ('Union of the Firm Hand') (1931), a fictional representation of the economic and social history of the Weimar Republic. In the Republic's highly politicised atmosphere, some works gained a notoriety they hardly deserved, the reception of Remarque's *All Quiet on the Western Front* in 1929 being particularly illuminating. Left-liberal critics initially welcomed the book as an anti-war novel, provoking a critical backlash from the nationalist right, who denounced it as a pacifist tract. Remarque's essentially unpolitical bestseller was thus transformed into a symbol of Weimar pacifism, becoming a focus for fundamental political divisions within the Republic. Such strident tones were rarely heard in English letters. The reception of R. C. Sherriff's *Journey's End* (or the restrained acclaim for Wilfred Owen's war poems) in the same year makes an illuminating cultural contrast.

The Weimar state itself was quick to acknowledge the political resonance of literary works. The prosecution of the poet J. R. Becher on grounds of 'literary high treason', following the publication of his book *Levisite*, or the banning of novels such as Hans Marchwitza's *Sturm auf Essen* ('Attack on Essen') under a political decree which was also used to ban the Brecht/Ottwalt film *Kuhle Wampe*, would have been unthinkable in Britain. There such scandals were reserved for alleged infringements of public decency, exemplified by the banning of *Ulysses* or the obscenity prosecutions in 1928 against *Lady Chatterley's Lover* and Radclyffe Hall's *Well of Loneliness*.

It is almost a cliché of literary history that the thirties were a decade of commitment amongst writers in Britain, though it is one which requires some qualification. The thirties were designated a decade, a discrete literary period, even before they had expired, John Lehmann attempting to establish its literary credentials with the anthology *New Writing in England*. Others were quick to follow. Looking back in 1940, F. R. Leavis designated the thirties 'the Marxist decade', though very few of its leading literary figures were Marxists; Arthur Calder-Marshall, writing a year later, was perhaps more accurate in calling them 'the pink decade'.

One of the leading English writers who was at least 'pink', Stephen Spender, wrote in retrospect of 'a literary movement called the thirties', the leading figures of which were of course Auden, Isherwood, Day Lewis – and Spender himself. Auden's group has indeed become emblematic of the literary thirties. The critic Samuel Hynes embraced this version of the decade in the title of his study *The Auden Generation: Literature and Politics in England in the 1930s* (1976). The Trinity of Auden, Isherwood and Spender inevitably also appear on the cover of Valentine Cunningham's *British Writers of the Thirties* (1988). English poetry in the thirties, as represented by Auden, Spender, MacNeice and Day Lewis, and perhaps embellished by the names of John Cornford and Julian Bell, certainly seems to corroborate the thesis of a political decade in literature. However, a literary period – if indeed any such thing exists – is not defined solely by its poetry, but equally by its plays and its prose fiction.

London theatre in the thirties was politically and aesthetically conservative, its repertoire consisting largely of drawing-room comedies, thrillers and musical revues. West End theatre management was parochial and unadventurous, dominated by a commercial ethos in which success at the box office was paramount. In such circumstances, the production of modern foreign plays was limited to the 'little theatres' and Sunday evening play societies, both run on club lines. The shortcomings of the English theatre were more than evident to the foreign observer. Bertolt Brecht, visiting London in 1934, called the situation 'antediluvian' (*'vorsintflutlich'*).

Although Berlin had become the theatre capital of Europe in the twenties, modern German drama was still virtually unknown in London, Brecht's own work providing a case in point. In 1933 the Brecht-Weill ballet *Die sieben Todsünden* (*The Seven Deadly Sins*) was produced at the Savoy Theatre under the title *Anna Anna* – playing for just three performances. Early in 1935 the BBC broadcast the first concert performance of *The Threepenny Opera*, which was comprehensively damned by the leading music critic Ernest Newman. The first production of a Brecht play, the highly untypical *Señora Carrar's Rifles*, took place at Unity Theatre in 1938 as part of international solidarity for the Spanish Republic: it was a play for Spain, which merely happened to be by a German author. Thereafter there was a gap of nearly twenty years before Brecht's work was finally introduced to the British public by the Berliner Ensemble.

As in any other period, most of the literary output of the thirties satisfied the need for escape and reassurance. Much of it followed a tradition of popular writing ranging from the detective novel to romantic fiction – genres encapsulated in the books of Agatha Christie and Daphne du Maurier. *Murder in the Vicarage*, which first introduced Miss Marple, prefaced the decade in 1930; the politically fateful years 1936 and 1938 also saw the publication of *Jamaica Inn* and *Rebecca*. Predictably, English comic writing continued to minister to the need for escapism. P. G. Wodehouse, who continued the amiable career he had begun almost two decades earlier, described his literary method as 'making a sort of musical comedy without music and ignoring real life altogether'.

In reviewing the thirties, it is also easy to forget that literary lions such as Shaw and Wells were still writing – and to many foreign observers remained the representative figures of English writing; their names will appear more than once in the following pages. Aldous Huxley and Virginia Woolf, both associated with the stylistic innovations of the twenties, also continued to write in the thirties, but their novels of the period are usually discussed only to compare them unfavourably with their earlier work. Perhaps more specific to the thirties is the number of widely-read novelists writing within the nineteenth-century tradition of realism, such as J. B. Priestley, Storm Jameson (whose name will also appear), A. J. Cronin, Howard Spring and Louis Golding, whose *Magnolia Street* became, like Priestley's *Angel Pavement*, a bestseller of the period.

The mere compilation of this list confirms that English writing did not lack social comment or concern: the single year 1933, for example, saw the publication of Walter Greenwood's *Love on the Dole*, Priestley's *English Journey* and George Orwell's *Down and Out in Paris and London*. Greenwood's novel was a bestseller, being turned into a play frequently performed by left-wing theatre groups. However, whatever the author's outrage at the social consequences of unemployment, it is ultimately an unpolitical book. Priestley's now-classic account 'of what one man saw and heard and thought and felt during a journey through England in the autumn of 1933' is a searching and sometimes bitter review of industrial decay and the human suffering it causes. *English Journey* proved to be a detour from which Priestley quickly returned to the beaten track: for the rest of the decade he worked largely for the theatre, writing several successful comedies in which social criticism is at best muted. Moreover, both Greenwood's and Priestley's works have a doggedly domestic perspective – in a year that saw fascism come to power in much of Central Europe. As to Orwell, always classified as a quintessentially 'thirties writer', *Down and Out* marked his literary debut. During the decade, his work alternated between documentary reportage (*The Road to Wigan Pier, Homage to Catalonia*) and fictional realism (*Keep the Aspidistra Flying, Coming up for Air*), but all of it was written in and about the political events of the decade. *Coming up for Air* is a novel permeated by the sense of approaching war. Orwell's narrator George Bowling is haunted by images of war: bombs, machine-guns firing from bedroom windows, rubber truncheons beating down.

Graham Greene's fiction of the thirties also has the authentic whiff of the period. With the exception of *Brighton Rock*, his novels (or 'entertainments' as he called them) are not concerned with the questions of Catholic conscience which later obsessed him. They are political thrillers, permeated by an atmosphere of fear and violence, a feeling of undeclared war. D., the protagonist of *The Confidential Agent*, for example, 'carried the war with him. Wherever D. was, there was the war. He could never understand that people were not aware of it.' He is haunted by the same visions of bombing-raids and shell-bursts as George Bowling. Significantly, the narrative opens with the arrival of a cross-channel ferry in Dover, the first port of call for any refugee arriving from Europe. The dominant theme of all Greene's 'entertainments' is the clash of the individual with dark totalitarian forces, summarising a dominant political experience of the decade. Greene and Orwell are among the very few thirties writers whose concerns echo the experience of Central European authors, but significantly *Coming up for Air* and *The Confidential Agent* were both published in 1939.

In truth, the thirties were not so much a discrete literary period, as two distinct periods intersecting and overlapping. Up to the middle of the decade, English writing had lacked any definitive political compass. Ernst Toller, the political writer *par excellence*, who lived in London from 1933 to 1936, was perceptive enough to register the change of attitude which took place during these years. Speaking at the International Writers' Conference in London in June 1936 (an event which surely documented the very change he spoke of) he commented that anyone reading the newspapers or visiting the theatre or talking to the man in the street might conclude that Britain was immune to the social upheavals which convulsed Europe: 'This country lives in a state of almost comfortable calm.' But beneath the surface, he detected an undercurrent of change which was particularly marked amongst young writers. Toller knew both Isherwood and Auden, indeed the latter had written the lyrics for Toller's anti-war play *No More Peace*, then running at one of London's leading 'little theatres'.

A perceptible change in the literary culture was certainly apparent in 1934–35: virtually all the major political props of the thirties literary stage date from the middle years of the decade. Thus *Left Review*, the very model of a Marxist literary journal, began publication in October 1934, the same year that saw Colletts bookshop established in Charing Cross Road. Unity Theatre, founded to bring political drama to the audiences other theatres could not reach, did not open until February 1936, the same month that brought the first mention of the Left Book Club – an enterprise for which, incidentally, there had been several precedents in Germany, most notably the Büchergilde Gutenberg. Conspicuously, all of these enterprises roughly parallel the emergence of the Popular Front, promulgated at the Comintern Conference of July 1935.

In fact, political commitment was very much the prerogative of a younger generation of English writers, blossoming only after 1934–35, and finally focused by the Spanish Civil War. In some cases, commitment was cut short: John Cornford, Julian Bell and Christopher Caudwell were killed in Spain. In others, it went stale, most obviously in the case of Auden himself, who sailed for America in January 1939, turning his back on Europe – and also on commitment. Such willing self-exile in another English-speaking country stands in stark contrast to the enforced separation of German-speaking authors from their homeland and native language.

Looking back from the prudent perspective of New York, Auden famously dismissed the thirties as 'a low, dishonest decade'. His friend and literary collaborator Christopher Isherwood came much closer to defining the decade – if only in retrospect. In 1946 he published the novel *Prater Violet*, a semi-autobiographical account of his work as a scriptwriter for Gaumont-British on the film *Little Friend*. His protagonist Friedrich Bergmann is a larger-than-life figure, described as 'a tragic Punch'. He is in fact a portrait of the Austrian writer and film director Berthold Viertel, whom Isherwood presents as the representative of a literary and political period:

> There are meetings which are like recognitions: this was one of them. Of course we knew each other. The name, the voice, the features were inessential: I knew that face. It was the face of a political situation, an epoch. The face of Central Europe.[10]

The same face haunts the pages of this present study.

Part One

The Flight of the Intellectuals

DEPARTURE . . .

Adolf Hitler's accession to power in Germany on 30 January 1933, bringing to an end the parliamentary democracy of the Weimar Republic, was not only a political watershed, but also a radical disruption of cultural continuity. Nazi cultural policy was dedicated, from the first, to the ruthless elimination of all works tainted with 'cultural Bolshevism', a term which embraced anything connected, however tenuously, with artistic Modernism. The Nazis perceived literature as the most influential, and therefore potentially the most subversive of the arts. Even before the 'Seizure of Power', they had publicly threatened their literary opponents, most ominously when the *Völkischer Beobachter* had published a list of 'those representatives of a decadent and declining era' whose work they would suppress – a list including the names of many of the leading representatives of Weimar culture.

Many writers and intellectuals were slow to acknowledge these threats. On hearing the news that Hitler had become Reich Chancellor, the dramatist Georg Kaiser had commented, with memorable miscalculation: 'A skittle club has changed its committee.'[1] Most intellectuals had merely temporised, preferring to wait and see what would happen; many had been convinced that the new government would last no longer than those which had preceded it in the dying days of the Weimar Republic. One or two had taken the Nazis' threats at face value: the novelist Heinrich Mann, who then probably enjoyed a greater reputation in Germany than his brother Thomas, had fled in February. He had left Germany without luggage, carrying only an umbrella, in order not to draw attention to his departure. Others had prudently decided to

make a short stay abroad, accepting lecturing or broadcasting engage-
ments outside Germany. Thus the novelist Lion Feuchtwanger was in
the USA, the dramatist Ernst Toller in Switzerland, while Thomas
Mann had withdrawn to his house in Kusnacht, near Zurich.

Not all had been so circumspect. Many writers who opposed the new
regime gathered on 20 February 1933 for a meeting of the Schutz-
verband deutscher Schriftsteller (Association of German Writers). 'We
don't know in detail what will happen,' declared the journalist Carl von
Ossietzky, 'but let us swear one thing: whatever path we may tread in
the next few days and weeks – into prison, concentration camp or
emigration – let us remain true to our convictions.'² Ossietzky, like
every other speaker at this meeting, was arrested only eight days later.
On the night of 27 February 1933 the Reichstag was burnt down. It has
never been satisfactorily established whether the Nazis themselves were
responsible, but it is certain that they exploited the event to settle
accounts with many of their political opponents. Even before the flames
had been extinguished, police and SA units, working from lists which
had long been prepared, arrested some 4,000 prominent left-wingers,
including over 130 writers and journalists, ranging from Communists
like Ludwig Renn and Willi Bredel to pacifists like Carl von Ossietzky
and Otto Lehmann-Russbüldt.

Thereafter, the Nazis had moved rapidly to extend their hegemony
into every corner of German society. The crucial role they assigned to
culture, and their intuitive respect for the power of the written or
spoken word, are confirmed by their measures to police, and then to
monopolise, cultural production and diffusion. They had begun by
purging the Prussian Academy of Arts, forcing the novelist Heinrich
Mann to resign as President of the Academy's Literature Section, and
excluding other prominent writers whom they considered racially or
politically undesirable. In April the official *Börsenblatt des deutschen
Buchhandels* published a blacklist of writers whose works were to be
withdrawn from bookshops and libraries. The first climax of this
Gleichschaltung of German letters was reached with the book-burnings
on 10 May, when students organised by the Nazi Party plundered
university libraries of banned books and consigned them to the flames in
huge bonfires.

To extend their control over the written and spoken word, the Nazis founded the Reichsschriftumskammer (Reich Chamber of Literature), a guild-like organisation to which writers and publishers had to belong in order to exercise their profession. Membership was explicitly denied to 'non-aryans', to writers classified as 'Marxist' and to all those who had expressed their opposition to National Socialism. All members were required to make a declaration of loyalty to the new regime, a provision intended to ensure that only works which conformed to rigid Nazi criteria could be published in Germany.

In the weeks following the Reichstag Fire, many writers who had previously hesitated to leave Germany now resigned themselves to emigration. What had previously been a trickle of refugees swelled to a flood, as leading writers and artists fled from Germany in the greatest cultural emigration since the fall of Constantinople. The American journalist Dorothy Thompson, who witnessed these early days of Nazism, wrote that 'practically everybody who in world opinion has stood for what is currently called German culture prior to 1933 is now a refugee'. Almost all these exiles had exile thrust upon them. Some were forced to flee to escape imminent arrest or death, but for others the process of exile was more gradual and more prosaic, and they would leave Germany only after it became incontrovertibly clear that they could no longer publish their work and had therefore lost their livelihood.

The proscription of leading authors was followed by their expulsion from the 'national community'. In August, the Nazis issued the first list of those deprived of their German nationality, including among the thirty-three names those of five of Germany's most famous living writers – Heinrich Mann, Lion Feuchtwanger, Ernst Toller, the satirist Kurt Tucholsky and the respected theatre critic Alfred Kerr.

ALFRED KERR: THE KING OF CRITICS

Alfred Kerr was Germany's most famous theatre critic in the years of the Weimar Republic, though he came in fact from an older literary generation. Born in Breslau in Silesia in 1867, Kerr was a child of the 'Gründerzeit', the first years of the Hohenzollern Empire, in which

Germany had finally claimed its place among the great powers of Europe. Brought up in provincial Breslau, he had come to Berlin before he was twenty to seek literary fame and fortune. As the theatre critic of the daily paper *Der Tag*, he had established himself as the capital's most authoritative critical voice, whose incisive analysis and highly individual style raised criticism to an art form. He indeed considered himself an artist, always insisting that 'only he who can create a work of art should be allowed to pass judgement on one'.[3] Kerr was not only a master of language but a highly individual stylist. The novelist Robert Musil contended that a review by Kerr could be distinguished from anyone else's at twenty yards distance. Kerr's review would be contained in a series of aphoristic comments, divided carefully into paragraphs which were numbered consecutively with Roman numerals.

As a critic, Kerr had used his voice to promote the avant-garde: he had championed Ibsen and Strindberg, Schnitzler and George Bernard Shaw, whose reputation in Germany he claimed was almost entirely due to him. Above all, he had lauded Gerhart Hauptmann, developing a close friendship which failed to withstand the advent of Nazism. As editor of the literary journal *Pan*, he had also encouraged new poetic talents, such as the poet Klabund and his fellow-Silesian Max Herrmann-Neiße, his friendship with the latter persisting into their mutual exile in London.

The famous critic was also a passionate and frequent traveller, who wrote a number of travel books recording impressions of his visits – amongst others those to England in 1913 and 1922.[4] In 1928 he summed up his own success thus: 'Ultimately, I always had more ready money than I could use – which in my ignorance I left lying around until a friend advised me to put it into the bank. I would travel four months of the year wherever the fancy took me, to the four corners of the earth. I did nothing but fill diaries with scribble.'[5] The comment captures all Kerr's insouciance – and the impractical nature which would make it so hard for him to adapt to the exigencies of exile.

The most famous image of Kerr is the portrait painted, when he was forty years old, by Lovis Corinth. Kerr strikes a studiedly aristocratic pose, eyes looking over the head of the viewer, giving more than a hint of preciosity. The various photographs of him taken in the twenties and thirties all confirm this radiant self-assurance, showing a spruce and cultivated gentleman, waistcoat always buttoned high, tie or cravat knotted with meticulous care: a portrait of dandyish refinement. The eyes observe in frank curiosity, the gaze is self-aware, but also aware of what it sees.

Throughout the nineteen twenties, Kerr wrote a regular theatre column for the *Berliner Tageblatt*, probably Germany's most respected daily paper. Long before the end of the decade, he had transcended fame and become an institution. The dramatist Julius Hay remembered the première of his play *Gott, Kaiser und Bauer* in December 1932: 'Before the play started, you could see Alfred Kerr standing to one side at the front of the auditorium, his face turned towards the audience. The king of critics was appearing to his people.'[6]

Like most institutions, Kerr inspired extremes of devotion, but also of hatred. From 1928 he had broadcast frequently on Radio Berlin, becoming a master of the new medium. His regular 'Tagesglossen' (daily commentaries) were an authoritative commentary on political events, in which he castigated the nationalist Right. Kerr's contrived, epigrammatic style epitomised the 'Asphaltliteratur' (big city literature) which the Nazis detested: the polemical scorn he poured on them made him one of their most hated adversaries, placing him in particular danger after January 1933.

On Wednesday, 15 February 1933, Kerr was at home in the Douglasstrasse in the exclusive Berlin suburb of Grunewald, a house he had lived in for over twenty-five years. His last theatre review had appeared in the *Berliner Tageblatt* some two weeks earlier, since when he had been confined to bed, suffering from a prolonged attack of influenza. When the telephone rang that evening, Kerr left his bed to answer it. The caller did not give his name, but identified himself as a member of the Berlin police force. He was calling to warn Kerr that he should leave Germany immediately: the police had already decided to confiscate his passport the following day. Having delivered his warning, the anonymous caller rang off.

Kerr had every reason to take the warning seriously. It was not long ago that Josef Goebbels had declared that Kerr, along with such subversive celebrities as the novelists Heinrich Mann and Arnold Zweig, and the veteran pacifist Helmuth von Gerlach, should be stood up against a wall and shot.

Kerr did not go back to bed. Waiting only long enough to pack a few necessities in a rucksack, he left Berlin by the next available train. Three and a half hours later he was across the Czech border in Bodenbach. Always a most dutiful husband, he sent his wife a carefully-worded telegram saying that he had arrived safely. His own immediate feeling was one of relief: 'On that evening I felt the great joy of being outside Germany – and drank in relief a large, large glass of Pilsener.'[7] He would not return to Germany until after the war – and then only to die.

MAX HERRMANN-NEIßE: THE POET AS OUTSIDER

Of all the German-speaking writers who sought refuge in London from 1933, none was more firmly rooted in German language and culture – and none was less prepared for exile – than the poet Max Herrmann-Neiße. He was born Max Herrmann in 1886 in the historic Silesian cathedral city of Neiße. His father ran a small beer-wholesaling business, but Herrmann-Neiße was always proud to assert that he could trace his descent, on both sides of his family, from Silesian peasant stock. His feelings about his native city were always ambivalent, but he signalled his indissoluble ties to it by adding its name to his own to form his pen-name.

Max Herrmann-Neiße was a frail figure, whose growth had been stunted from childhood. As a grown man he stood no more than four foot ten and weighed barely fifty kilos (seven stone twelve pounds). A hunchback, his head too large for his body, his grey eyes peering myopically from behind thick glasses, he seemed a vulnerable figure, strikingly captured in portraits by his friend George Grosz and the Expressionist painter Ludwig Meidner – who would later share the misfortune of exile in London.

Herrmann-Neiße was a natural outsider: an only child, brought up as a Protestant in a fervently Catholic town, a poetic temperament in a prosaic world. From early childhood, he had been something of an outcast, subjected to the scorn and cruelty of his schoolmates on account of his hunchback. His earliest poems, formally influenced by Heine and Detlev Liliencron, were an attempt to come to terms with his suffering at his physical deformity. Poetry always retained for him this element of consolation. From 1906 to 1908 he studied literature and art history in Munich and Breslau, returning to Neiße in 1909 where he lived as an independent writer. He actually remained in his native town until the age of thirty, finally leaving – in 1917 – only after the death of his father, compounded by the subsequent suicide of his mother. By that time, he had already established a reputation as a local oddity – and as a poet.

Some of his early poems were published in the pre-war years in Expressionist periodicals such as *Die Aktion* and *Pan*, but remained known only to a small circle of initiates until they were brought to the attention of a wider public by the advocacy of Alfred Kerr, who demanded rhetorically why the devil no publisher had seen fit to take up this poet. Shortly after, the S. Fischer-Verlag did see fit to publish the lyric collection *Sie und die Stadt* ('She and the City'). The city was Neiße; she was Helene (Leni) Gebek, who was to follow him to Berlin and marry him there in 1917. Berlin was to remain their home until 1933.

Herrmann-Neiße later maintained that it was only Leni who had saved him from a complete breakdown after the death of his parents. To support himself and his wife he had taken 'a subordinate, pitifully paid position' in the editorial department of his publisher S. Fischer, where he survived 'under the most degrading conditions' until October 1919.[8] Shortly after, he had achieved something of a cult success with his play *Albine und Aujust*, in which he created a minor sensation by appearing on stage as himself, commenting on the actions of his characters. Thereafter, he had lived as an independent writer, eking out a precarious existence on the literary margins.

During these years in Weimar Berlin, Max Herrmann-Neiße became a familiar figure on the bohemian fringe. He appears in many Berlin memoirs of the period: holding court at his 'Stammtisch' in the Mampe Stube or the Café Wien. He took a lively interest in the theatre, particularly in the satirical cabaret of the twenties, enjoying the friendship of many of its most famous performers, such as Willi Schaeffers, Paul Graetz, Paul Nikolaus and the poet Joachim Ringelnatz, who was a regular drinking companion. Herrmann-Neiße was equally fascinated by the world of painting. Among his close friends were Heinrich Zille, famous for his genre scenes of Berlin, and George Grosz. He was a frequent visitor to Grosz's studio and posed several times for the artist, in whose company, he declared, he felt 'completely at home'. Grosz's first major oil painting was a portrait of the poet; included in the original 'Neue Sachlichkeit' exhibition at the Städtische Kunsthalle in Mannheim, it was acquired by the gallery in 1925 and still hangs there.

Despite these friendships, Herrmann-Neiße was an outsider by temperament, a disposition strongly reinforced by the exclusion of physical deformity. The feelings this induced found frequent expression in his literary work: in 1919 he published a collection of poems under the title *Verbannung* ('Exile') and two years later a short novel called *Der Flüchtling* ('The Refugee'), titles prefiguring the fate which finally befell him.[9] During the twenties he had consolidated his reputation as a poet, his work receiving the Eichendorff prize in 1924 and the Gerhart Hauptmann prize in 1927. He also contributed essays and theatre criticism to newspapers and periodicals like the *Berliner Tageblatt*, *Die Weltbühne* and *Die literarische Welt*. But such literary jobbing-work failed to provide financial self-sufficiency, forcing him into the humiliating dependence on wealthy patrons which would also characterise his London years. Writing in 1928, he noted with bitter self-deprecation that his position was the same as it always had been: 'in economic uncertainty and dependent on the good will of others'.[10]

When the Nazis came to power, Herrmann-Neiße and his wife were living in a small flat on Berlin's fashionable Kurfürstendamm. Superficially, there seemed no immediate cause for alarm. While the Nazis had excoriated his work, condemning him, in their fervent antisemitism as a crypto-Jew, neither he nor his wife were in fact Jewish. Neither had publicly expressed opposition to the Nazis, indeed any overt political commitment of his had ended more than a decade earlier. As a nature poet, he could even have found favour with Nazi advocates of 'Blut und Boden' ('blood and soil'). Yet Leni was haunted by the premonition of impending disaster. Herrmann-Neiße himself felt repelled by the tenor of Nazi rhetoric and deeply disturbed by their brutal and aggressive triumphalism which, in a poem written only a few days before the Reichstag Fire, he called 'the victory of Evil'.[11]

The Reichstag Fire and the ensuing wave of arrests seemed to confirm their worst fears. The couple left Germany two days later, entrusting their flat to the care of a friend. In the haste of departure they abandoned almost all their belongings, including most of Max's papers and manuscripts. As they left Berlin on the night train to Switzerland, Herrmann-Neiße could hardly have suspected that he would never see Germany again. Like many others, he thought of their flight as a temporary expedient, an enforced vacation from which they could return 'once the nightmare was over'. In fact, he would spend the remaining eight years of his life in exile – an essentially unpolitical writer whose life and work were hopelessly circumscribed by the course of political events.

KARL OTTEN: WRITER OF CONVICTION

Unlike Max Herrmann-Neiße, Karl Otten was a writer whose work always had a political dimension. Otten was a man of great moral integrity, a lifelong pacifist who had consistently maintained his convictions even in the face of persecution. Born in 1889, Otten belonged to a generation in Germany which was motivated by political idealism and which, during and after the First World War, equated revolution with humanitarianism. He was a writer of great versatility, who had won fame as a lyric poet before becoming a working journalist and then in turn a novelist, dramatist and successful film-writer.

Otten was born in Oberkrüchten, a village near the Dutch border. The first of two children of a customs official, he spent much of his childhood in Cologne. He never lost his feeling for his native Rhineland, always asserting his identity as a Rhinelander, with all the latter's innate suspicion of Prussian hegemony in Germany.[12]

In the years immediately before the First World War he studied Social Sciences and Art History in Munich, Bonn and Strasbourg, a time which he later called 'one of the few peaceful periods' of his life. In Munich, he was not an assiduous student, attending few lectures, preferring to mix in bohemian circles. He joined the anarchist 'Gruppe Tat', meeting prominent anarchist 'literati' like Erich Mühsam and Franz Jung, whose libertarianism always coloured his subsequent political views.

These were the years in which Otten began to make a name as a writer, contributing poems and sketches to avant-garde journals. On a journey to the Balkans in 1912, he travelled to Albania and stumbled into the Albanian war of independence against Turkey, a key experience which was to make him a lifelong pacifist and which he recorded in *Die Reise durch Albanien* ('Journey through Albania') (1913). The book was published in a limited edition of two thousand copies; though hardly a commercial success, it did achieve a certain *succès d'estime*, establishing Otten's name as a writer.[13]

Die Reise durch Albanien contained illustrations by the artist Franz Henseler, with whom Otten shared a house in Bonn, where he had transferred his studies in 1913. While in Bonn, Otten also enjoyed the friendship of the Expressionist painter August Macke, whose circle included Franz Marc and Max Ernst. Macke made two portrait sketches of Otten, who appears to have exerted a certain fascination for artists.[14] The best-known images of him are, however, the three sketches made by the Viennese artist Egon Schiele in 1914. Schiele has caught his subject in mid-discussion, capturing the expressive, fluttering hands and the sensitive, attentive face. In both sketches, he portrays Otten in half-profile, a pose which draws the viewer irresistibly into the conversation. The face is finely drawn, the spectacles adding to the air of erudite sensitivity. Otten remembered this time of his life nostalgically as a 'summer without autumn', a few golden months truncated by the outbreak of the First World War. Macke was killed in action in September 1914, Marc shortly after; Henseler survived the war, but died within a few months. 'There was no end to the dying,' Otten commented tersely.[15]

He himself had been a resolute survivor. On 1 August 1914, the day war was declared, he was arrested in Strasbourg for distributing pacifist leaflets. Charged with 'incitement to disaffection', he was imprisoned without trial, first in Strasbourg then in Tübingen, until late 1915. Despite many months in prison, much of it in solitary confinement, Otten did not retract his beliefs; indeed the experience of imprisonment served merely to confirm them. After his release, he returned to his native Rhineland, being assigned, somewhat bizarrely, to the Censor's Office for Foreign Post in Trier.

Privately, he continued to write radical anti-war poems, many of which appeared in the journal *Die Aktion*. Otten's association with the journal, and its editor Franz Pfemfert, pre-dated the war. Under Pfemfert's editorship, *Die Aktion* embodied the symbiosis of culture and politics so typical of German literary and artistic circles at that time. Otten became a close friend of Pfemfert's and a regular contributor to the journal. In November 1917, *Die Aktion* produced a special Karl Otten number, containing poems and short prose pieces, its front cover bearing the portrait by Schiele which has remained the image by which he is best remembered. Shortly after, Otten published his first collection of poems under the evocatively Expressionist title *Die Thronerhebung des Herzens* ('The Heart's Elevation to the Throne'). The provocatively pacifist tendency of the volume enraged the authorities. Copies of the book were impounded; Otten was arrested and brought before a court martial, which ordered his forcible conscription. He was assigned to a labour battalion in Koblenz, an experience which he described retrospectively: 'There, among other things, I had to unload hospital trains with dying prisoners ill with dysentery; we ran across the lines with the stretchers, between shunting trains and attacking aircraft.'[16] Eventually, Otten fell ill himself and was finally freed by the 1918 revolution.

Like many young intellectuals in 1918, Otten was a utopian and emotional communist, greeting the revolution with almost unbridled enthusiasm: 'As for my life, I can only say it is dedicated to the struggle and triumph of the poor, the proletariat. . . Ever since I could think, I have loved Russia and my first demand of every revolutionary poet is that he should share this love.'[17]

By 1919 he had also become something of a literary celebrity, though his reputation rested on the slimmest of oeuvres. He had published only a single volume of verse and two short volumes of prose, the last of which, *Der Sprung aus dem Fenster* ('The Jump from the Window'), had also appeared in 1918.

Otten's literary star had waned during the twenties. In 1916, he had married the Austrian artist and designer Marie (Mitzi) Friedmann, settling with her in Vienna in 1919. Though she bore him a son, Hugo Julian, later that year, the couple separated three years later and Otten left Vienna for Berlin, where, apart from short intervals, he lived until March 1933.

For most of these ten years he made a living from literary journalism, contributing to a list of newspapers and periodicals that reads like a compendium of the liberal press which Hitler was so completely to destroy: newspapers such as the *Berliner Tageblatt*, *Vossische Zeitung* and *Frankfurter Zeitung*, and periodicals like *Das Tage-Buch* and *Die literarische Welt*. The pattern of Otten's life resembled that of many other literary figures in the Weimar Republic: he travelled widely, writing plays, stories and novels, as well as extensive literary journalism. Two of his novels, *Eine gewisse Viktoria* (1930) and *Der unbekannte Zivilist* (1932), were serialised in the *Berliner Tageblatt*, but due to the rapidly deteriorating political climate neither was published in book form.

During these twilight years of the Weimar Republic Otten once more became famous. In 1931 he published a biography of Toussaint L'Ouverture, the black revolutionary who had led a slaves' revolt in Haiti, under the title *Der schwarze Napoleon* ('The Black Napoleon'). The book created great interest, encouraging Otten to turn the material into a play which was premiered in Hamburg on 9 January 1933, but was rapidly withdrawn following Hitler's assumption of power at the end of the month. The revolutionary theme had also attracted the attention of the Soviet film director Sergei Eisenstein, who planned to make a film based on it in Hollywood. The project was one of several Eisenstein took with him to America, but it was never realised, foundering when Hollywood – predictably – took fright at the radical implications of the story.

In the meantime, Otten had himself achieved fame in the cinema; entering a competition for a film scenario to demonstrate 'the stupidity of national frontiers within Europe', he submitted a story based on an incident in which a German rescue team had come to the aid of French miners trapped underground by a gas explosion. The prize was not awarded, but the director G. W. Pabst selected Otten's scenario as the basis of his film *Kameradschaft*, which Otten co-scripted with Ladislaus

Wajda and Peter Martin Lampel. *Kameradschaft*, a powerful exposition of the international solidarity of labour, became the cinema sensation of 1932. Otten's fame once more proved fragile: the international success of *Kameradschaft* provoked the Nazis into banning it, along with all Pabst's other films, as soon as they took power. Such developments came as no surprise to Otten who had long foreseen the destructive potential of Nazism. By the summer of 1932 he was already resigned to leaving Germany if Hitler came to power. From December 1929 Otten had been part of the artists' colony in the Berlin district of Wilmersdorf. Here some two thousand artists, musicians, actors and writers lived in three huge apartment blocks in an attempt to develop new forms of artistic activity in direct collaboration with the working class. Otten had appealed strongly for intellectuals to make common cause with the workers against the threat of fascism: 'Organise the opposition of the spirit.'[18] The 'artists' colony' had naturally not escaped the attention of the Nazis.

On 12 March 1933, Otten left Germany: posing as a tourist, he took the morning train from Berlin to Paris. It was a timely escape. Three days later SA stormtroopers raided the 'artists' colony', making numerous arrests and confiscating incriminating material. They searched also for Otten, ransacking his flat before departing empty-handed. Otten was already safely in Paris, where he was joined five days later by Ellen Kroner, whom he had met in 1930 and who was to become his second wife. Ellen left Germany on the pretext of taking a three-month convalescence, carrying currency to the value of 900 Reichsmark. Once reunited, the couple left Paris, travelling via Barcelona to the island of Majorca: an escape planned well in advance for just such a contingency.

ROBERT NEUMANN: WITH THE PENS OF OTHERS

When the Austrian writer Robert Neumann arrived in London in August 1933, he was not yet a refugee, but a successful writer pursuing a challenging and lucrative commission. In Germany, Neumann was indeed a bestselling author, who was then at the peak of a literary career on which he had embarked only a few years earlier. His decision to become a writer had actually been something of an afterthought, taken only after the collapse of a promising business career.

Born in Vienna in 1897, Neumann was the son of a well-to-do Jewish family, growing up in the relative affluence of the city's ninth district. His father Samuel, a director of the state bank, was a man of strong socialist principles who had been one of the founder members of the Austrian Social Democratic Party. In 1915 Robert Neumann had begun to study medicine, switching after two semesters to German literature. He had also started to write, joining an informal literary circle which included the novelist Hans Flesch-Brunningen, whom Neumann would encounter again, twenty years later, in exile in London. Neumann certainly considered a literary career at this stage, publishing two volumes of poetry, each of which proved a financial disaster for its respective publisher. In 1920, after marrying his first wife Stefanie, he had put aside any literary ambitions, embarking instead on a business career. (Shrewd business calculation was to remain characteristic of Neumann's later literary dealings.) In 1922 he established the import-export company R. Neumann & Co, which flourished in the years of the inflation. When the firm went bankrupt in 1925 after some rather shady transactions, Neumann decided that the time had come to realise his literary ambitions.

In the next two years he endured great hardship before finally launching his literary career in 1927 with a bestselling book of parodies, *Mit fremden Federn* ('With the Pens of Others') in which he cleverly parodied the styles of various contemporary authors, ranging from Rilke to Karl Kraus and from Thomas Mann to Carl Sternheim. Neumann was a versatile and above all prolific writer, consolidating his initial success with a stream of novels and stories. During the next five years he published no fewer than eleven books, culminating in a second book of parodies *Unter falscher Flagge* ('Under False Colours') which proved as accomplished and as successful as the first. Neumann could never escape this initial success and although he wrote some thirty books, his name remained associated in post-war Germany with parody. His rapidity of conception, technical virtuosity and talent for literary impersonation were to stand him in good stead in the harsh climate of exile.

In January 1933 Neumann was at the height of his success, carrying out an extended lecture tour of Germany which ended in Berlin. Reaching the capital on the day before Hitler became Reich Chancellor, he insouciantly told an interviewer that he saw no cause for political concern: he had just travelled the length and breadth of Germany, meeting hundreds of people – and not a single Nazi among them. He was rapidly sobered by Hitler's accession to power. Fearing that the cynical and scurrilous wit of his work – and particularly his merciless parody of Nationalist writers – would make him a political target, he took the next train back to Vienna. His prudence was not misplaced. Shortly after, a man who had the misfortune to share his name was murdered by Nazi thugs in an apparent case of mistaken identity. Neumann's works were included in the first Nazi blacklist on 26 April 1933. Josef Goebbels is reported to have said that, from now on, Neumann would be able to write only in Hebrew.[19] Neumann did not return to Berlin for almost thirty years.

He spent the following months in Vienna, completing a new book, *Die blinden Passagiere* ('The Stowaways') and wondering where he could publish it. The German market was now inaccessible, his Viennese publisher Zsolnay – in deference to the volatile political situation – was cautious. While many refugees from Nazism were forced to flee in fear of their lives, Neumann later admitted that 'my own journey into exile was made initially in the most comfortable manner'.[20]

During that summer he received an offer from a London literary agent, Elias Alexander, to write a biography of the financier and arms dealer Sir Basil Zaharoff, a figure of some public prominence, for the British publishers Rich & Cowan. Neumann knew little about Britain and even less about Zaharoff, but – always something of a literary adventurer – he did not allow such considerations to deter him. He had good reason to accept. The loss of his German readership, and with it his German royalties, was beginning to make itself felt: 'Poverty once again stared me in the face.'[21]

Neumann, whose fame in Germany rested on his parodies, was still virtually unknown abroad. Parody is a genre so culturally specific as to be virtually untranslatable – certainly, Neumann's books of parodies have never been translated. He arrived in London on August Bank

Holiday 1933 to sign a contract for the Zaharoff book, intending to stay only long enough to research and write it. In fact, he was to remain in Britain for the next twenty-five years. London was a completely alien city. Many years after, returning to a post-war Germany which he found equally alien, Neumann recalled his feelings on this first day in London: 'There I stood, unable to speak a word of English, friendless, speechless – the Nazis had robbed me of my voice.'[22]

There are few indications about Neumann's life during these early months in London. Virtually none of his letters from that time have survived and he made few retrospective comments, tacitly emphasising that he considered his move to London as an improvised expedient, a tentative first step in the rerouteing of a literary career temporarily halted by the aberration of Nazism. At the end of 1933 he returned to Austria to see his wife and son, who had remained behind in Vienna. He was still there when, on 12 February, a brief but bloody civil war erupted onto the streets of the city.

The situation in Austria had deteriorated since the previous summer. Faced by the threat of Nazi encroachment, Chancellor Dollfuß had introduced his own brand of Austrian fascism, eliminating parliament and inaugurating a one-party state. A central aim in this transition to an 'authoritarian democracy' was the repression of the Social Democratic Party, the last pillar of the democratic Austrian Republic established in 1919. The Dollfuß government deployed regular troops and the para-military 'Heimwehr' against a supposed uprising of the Social Demo-cratic 'Schutzbund' or workers' militia, crushing it in three days of violent street fighting in which artillery was used to bombard working-class dwellings.

Neumann played no direct part in these events, but fearing that his known Social Democratic connections would make him a political target, he packed his bags to return to London, making arrangements for his wife and child to follow him. When the train on which he was leaving Austria reached Salzburg, he was joined in his compartment by his fellow-author Stefan Zweig, he too making the journey of no return into exile.

STEFAN ZWEIG:
THE WORLD'S MOST TRANSLATED LIVING AUTHOR

Stefan Zweig was undoubtedly the most famous German-speaking author to seek refuge in Britain from the Nazis. Arriving in London in October 1933, he had already passed his fiftieth birthday and enjoyed a worldwide literary reputation. His work had been translated into over thirty languages – in fact, as he claims in his autobiography *Die Welt von Gestern* (*The World of Yesterday*), he was at that time the most translated living author in the world.[23] Zweig was Viennese by birth and by temperament: an elegant and cultivated gentleman whose surface charm was tempered by deep melancholy. Born the son of well-to-do Jewish parents in 1881, Zweig had grown up in the golden autumn of imperial Vienna, the 'world of yesterday' which would remain the subject of much of his fictional prose.

Zweig had come to public attention at the age of nineteen with his first book of poems. In the following years he enjoyed the friendship of some of Vienna's most outstanding figures: Arthur Schnitzler, Hermann Bahr, Theodor Herzl and, above all, Sigmund Freud, whose ideas and personality exerted a strong influence on him throughout his life. In the years before 1914 Zweig had also travelled widely, visiting the USA and India as well as the major European capitals. Among the many friends he made during these travels were many of the European cultural elite he aspired to belong to: W. B. Yeats, Henri Barbusse, Jules Romains, Romain Rolland, Benedetto Croce. An urbane and cultivated man, who spoke French, English and Italian, Zweig considered himself a European, whose task was to contribute to the cultural unity of Europe. He frequently put his own literary work aside to devote himself to mediation between foreign artists and writers and the German-speaking world. He published a series of monographs (on Paul Verlaine, Emil Verhaeren, Frans Masereel) and translations (of Baudelaire, Verlaine and Romain Rolland). He would later publish adaptations of authors as varied as Ben Jonson and Pirandello.

The First World War came as a profound shock, shattering Zweig's dream of European cultural unity and confirming his deep-seated pacifism. In 1917 he left Austria for the safety of Swiss neutrality, living

in Zurich, where his pacifist drama *Jeremias* ('Jeremiah') was first produced in February 1918. As the war drew to an end, he looked forward
to 'the long-promised empire of justice and brotherhood'[24] but the
reality of the post-war world proved a disappointment, and he withdrew increasingly into his friendships and his literary projects.

In 1919 he returned to Austria, and the following year married
Friderike von Winternitz, settling with her and her two daughters in a
villa on the Kapuzinerberg outside Salzburg. In the following decade,
he established an international reputation as a master of the short novel,
consolidating his success at the end of the decade with his historical
biographies *Fouché* (1930) and *Marie Antoinette* (1932). While he had
continued to travel extensively, his travels had now assumed a different
complexion. 'I was no longer a stranger in these countries, everywhere I
had friends, publishers, a public. I came as the author of my books and
not as the anonymous inquisitive visitor I had been before.'[25] He had
indeed become a literary celebrity, a prolific author with an expectant
public and an assured income.

During these years of fame and success, Zweig's house on the
Kapuzinerberg became a meeting-point for some of the leading cultural
figures in Europe. Among the friends and acquaintances who enjoyed
Zweig's hospitality were Thomas Mann, Romain Rolland, Emil Lud-
wig, Georg Brandes, Jakob Wassermann, Schalom Asch, Paul Valéry,
Arthur Schnitzler and Franz Werfel, as well as composers like Bartok,
Ravel, Richard Strauss, Alban Berg and the conductors Toscanini and
Bruno Walter. Few English writers made the journey to the Kapuzin-
erberg: H. G. Wells and James Joyce were both occasional guests, but
neither counted among Zweig's intimates. Zweig himself felt that
English writers stood outside the European mainstream and that
Britain belonged only marginally to the Europe whose spiritual unity
remained his lifelong goal.

Zweig's exile in London was initially a voluntary one. When he
arrived there in the autumn of 1933, he planned only a short stay, a visit
no different to many others in the restless itinerary of his life over the
preceding fifteen years. The seismic events in Germany had already
shaken Austria, and Zweig had been among the first to feel their effect.
He was horrified at the Nazis' early excesses: 'what is happening

beggars every description, any kind of law or liberality has been suspended,' he wrote to Frans Masereel.[26] Moreover, he was convinced that these events would soon be repeated in Austria, a foreboding strengthened by the border location of Salzburg. From his house on the Kapuzinerberg Zweig could look over into Germany: Berchtesgaden, where Hitler had built his mountain retreat, was clearly visible to the naked eye.

Nonetheless, Zweig initially felt 'the strongest disinclination to emigrate', confirming that he would do so 'only in the most extreme emergency'.[27] Zweig's attitude illustrates the dilemma of German liberals in the face of Nazism: the very values they proclaimed hindered any adequate public response. Although appalled by Nazi crudity and brutality, he kept his feelings very much to himself. He had always avoided direct political involvement, convinced of the autonomy of art, and believing that the artist must remain 'a man above party'. Now he conspicuously refrained from the public condemnation which many exiles expected of him, preferring to withdraw into the privacy of his literary work. In April 1933 he wrote to Romain Rolland: 'I shall pass over in silence everything that we have suffered morally. Remaining true to myself, I refuse even now to hate a whole country, and I know that the language in which I write prevents me from cutting myself off from a people – even in its madness.'[28] He maintained his silence even when his books were included among those publicly burnt in the Third Reich. 'I would gladly have done without this advertisement,' he commented to his old friend Franz Servaes. 'You know I am a man who values nothing more highly than peace and quiet.'[29]

In Austria he found the atmosphere more and more oppressive, disrupting the intense concentration he had always needed to write. Even his domestic circumstances had deteriorated; his relations with his wife Friderike had become increasingly strained. In the circumstances, Zweig was more than usually ready to winter abroad.

Nonetheless, his decision to winter in England was surprising. Like Kerr, Zweig was an ardent francophile. Among his early works of cultural mediation had been translations of Baudelaire and Verlaine. He had always felt a particular affinity with Paris which he regarded as his second home and where his many friends included such literary notables as André Gide, Valéry, Jules Romains, Georges Duhamel and Roger Martin du Gard. His books were almost as popular in France as in the German-speaking world.

He was much less at home in Britain. Though he had visited England twice as a young man, he had found the English cold and enigmatic, their universal reserve difficult to penetrate. Significantly, he had found no reason to return to the country for over twenty-five years. He had little interest in British affairs and knew virtually no one in London. Only a year earlier he had told Erich Ebermayer that he could not help him to place a novel in Britain, since he had no contacts there.[30] Though some of his books (most recently *Fouché*) had been published in London, they had made little impact, selling only a fraction of the copies sold in France or Italy or the United States. He himself noted that, while he enjoyed the personal friendship of his publishers in all these countries, he had never even seen a representative of the firm which published his works in London. However, precisely this lack of involvement constituted the attraction of London which, unlike Paris, seemed to offer the anonymity and seclusion in which he could work undisturbed. When he registered at Browns Hotel on 20 October 1933 he intended to stay only a few weeks. In fact, he had taken his first step into exile.

A shy, even withdrawn man, Zweig made little attempt to seek society. His detachment from the life around him was a welcome relief from the personal and political tensions of Austria. The very qualities which had alienated him during his earlier visits to London now seemed positive virtues. After a few days, he 'felt a sense of exceptional well-being'.[31] He worked regularly in 'the beautiful seclusion' of the British Museum Reading Room and it was here that his lifelong interest in autograph manuscripts drew his attention to an eye-witness account of the execution of Mary, Queen of Scots. His interest stimulated to pursue the topic, he found that there was no reliable account of her life – and plunged immediately into another of the historical biographies he had firmly intended to renounce.[32] Contrary to his usual practice when staying abroad, he moved out of his hotel after only a week and rented a small flat at 11 Portland Place. By the time he left London in December, he was already planning to come back: events in Austria would transform this return into a flight into exile.

Zweig had spent some time at his home in Salzburg before travelling on to Vienna. His elderly mother still lived in the capital and Zweig, having been obliged in November to part company with his publisher in Germany, was eager to set up new publishing arrangements in Austria. He thus found himself in Vienna at the time of the February 1934 events which heralded the rise of Austro-fascism. Cocooned in the calm of the city's eighth district, Zweig contrived to see and hear nothing of the fighting and indeed learned of it only when he found himself unable to leave Vienna because there were no trains running. It was only after he had returned home to Salzburg that the consequences of these political events caught up with him. He was woken the next morning with the news that four policemen were at the door. He received them in his dressing-gown and learned to his amazement that they had orders to search his house on the pretext of looking for concealed 'Schutzbund' weapons. He later recalled that they threw open every cupboard and every drawer, even those of his handsome writing-desk which had once belonged to Beethoven. Finding nothing, they withdrew.

Zweig, who had always fastidiously avoided any political involvement, was so disturbed by this bizarre and sinister intrusion that he began, that very evening, to sort his papers. Two days later he left for London, leaving behind Friderike and her daughters and abandoning the house which had been his home for the last fifteen years. Once back in London, he wrote to Romain Rolland: 'I intend to remain here whatever happens in Austria.'[33] Shortly after, he wrote to the authorities in Salzburg to inform them that he no longer lived there.

. . . AND ARRIVAL

When the great exodus of artists and intellectuals from Nazi Germany began in 1933, Britain was neither an obvious nor a particularly favoured place of refuge. In the early months of exile, refugees had settled largely in the countries immediately bordering Germany, notably Holland, France, Switzerland and Czechoslovakia, from where they hoped to follow or even influence events in the Third Reich, a situation memorably captured by Bertolt Brecht:

Restlessly we wait thus, as near as we can to the frontier
Awaiting the day of return, every smallest alteration
Observing beyond the boundary. . .[34]

Certainly, few of them thought they were starting a long exile: most
expected to return to Germany in a few weeks, 'once the fuss was over'.
Few of them initially considered the country in which they had arrived
as anything but a temporary refuge, and therefore made little effort to
accommodate themselves to its customs or even to learn its language
beyond the basic needs of practical communication.

As the Nazi regime consolidated itself, and hopes of an early return
receded, the émigrés were forced to reappraise their position. During
the summer and autumn of 1933, many of them began to move on, often
'encouraged' by the refusal of the authorities to extend their residence
visas. But even at this stage, relatively few émigrés chose to come to
Britain. The reasons for this were only superficially geographical.
Britain was economically and culturally remote from the European
continent, preoccupied with its role as the centre of a world-wide
empire. Equally important was the restrictive nature of British immigration policy, which placed considerable obstacles in the way of any
refugee wishing to come to the United Kingdom.

Immigration policies in the thirties were determined largely by the
provisions of the 1919 Aliens Act, which had modified the liberal idea
of asylum in favour of controls on the flow of immigration. Visitors to
Britain were admitted with few formalities, but permission to stay was
normally granted only to those who could prove that they had adequate
means of support. Such permission was subject to the condition that the
applicant did not try to seek employment: in order to protect British
workers at a time of high unemployment, work permits were given only
for a limited number of occupations, and not at all for most.

The effect of this policy was to limit the number of German refugees
entering Britain. According to the most reliable estimates, some forty
thousand refugees had left Germany by the end of 1933, only two
thousand of whom had settled in Britain, compared with ten times that
number in France.[35] Even by the end of 1935, after the enactment of the
infamous Nuremberg Laws, there were still only about four thousand

refugees in Britain, rising to some five thousand five hundred at the end of 1937: figures which compared with much larger concentrations in France or even Holland.[36]

British immigration policies certainly meant that German émigrés who were admitted represented something of a commercial and intellectual elite. They included a number of businessmen with capital who were generally welcomed and admitted without difficulty. About half of those who came in 1933-34 had an academic profession, leading a contemporary observer to conclude: 'England is the country of academic emigration.'[37] Many émigrés found, however, that their professional skills were not automatically transferable. Some, like doctors and dentists, already facing the problems of differing professional norms, also encountered the entrenched resistance of professional groups. Teachers and professors enjoyed a greater degree of practical sympathy, not least through the efforts of the Council for Academic Assistance which attempted to find new posts or research facilities for displaced scholars. Even so, many academics found the differences of language and culture almost insuperable. World-famous scholars were thrust abruptly into a context in which their knowledge seemed literally to have shrunk.

Only in the autumn of 1933 did the first trickle of literary refugees begin to arrive in Britain: Stefan Zweig, Robert Neumann, Max Herrmann-Neiße and Ernst Toller all arrived in London within six weeks of one another. By early 1934, they had been joined by a handful of other writers, such as Hans Flesch-Brunningen, the journalist Rudolf Olden and the young novelist Ruth Feiner. Although there were, as we shall see, some personal contacts between them, they were never to constitute a coherent group, united around a literary or political agenda, such as gathered in other European capitals, like Paris or Prague or Moscow. Cut off from their literary roots, these authors found themselves forced to accommodate, in different ways, to a new cultural environment.

Part Two

The Waiting Room

1933–1936

The cultural climate in Britain in the thirties was unwelcoming for the German writer. The German community which had existed in Britain throughout the Victorian and Edwardian periods, numbering some sixty thousand in 1914, had been decimated in the First World War. In 1933/34 the German-speaking population of London numbered some five thousand: too small and too scattered to make German publishing commercially viable.

There was a lack of cultural links between Britain and the German-speaking world. Few German authors had personal or literary connections with Britain, fewer still had any strong cultural or linguistic affinities. The reasons for this lay in the nature of English culture in the inter-war years, which was at once insular and imperial. British publishers looked outward towards the English-speaking world: their subsidiaries or associates were in Melbourne, Johannesburg, Toronto or New York. British writers, working within an imperial cultural tradition, generally sought little contact with their continental counterparts. (The very locution 'continent' signified Britain's distance from involvement in Europe.)

One of the notable features of British publishing in the inter-war years is the lack of any European dimension. The most obvious measure of this cultural insularity was the reluctance to publish books in translation, an aspect of cultural history which has received strikingly little attention. With the exception of one or two small publishing houses, the business of British publishing at that time was confined largely to work which had been written in English. The proportion of translations in publishers' lists amounted to a mere two to three per cent of total production, roughly half the comparable figure in France or Italy or Germany.[1] (Some seventy years later, the relative situation has hardly changed.) Moreover, if the educated Englishman had any knowledge of a European language or literature, it was French. German culture was regarded with incomprehension, and even distaste, compounded by a lingering hostility from the war.

Many of the writers who fled from Germany in 1933 were already successful authors who had established a reputation in the German-speaking world, but relatively few of them were known outside it. Shortly after leaving Austria, Stefan Zweig observed wryly that he was one of the ten authors writing in German who could afford to be exiled.[2] Zweig was indeed an international celebrity, who could live comfortably on his foreign royalties, but the only names one could add to his were those of his namesake Arnold, the novelist Lion Feuchtwanger, the brothers Thomas and Heinrich Mann, and Erich Maria Remarque, whose reputation rested on the phenomenal success of a single book, the international bestseller *All Quiet on the Western Front*.

If relatively few German authors were published in translation, even fewer appeared in *English* translation. 'Franz Kafka's name, so far as I can discover, is almost unknown to English readers': so runs the opening sentence of Edwin Muir's introduction to the first English edition of *The Castle*, published in 1930. Kafka was not an isolated example. German writing had been virtually ostracised in Britain after the First World War; even world-famous authors like Thomas Mann and Hermann Hesse were little known. Although Mann had won the Nobel Prize in 1929, only his best-known works had been published in Britain before 1933: *Buddenbrooks*, *The Magic Mountain* and a volume of short novels. Hesse's *Steppenwolf* had been translated in 1929 but only one other book of his had appeared. Heinrich Mann's *Im Schlaraffenland* had appeared as *In the Land of Cockaigne* in 1929, one of the first books ever published by Victor Gollancz; *Professor Unrat* appeared in 1932 under the title *The Blue Angel* (exploiting the success of the film which had made Marlene Dietrich famous). Lion Feuchtwanger had already won international fame with *Jew Süß*, followed by *Success*, which had appeared in English translation in 1927 and 1929 respectively. It is striking that most of these works had appeared under the imprint of Martin Secker, a small publisher with an outstanding literary list and a reputation for commissioning translations of distinguished foreign novels.

The years 1928–29 were something of a turning-point, marking the beginning of what was somewhat fancifully described as 'a literary invasion'. A decade after the armistice, the German book market was flooded with fictional representations of the Great War. Many of these were rapidly published in English, beginning with Arnold Zweig's famous pacifist novel *The Case of Sergeant Grischa* in 1928, and continuing the following year with Ludwig Renn's *War*, Ernst Jünger's *Storm of Steel* and the international bestseller *All Quiet on the Western Front*.

The reception of these novels was highly ambivalent, culminating in what became known as the War Books Debate. The critic of *The Times Literary Supplement*, reviewing Ernst Johannsen's novel *Four Infantrymen of the Western Front 1918*, spoke for many:

> Frankly this book has every vice which German war fiction has displayed in the last two years. It is wordy, brutal, hysterical and at times improbable. It is full of philosophical discussions of which the basis seems to be that 'mankind is garbage'.[3]

The wave of German war novels had begun to recede by 1932. Attitudes to war literature were changing, influenced by the rise of fascism and Nazism.

Despite its international reach, British publishing was still a relatively small-scale business: a cosy and rather conservative world which, in the words of Fredric Warburg, was still very much 'an occupation for gentlemen'.[4] It was a world dominated by the individual owner or director, for whom publishing was a consuming passion, at once both hobby and profession. The dominant figures of the trade, men like Newman Flower of Cassells, Stanley Unwin of Allen & Unwin, or Jonathan Cape, were increasingly joined by newcomers such as Victor Gollancz, who had started his business in 1927, and Hamish Hamilton (founded 1931). Such individuals were a mixture of entrepreneur and patron, closely involved in building up their list and quite prepared to indulge their own taste or preference. As it happens, several of these dominant figures had personal connections with German and Germany. Stanley Unwin had studied the book trade there; Hamish Hamilton had read Modern Languages at Cambridge.

Even before 1933 Gollancz's list included a number of books on social, political and economic subjects, which were 'designed to convert people on a big scale to socialism and pacifism'. Hitler's assumption of power naturally directed Gollancz's attention towards Germany. In 1933 he published *The Brown Book of the Hitler Terror*, under the auspices of the World Committee for the Victims of German Fascism. This was followed in 1934 by Vernon Bartlett's *Nazi Germany Explained* and Naomi Mitchison's *Vienna Diary*, which recounted the February events in Vienna and her own experience of their aftermath. In 1935 Gollancz ceased to trade with Germany altogether, on political grounds. In the same year he inaugurated discussions which led to the founding of the Left Book Club.

Nor was Gollancz the only publisher to pursue an overtly political agenda. In 1933-34 Bodley Head published a series of books on Germany, largely at the instigation of Ronald Boswell, who had been the firm's most influential director since the death of John Lane in 1925. The books were mostly factual and politically topical, including Alfred Apfel's *Behind the Scenes of German Justice*, Leopold Schwarzschild's *End to Illusion* and a compilation of documents relating to the Reichstag Fire Trial. However, most of these books lost money – the title *Hitler Rearms* sold just fifteen copies in 1934 – their poor sales suggesting that the reading public had considerably less appetite for events in Germany than certain publishers.

There were other factors restricting the access of the German-speaking author to the British market. Cultural attitudes in Britain were not only insular but highly conservative, resulting in inherent suspicion of anything which smacked of cultural modernism. Much of the press tended to ignore books which were aesthetically or politically radical, and many booksellers were unwilling to stock them, attitudes which naturally affected both reading tastes and publishers' lists. However, British publishing in the thirties also showed strong signs of innovation, certainly from the middle of the decade. In July 1935 Allen Lane founded Penguin Books, inaugurating the era of the paperback.

Although fellow-publishers were initially sceptical, they were soon forced to admit the success of this publishing revolution. It was also in 1935 that Victor Gollancz first initiated discussions about the formation of a book club to publish left-wing books, a project culminating in the founding of the Left Book Club. Various book clubs had been launched in the thirties, among them the Reprint Society, based on special editions of acknowledged successes, the Readers Union, and the Folio Society. The Left Book Club was intended from the first as a means of providing political education: members received the club's monthly selection at a price of 2s 6d, half the price of the normal edition. The Club was inaugurated in May 1936, one of its earliest selections being Rudolf Olden's *Hitler the Pawn*, which had been published the previous year in German in Amsterdam.

The reluctance of British publishers to brave the deep waters of translation was endorsed by the leading literary critics, who were very much the arbiters of public taste. Such influential voices as James Agate, Gerald Gould or F. R. Leavis were strikingly monocultural. The critical position adopted by Leavis and his *Scrutiny* group, for example, was based on the concept of cultural tradition advanced by T. S. Eliot – but had narrowed it by stripping away Eliot's European perspective.[5] Younger critics such as Raymond Mortimer and Cyril Connolly had distinct francophile tendencies, but even Connolly's predilection for French and Latin literature, well documented in *The Unquiet Grave*, did not extend to German culture.[6] His review of a book by the young German writer Ruth Feiner, catches the essence of English literary criticism in the thirties:

> *Cat Across the Path* is the first novel by a young German woman about two rival jazz pianists of Berlin. It is rather more able than one would expect but it is difficult to see why [it] should have been translated.
> There are still so many American novels which one can't get here, that one would rather have more of them and fewer tales of Central Europe.[7]

The problems facing German writers in securing publication in Britain were further exacerbated by the dearth of outstanding translators. In compiling a list of literary translators from German, the two couples Edwin and Willa Muir, and Eden and Cedar Paul spring immediately to mind, followed perhaps by the names of Eric Sutton (who had translated *Sergeant Grischa*) and A. W. Wheen (the translator of *All Quiet on the Western Front*). However, apart from these, it is hard to think of any other well-known translators from German. Translation may sometimes have been a labour of love. More often it was jobbing-work: badly-paid and poorly regarded. Many of those responsible for the translation of German books in the twenties and thirties translated only one, or at most two works.

In general, German literature received little attention in Britain, a legacy of both cultural insularity and wartime hostility; the reception of Stefan Zweig provides a case in point. While he was already a world-famous author when he arrived in London, he had certainly found much less resonance there than almost anywhere else. In a letter to his British publisher Cassells in January 1932, Zweig commented that 'till now Great Britain was the country where I found less answer than anywhere. Here in France my books have now a great sale (*Fouché* 26,000 in one year . . . in Russia, Italy and America the same)'.[8] There is no doubt that Cassells worked hard to correct this situation, particularly after Zweig's arrival in London in 1933. Nonetheless, it was another two years before the success of *The Queen of Scots* finally earned him the kind of reputation in Britain he had long enjoyed elsewhere.

STEFAN ZWEIG: 'MILES AWAY FROM POLITICS'

Arriving back from Austria at Victoria Station in February 1934, Stefan Zweig was acutely aware that his exile had now begun in earnest. He later recalled that he saw London with new eyes: 'You look differently at a city in which you have decided to live than one in which you are merely a visitor.'[9] He returned initially to the flat he had rented in Portland Place, which was small and sparsely furnished, consisting of a bedroom and a study just large enough to hold a few essential books and a writing-desk. Opening the door on this first evening, he felt that he had been transported back into his own past, so forcefully was he reminded of his first flat as a young student in Vienna. His life seemed to have turned full circle, as though everything he had experienced or achieved in the intervening thirty years had suddenly been erased.[10] He sensed that his life had entered a new provisional phase: while his decision to leave Austria was final, he was still unsure how long he would stay in London.

Zweig's voluntary exile was not merely a prudent withdrawal from the political uncertainties of Austria but a conscious attempt to escape the constraints of property and family commitments. Just turned fifty, Zweig – like many men of his age – was obsessed with the idea that he had lived his life wrongly and that he should make a fresh start. Abandoning Salzburg and the last fifteen years of his life, he had also consciously renounced his domestic responsibilities. He had increasingly come to regard his marriage as restrictive and his property as burdensome. One of his step-daughters later remembered that he would often shut himself away in his room, refusing to speak to the family for days on end.[11]

In turning his back on Salzburg, Zweig had also renounced many of his former pleasures and possessions. Zweig the famous author was also an avid and discriminating collector of books and manuscripts. Over the years he had acquired an extensive library of some ten thousand volumes, but his greatest pride was undoubtedly his collection of autograph manuscripts. His collection of literary manuscripts, comprising pieces by many of his outstanding contemporaries in Germany and Austria, was surpassed only by his musical collection which included valuable items by Mozart and Beethoven.

Zweig himself would later depict his voluntary exile as a pursuit of the ideal of personal and creative freedom: 'Personal freedom was the most important thing on earth to me.'[12] During the early months of his exile in London, he certainly experienced a new sense of liberty, a feeling of having shed the ballast of the past.

> England is fantastic for a person who wants to work. . . I feel very well.
> I feel freer than ever without my books, without my house, without my collections. I've had enough of all that for some years to come.[13]

Unencumbered by commitments to family and friends, he could devote himself exclusively to his work, finding the very lack of space in his flat conducive to concentration.

As his compatriot Franz Werfel later observed, Zweig seemed to possess all the prerequisites of a successful life in exile. He had travelled widely and possessed friends and contacts in many countries. He had come to Britain as an author of international reputation and substantial means: a visiting celebrity, not a refugee. Throughout his years in London, he remained virtually free of financial problems, international royalties and lucrative lecture tours giving him an economic security which was the envy of his fellow-exiles.

The true extent of his income can be inferred from his correspondence with his American publisher Ben Huebsch, who wrote in November 1933 that the film rights to the short novel *Letter from an Unknown Woman* had been sold for a fee of $7,500: 'Please let me know whether we should forward the proceeds to you or hold the money for future instructions.'[14] A few months later Huebsch sent him a contract for a new book which studiously avoided naming any specific advance: 'We refrained from stating an amount solely because we do not wish you to be restricted to any particular sum. You are at liberty to draw on future earnings as your discretion may dictate.'[15] Financial independence also gave Zweig great creative freedom, enabling him to decline even lucrative offers if they failed to match his literary aspirations. He felt able, for example, to refuse an offer from a Hollywood studio to write film scripts for ten weeks at a salary of $3,000 a week plus travel expenses, though he confessed that it 'demanded moral willpower to let quite such an awful lot of money go out of the window'.[16] Shortly after his return to London, Zweig was joined briefly by his wife, Friderike, who neither understood his compulsion to leave Salzburg nor appreciated the finality of his decision. Friderike had brought with her a handful of Stefan's prized possessions, such as the Blake drawing of King John which he had acquired during his first stay in London and which had hung in his study ever since. However, she sensed the growing distance between them and saw all too clearly where it might lead: 'Stefan wants to sell the house,' she wrote to a friend. 'He's behaving brutally and I fear the estrangement which this behaviour will bring. I shall make a new home for myself alone, though God knows where. Stefan is living in an imaginary emigrant's psychosis, and I just enjoy my home.'[17]

In fact, Zweig had long since ceased to regard Salzburg as his home, increasingly disturbed by the border location of the city and the political reverberations of its proximity to Germany. 'The feelings of agitation get into the house through every gap and crack, however tightly one

closes the windows of the spirit,' he told his fellow-writer Hans Carossa.
'One is living, so to speak, on a military bridgehead and that is not
particularly beneficial for one's work.' He had found it 'a spiritual
necessity' to escape to the 'calm security' of England, with its 'totally
apolitical atmosphere'.[18] In a letter to his former publisher Anton
Kippenberg, he was even more fulsome in his praise of London:

> The city is wonderful. You can live just as you want and are miles away
> from politics. . . I haven't felt better for years in any place. The reserv-
> ed, tactful, discreet and friendly manner of the English is, after the
> nervous tension of Vienna and Paris, as good as being in a sanatorium.[19]

'In the long run,' he told Rolland, 'one would suffer from this cool-
ness of temperament, but at the moment I find it soothing.'[20] He was
indeed more than happy in his sanatorium, happy to recuperate from
the stresses of the German-speaking world and to insulate himself from
events there. The Nazi *putsch* in Vienna and the assassination of
Dollfuß, though widely reported in the London press, find virtually no
mention in his correspondence. During these early years of exile, he was
more than happy to endorse British detachment from the affairs of the
continent, considering it a political articulation of his own philosophy.
'They have only one aim here – to keep out – and that is mine too as a
writer,' he wrote to Friderike.[21] Two years later, British isolationism
would appear much less attractive.

Zweig's determination 'to keep out', his apparently passive attitude
to events in Germany and his determination to withdraw into his own
work, had provoked hostile criticism from many of his fellow-exiles.
After the book-burnings in Germany Zweig had seemed resigned to the
loss of his German readership but nonetheless reluctant to turn his back
on the country. For many months he felt unable to sever his connection
with Insel Verlag, which had published his work for the last twenty-
eight years. When the break was finally forced upon him, he wrote to
Anton Kippenberg that it was 'among the most painful things I have
ever had to suffer in intellectual matters'.[22] Even then he continued to
correspond with Kippenberg, admitting that he still hoped his books
would one day appear again under the Insel imprint.

For all his regrets, Zweig's business sense was strong enough to
prevail over such sentimentality. While in Vienna in January 1934 he

had persuaded Herbert Reichner, the editor of the Austrian journal *Philobiblon*, to set up his own publishing house, with Zweig as his flagship author. Moreover, at Zweig's instigation, Reichner registered the new firm not only in Vienna and Zurich – but also in Leipzig, thus providing a (modest) channel for the distribution of Zweig's work within Germany itself. This back door remained open for some two years and was finally closed only after complaints by Nazi literati that Reichner was 'flooding Germany with publicity for the work of Stefan Zweig and other Jews'; early in 1936 all copies of Zweig's books in Reichner's Leipzig warehouse were impounded.

Reichner's first publication in 1934 was Zweig's historical monograph *Triumph und Tragik des Erasmus von Rotterdam* (English title: *Erasmus*) which he had written in the first year of the Third Reich, completing it during the autumn in London. At first glance, *Erasmus* shows considerable continuity of style and subject-matter with Zweig's work before 1933, continuing the series of biographical studies he had begun with *Fouché* and *Marie Antoinette*. Closer inspection confirms the book's contemporary significance, placing it firmly in the context of Nazism and exile. Zweig himself commented that 'anyone who can read will recognise the analogy to the history of our own times'.[23]

Zweig's critics had openly accused him of living in an ivory tower, or even of trying to accommodate himself to the regime in Germany: of tolerating the intolerable. His actions were indeed open to misinterpretation. While expressing his distaste for Nazism in private, he had remained conspicuously silent in public, determined to devote himself exclusively to his literary work. He had always remained aloof from politics – admitting that for years he had not even exercised his right to vote – in the belief that the artist must remain a man above party.[24] As time passed, his attitude had become more equivocal. After first promising to contribute to the journal *Die Sammlung*, which Klaus Mann had founded as a focus for anti-Nazi opposition in exile, Zweig had then withdrawn his support on the grounds that the journal was too overtly political. When a private letter he had written in this connection to Kippenberg was made public by the Nazi authorities, Zweig was accused of seeking to propitiate the Nazis in order to maintain a market for his books in Germany. Klaus Mann scornfully accused him of 'falling over backwards not to offend Goebbels'.[25] 'Since then I count as a traitor to the exiles,' Zweig wrote gloomily in a letter from London.[26]

Zweig did not seek to defend himself publicly against the increasingly virulent attacks on him in the exile press; typically, he chose to answer his critics in literary form. His *Erasmus* is an extended self-apology in the guise of a literary monograph. When he began work on the book, Zweig intended to erect 'a modest monument' to a man whom he regarded as his spiritual forebear.[27] He later called the book 'a confession of faith, an attack on fanaticism'[28] and certainly, as work progressed, it assumed more and more the character of a personal statement.

Zweig presents his subject as 'the first conscious cosmopolitan and European', a role model and intellectual precursor of his own philosophy of liberal humanism. He does not conceal his admiration for the scholar whom he cites as 'a man of understanding and mediation, a man of moderation and the middle ground', open to any idea and 'opposed only to the enemy of all free thought, fanaticism'. Consciously echoing the words of his friend Rolland during the First World War, he invokes the position of the writer 'not to one side of the parties, but above them, au dessus de la mêlée'. The antagonist of Erasmus, and the enemy of humanism, is the religious fanatic Martin Luther. Zweig's Luther is in no sense a rounded historical portrait. He is neither the theologian and reformer, nor the great teacher but 'the fanatical man of action' (*der fanatische Tatmensch*), a phrase in which contemporaries easily recognised the intended analogy with Nazism. *Erasmus* ends on a subdued note which illuminates Zweig's own intellectual dilemma: 'But in his heart of hearts Erasmus had long known that, at a time of universal madness, it was pointless to exhort men to embrace humanity. He knew that the great and sublime ideal of humanism was defeated.' Zweig's exposition of liberal humanism therefore ends on a note of cultural pessimism, expressing his feeling that the world he stood for was vanishing in the face of the aggressively competing ideologies of the thirties.

If the conception of *Erasmus* was coloured by the political debate amongst émigrés, its reception was no less so. The critic Ludwig Marcuse spoke for many exiles when he interpreted the book as an appeal for neutrality on their part. Zweig was dismayed by this verdict, complaining privately that the book had been 'grievously misunderstood'[29] and that it had never even occurred to him to treat neutrality as axiomatic.

In his autobiography *Die Welt von Gestern* (*The World of Yesterday*), Zweig later depicted his life in London as one of self-restraint, an almost monastic existence, bereft of friends and social contacts. In fact, his life during the first eighteen months of his exile was anything but reclusive. He manifestly enjoyed the cultural life of London, his letters to different correspondents recording visits to a succession of concerts and to the opera at Covent Garden. He had always had a great affinity with music, which was reflected in his wide collection of musical manuscripts and his friendships with such musicians as Bruno Walter, Toscanini and Richard Strauss. He was also enchanted by the open-air theatre in Regent's Park, particularly enjoying a production of *The Tempest* in which he admired the performance, as Prospero, of John Drinkwater, who was to become one of his few English friends. He called the location 'the most perfect open air theatre in the world . . . a jewel amid the greenery with a magical stage'.[30] Writing to Richard Strauss, he even suggested that it would make an ideal setting for the composer's *Ariadne*.[31]

Zweig's friendship with Strauss and their collaboration on the opera *Die schweigsame Frau* (*The Silent Woman*) was to prompt one of the strangest episodes in the cultural history of the Third Reich. Strauss, still at the height of his powers, was Germany's greatest living composer. His seventieth birthday had just been celebrated with great pomp in the Third Reich, and his collaboration with a writer whom the Nazis stigmatised as a Jew therefore seems a spectacular musical *mésalliance*.

Strauss's association with Zweig had begun in 1931, shortly after the death of his long-standing collaborator Hugo von Hofmannsthal. The composer had asked Zweig to suggest a possible subject for an opera, whereupon the latter had proposed an adaptation of Ben Jonson's comedy *Epicoene, or The Silent Woman*. Zweig was of course no stranger to Jonson's work and he had little trouble in convincing Strauss of the comic possibilities of the subject.

Zweig began work on the libretto in 1932 and during the autumn sent Strauss the first two acts, which the latter greeted with the same enthusiasm as the initial outline, calling it 'delightful, a born comic opera . . . which lends itself to music like neither *Figaro* nor the *Barber of Seville*'.[32] During January 1933 Strauss also received the final act, commenting: 'The third act too is successful. My thanks and congratulations.'[33] He had already begun composing the music, a task which it took him until October 1934 to complete. In these two years of political upheaval, the cultural landscape of Germany had been transformed. The theatre had been cleansed of all works considered subversive, including any written by 'non-aryan' authors. Zweig had assumed that the fate of *Die schweigsame Frau* was thus sealed, but he had reckoned without the determination, and influence, of his composer. Strauss had embraced the new Germany with some opportunism, allowing the regime to appropriate his international prestige by accepting the influential post of President of the Reichsmusikkammer, one of the new cultural organisations which the Nazis had established to enforce their hegemony in the arts. Strauss expected that in return the regime would allow him to continue his work undisturbed and moved with tactical skill and an absence of moral scruple to ensure that an exception could be made to allow his new opera to be performed. After lengthy discussions, and only after the matter had been referred to the Führer himself, the performance was finally sanctioned and the première fixed for 24 June 1935 at the Staatstheater Dresden.

While sharing Strauss's view of the autonomy of the work of art, Zweig himself had played a typically passive role during these months. He was under pressure from fellow-exiles to withdraw his libretto, but felt unable to do so, both for contractual reasons and from personal loyalty to Strauss, for whom he always retained the highest regard. In fact, his feelings about the opera were highly ambivalent. He told Joseph Leftwich that he hoped it would not be performed; he was certainly sceptical that even Strauss's undoubted prestige could ensure that it would be. His scepticism was not unfounded. When the theatre bills were printed, Zweig's name was left off, and was only reinstated at the last moment, when Strauss furiously insisted that he would otherwise boycott the première.

The production was a brilliant success, despite the conspicuous absence of the Nazi *nomenklatura*, but after four performances, the opera was taken off without explanation and all further performances banned. Shortly before the première, Strauss had written in unguarded terms to Zweig, ironically undermining his own official position ('Do you think Mozart consciously composed in an 'aryan' way?') and repeating his determination to keep Zweig as his librettist.[34] The letter never arrived, being intercepted by the Gestapo and unleashing a political storm which forced Strauss to announce his resignation as President of the Reichsmusikkammer 'on grounds of ill-health'.

The episode of *Die schweigsame Frau* is merely a footnote to the cultural history of the Third Reich, but it significantly affected the development of Zweig's attitude to art and politics. His letters to Strauss confirm that he shared the latter's robust aestheticism, which held that the quality of the work of art was paramount and politics were merely an alien additive. However, he remained sceptical that even Strauss's personal prestige could ensure the performance of a work by so notable a non-aryan as himself. While Strauss continued to insist that Zweig was the only librettist with whom he would work, the latter was realistic enough to acknowledge that nothing could come of further collaboration. The experience seems to have hardened Zweig's political attitude. At the height of the scandal over *Die schweigsame Frau* he was already working on a sequel to his *Erasmus* entitled *Castellio gegen Calvin* (*The Right to Heresy*), in which he elaborated the ideal of militant humanism increasingly espoused by anti-Nazi liberal intellectuals such as Heinrich and Thomas Mann.[35]

The central figure of Zweig's new work, Sebastian Castellio, was – unlike Erasmus – an obscure scholar who, in an act of rash courage, had accused John Calvin of murdering a man whom he had ordered to be burnt as a heretic. *Castellio gegen Calvin* is, even more clearly than *Erasmus*, an attempt at self-justification: Zweig's protagonist personifies his ideal of intellectual freedom. If Erasmus was 'a veiled self-portrait',[36] a picture of the man he actually was, Castellio, he confessed, represented 'the man I should like to be'.[37] Like all Zweig's biographies, *Castellio* was based on careful historical research, carried out during a three-month stay in Zurich in the summer of 1935. His research concentrated on the little-known figure of Castellio, for whom Calvin was to be merely a dramatic antagonist. Zweig's Calvin, like his Luther, is not an historical portrait, but an analogy for the intolerance and fanaticism of the twentieth century. He is a tyrant and dictator, suppressing freedom of thought and belief by means of terror, an early example 'of the total *Gleichschaltung* of a whole people'. If Calvin is a forerunner of totalitarian philosophy, Castellio's principled opposition to fanaticism represents the 'militant humanism' which Zweig increasingly sought to espouse. In contrast to *Erasmus*, *Castellio* ended in muted optimism, suggesting that moderation would eventually outlive fanaticism, however powerful the latter might seem. *Castellio gegen Calvin* was perceived – a misunderstanding eloquent of the politicised context of literary discussion amongst exiles – as a declaration of solidarity in the fight against fascism. 'I am glad,' wrote Lion Feuchtwanger, 'that you have placed yourself so unmistakeably on our side.'[38]

If Zweig was already a world-famous author when he came to London, his fame was nonetheless more muted there than almost anywhere else. During the twenties his work had appeared only spasmodically in English translation and his name had remained comparatively unknown. One of the major obstacles to his fame in Britain was that of literary form. His reputation in the German-speaking world rested on his mastery of the *Novelle*, a genre with a long tradition in Germany, but one rarely adopted by English writers and virtually impossible to place with British or American publishers who felt it was uneconomic in length. Zweig frankly acknowledged the commercial difficulties of the *Novelle*: 'My beloved and unhappy format, too big for a newspaper and too small for a book.'[39] Writing to Cassells in January 1932, he predicted that 'my first real success . . . in England will be a great biographie (*sic*) I prepare'.[40] The 'great biographie' was *Marie Antoinette*, yet it was not to be this book which finally established his popularity in Britain but, more fittingly, *Maria Stuart*, the project which had first motivated him to return to London.

During 1934 Zweig made excellent progress on the book, dictating much of the first draft to his new secretary. Zweig was a careful and methodical author, whose writing habits had long been established. He always preferred to dictate the first draft of a book, which he would then spend considerable time revising and editing. After completing the initial research for *Maria Stuart*, he urgently needed a secretary. Ironically, it was Friderike who took charge of the matter, engaging a young woman called Lotte Altmann, whom she found through the Jewish Refugees Committee based at Woburn House. In so doing she unwittingly initiated the final breakdown of her marriage to Stefan: it was Lotte to whom he increasingly turned and who eventually became his second wife.[41]

Lotte Altmann was then twenty-six years old. The granddaughter of a rabbi, she had emigrated to London from Frankfurt with her brother in 1933, spending several months at Whittingham College, Hove, in order to learn English. She was apparently an ideal secretary for Zweig: well-educated, hard-working, tactful and reserved.[42] She also quickly became his devoted admirer, ready to tolerate and even anticipate his changes of mood, compliant where Friderike had often seemed assertive. Inevitably, her relationship with Stefan soon took a more intimate turn.

Throughout 1934, Zweig worked intensively on the manuscript of *Maria Stuart*. In March, he reported to Huebsch that work was 'proceeding steadily',[43] though he had written only an outline of the whole thing, in order to fix the structure, and still hoped to find the right tone. He told Kippenberg that he thought it would become 'a solid and decent book'.[44] His optimism about the book sprang partly from his feelings of well-being in London; he worked in the Reading Room of the British Museum, 'the most beautiful library in the world, where one doesn't feel the political idiocy and can still concentrate'.[45] In the late summer, he travelled to Scotland with Lotte to visit the historical locations of the book in search of local colour and atmosphere. However, as the book neared completion, his pleasure in the calm and restrained atmosphere of London began to pall. English courtesy and discretion now seemed merely a device to push unpleasant considerations into the background; the universal reserve towards foreigners merely a lack of understanding of their problems. 'This country has begun to bore me,' he wrote to Rolland shortly after returning from Scotland. What he had hitherto perceived as London's restful atmosphere had become tedious, 'the white walls of the sanatorium' were suddenly 'unbearable'. He could, he wrote, no longer breathe the air of England, which lacked the spice of vitality.[46]

As so often, Zweig's acerbic comments coincided with feelings of creative crisis. While the manuscript of *Maria Stuart* was now virtually complete, the work had convinced him that he should abandon 'the mass production of biographies'. He had lost interest in the fashionable success which the genre offered and wished to return to work which he found creatively more satisfying.[47] To alleviate his crisis, Zweig turned to the remedy of travel.

He had always been an eager traveller, recording his impressions of the places he visited in lucid and enormously successful travel books and articles. In exile, travel became almost a compulsion, a palliative for the periods of dark depression which increasingly haunted him. Unlike most of his fellow-emigrés, for whom exile was a decline into poverty, Zweig was able to travel almost at will. In December, he left London for the South of France on his way to a lecture tour of the United States.

Zweig's unpublished impressions of New York, which he was visiting for the first time since 1911, confirm his lively and acute observation. Despite a busy lecture schedule, he did not forget *Maria Stuart*, conducting negotiations with Ben Huebsch regarding the American rights for the book. The Queen of Scots was also the subject of some of his lectures. On the voyage home, he reflected that the journey had been useful, 'even if it could not solve the deep artistic and personal crisis in which I find myself'. He was firmly resolved to abandon biography in favour of more creative writing: 'a novel would be the absolutely ideal thing for me'. In conclusion, he noted that 'it was good for me, this pause, and it will also be good for M[aria] St[uart]'.[48]

Maria Stuart was finally completed shortly after his return to London in the New Year; by March he was already in Vienna to read the proofs and oversee the publication the following month. The edition was handsomely designed but Zweig found his own pleasure in it tempered by the knowledge that it could not appear under the Insel imprint.[49] The English edition, once more in a translation by Eden and Cedar Paul, appeared in October under the title *The Queen of Scots*. The book had created great interest, the advance orders far exceeding those for any other book of Zweig's. Sales were also enhanced by the almost unanimous praise of the critics. The Elizabethan historian A. L. Rowse congratulated Zweig 'on having mastered the intricacies of our history at this time, and for the most part to have written about it as to the manner born'; another Elizabethan scholar, J. E. Neale, lauded the book's 'brilliant qualities': 'there are many sentences that one would have given a great deal to have written', adding that 'the translation is beyond praise'.[50] High praise indeed for both author – and translators. The work of Eden and Cedar Paul, who translated most of Zweig's work in the thirties, has been largely unsung. Zweig's biographer Donald Prater is critical, asserting that none of Zweig's English translators did justice to his work, but Zweig himself, who worked closely with the Pauls, found little fault, and even recommended them to his friend Victor Fleischer in 1940. There is no doubt that the impact made by *The Queen of Scots* was due, in no small measure, to their accomplished translation.

The book's runaway success assured Zweig's reputation in his adopted country, at last making him as widely read in Britain as he already was elsewhere. When Friderike arrived in Dover in January 1936, the immigration officer she encountered told her that he was proud to welcome Stefan Zweig's wife to Britain. By the end of that year, *Maria Stuart* was an international bestseller, having already been published in sixteen languages.

By October 1935, Zweig had abandoned all pretence that his stay in London was a temporary arrangement, taking a new flat at 49 Hallam Street, just round the corner from the old one.[51] He wanted to stay close to the centre of London and had consulted various estate agents. The new flat was in a block still under construction, so that Zweig could not move in before the New Year. These rather leisurely arrangements confirm that Zweig intended the flat to be the permanent base which it indeed became for the next three and half years. It was more spacious than the small flat in Portland Place, comprising four rooms: a large study, a dining and reception room and two bedrooms.

Quite forgetting his comments of a year earlier, he wrote to Rolland:

I have chosen London because of its libraries, and – though it seems paradoxical – because the people are completely indifferent and one can live in this enormous city absolutely for oneself. I can't complain. *Maria Stuart* has become a great success here, but it doesn't intrude on one's life (as in Paris or Vienna). No one rings up, no one visits you. You just meet a few friends.[52]

He could retain his privacy and the personal freedom he prized above all else. Later he would tell Rolland that 'life in London is wonderfully monotonous. I go out rarely and see almost nobody. Here you can be forgotten. . . I read a lot and study a lot and am happy to have many plans.'[53]

The decision to settle in London inevitably also meant the liquidation of his house on the Kapuzinerberg. Following the purchase of his new flat, Zweig had returned for the last time to Salzburg to make a selection from his books and other belongings, instructing Friderike to forward the items to London. She, still anxious to preserve the remnants of their marriage, came to London in January 1936 to prepare the new flat for Stefan's return from the South of France. She attempted to turn the study into a replica of Zweig's library on the Kapuzinerberg, with the same red wallpaper and the landscape by Masereel hanging over the bookcases, which, however, held only a tenth of the roughly 10,000 volumes which his library in Salzburg had contained.[54] Friderike's attempt to recreate Zweig's library on the Kapuzinerberg suggests her continuing hope of reviving their relationship. She in fact stayed on in London for several weeks but was finally forced to acknowledge that she was no longer central to his life, that the thread of loyalty between them had snapped. When she finally left in May, it was still unclear precisely what the future of their relationship was to be.

While the success of *The Queen of Scots* had assured Zweig's reputation in Britain, he had no wish to become part of the English cultural scene. He had always acknowledged that his roots in Austro-German culture ran deep, maintaining that his only true homeland was, and would remain, the German language. It is indeed one of the great ironies of German-speaking exile that Zweig, the self-styled cosmopolitan, 'the great European', as his friend Jules Romains called him, always remained imprisoned in his native language.

He was in fact a more than competent linguist and during his early months in London made serious efforts to improve his rather rusty English. 'It is part of my "inner hygiene" and of my resolve to improve my English, that I will have no papers, periodicals or books forwarded to me here,' he wrote to Ebermayer.[55] However, these efforts soon lapsed: English was never to be more than a language of practical communication. He told Emil Ludwig that he liked the French better than the Germans, and the English better than both, but he nonetheless kept his distance, remaining studiously uninvolved in British affairs.[56]

In his autobiography *Die Welt von Gestern* (*The World of Yesterday*), Zweig notes that England was 'the only country in the "old world" in which I never published an article of a topical nature in a newspaper, never spoke on the radio, never took part in a public discussion'.[57] He describes his life in London as 'one long self-restraint' (*eine einzige Zurückhaltung*); he was indeed always conscious of the vulnerability of his position as a refugee, and the reticence which it imposed. He also suggests that he lived a life of self-imposed isolation, maintaining only formal contacts with his British publishers, having few, if any, English friends and refraining from speaking or appearing in public – statements which require considerable qualification.

In fact, he came to enjoy good relations with his British publishers, Cassells, lunching regularly with its chairman Newman Flower and his son Desmond. 'My stay here was extraordinarily pleasant, although I lived a secluded life. I still saw the best people. I now have a very pleasant personal relationship with the Flowers,' he wrote in December 1933.[58] Newman Flower was a publisher who felt confident enough to indulge his own taste. At the recommendation of Ben Huebsch, he had read one of Zweig's short novels and had been so impressed that he asked Zweig to become a Cassells author. Zweig also enjoyed friendly relations with Flower's son Desmond, a friendship based on a mutual passion for autograph manuscripts (Zweig actually presented the younger Flower with one or two valuable pieces). Desmond Flower recalled that he used to visit Zweig regularly at Hallam Street, usually on his way home from work.[59] At one time, Zweig allowed him to use the flat during his absence from London. Zweig himself declared: 'I feel not only as a Cassells author but as a real friend of you all and I hope there will still be much opportunity in this life to prove it.'[60] Another English friend was the journalist Joseph Leftwich, who remembered that from the time of Zweig's arrival in London, they saw each other almost daily, remaining in touch when Zweig was out of town.

On the other hand, Zweig did not seek the company of English writers, whose concerns he did not share, and who he felt belonged to a different cultural tradition from their European colleagues. There were exceptions, such as Hugh Walpole or the writer and actor John Drinkwater, whose plays he admired and with whom he shared an interest in historical biography. His speech at a memorial evening for Drinkwater in 1937 is a moving tribute to their friendship. He had always disliked being linked with parties and associations, and conspicuously avoided contact with writers' organisations, such as PEN. (Even when he accepted an invitation to the PEN Congress in Buenos Aires in 1936, he was careful to remain as far as possible in the background.) Newman Flower recalled that literary London would have been glad to honour Zweig and that he was offered public dinners and receptions, but always refused them, jealously guarding his privacy – and the German linguistic ambience he was anxious to preserve. In his personal sphere he continued to think, speak and write in German. Not only Lotte, his secretary, but all his closest friends and contacts in London were fellow-exiles – Herrmann-Neiße, Neumann (with whom he would occasionally dine in Lyons Corner House) and old friends from Austria like the writer and publisher Victor Fleischer.

During these early years of exile, Zweig became increasingly preoccupied with his Jewish heritage. As a young man in Vienna he had known Theodor Herzl, but despite his personal admiration for him, Zweig had never felt any affinity with Zionism. Like many assimilated Viennese Jews, he had identified completely with Austro-German culture, but his virtual expulsion from it had forced him, like other exiles, to acknowledge his Jewish identity.

His initial attitude to Nazi anti-semitism was, however, cautious, even ambivalent. Shortly after arriving in London, he commented in a letter to Romain Rolland, that he wished to see strict limitations imposed on Jewish immigration into Britain, lest a flood of Jewish refugees should provoke the very anti-semitism from which they had fled:

> There's no room for any more new arrivals. Without a certain breathing space the liberal spirit in France and England will be poisoned. Our whole task now consists in slowing down and regulating emigration –[61]

His caution matched that of official British Jewry: the Board of Deputies of British Jews was also in favour of controlling the flow of refugees.

The fate of the Jews, once more persecuted, once more forced into the diaspora of exile, continued to concern Zweig. Joseph Leftwich recalled that, when the Vilna Yiddish Theatre came to London on tour in 1934, Zweig was a frequent visitor, fascinated by this manifestation of a vibrantly Jewish culture. He even made a speech at a reception for the company in the Whitechapel Art Gallery. Leftwich, who saw much of Zweig in these years, suggested that he was moving closer to Zionism, and although the suggestion must be viewed in the light of Leftwich's own adherence to Zionism, the hypothesis is supported by Zweig's choice of theme for his next book, *Der begrabene Leuchter* (*The Buried Candelabrum*), on which he began work in 1935. The book retells the Jewish legend of the seven-branched menorah or candelabrum of Moses. Zweig had already used legend as literary material fifteen years earlier, when he had reworked a tale from Indian legend in *Die Augen des ewigen Bruders* ('The Eyes of the Eternal Brother'), but his choice of theme in *The Buried Candelabrum* is far more significant. The menorah is the emblem of the Jewish faith, symbolising the sense of community which it fosters. Stolen during the sack of Rome, and taken to Byzantium, the candelabrum is finally brought back in secret to Jerusalem, where it is buried by night, awaiting the time when the Jews are once more united, when the chosen people will once more inherit the Promised Land. Zweig completed the book in the summer of 1936.[62] Embellished by woodcuts by Margarete Hammerschlag, *The Buried Candelabrum* was published the following year in both Vienna and London. Cassells produced the book in a bibliophile edition of a thousand copies – a confirmation of the literary standing Zweig now enjoyed in Britain.

Further evidence of Zweig's preoccupation with his Jewish identity is provided by a speech he gave in 1936 on the occasion of the fiftieth anniversary of the 'Poor Jews Temporary Shelter' in Whitechapel.[63] The Shelter had been founded to promote the welfare of Jewish refugees from Eastern Europe, offering them assistance before they travelled on. Talking to Jewish migrants on the boat for England, Zweig had found that almost the only common knowledge among this great army of the homeless was that they could find refuge in the Shelter. Zweig admitted that, despite living in London, he had never heard of the Shelter, and spurred by a sense of shame, had gone to see it for himself.

His speech confirms the extent, and limitations, of his interest in Zionism. It reveals great empathy with the plight of the Jewish refugee, whose particular vulnerability he acknowledged. He also recognised the sense of Jewish solidarity which the Shelter exemplified, but it was for him subsumed into a wider human interdependence: he described the Shelter as 'this unknown and incomparable monument to human solidarity'. Zweig's identification with the fate of the Jews was not merely an intellectual concern. During his tour of Brazil in 1936, he gave a reading from *The Buried Candelabrum* to an audience of 1,200 people in Rio, insisting that the proceeds should go to aid Jewish refugees.

Stefan Zweig's dalliance with the German market after 1933 was not unique. Thomas Mann had been equally reticent, refraining from any public condemnation of Nazism for over three years. As long as his publisher Bermann Fischer stayed in Germany, Mann pursued the vain hope that he could maintain links with his reading public there, an attitude which was incomprehensible to many fellow-exiles.

Most of the other writers who had fled from Germany in 1933, had no such option: their work had already been proscribed by the regime, a measure entailing the loss of publishing outlets and royalty income. Most important, it meant the abandonment of precisely what Zweig and Mann still hoped to maintain: a readership with whom they shared a common language and cultural heritage.

There remained a German reading public outside Germany – not only among the growing number of German exiles, but in Austria and Switzerland, and among the large German-speaking minorities in Czechoslovakia, Hungary, Romania and elsewhere in Eastern Europe. It was the existence of these markets which made possible the emergence of exile publishing. In the summer of 1933, exile publishing houses sprang up in all the main centres of emigration – in Prague, Zurich, Paris and above all Amsterdam. In London there was no such initiative. It was not until 1941, when successive waves of emigration had swollen the number of refugees to over seventy thousand, that the first German books were published in Britain.

Many exile publishing ventures were predictably short-lived. The opportunities for publication and distribution were limited, circumscribed by the emergence of right-wing regimes, and further undermined by the growth of Nazi influence in Central and Eastern Europe. Allert de Lange and Querido, the two main exile publishers, both based in Amsterdam, were established as German sections of existing publishing houses, which spared them various publishing overheads. Even so, they were rarely able to exceed a print run of four thousand copies, even for a popular novel or biography, thus severely limiting any advance or royalty they could pay to the author.[64]

The material and creative problems of exiled writers were also compounded by the deliberate efforts of the Nazi regime to silence them. These efforts were directed and coordinated through German embassies and consulates which carefully monitored the activities of anti-Nazi refugees, reporting back to their masters in Berlin. On more than one occasion, German diplomats called on the Foreign Office in London to complain of the 'anti-German' activities of some refugees, demanding that they should be required to refrain from political activity while in Britain – and if they failed to comply, should be deported.

Where diplomatic efforts failed, economic pressure was exercised. German-language publishers outside the Third Reich were threatened with boycott by the German book-trade if they published proscribed authors. Fritz Landshoff, Director of Querido Verlag, reported that booksellers in various countries, including Britain, were told that their supplies of German books would be withdrawn if they continued to stock works by anti-Nazi exiles. Foreign newspapers were threatened with punitive retaliation if they so much as published reviews of books by exiled authors – and some, even those of the standing of the *Neue Zürcher Zeitung*, refrained from doing so.

Such pressure could of course most effectively be applied in German-speaking countries. In 1934, Switzerland proscribed the publication, in books or newspapers, of any material which might harm Switzerland's relations with other countries. But also elsewhere, notably in Holland and Greece, Nazi pressure resulted in the prosecution of anti-Nazi exiles for the publication of material hostile to the Third

Reich. Hans Liepmann's novel *Das Vaterland*, published in Holland, was impounded and its author sentenced to imprisonment for allegedly 'insulting the head of state of a friendly power' (i.e. Hindenburg).[65]

In their attempts to silence their most dangerous opponents abroad, the Nazis even went to the lengths of assassination and abduction. The philosopher Theodor Lessing was murdered at his home in Marienbad and there were several cases of political kidnapping, most famously that of the journalist Berthold Jacob, who was lured to a rendezvous in Basel and abducted across the Swiss border into Germany. The activities of Nazi agents, sometimes recruited from amongst the ranks of the emigrants themselves, had caused grave disquiet in various European countries. While Britain had not yet become a major centre of German emigration, the abduction of Berthold Jacob in March 1935 had had a particular resonance there, as the Gestapo agent Hans Wesemann, who had lured Jacob to his fateful rendezvous, had been living and operating in London. The climate of unease increased shortly after, when two anti-Nazi refugees, the former Reichstag deputy Mathilde Wurm, and the journalist Dora Fabian, who had been investigating Wesemann, were found dead from poisoning in their flat in Great Ormond Street. While the coroner returned a verdict of suicide, there were many who suspected foul play. The British authorities played down the political dimensions of the case, but the deaths of the two women nonetheless gave rise to grave anxieties about the activities of Nazi agents in Britain. Newspapers printed sensational stories ('Is there a secret foreign Terror in our midst?' asked the *Daily Express*, 6 April 1935), questions were asked in Parliament and at least two unofficial enquiries into the deaths were begun.[66]

Theatre managers were pressurised not to produce plays by exiled writers. In Zurich, performances of Friedrich Wolf's *Professor Mamlock*, a passionate exposition of Nazi anti-semitism, were violently disrupted by groups of Swiss fascists. There were no such scenes in London, but there were more subtle pressures, which may well have resulted in examples of pre-censorship: a production of Ferdinand Bruckner's anti-fascist play *Die Rassen* which Robert Klein, former director of Berlin's Deutsches Theater, planned to produce in London, never took place, apparently because the theatre management was reluctant to produce a play with such explosive political content. Such cases of pre-censorship, though difficult to substantiate, were probably few and far between. Certainly, despite such pressures, anti-Nazi plays were performed in Britain – for example *Professor Mamlock* at the Westminster Theatre in 1935 and Toller's *No More Peace* at the Gate Theatre the following year.

These developments meant the gradual contraction of even the limited market available to exiled authors, increasing their dependence on publication in translation. Even here, the author's prospects were limited, and particularly so in Britain, where the number of translations which appeared represented only a tiny proportion of the total publishing output.

The intrinsic problems of publishing work by German émigrés were compounded by the effects of the Depression, which began to deepen in 1934. Desmond Flower records that the illustrated book was an early casualty of the recession, which by 1935 was biting deeply into Cassells general list.[67] The year 1935 was in fact the economic trough of the recession in British publishing: thereafter things began to improve a little, peaking in 1937, before declining again in the immediate pre-war years. It was against this political and economic background that the exiled German or Austrian writer had to struggle for survival.

ROBERT NEUMANN: LOST IN TRANSLATION

Robert Neumann returned to London in February 1934 determined to re-establish a literary career which had been derailed by events in Germany and Austria. At the time, he still spoke little English; six years later he began his first novel in the language, going on to achieve wide recognition as an 'English' novelist. The story of this literary metamorphosis is an instructive paradigm of the obstacles facing the exiled writer – and the opportunities available to those sufficiently versatile to master the craft of writing in another language.

In 1934, Neumann was scarcely (in Zweig's phrase) 'one of the ten authors writing in German who could afford to be exiled'. He was little known in Britain: although no fewer than five of his books had already been published in English translation, they had made little impact on the British reading public. The reasons for this lay partly in the economics of publishing: most of Neumann's work had appeared with a small publisher, Peter Davies, who lacked the resources to promote a foreign author in the British market. Some of Neumann's distinctive style must also have been lost in translation: each of the five books had been assigned to a different translator, some of whom never translated another book. The novel *Die Macht* was translated by the English writer Dorothy Richardson, who was more used to translating from French than German. At the request of the publisher, she undertook both to translate and to condense the novel, shortening it by more than a third. When Neumann saw the published version, he insisted that the entire edition be scrapped.[68]

Despite such misfortunes, Neumann found himself increasingly forced to write for the translator. The pattern of publication of his work up to 1939 exemplifies the rapid contraction of German-language publishing outside the Third Reich and the German author's growing dependence on the English-speaking market. In these five years Neumann wrote four books, only three of which were able to appear in German – and all of those in Switzerland. All four were published in English, though each with a different publisher. This small odyssey around English publishing houses confirms that Neumann did not find automatic acceptance for his work. Some of his difficulties were of his own making. His correspondence with publishers suggests that he was a 'difficult' author, who sometimes made elaborate demands and whose feelings were easily ruffled. Other problems were intrinsic to the work itself, exemplifying the cultural difficulties of adapting style and content to the requirements of the English market.

In the early months of 1934, Neumann worked intensively on *Zaharoff the Armaments King*. Always a rapid and fluent writer, Neumann completed the manuscript by the spring of 1934, only to find that it was immediately the object of dispute and litigation. The problem lay in Neumann's treatment of his subject. Formerly managing director of Vickers (then one of the world's largest armaments manufacturers), Zaharoff was an ambiguous figure on the world stage: international arms dealer, philanthropist and patron of the arts, a former owner of the Monte Carlo casino and the man behind the scenes in many a political deal. The shadowy nature of his activities served only to enhance his fascination: at this time there were at least three books about him in preparation. Neumann certainly admitted that he was fascinated by his subject, for whom he even felt a certain affinity: he later commented that the book showed 'an adventurer cruelly tracking down an adventurer'.[69] A publisher's reader called it 'an important and even valuable book . . . half a detective story, half a contribution to history'.[70] It is in fact a judicious mixture of fact and fiction, interweaving historical documents, newspaper reports and fictional scenes into a polemical indictment of Zaharoff and his involvement in the international arms trade. Neumann portrays his subject as a shady dealer, a swindler on a grand scale, ruthlessly accumulating money and power.

The book's polemical tone alarmed Neumann's publishers, Rich & Cowan, who, fearing a libel suit, declined to publish the manuscript unless he revised it to include material supplied by Zaharoff himself. When Neumann refused, the publisher threatened to sue him for failing to supply a publishable manuscript, but Neumann, who for all his cynicism was not without principle, still refused, maintaining that the proposed revisions would destroy 'the intrinsic truth' (*innere Wahrheit*) of what he had written. The resulting legal action, lasting almost three years and ending only with Zaharoff's death in 1936, cast a long shadow over Neumann's early years in Britain. Fortunately, he was not without friends. His case was conducted by the left-wing barrister D. N. Pritt, who refused to accept any payment for his services.

Economically stranded by the withdrawal of his original publisher, the resourceful Neumann hastened to prepare a serial version of the book, which he had had translated at his own expense. In the course of 1934 he negotiated with *The Strand Magazine* which was interested in acquiring the serial rights for the reported sum of £5,000, but these negotiations finally fell through, apparently for legal reasons.[71] By this time, however, Neumann had placed his original manuscript with a Swiss publisher, who published a German edition without any repercussions, encouraging Neumann to offer the book to another British publisher, George Allen & Unwin.

Stanley Unwin was then at the height of his eminence in the

profession, having been President of the Publishers Association in 1933. In a letter to him, Neumann conceded that the book was 'audacious' in places, but assured him that Pritt was willing to vet the manuscript to remove any potentially libellous passages. The Allen & Unwin director Charles Furth replied that 'whatever the commercial prospects, this is the type of work with which we like to be identified'.[72] This was probably true, though it should be added that Stanley Unwin had a reputation for building up his list with unusual commercial shrewdness, rarely publishing a book on which he lost money.

Allen & Unwin finally published *Zaharoff the Armaments King* in September 1935, the text having been vetted by Pritt and Dorothy Woodman to limit the possibility of libel action. The critical reception was mixed, clearly depending on political perspective. While Raymond Postgate praised the book as 'a serious and important study of one of the strangest figures of this century', the reviewer of *The Times Literary Supplement* dismissed it as a polemic, asserting that its only interest lay in 'the light which it throws on the author's psychology and especially his readiness to attribute diabolism to the makers of armaments'.[73] Charles Furth cited the latter review as an example of 'one of the difficulties of selling Radical books outside the Labour market'.[74] *Zaharoff* was none the less clearly a success. During 1935 there was also an American edition, quickly followed by translations into French, Dutch, Czech and other languages. In Britain, the modest first printing of 1,500 copies was sold out within six months and the book was reprinted twice in 1936. Unwin later sold the book to the Readers' Union and by 1939 over thirty-five thousand copies had been sold in Britain alone.

The success of the book eased Neumann's financial problems, but did not ensure the publication of his other work in Britain. He offered Unwin a volume containing three of his short novels, all previously published in German. The comments of Unwin's reader, on this occasion Edward Crankshaw, serve to illustrate the cultural obstacles confronting the foreign (and particularly the German) writer in adapting to the English market. Crankshaw called the short novel *Karriere* ('Career') 'a sort of Teutonic version of *Gentlemen Prefer Blondes*' and felt that it was 'very strong meat indeed' for English readers.[75] When Neumann offered the same volume to Victor Gollancz, he too rejected it because he too disliked its amoral tenor. However, he was happy to accept Neumann's new novel *The Queen's Doctor*, which he had written at great speed in 1934.

The Queen's Doctor is an historical novel, recounting the rise and fall of Johann-Friedrich Struensee, doctor at the court of Christian VII of Denmark, who used his position as the Queen's favourite to introduce Rousseauesque reforms, only to fall from favour and be executed in 1772. Neumann's reason for choosing this subject-matter was purely pragmatic. The historical novel was a popular genre with a broad reading public largely uninterested in contemporary events in Europe. It was one adopted by a number of exiled writers, since it allied an appeal to popular taste with the opportunity to present contemporary political questions through the device of historical distance. However, *The Queen's Doctor* was only superficially concerned with historical analogies for Nazism. Neumann saw the historical novel primarily as a means of writing a commercial success. He had written the book at the suggestion of Stefan Zweig, whose recent success with *Marie Antoinette* confirmed the appeal of historical subject-matter for a largely middlebrow audience.

Struensee (to give the book its original title) was first published in German by the exile publishers Querido in 1935. The modest advance Neumann received served to heighten his awareness of his economic dependence on the English-speaking market – and consequently on the translator. Such was his concern about the quality of the translation that he asked to see the work of the translator, Edwin Muir, in manuscript. 'The fate of the book is of very great importance to me,' he wrote to Muir, asking him 'to adapt certain passages to English requirements rather than simply translate them'.[76] While acknowledging Neumann's legitimate concerns, Muir had problems of his own, which were partly those intrinsic to literary translation: 'Neumann's style is so idiosyncratic and strives for so much nuance that it needs a great deal of care . . . to get it right.'[77] In fact, it required so much care that Muir eventually had to ask for more time, so that the publication, originally planned for autumn 1935, had to be postponed until the following year. When Muir delivered his final version, Gollancz congratulated him on 'a brilliant translation'.[78] Muir's translation was in places extremely free. He had actually condensed the novel, paring down the excesses of Neumann's somewhat florid style. Despite the care he had devoted to the translation, Muir did not like the book itself, calling it 'meretricious through and through, without a spark of creative talent, but with an infinity of clever dressing up'.[79] Although the critics were much kinder, congratulating Neumann on his treatment of a little-known historical episode, the book achieved only modest sales. Neumann partly blamed Gollancz, whom he portrayed in his memoirs as a publisher of many causes, but always totally committed to the most recent one: 'Gollancz was going to conquer the world with *Struensee*, but he forgot about it after the first 1,300 copies because there was something new to be fought or to be saved.'[80] In retrospect he was prepared to admit that the novel was one of his worst, 'a potboiler which didn't boil – until after the war' when it was reprinted in Germany, its potential as a costume drama attracting two separate film versions, one in Germany in 1957 and one in Britain two years later.[81]

Neumann's personal life during these early years in London was no less bounded by the material and cultural exigencies of exile. Though he received a useful advance for the Zaharoff book, his subsequent dispute with the publisher soon drained his resources, causing the financial problems which dogged him throughout the decade. In an alien city, whose language he had not yet mastered, Neumann sought refuge in a modest boarding-house in Paddington, run by a German film actress from the silent days, called Lo Hardy. It was very much a German-speaking haven, inhabited exclusively by German and Austrian refugees. Lo Hardy's rates were thirty shillings a week, including breakfast. Every evening the guests would assemble for a hot meal at which, inevitably, German was always spoken. Among the guests Neumann encountered there in 1934 were the young actress Lilli Palmer, then on the brink of stardom in the British cinema, and the colourful Stefan Lorant, a pioneer of photo-journalism, now best remembered as co-founder and editor of *Lilliput* and *Picture Post*.

Neumann had few contacts with English writers at this time, but among those he did meet was Dorothy Richardson, whose translation of *Die Macht* had so offended him. Surprisingly, they got on extremely well. Richardson was apparently equally charmed by Neumann's physical presence and his colourful account of his past: not only was he 'gigantic' and a past swimming champion, but 'he was also a sailor, like Conrad'. Neumann was indeed a man of imposing stature, who in his youth had been a champion swimmer. (It was while working as an instructor for a ladies' swimming club in Vienna that he had met his first wife, Stefi.) He was, moreover, a witty and entertaining conversationalist, possessing considerable Viennese charm to which women were particularly susceptible. Dorothy Richardson called him 'a most delightful creature', declaring that both she and her husband 'fell in love with him'.[82]

Neumann's limited English meant that – apart from German-speakers like Dorothy Richardson – his social contacts at this time were confined almost exclusively to fellow-exiles. Among those whom he met regularly were the journalist Rudolf Olden, Max Herrmann-Neiße and Stefan Zweig. In the context of their native Austria, Zweig and Neumann had met only rarely, apparently finding little in common. Zweig may well have viewed his colleague as something of a literary parvenu: he was certainly not one of the privileged few invited to visit Zweig in his house on the Kapuzinerberg. Suddenly thrown together by the vagaries of exile, the two men – both natives of Vienna – began to see much of each other, their friendship even blossoming into collaboration. They would sometimes dine in Lyons Corner House in the Strand, 'that cheap and gilded eating palace' which became a favourite haunt of German-speaking exiles.[83] Zweig was, like Neumann, a film enthusiast and they regularly went to the cinema together, once to see Garbo in the title role of *Queen Christina*. The avid reaction of both men, which Neumann remembered many years later, confirms both the power of Garbo as a cultural icon, and the extraordinary attraction which the cinema held for many intellectuals in the thirties.

Neumann even tried his hand at film writing at this time. The British film industry was enjoying a boom, inaugurated by the extraordinary success of Alexander Korda's *The Private Life of Henry VIII*. Neumann's interest was no doubt also encouraged by the example of the numerous German exiles who had already established a foothold in British films. In 1934 he worked on the film *Abdul the Damned* which in truth was hardly a British film at all: produced by Max Schach, directed by Karl Grune and starring the famous Austrian actor Fritz Kortner. Neumann supplied the story for the screenplay: an exotic confection set in Turkey, in which a Viennese opera star saves the life of her lover by joining the sultan's harem. In view of his problems with English, Neumann was fortunate that those collaborating on the screenplay included the playwright Ashley Dukes, whose translations and adaptations had done much to introduce German drama to the English theatre in the twenties. Kortner, still struggling to master the rudiments of the language, learned his lines sentence by sentence. 'And then the assistant director would put his head round the dressing-room door and say: "Mr Kortner, we've changed these three sentences and taken that line out and added these few words here, so it's no longer that, it's this –" And he was gone, leaving Kortner in despair: "How do I learn this at the last minute and how do you pronounce it anyway?"'[84]

It was Neumann's first direct experience of the film industry, and like so many of his generation he remained dazzled by the artistic and commercial potential of the medium. During 1935–36 he attempted to sell the film rights to his stories and novels to Hollywood. Warner Brothers, always more inclined than other studios to make films with a social message, were interested in filming *Zaharoff*, but in 1937 finally dropped the idea because the social climate in Europe seemed unfavourable.[85] In 1936 Neumann suggested to Stefan Zweig that they should collaborate on a film version of *Manon Lescaut* – and they did indeed produce a script, working in the seclusion of Zweig's flat in Portland Place. Coming across the script many years later, Neumann was struck by the 'fine writing' it contained: 'It was cooked in so much of the best butter that it had once again a style, a dignity, a touch of distinction.'[86] However distinguished, the script was never filmed, though it was offered to producers in both Hollywood and Paris. A typescript copy, stamped with the name of a Beverly Hills agent, still survives, having found a last resting place in the obscurity of an archive in Vienna. Neumann's only apparent success was the sale of a story on the life of Alfred Nobel to the London company Capitol Film, but by 1937 the British film industry was deep in recession, Capitol Film on the verge of bankruptcy, and *Dynamite Nobel* was never filmed.

In 1936 the first German and Austrian exiles began to leave Europe for the USA. Famous writers, such as Ernst Toller, Bruno Frank and Ferdinand Bruckner arrived in Hollywood to work as scriptwriters for the major studios. Neumann too was keen to move there, engaging various agents to negotiate a screen-writing contract on his behalf. But the early gold-rush days in Hollywood were over. 'As you must know,' wrote one well-known agent, 'the problem of selling authors and playwrights for personal service contracts in Hollywood is, at the moment, not as easy as it used to be.'[87] When Neumann finally did receive the offer of a contract with MGM in 1940, it was too late. In post-war years, Neumann wrote several screenplays, but only two were actually filmed: for all his talent as a storyteller, his writing lacked dramatic tension. The glittering prizes of the film world always remained tantalisingly beyond his reach.

In August 1934 Neumann was joined in London by his wife Stefi and their son Heinrich, then twelve years old. However, the couple's reunion quickly confirmed that they had grown apart and their relationship finally deteriorated so much that Stefi left again in February 1935. Neumann's friendship with the German journalist Franziska Becker, nicknamed Rolly, also dates from this time, though it is uncertain how far their relationship was the cause or merely the consequence of the rift between Neumann and his wife. Rolly, who had arrived in London in 1933 with her husband, a film director, was then working as a publisher's reader for Allen & Unwin. One of her tasks was to read *Zaharoff the Armaments King*, which she warmly recommended for publication. Shortly after she was invited to meet the author, who carried a strong impression away from their first meeting, remembering her as 'slim, slight, dark, and how young'.[88] Neumann was particularly attracted by her youth; he was married four times, the last three to women much younger than himself. Indirectly, it was Zaharoff who had brought the couple together and there was thus a certain symmetry to the fact that Rolly finally left her husband to live with Neumann on the very day Zaharoff died. She was to remain Neumann's companion for the next fifteen years, marrying him in 1941 and divorcing him in 1952.

During these early years of his exile, Neumann was technically not yet a refugee. Although (unlike Zweig) he was not able to publish his work in Austria, he retained his Austrian passport and was free to return there at any time. In summer 1935 he spent several weeks in Alt-Aussee in the Salzkammergut and stayed more than once in Vienna in 1935–36. While the purpose of these visits was to spend time with his wife and son, he was obviously also unable to withstand the pull of his native city.

These were strangely twilight years in Vienna, a time of moral and political ambiguity. As Hitler took and consolidated power in Germany, Austria had tried to assert its national independence. In 1933 the Dollfuß government had suspended parliament, inaugurating the authoritarian and hierarchical *Ständestaat* (corporate state). The failure of an attempted Nazi coup in July 1934 apparently left Austria free to follow its own road to fascism. While many political opponents of the *Ständestaat* had been forced to flee from Austria after February 1934, some cultural refugees from the Third Reich, particularly actors and other theatre workers, had actually found refuge there. Although the constitution of the *Ständestaat* was explicitly undemocratic, its laws were not openly anti-semitic; censorship was certainly in force, but it was more discreet, even dilatory than in Nazi Germany. Prominent playwrights, such as Zuckmayer and Horvath, whose work was banned in Germany, could still be performed in Vienna; well-known Jewish authors, such as Werfel and Zweig, had few difficulties in publishing in Austria.

The young novelist Hilde Spiel, who left Austria for London late in 1936, experienced these years in Vienna as 'a confused and blurred time', full of 'half measures, distortions and aberrations'.[89] In the city's coffee-houses and salons, avowed opponents of the regime mingled openly with its supporters in fevered, if ambivalent debate. In this prelude to Nazism, the Viennese continued to pursue their traditional pleasures, as though unaware that they were living on borrowed time. Spiel notes more than one occasion when Neumann, during his brief visits to Vienna, joined her and others in the fashionable bars of the city until the early hours of the morning, once when she was celebrating the acceptance of her doctorate.

Such insouciance did not go unpunished. While staying with his wife during one such visit in 1936, Neumann was woken in the early hours of the morning, arrested by armed police and held for twelve hours until he could prove beyond doubt that he was not the German Communist leader Heinz Neumann, for whom he had mistakenly been arrested. Neumann remarked drily that it was the closest he ever came to being mistaken for a Communist. The sinister absurdity of this incident was sufficient to deter him from revisiting his native city. When he finally returned long after the war, he had assumed a new identity as a British citizen and an English author.

The climate of British culture in the inter-war years was not one which allowed foreigners to assimilate easily. While this is famously true of the London art world, it was no less true of literary circles. British authors generally sought little contact with their continental counterparts, a situation which hardly changed with the arrival of émigré writers in Britain. One exception to this rule was the PEN Club, founded in 1921 by Catharine Dawson Scott to give authors of different nations the opportunity to meet and understand each other. A PEN centre had been founded in Germany in 1925. Eight years later, its President, Alfred Kerr, and Secretary, Herwarth Walden, were among the first refugees to flee the country. The issue of freedom of speech in general, and its suppression in Germany in particular, were the questions which politicised the PEN in the thirties, culminating at the International PEN Congress in Ragusa, when Ernst Toller delivered a passionate denunciation of the book burnings in Germany, forcing the official German delegation to walk out demonstratively in protest. The German centre later withdrew from the International PEN, leaving a vacuum which was filled by German writers in exile.

In December 1933 the International PEN Secretary Hermon Ould received a letter announcing plans to establish a PEN group of German writers in exile, and requesting official recognition of the group 'as representing free German literature in the spirit of the Internationale (*sic*) PEN Club'.[90] Such recognition was duly granted a few months later. The four signatories to the original letter were among the most prominent of German literary exiles: Ernst Toller, Lion Feuchtwanger, the journalist Rudolf Olden – and the poet Max Herrmann-Neiße.

MAX HERRMANN-NEIßE: 'MY LIFE IS EVER EMPTIER'

When Max Herrmann-Neiße landed in Dover on 19 September 1933, he was setting foot in England for the first time: he would spend the remaining eight years of his life in London, where he died on 8 April 1941. He was a voluntary exile from the Third Reich, which he had left, not to escape immediate personal danger, but because of his strong moral revulsion against Nazism. Summarising his feelings later, he wrote that human dignity required him to leave a country 'which has been enslaved by an aggressive, lawless, intolerant system, hostile to freedom and ruthless in its worship of power'.[91]

The early months of the Nazi regime had confirmed his worst fears. Writing to his wife following the book burnings in Germany, he declared flatly 'that there is no question that *I* shall ever return to the country as long as these conditions prevail, and that may well be at least the next decade'.[92]

Like many other émigrés, Herrmann-Neiße had gone first to Zurich – 'the beloved city' which he celebrated in so many of his early poems of exile. He would gladly have stayed there, but the Swiss authorities had granted him only a temporary residence permit and refused to extend it. After short stays in Holland and Paris (where he had also felt a sense of well-being), he travelled to London to rejoin his wife, who had arrived there some weeks earlier.

He had come to London at the invitation of his long-term friend and benefactor Alphonse Sondheimer, a dealer in precious stones, who was reputed to have made a fortune in deals disposing of the Habsburg crown jewels after the collapse of the Austro-Hungarian Empire in 1918. Sondheimer was not only shrewd and resourceful, but also unusually far-sighted: though well established in Berlin, with premises in the prestigious Tiergartenstrasse, he left Germany abruptly early in 1933 and transferred his business to London. There he took a furnished flat at 83 Duke Street, in which he now offered Max and Leni a room. It was intended to be a temporary refuge, a place in which they could spend the winter: in fact, the couple were to become permanent guests.

Arriving in London in September after the calmest of Channel crossings, Herrmann-Neiße sensed that his exile had only now begun in earnest.

> This is actually the beginning for me of life in exile, for everything else, even Paris, was in one way or another what I was used to, a substitute for home, Continent. But here it is a quite quite different world, an unfamiliar, closed world, with absolutely no connection to mine.[93]

England was indeed a completely alien world, in which he was never able to feel even remotely at home. Sensing how out of place he would be, he had been reluctant to come to London, finally coming only at Leni's insistence. He had always shrunk from taking decisions, preferring to temporise and finally submitting to decisions made by others – only, as he engagingly admitted, to complain of them afterwards. Herrmann-Neiße's reservations about living in London were not merely cultural. His friendship with Alfons Sondheimer, on whose patronage he had come to rely, dated from the late twenties. Their relationship was not without its ambiguities, Sondheimer having enjoyed an intimate relationship with Leni, which, in the free-and-easy atmosphere of Weimar Berlin, Max had known and tolerated. In the cold light of exile, however, he saw this relationship in a different perspective, fearing that he might lose Leni altogether.

His early months in London were very much a provisional arrangement. Like other émigrés, he was granted only a temporary residence permit, which required periodic renewal and carried the stipulation that he should undertake no work, paid or unpaid. The restrictions were unnecessary, for he had no prospect of finding employment. He spoke little English, and though he took lessons, he was soon forced to acknowledge that he had difficulty in learning it at his age. His problems were not so much with the written language, as with the rhythms of English speech. After more than a year in London, he was forced to admit:

> If someone speaks English to me, I still hardly understand a word, or if I see an English film, or have to say something, I have a problem . . . and so I hang around here, good for nothing and completely superfluous.[94]

When he came to England, he had little affinity with English culture, noting ruefully that even Shakespeare was a taste he had failed to acquire. Throughout his eight years in London, he retained a sense of inadequacy in the language. Though he eventually managed (much to his own surprise) to master English sufficiently to read Shakespeare in the original, he never felt really at home in speaking it. 'Oh, I shall never learn to speak English properly,' he interjects in his poem 'Ich lese Shakespeare'.[95] If the language was unmanageable and the culture unfamiliar, the English themselves seemed distant and impenetrable, the inhabitants of another world. Writing to Klaus Pinkus, he admitted that he envied him the opportunity to be in Zurich: 'There I could finally once more pour my heart out and talk to *Europeans*. Over here, it's a different continent and a different breed, you might almost say another form of life.'[96] Unlike Zweig, he found the calm, restrained atmosphere of London anything but a relief: it seemed almost a reverse image of his own emotional turmoil. Like most other émigrés, he felt defeated by the political complacency. The polite interest in the political problems of the Continent, and the widespread feeling of immunity from them, seemed *prima facie* evidence of political naivety.

The early poems Herrmann-Neiße wrote in exile document his feelings of unease and isolation in the stern grey city where fate had stranded him. The exile's life was uncertain and impermanent:

Schwer ist es an diesem Ort,
wenn die Abendnebel sinken,
sich bei fremdem Volk und Wort
um die Einsamkeit zu trinken.

It is hard in this place, / when the evening mists descend, / amidst a foreign people and an alien tongue / to drown one's loneliness in drink.[97]

Sitting alone in Hyde Park amid the impersonal swirl of the city's relentless activity, he felt wretchedly homesick:

Ich saß Byron gegenüber
auf der Promenadenbank:
Autos jagten wild vorüber,
und mein Herz war heimwehkrank.

I sat opposite Byron / on the park bench: / cars hurtled wildly past / and my heart was sick for home.[98]

Subjectively he seems to have perceived London as virtually boundless, feeling alienated by the apparently endless succession of streets, the rows of terraced houses, replicating into infinity:

Fremd ist die Stadt und leer
Ich gehe ohne Sinn
in ihrem Nichts umher,
dem ich verfallen bin. . . .
Das Laute ist nur laut
und lärmt an mir vorbei
Haus ist an Haus gebaut
zu öder Wüstenei.

The city is alien and empty. / I walk pointlessly / about in its nothingness, /
by which I am enslaved. . . / The sounds are merely loud / passing me
noisily by / house follows house / in a desolate wasteland.[99]

The image of London as a wasteland (*Wüstenei*) is a recurrent one in his
exile poems.

These poems suggest that, during his early months in London,
Herrmann-Neiße made little attempt to adjust to his new surroundings.
Spiritually and emotionally he remained in Germany, returning in his
imagination to the narrow streets and familiar corners of his native
Neiße. He had begun work on a novel called *Die Bernert-Paula* ('Paula
Bernert'), in which he traced, through the figure of his eponymous
heroine, the history of a 'Silesian provincial town' from the turn of the
century to the Nazis' seizure of power.[100] Despite its setting, and often
precise topographical references, the book is not so much a portrayal of
Neiße as of the small-town atmosphere which had nurtured first
nationalism and then Nazism. The novel's 'Silesian provincial town' is
therefore a microcosm of Germany at large. He gave the novel the subtitle 'Eine Geschichte zum Vorlesen?' ('A Story to be Read Aloud?'): as
one might read to children, for both pleasure and moral instruction.

He worked rapidly, completing the first draft of the manuscript in
March 1934, making a fair copy in three large school exercise books. In
his final paragraph, he suggested that the book had gone its own way:
'In its course, we discussed more that was tricky, repulsive to the
sensitive disposition, than I had originally expected. The subject-
matter demanded it. . . Is it none the less still a story to be read aloud
everywhere?'[101]

Klaus Völker, the recent editor of Herrmann-Neiße's works, suggests that he initially hoped the novel might be broadcast on one of the

German-language stations, such as Radio Saarbrücken, which could easily be heard inside Germany, but there is no evidence that he actually submitted the novel for broadcast or publication.[102] In fact, he seems to have written it for his desk drawer, keeping its very existence to himself, making no mention of it in his letters. He was always loath to discuss work in progress, fearing that to talk about it might disrupt the creative process. It is also clear that after completing the manuscript he had doubts as to its literary merit. In a letter to Leni in July 1934, he asked her to bring the manuscript with her to Zurich, as he wished to show it to his friend Friedrich Grieger:

> Writers are as attached to their awkward and sloppy offspring as any other father . . . and are always trying to get a more favourable verdict on the child from someone or other. But I leave it up to you to decide whether we shouldn't just pass over it in charitable silence.[103]

For Herrmann-Neiße, the novel was an extended reflection on Germany, and an escape from the unwelcome reality of exile. It was to remain unpublished for more than fifty years.

From the first, Herrmann-Neiße had been among those who discounted the idea that Nazism would collapse quickly, and the events of his first year in exile had only strengthened his view: 'Incidentally, my pessimistic conviction of the duration and stability of the Hitler regime constantly increases. Fortunately, so does my final spiritual release from things which are past and hence radically settled.'[104] The spiritual release included his parting from many 'false friends', who had made their peace with the new regime or even endorsed it. 'How many friendships have been ruined / since treachery is well rewarded.'

Herrmann-Neiße insisted that he too could have won recognition in the new Germany, if he had been prepared to compromise with it:

> I too could be a recognised German poet now, with my nature poetry and my Silesian peasant forebears, but I could never allow myself to be promoted, even tacitly, by a system which I regard as truly diabolical.[105]

He and Grieger, whose friendship dated from their days together in Neiße, continued to correspond until 1939. Grieger visited Berlin from time to time, and undertook – at some personal risk – to return to Herrmann's flat to rescue some of the important notes and manuscripts which he had left behind and which Grieger forwarded piecemeal to him in London. It was Grieger who was to edit one of the first selections from his friend's work to appear in the post-war Federal Republic.

By early 1934 it had become clear that the Herrmanns' stay in London was to be more permanent, and it was decided that they and Sondheimer would move from his small Mayfair flat which was proving increasingly cramped for three people. On 20 April this curious *ménage à trois* moved into a four-roomed flat in a newly-built apartment block in Great Cumberland Street. The flat was on the sixth floor, with views across Marble Arch and into Hyde Park. The Herrmanns had their own room which now contained the bed from their Berlin flat; on the wall was the pencil drawing of the poet by George Grosz which had previously hung over Herrmann-Neiße's writing-desk in Berlin.[106]

Herrmann-Neiße viewed the change of flat with some ambivalence. While grateful for Sondheimer's generosity, he felt uncomfortable with his position as permanent guest, complaining in a letter to Grieger that he had lost even the semblance of independence: 'Previously, in my own flat, I had at least the illusion of a certain independence, but now. . .'[107] His humiliation at this dependence was undoubtedly increased by the ambiguities of their relationship and the knowledge that the renewal of his residence permit was subject to Sondheimer's sponsorship.

Herrmann-Neiße was already well versed in the doubts and despairs of exile. Among those he had met in the first wave of exile in Zurich was an old friend, the noted cabaret artist Paul Nikolaus. Famous for his scathingly witty commentary on public affairs and public figures, Nikolaus had realised that there was no place for him in the new Germany. Ultimately unable to face the prospect of exile, he had committed suicide: 'I cannot in future live in Berlin,' he wrote, 'and I cannot live without Berlin – so I'm going.'[108]

Publicly Herrmann-Neiße seemed reconciled to his exile, even ready to count his blessings:

> And so I eke out an existence here as a 'visitor'. . . My life is of necessity very respectable, walks in Hyde Park, sometimes a visit to one of the many fine galleries, or to the cinema, in the evenings almost always at home, where there is at least some good dark bottled stout.[109]

In the privacy of his poetry, he was more pessimistic, submitting to feelings of inexorable decline:

Not und Angst beflecken
meines Lebens Rest.
Was ich jetzt ertrage
macht mich alt und krank.
Alle meine Tage
atmen Untergang.

Want and fear stain / the rest of my life. / What I now endure / makes me
old and ill. / All my days / breathe doom.[110]

The move into the new flat forced him to acknowledge the impasse he
had reached: unable to reconcile himself to living in London, but also
unable to escape from it. Taking stock of his life on the occasion of his
forty-eighth birthday in May, he wrote:

Immer leerer wird mein Leben
Immer mehr Gefangenschaft
Und schon hab ich, Trost zu geben
mir und anderen – keine Kraft

My life grows ever emptier / more and more an imprisonment / and I have
lost the strength / to give consolation – to myself or others[111]

He continued to suffer from feelings of homesickness which would
return with particular intensity at Christmas or other festivals. Writing
to his fellow-poet Alfred Wolfenstein at Christmas 1934, he confessed
his deep unhappiness: 'Here unfortunately there is no real Christmas
spirit, the weather is warm, damp and foggy, I am discontented – with
God and the world and above all with myself, finding everything
that's happening in the world repulsive.'[112] Writing shortly afterwards
to the novelist Paul Zech, he confided that he did 'not feel very happy
in this frighteningly large, unwelcoming, businesslike London'. He
was not ungrateful, acknowledging that England offered a refuge
which enabled him to preserve his moral integrity and intellectual
freedom: 'Here I am far removed from the barbarity, can be a pacifist,
democrat, lover of freedom, antimilitarist and have no need to incur
the guilt of the shameful brown regime.'[113] But all his letters
nonetheless make clear his feeling of isolation 'in this hospitable but
cruelly alien land'.[114]

It was not only the physical environment of London which he found alienating but the lack of good company and congenial meeting-places, such as the cafés and beer-houses of Neiße and Berlin. He made little effort to cultivate English acquaintances, defeated by a language he felt he would never master. But he also saw little of his fellow-exiles. He occasionally met fellow-writers like Toller and Olden or, more rarely, Bruno Frank and Feuchtwanger, but such meetings were transitory, subject to the ebb and flow of exile. In these first two years in London, he saw much of the cabaret artist Paul Graetz, who had begun a new film career in England. Graetz had been an immensely popular artist who had personified the very spirit of Weimar Berlin. Herrmann's meetings with Graetz were nostalgic occasions, though he found the latter's enthusiasm for London quite incomprehensible.

Herrmann-Neiße would also occasionally see other acquaintances from the German film and theatre colony in London, such as Leopold Jessner, Fritz Kortner and Berthold Viertel – until one by one they began to leave, moving on to New York or Hollywood. Such meetings were anyway relatively rare in this sprawling metropolis in which everyone seemed to vanish in pursuit of their own affairs. Herrmann-Neiße was often thrown back on his own devices, as he reported – not without self-pity – to Klaus Pinkus: 'Apart from that, I am on my own a lot, walk in Hyde Park or round the wide districts of this cruelly large and, for foreigners, rather unwelcoming city.'[115]

Almost his only pleasure in London were the parks, where he would he would often walk for hours on end. All his London addresses were within five minutes' walk of Hyde Park and in fine weather he liked to spend the afternoons sitting on a park bench, reading. He was a keen observer of the passing scene, sometimes recording it in the genre pictures of his verse. Most of the poems he wrote about London are in fact poems about its parks: many were actually written there. He always took his notebook and would often sit on a bench to note an appropriate line or draft a complete poem. It was here, insulated from the surrounding city, that he achieved moments of happiness, that he could feel reconciled to his environment. But even such moments were fragile, tempered by the awareness of being an outsider, separated from those around him by the gulf of language and experience.

Mittags auf der Bank im Park, geborgen,
mit den andern hier in Friedlichkeit,
fühl' ich mich zuhaus und ohne Sorgen,
es erfragt bei mir ein Kind die Zeit,
Liebespaare lassen sich nicht stören,
und ein Hündchen wagt mit mir ein Spiel –
ein Verbannter fordert ja nicht viel!
Dennoch darf ich nie dazu gehören.

At midday on a park bench, secure, / peacefully here with the others, / I feel carefree and at home, / a child asks me the time, / lovers do not mind me, / a dog tries to have a game with me – / an exile doesn't ask for much! / Yet I shall never belong here.[116]

If his present seemed cheerless, his future offered little cause for comfort. He was periodically forced to question his decision to leave Germany for a life in the waiting-room of exile.

Zweifel plagt mich, ob ich richtig wählte,
als ich ganz der Fremde preis mich gab;
denn wenn andere ihr Entsagen stählte,
brachte meins mich näher nur dem Grab.

Doubt plagues me, whether I made the right choice / when I committed myself completely to exile; / if others were strengthened by their renunciation / mine has only brought me closer to the grave.[117]

His memories of Germany were still fresh, but he was realistic enough to concede that the country he so desperately longed to return to had already ceased to exist. Many of his friends were also in exile, others had remained in Germany, choosing to compromise with the hated regime. Some had fallen silent, like his old friend Ringelnatz, whose death in November 1934 he mourned as the loss of another piece of the Berlin he had loved. His beloved Germany had been usurped by a murderous clique: 'They have turned my homeland into a hell / the peaceful valley into a haunt of murderers.' ('Sie haben die Heimat zur Hölle gemacht / zur Mördergrube das friedliche Tal.')[118] Written in July 1934 as a direct comment on the Night of the Long Knives, this poem was one of Herrmann-Neiße's few allusions to contemporary political events in Germany.

During his early years of exile, Herrmann could still occasionally escape from London to his beloved Zurich, where he spent three months in 1934, and where he returned the following year. Such visits were a psychological lifeline. Here he could once again hear German spoken, could once more meet and talk with old friends, like the theatre director Gustav Hartung, the author Leonhard Frank and the actor Albert Bassermann, could once more enjoy the German theatre and cabaret from which he was cut off in London. Here he could rest and recuperate, storing up summer memories to tide him over the long London winter.

Herrmann-Neiße was very much a small-town dweller, for whom the charm of Zurich lay in its combination of intimate atmosphere and big city bustle, 'the mixture of little Paris and Neiße'. He loved the narrow streets with their small cafés and bars which reminded him of Neiße and Breslau, but what he perhaps loved best was the delicate fusion of the city with its surrounding countryside. The beauty of nature had always been one of his main sources of poetic inspiration.

Inevitably, his visits to Zurich tended to heighten his antipathy to London. If 'the beloved city' evoked memories of the lake and the view of the surrounding mountains, London was a wilderness of stone and concrete which inspired only images of imprisonment:

> Städte gibt es, die wir lieben,
> doch sie bleiben uns verwehrt,
> daß man rastlos umgetrieben,
> sich in Sehnsucht nur verzehrt
> nach dem See, den Hügelgassen,
> stets durchweht vom Bergeswind,
> während hier die Häusermassen
> uns Gefängnismauern sind.

There are towns which we love / but which are denied to us / so that – driven restlessly – / one is simply consumed by longing / for the lake, the steep streets / through which the mountain winds blow, whereas here the mass of houses / enclose us like prison walls.[119]

His occasional visits to Zurich were largely paid for by Sondheimer. Though Herrmann-Neiße was not slow to acknowledge his friend's generosity, he also felt increasingly bitter at his own financial dependence, a situation which doubtless acquired added piquancy from his friend's continued admiration for his wife. Max had always relied heavily on Leni's support and companionship. He always insisted that it was only she who had saved him from a complete breakdown after the death of both his parents. Above all, she had been a constant source of poetic inspiration. His unpublished works contain no fewer than 137 poems dedicated to Leni, spanning the whole period of their relationship between 1912 and 1940.[120]

To outsiders, they must have seemed an extraordinary couple. Leni was a strikingly handsome woman, tall and blonde, her looks and stature both accentuated by the stunted and deformed figure of her husband. His feelings for her are recorded in his letters to her over a period of thirty years, letters which she carefully preserved, though her replies have been equally carefully suppressed. His letters are an account of a close, almost obsessive relationship. The correspondence is intermittent, since they would write only when they were apart, but at such times Max would write almost daily, often covering several sheets of writing-paper with his small neat handwriting. His letters record the mundane details of his daily life, an account of time passed waiting for her to return:

> I cleared everything away, moved over to our room, had to chase a bit after the cat, who wanted to play, and then pissed charmingly on the tray. He ate his liver, gave his usual demonstrations of pleasure and is now asleep. I am sitting at my desk, the schnapps (*Korn*) tastes damned good, so does the stout, the room is cosy and warm.[121]

His letters, frequently addressed to 'my dearest best little Leni', express his affection and concern, but also his feelings of guilt at being unable to provide for her and his sense of being a constant burden to her: 'I have always been a great burden to you, a source of disquiet and a cause of constant worries and difficulties for you.'[122] He is perpetually concerned at the state of her health – more than one of her trips abroad was to consult a specialist in Zurich. Throughout his later letters runs an undercurrent of disquiet at the development of her relationship with Sondheimer.

During these years, Herrmann-Neiße's life followed an uneventful, even humdrum pattern, an existence ordered by regular habits and bounded by the constraints of communication in a foreign language.

His only contacts with English writers were the passing acquaintances mediated by the PEN Club. The English PEN, and particularly its Secretary Hermon Ould, was genuinely anxious to integrate the émigré writers, ensuring that they were invited regularly to the monthly dinners which were the main events in the PEN calendar. Herrmann-Neiße found himself ill at ease on such occasions, writing to his wife after one dinner:

> Yesterday evening it stopped raining and I went dry-footed to the PEN Club dinner. There were a great many people there. I was once again seated at a table with Wells and also Leonhard Frank, but unfortunately between two awful old women. I just about communicated in broken English; the food was as bad as ever. . . I was even mentioned in the speech of welcome ('what brings me such glory?'), spoke afterwards with Wells and his Baroness [Moura Budberg] . . . Frischauer, Robert Neumann, had a drink later with Leonhard Frank.[123]

His letters record other occasional outings, such as a visit to Bruno Frank's successful play *Storm in a Teacup*, for which the author had sent him tickets, or a variety performance at the Victoria Theatre, where Marlene Dietrich was among the audience, stopping to chat when she saw him in the foyer during the interval. There were few such highlights. He noted bitterly that the isolation of his life in London resembled very much the seclusion of provincial Neiße, in which he had felt 'buried alive' (*eingesargt*). Then he had been able to flee to Berlin; now there was no escape. More than once, during these years, he referred to London as his St Helena.

His evenings were spent mostly at home, reading or writing or listening to the radio, alleviating his loneliness with a bottle of beer or stout, sometimes laced with *Korn* or whisky. He was not an abstemious man and drink remained one of his small pleasures. He would usually start writing late in the evening, after the others had gone to bed, often continuing to work far into the night. Here, 'seven floors high above the streets of London',[124] the view would sometimes prompt thoughts of suicide, but usually these lonely vigils into the night were his happiest times, when he could temporarily forget the relentless horror of the world outside and concentrate on what he felt was his vocation.[125]

Despite his unhappiness and feelings of emotional displacement,

Herrmann-Neiße remained astonishingly, even defiantly productive, continuing to write poems even though he knew there was little prospect of getting them published. He would often enclose one of his poems in his letters to friends and acquaintances. Writing to Sondheimer from Switzerland in 1934 he enclosed a poem with the terse comment: 'Shame that not a bloody soul wants to publish it.'[126]

Max Herrmann-Neiße's years in London exemplify in many ways the fate of the poet in exile. If the work of the poet is more closely embedded in his native language, he experiences exile from it even more intensely than the novelist. Attuned to using language connotatively, rather than denotatively, he is unlikely to countenance writing in a foreign language. Conversely, poetry is much less likely to be translated, afflicted with both the intrinsic difficulty of translation and the financial hazards of publication. For Herrmann-Neiße, as for other exiled German poets, the only real prospect of publication was in the burgeoning number of exile periodicals.

While in Switzerland, he attempted to place some of his work with the *Basler Nationalzeitung* and the *Neue Zürcher Zeitung*, but in vain. Eduard Korrodi, literary editor of the latter, told him that it was impossible to publish more than a fraction of the work he received. In fact, Korrodi was unsympathetic to exile literature, which he considered too overtly political, preferring to publish the more 'traditional' voices still sanctioned in the Third Reich.

As time passed, Herrmann-Neiße was able occasionally to place poems in exile periodicals, such as the *Neue Tage-Buch*, *Pariser Tageblatt* and *Die Sammlung*, but such successes were sporadic and proved an unreliable source of income: after two years, *Die Sammlung* was discontinued, while the *Pariser Tageblatt* collapsed in insolvency and mutual recrimination. During 1934–35, Herrmann-Neiße also attempted to secure book publication for his work, submitting a collection of his recent poems to both the main exile publishing houses in Holland, Querido and Allert de Lange. The Querido director Fritz Landshoff was certainly impressed, commenting that 'the collection is quite simply beautiful'.[127] Nonetheless he felt unable to commit Querido to publishing a book which, in the context of exile publishing, represented a considerable financial burden. De Lange also rejected the manuscript. Herrmann-Neiße commented bitterly: 'Alas for me that I am a poet, and what is worse, a German poet.'[128]

He did consider the possibility of translation, but he confessed that he knew nothing of the London literary scene, and seems to have made no serious efforts to find a translator, for the subject is not mentioned again in his correspondence. In fact, translation was hardly a realistic option. Herrmann's work was unknown in Britain, and therefore virtually unmarketable. Significantly, his work has never been translated into English – or indeed into any other language – doubtless because, despite its lucidity and apparent simplicity, it is too culturally specific. Nor is it true that he could have improved his chance of being translated if he had written more prose. He always insisted that poetry was his *métier*, but even the prose works he wrote in exile remained unpublished.

It was many months before he could find a publisher for his poems, his collection finally being accepted by the Swiss publisher Emil Oprecht, who published a variety of exile literature. Oprecht provided a moral and financial lifeline to an increasing number of exiled writers, but he also possessed a hard head for business. He agreed to publish Herrmann's collection *Um uns die Fremde* in a limited edition of five hundred copies, but only because it was effectively underwritten by Sondheimer.[129]

The volume was published in May 1936 to coincide with Herrmann-Neiße's fiftieth birthday, an occasion which did not pass unnoticed in London. The bookseller Hans Preiss, whose International Bookstore in the shadow of the British Museum was a popular rendezvous for German émigrés, arranged a public reading to mark the event, held on the London premises of the YMCA. According to Herrmann-Neiße himself, the audience was so large that many had to be turned away at the door. The YMCA observed strict temperance, but Herrmann-Neiße had managed to bring a bottle of beer in his briefcase with which he was able to 'wet his throat'.[130] Stefan Zweig delivered the opening address and Ernst Toller gave a brief appreciation of Herrmann-Neiße, before the poet was called upon to read some of his recent work. Zweig remembered the occasion vividly, recalling that there was something infinitely touching about 'the misshapen little man, hunched forward over the lectern, his sharp grey eyes shining on that evening with a special brightness and tenderness', seeming 'visibly moved' by the rare chance to read his work to an attentive and receptive audience.[131] It must indeed have been an emotional occasion for both the poet and his audience, briefly transporting them back to the homeland they had once shared. Herrmann-Neiße declared himself more than happy with the occasion:

> It all gives me new courage to face life, increases the demands I must make on my own work, obliges me to justify the praise, the comradely readiness to help and the abundance of trust.[132]

After the reading, a small group of friends, including the artist Martin Bloch, had been invited back to Bryanston Court. It was a cheerful evening, well laced with beer and spirits, which broke up about one o'clock. Herrmann-Neiße had seemed buoyed up by the occasion, but once alone again he had plunged back into depression, expressing his feelings in one of the poems which now become more and more like daily entries in a diary. The only gift he wanted, he wrote, was one which nobody could give him:

> Aus den Gefangenschaften
> hat niemand mich befreit.
> An jeder Wohltat haften
> die Flüche dieser Zeit.
>
> *No one has freed me / from my imprisonment. / To every good deed clings / the curse of these times.*[133]

In September 1936, Herrmann-Neiße drew up the meagre balance of his first three years in London: 'I think I could live here for fifty years without ever feeling at home.'[134]

ALFRED KERR: 'AN IRREPROACHABLE AND HARMLESS YOUNG MAN OF 67 YEARS'

Alfred Kerr had not stayed long in Czechoslovakia. From Prague he had moved to Vienna and from there to Zurich, where he had finally been joined by his wife Julia, and their two children Michael, then aged twelve, and Anne Judith, aged ten. Kerr had few illusions about the Nazis and they, in turn, had soon confirmed his worst fears. In May, his books were among those thrown onto the bonfires of the Third Reich. In August, his German nationality was revoked, and his property confiscated. His name appeared with thirty-two others on the first expatriation list published in the official *Reichsanzeiger*, an indication of how much the Nazis detested him – and still feared his influence.

Kerr had been all too aware of the problems of exile, particularising them in one of his earliest articles after fleeing Germany:

> You don't go into exile for pleasure. (Only, the pleasure of staying would be even smaller.) You love the country you grew up in; you are attached to places where you pay taxes. And: always having to write in a foreign language – ?[135]

Separated from the theatre which had been his livelihood for forty years, Kerr now found himself – at an age at which most men had already retired – abruptly facing the problem of subsistence. Unable to stay in Switzerland because of the publishing restrictions imposed on refugees, he attempted to establish himself in Paris, which had meanwhile become one of the main centres of German emigration.

Like Stefan Zweig, Kerr was an ardent francophile, fond of quoting the phrase 'every man has two countries, his own and France' – adding: 'particularly if he has lost the former'.[136] During his early months in Paris, he had met with great sympathy and some success. He spoke and wrote French fluently – the result of having had a French governess as a child – and was able to place a number of articles in French newspapers and periodicals, including *Le Figaro*, *Le Temps* and *Nouvelles Littéraires*, as well as the Brussels paper *Le Soir*. He had also contributed to the exile press, notably the daily *Pariser Tageblatt*, founded in exile by Rudolf Mosse, the publisher of the *Berliner Tageblatt*, which had now been 'aryanised' by the Nazis. On the strength of his initial success, Kerr was able to bring his family to Paris – only to be plunged immediately into the financial difficulties which were to persist throughout his life in exile.

Declining economic confidence had forced many French newspapers to close their columns to foreign contributors. Kerr summarised the situation in a letter to Albert Einstein:

There is hospitality, even to the point of banquets. But there is not the slightest economic basis. The articles I wrote in French may have won over a few readers, but they earned me very little. Here there is crisis, dwindling royalties, lack of confidence.[137]

Furthermore, the exile periodicals to which he contributed often lacked financial stability; the *Pariser Tageblatt*, in which much of his work appeared, did not always pay promptly, or even at all. By July 1934, Kerr's slender resources were exhausted and he was forced to write begging letters to friends, asking for money to tide him over, requests which he renewed more than once.[138] It was at this time that Kerr first considered the possibility of further emigration to the USA or Britain.

Despite the gathering recession, Kerr did succeed in publishing two books. In the summer of 1934, he finished compiling *Die Diktatur des Hausknechts* ('The Dictatorship of the House Servant'), a miscellany of prose, verse and polemic which included many of the pieces he had written during the first year of exile. The volume was beset by the usual difficulties of exile publishing. Aimed at a German-speaking audience, it was published in Brussels in an edition of four thousand copies, but the meagre royalties did little to alleviate Kerr's growing financial problems. He himself remarked that the publisher's advance, paid in January, had been spent long before the book had even appeared.[139] He was forced to acknowledge that the audience for his brand of virulently anti-Nazi polemic was very restricted, and had become even more so in the light of political developments in Austria.

Kerr was much more optimistic about the prospects for his biography of Walther Rathenau, the German-Jewish industrialist and statesman assassinated by extreme nationalists in 1922, hoping that it would provide some economic security for himself and the family.[140] 'This book should provide for material necessities,' he wrote to Kommer.[141] He evidently felt that his subject's international stature would ensure a potential audience far beyond the small and scattered circle of German exiles. Before the end of the year it had been accepted by the exile publishing house Querido, but Kerr found the terms 'very modest', his advance being limited to 200 Dutch guilders, while the balance was to follow in the form of small monthly payments. The edition was once again limited to four thousand copies.

Kerr's hopes evidently rested on translation. He was able to stimulate some interest in an American edition, negotiations reaching an advanced stage, only to founder when Random House baulked at the inflated demands of the translator.[142] His hopes of a French edition proved equally transitory: the typescript of the French version still languishes amongst his unpublished papers in Berlin.

It was Kerr's desperate economic plight and the meagre returns from his literary work which undoubtedly spurred his interest in writing for the cinema. He first turned his hand to scriptwriting in 1934, at the suggestion of Rudolf Kommer, a journalist and theatre agent who had befriended him in exile. Kommer was a German-speaking Romanian, born in Czernowitz, whose connections were to make him a sought-after, if dubious patron of exiled writers. Kerr had always been a great film enthusiast, and the idea of writing for the cinema greatly attracted him: 'In addition, I have never stopped thinking about film,' he wrote to Kommer. 'That would fascinate me, because the combination of scene and dialogue offers the potential to be concise.'[143] His enthusiasm for the medium of film evidently outweighed his considerable mistrust of the practices of the film industry: 'The trouble with film proposals is that the ideas they contain mostly get stolen. So it all depends on the decency of the producer.'[144]

It is at this point (July 1934) that Kerr's correspondence contains the earliest mention of two film projects which increasingly preoccupied him over the coming months. He had first tried to place a work called *Der Chronoplan* ('The Chronoplane'), originally conceived as a libretto for an opera which his wife had composed. An earlier work of hers had been performed in Berlin, but Hitler's seizure of power had dashed any prospect of staging *Der Chronoplan*. In exile, Kerr had first attempted to publish the text independently, offering it to Klaus Mann for publication in the journal *Die Sammlung*. He described it as 'not so much an opera text . . . as a critique of the present in operatic form'. He summarised the plot as follows:

> Einstein, the main character, in the company of Shaw, etc., crash lands, in the time-machine he has built, on English soil about 1800. Encounter with someone who will later write verse: Byron. Byron's misfortune in the present: in a golf club near Berlin. Disappointment in love and

moral disappointment. Angry, he travels back in the time-machine to his equally unpleasant century.[145]

The work greatly preoccupied him and was so frequent a subject of discussion in the family that Kerr's daughter Judith still remembers it as 'the thing which overshadowed my entire youth'.[146] It was also one of the works he recited when requested to give a series of readings at Strasbourg University.[147] As Kerr's interest in the cinema crystallised, he began to visualise the text in cinematic terms, though he seems to have made little effort to revise it for film treatment. In 1934 he made perfunctory attempts to place the script in Britain, evidently regarding it as eminently suitable for an English film, since the dramatis personae included Byron and Shaw.[148] It is difficult to say how seriously Kerr took the project: the surviving typescript versions are all in German, though there is also a synopsis in English, which was probably written by Julia Kerr. (Though written in good English, it shows several signs of interference from German.) Early in 1935, Kerr even opened negotiations with the Hollywood production company Universal Pictures. There were initial difficulties, such as the refusal of George Bernard Shaw to allow himself to be portrayed in the film, though these ultimately proved unimportant, since Universal Pictures did not pursue its interest in the project.[149]

During these months Kerr was also working on an original film script, written partly as a reaction to the prevailing fashion for films and plays dealing with 'great men'. In the summer of 1934, he had discussions with French film-makers (notably Alfred Savoir) regarding a scenario entitled *Sa mère Letitia*, which would portray the life of Napoleon's mother and which Kerr described as 'a Napoleon film without Napoleon'.[150] During the next twelve months, Kerr developed this idea into a full-blown film treatment. In August 1935, he read the script's 'extended treatment' to a representative of the Hollywood production company Radio Pictures and was delighted with the positive response: 'He's very keen on it,' he told Kommer.[151] Kerr's comments suggest a certain innocence of the ways of the film industry, in which options were taken swiftly – and often equally swiftly abandoned.

For some months, Kerr had been seriously considering the possibility of further emigration to Britain or the USA, as a means of escaping the economic impasse which confronted him in France. In August and September 1935, he conducted lengthy negotiations with various film producers for the rights to his film script *Letitia*.[152] In October the script was finally acquired by the Hungarian-born producer Alexander Korda, who since the success of *The Private Life of Henry VIII* had become the prime mover in the British film industry. Kerr received a thousand pounds for the film rights and was to be paid a further thousand if the profits exceeded fifty per cent.[153] It was this unprecedented windfall which finally persuaded him to uproot the family once more and settle in London.

Kerr had visited England on several previous occasions, the last in 1922, when he had recorded his impressions in the travel book *New York und London*. While he expressed almost unbridled enthusiasm for America, his feelings for Britain could best be described as those of benevolent neutrality. 'Fateful places. New York and London. My heart, with all the bold and roaming spirit which a man loves, is with America. But a quiet homely thought goes also to the British island.'[154]

In 1922 he had come as a traveller and observer; in 1935 he came as a refugee. He had left Paris, with great regret, after what he later described as 'two wonderful years': not the least of his reservations in coming to London was that, while he spoke French fluently, his English was only roughly serviceable. However, his wife Julia was a staunch Anglophile who had an excellent command of the language. Kerr himself was now almost sixty-eight, Julia thirty-two years his junior, and it was therefore considered that her earning prospects were considerably better in London.

Arriving with his wife in Newhaven in November 1935, Kerr had been asked to name a guarantor in Britain and had unhesitatingly named George Bernard Shaw, whose work he had been the first to champion in Germany. His letter to Shaw, informing him of this démarche, is worth quoting at length:

Dear Bernard Shaw,

   I am now in London . . . with my impresario (Mrs Kerr, my wife). I have greatly improved our situation by the healthful idea of writing films.

I should be very glad to see you again. May I ring you up one of these days?

On landing at Newhaven I was asked whom I knew in London. Amongst others I gave your dear name.

Should the Home Office (to whom i [sic] am applying for the permission to stay here for some time) ask you who I am, would you please tell them that I am an irreproachable and harmless young man of 67 years who has done much for the German language and little (but all he could) for GBS.[155]

The blithe self-assurance and the would-be lightness of tone, bear eloquent testimony to Kerr's self-perception: this is the letter of one literary institution acknowledging another.

The Kerrs were admitted to Britain without difficulty, apparently benefiting from a more liberal immigration policy which now welcomed refugees who had achieved distinction in the arts or sciences, and who might enhance Britain's international prestige. The Home Office quickly extended the couple's residence permits for a year, confirming that 'the Secretary of State does not desire to raise objection to Mr Kerr continuing his activities as a freelance writer', also approving the arrival of the Kerrs' children, who had initially been sent to stay with relations in France.[156]

Though bolstered by the advance paid by Korda, Kerr was rapidly confronted by the problem experienced by other exiled writers: the loss of his audience and the consequent loss of the very language he wrote in. Unlike his French, which he had learned as a child, Kerr's English derived largely from reading, having a pronounced literary flavour. His daughter remembers that he would give full value to the final syllable of past participles like 'revoked'. Although a regular reader of newspapers, he had few English friends or acquaintances. He had always been a somewhat solitary man, having few close friends: his daughter recalled that he was 'very self-sufficient'. Unfamiliar with colloquial English, he often found himself unable to understand what was said to him. Though his English undoubtedly improved considerably, he always remained self-deprecating about it, frustrated by the humiliating contrast with his acknowledged mastery of his own language.

At the time of his arrival in London, Kerr still hoped to find a place in the British cultural scene. On the strength of his contract with Korda he hoped, perhaps even expected, to gain a foothold in the British film industry, where other prominent exiles were already successfully established. Alexander Korda was now the leading 'British' film producer, his position contested only by his fellow-Hungarian Paul Czinner. Among other leading émigrés was the writer and film director Berthold Viertel (the model for Friedrich Bergmann in Christopher Isherwood's *Prater Violet*), who had already made his mark with such films as *Sanders of the River* and *Rhodes of Africa*. A number of outstanding actors had also appeared in English films, including Peter Lorre, Fritz Kortner, Anton Walbrook (originally Adolf Wohlbrück) and above all Elisabeth Bergner, who having emigrated with her producer husband Paul Czinner, had become almost as popular on the London stage and screen as she had been in Germany.

Kerr's initial hopes naturally rested with the Napoleon script, on which Korda had taken an option. Kerr intended his script to mark an entirely new direction in the cinema: 'This sketch seeks to put film on a new basis (in its mixture of tragedy and humour): it seeks to mingle the popular and the poetic, to make the responses apt, to assign a greater importance to the word.'[157] The surviving typescript is probably the 'extended treatment' referred to by Kerr, delineating individual scenes and including long passages of dialogue. It certainly reveals Kerr's considerable flair for scriptwriting: regrettably, it was never filmed. The reasons are difficult to ascertain, though Korda was already occupied with a string of other film projects, and Kerr's arrival in London coincided with a slump in the British film industry, a conjuncture which certainly ended any hopes that *Der Chronoplan* would ever be filmed.

Undeterred by these failures, Kerr continued to write for the cinema. His unpublished papers include several film treatments or synopses, all of which fall within the period 1936–37. They include *Thomas Becket* (1936), *Mamma* (1937), *Nadia* ('a realistic-fantastic comedy') (1937) and *Cagliostro. The Great Charlatan* (1937).[158] *Mamma* is a full-scale 'film treatment', based largely on autobiographical material, the two main characters, the mother Sheila, and her son Jim, deriving loosely from his own wife and son. Presumably to make the idea more acceptable to a British audience, the family is British, the son ultimately attending (like Kerr's son Michael) a British public school. The plot, with its strong motif of filial jealousy, may well contain biographical aspects. More significantly, the English school setting was certainly chosen in deference to British taste. It seems a shrewd choice, which might even have found a producer, given the tremendous success, two short years later, of such British films as *Tom Brown's Schooldays* and *Goodbye Mr Chips*. An even more promising subject for film treatment was *Cagliostro. The Great Charlatan*, dealing with the career of the eighteenth-century Italian adventurer. According to Kerr's own note, the surviving typescript is 'not a film treatment. Only the embryo of one'.[159] The subject was obviously chosen not least because of its British dimension. The typescript includes scenes of Cagliostro's stay in London during which he persuaded a number of rich men to invest in 'Egyptian freemasonry'.

Faced with such evidence of Kerr's fertile and wide-ranging imagination, one can only regret that none of these subjects was ever actually filmed. As we have seen, Kerr's attempts to find a foothold in the cinema in 1936–37 coincided with a slump in the British film industry, a conjuncture typical of the ill fortune he experienced in exile. While the promise of success in the cinema continued to nourish his imagination, it was to continue to prove elusive: one of the visions of exile which receded regularly before him.

Part Three

Isolation or Integration

1936–1939

ASPECTS OF APPEASEMENT

Political exiles from the Third Reich undoubtedly regarded themselves as the true representatives of Germany – of a different, better Germany, summarised in the title of Heinrich Mann's *Das andere Deutschland* ('The Other Germany'), a work which achieved instant fame amongst émigrés. Considering the large number of writers and journalists who had left Nazi Germany, it is scarcely surprising that many prominent émigrés in Britain felt that their first duty was to alert public opinion to the true nature of Nazism and the renewed threat of war which it posed. Their efforts were sometimes compromised by the limitations on political activity imposed by the Home Office as an implicit condition of their permission to stay in Britain. More often, they would founder on the lack of interest of much of British public opinion.

Such indifference was partly a result of British insularity. The separation of Britain from the European continent was more than merely geographical: it was a frame of mind. British attitudes in the thirties were those of a maritime nation, nourished on one hundred and fifty years of Imperial history, with its implicit assumptions of superiority. These differences were noted by all continental visitors almost as soon as they set foot in Dover or Folkestone. They felt that they had arrived in a different world which was totally remote from the familiarities of the European continent.

When the young lawyer Fred Uhlman, who was to marry into the English aristocracy, arrived in September 1936, he found England 'a stranger country than any I had known before, as far away from Europe as Peking', its people still apparently living in some golden Edwardian past.[1] This strangeness both derived from, and reinforced, British isolationism. If the traditional aim of British foreign policy was to preserve the balance of power in Europe, its corollary was that Europe should then be left to its own devices. The experience of the First World War had merely reinforced traditional British determination to keep a distance from the disputes of quarrelsome European neighbours.

The effects of such isolationism were not lost on the more perceptive émigrés. Writing for a German exile audience, the veteran pacifist Otto Lehmann-Rußbüldt noted with resignation:

> Winston Churchill once said that all England's special woes would disappear, if you could move the island away from Europe. That hits the nail on the head. Every political consideration – whether from the left or the right – is secretly dominated by the idea: 'Let the crazy continentals kill each other; what's it got to do with us?'[2]

Stefan Zweig was initially prepared to endorse Britain's lack of engagement with Europe, but his later attitude was less indulgent. Writing to a friend in Italy about the war in Abyssinia, he remarked that Britain remained 'carefree and swimming in wealth, proceeding unimpeded through the conflict, completely absorbed in its own business and pleasures'.[3] Symptomatic of such introversion was the abdication crisis of 1936, which for days monopolised the pages of the daily press. The journalist Rudolf Olden, involved in the campaign to gain the Nobel Peace Prize for the imprisoned pacifist Carl von Ossietzky, was forced to abandon his efforts momentarily, since the entire country was transfixed by the drama of the King and Mrs Simpson and had eyes and ears for nothing else.[4]

Anti-Nazi exiles were therefore confronted with a widespread indifference to the political affairs of Europe in general, and Germany in particular. Indifference was compounded by incredulity. Many exiles noted that their attempts to convince English acquaintances of the full extent of Nazi excesses often met with scepticism and even disbelief. The economist Moritz Bonn recalled that, if he criticised Germany, his English friends were apt to discount it as prejudice: 'I shut up.'[5] Max Herrmann-Neiße encountered the same reaction, transmuting the experience, like so much of his life in exile, into the verse which became his daily bread:

Da klang, was wir erzählten, übertrieben,
man lauschte zweifelnd, wenn auch wohlgesinnt:
man war noch immer Gentleman geblieben,
als welche jede letzte Schlacht gewinnt.

What we recounted sounded overblown, / they listened dubiously, however well-disposed: / remaining still the gentlemen / who always win the last battle.[6]

The attempts by German émigrés to convince British public opinion of the dangers of Nazism were also fatally out of step with the prevailing social mood in Britain which, still haunted by the slaughter of the First World War, was as yet unwilling to countenance a second. It was a mood which was perhaps most famously captured in the motion of the Oxford Union in February 1933 that 'this House will in no circumstances fight for its King and Country'. But this mood was by no means confined to Oxford or Cambridge. Eight months later a pacifist Labour candidate won an upset victory in the Fulham East by-election. Even more significantly, the organisers of the Peace Ballot in 1934–35 were able to secure over eleven million signatures in favour of peace through collective security. The General Election of 1935 was fought largely on the issue of rearmament; 1936 saw the establishment of the Christian-pacifist Peace Pledge Union.

The British public's view of events in Germany was also, in Martin Gilbert's telling phrase, 'fed on ignorance'.[7] Right-wing opinion saw Nazism as a bulwark against the spread of Communism. A number of British newspapers, reflecting the views of their proprietors, were either, like Lord Rothermere's *Daily Mail*, openly pro-fascist or, like *The Times*, implicitly so. *The Times* editor Geoffrey Dawson was so concerned to publish nothing which might prejudice good relations with Germany, that he frequently censored the dispatches of his Berlin correspondent, Norman Ebbutt, in order to avoid offending Nazi sensibilities.[8]

Some newspapers were, of course, sympathetic to anti-Nazi exiles – notably the *Manchester Guardian*, *News Chronicle* and *Daily Worker*, as well as respected political journals such as the *New Statesman*.

However, even these sections of the British press could not be guaranteed to publish contributions by exiles, largely because of the widespread feeling, noted above by Moritz Bonn, that such testimony was 'prejudiced' or somehow suspect. This inherent scepticism undermined almost any attempt at polemical journalism. Rudolf Olden, at the height of the campaign on behalf of the imprisoned pacifist Carl von Ossietzky, found that an article he had written specially for the *New Statesman* was rejected by it – only to appear later in truncated form in the *News Chronicle* (signed, presumably to add plausibility, by 'a special correspondent'). Olden commented gloomily: 'Nobody wants to listen to the clever emigrants, in any way at all.'9

The widespread ignorance of conditions in Germany, the incredulity at the claims of exiles, and the prevailing public mood in favour of peace were certainly all factors contributing to the policy of appeasement increasingly pursued by the British government. When Neville Chamberlain became Prime Minister, early in 1937, he proposed to pursue what he called 'a general scheme of appeasement', and the term has since remained fatally associated with his name.10 In fact, Chamberlain was merely continuing a policy already established by the previous government as early as 1933–34. Early Nazi atrocities, such as the book burnings or the Night of the Long Knives, were regarded with distaste but treated with diplomatic indulgence. The years 1935–36 saw the emergence of a broad political consensus in favour of propitiating the European dictators. While even such atrocities as Hitler's murder of his own henchmen might have been deemed an internal political matter, the question of German rearmament was obviously not. On 16 March 1935 Germany announced the reintroduction of general conscription, a measure which openly flouted one of the major clauses of the Treaty of Versailles. The British and the French, meeting at Stresa, made strong protests to Germany but ultimately took no action. Even these protests were vitiated a couple of months later by the conclusion of the Anglo-German Naval Agreement, in which Britain sanctioned an increase in German naval power far beyond the stipulated limits of the Versailles Treaty, a concession which can only have encouraged the Nazis to go much further. On 7 March 1936, German troops reoccupied the demilitarised Rhineland, breaking a pledge Hitler had made less than a year previously to abide by the demilitarisation zone. Although this action also provoked strong protests from Britain and France, neither country took military action to reverse it.

Perhaps even more revealing than the public actions of the British government were the private attitudes of leading British politicians. Lord Londonderry, who only a short while before had been a minister in the Conservative government, is reported to have sent Hitler a telegram congratulating him on his reoccupation of the Rhineland. The prominent Liberal peer Lord Lothian, frequently lobbied by German exiles, commented that the Germans were 'only reoccupying their own back yard'. The same Lord Lothian is a striking example of the readiness of many British politicians to take Hitler at his word: following a visit to the 'Führer' in 1935, he felt able to announce that 'Germany does not want war and is prepared to renounce it absolutely as a means of settling her disputes with her neighbours'.[11] Such naivety was baffling to German exiles. Fred Uhlman remembered the frustration of living in a country 'where people, who seemed to be sane in every other way, were willing to believe the word of a lunatic but refused to believe in concentration camps'.[12]

There was of course a political minority in Britain – mainly though not exclusively on the left – who were aware of the true nature of the Nazi regime and were receptive to appeals for help from German antifascists. They included left-wing figures such as Fenner Brockway of the Independent Labour Party and the Labour peer Lord Marley; liberal intellectuals like Lady Oxford, daughter of the former Liberal Prime Minister Asquith, and journalists like Amabel Williams-Ellis, Kingsley Martin, editor of the *New Statesman*, and above all Wickham Steed, a former editor of *The Times*. As an ex-foreign correspondent in Vienna and Berlin, Steed had unrivalled experience of German and Austrian affairs, and enjoyed close contacts with such prominent 'political' refugees as Gerhart Seger (a former Social Democrat deputy), the pacifist Otto Lehmann-Rußbüldt, and above all Ernst Toller. Toller was a frequent guest at Steed's famous Sunday lunches, which were occasions for wide-ranging political discussion. In her fragmentary memoirs, Toller's wife, Christiane Grautoff, records one such occasion:

After the long meal we all went solemnly into the drawing-room and settled comfortably in beautiful armchairs. . . ET was not sitting with me. From the corner of my eye I could see him talking to a venerable old gentleman. . . ET spoke well – and he liked speaking. To my dismay, I saw that he had embarked on a speech and had already moved into the centre of the room. Now he was speaking. Impressively. He spoke the truth, he depicted the brutality in the concentration camps. . . He was cautious, but sought to open a window of interest. Everyone was looking at him. He was on form now. His voice sounded good. . . And then it happened. A stout ex-consul, sitting in a round, soft, and oh! so comfortable armchair, began snoring so loudly that the Queen must have heard it in Buckingham Palace. He slept and snored and snored.[13]

Christiane's picture of the sleeping ex-diplomat seems an apt symbol of a Britain slumbering through the years of appeasement; it is no criticism of Toller, or other German exiles, that they were unsuccessful in awakening it.

Of course, British public opinion was neither uniform nor unchanging. Attitudes, particularly those on the political left, certainly began to change in the course of 1936. For one thing, faith in the idea of collective security, an important nostrum of the liberal-left, was effectively discredited by the impotence of the League of Nations in the face of fascist aggression in Abyssinia. But the event which did most to convert many on the left who had hitherto been convinced pacifists was the outbreak of the Spanish Civil War.

KARL OTTEN: THE SHADOW OF SPAIN

Karl Otten had planned his escape with Ellen Kroner to Majorca as early as the summer of 1932.[14] He had chosen Majorca on the advice of the writer Franz Blei, an old friend from his student days in Munich – and it was Blei whom the couple joined in the fishing village of Cala Ratjada, on the north-eastern tip of the island. Numerous artists and writers were already living on Majorca, attracted by the mild climate, the unspoilt natural beauty and the simple life-style.

Cala Ratjada boasted the largest artists' colony on Majorca, a motley collection of writers, painters and bohemians, who had begun to

congregate there in 1932. It included a number of other refugees from
the barbarities of the Third Reich: apart from Franz Blei himself, there
were left-wing journalists like Walter Pollatschek and Arthur Seehof,
and painters such as Heinrich Maria Davringhausen, Arthur Segal and
Rudolf Levy. Probably the most colourful character of all was the
writer, painter and adventurer Hugo Baruch, who called himself Jack
Bilbo. He would later make a name in London as an artist and gallery
owner, but during his stay in Cala Ratjada he ran the Wikiki bar, a
meeting-place for both the German and local communities, which also
served as a trading place for smuggled tobacco and cigarettes.

Cala Ratjada was notable for the beauty of its natural setting which
Otten was to evoke, in his novel *Torquemadas Schatten*, through the eyes
of his protagonist, Don Carlos:

> The deep silence all around, the rich fruitfulness and beauty of the
> valley which, with its yellow and green fields, pine woods and olive
> groves, its dusky orange trees and brown outcrops of rock, lies like a
> lightly curved shell between the eastern cape and the sierra, had
> enchanted the visitor. He breathed in the peace of the island, the calm
> of the last paradise, as the peasants here called it.[15]

In this earthly paradise the Ottens led a life of rural simplicity, growing
all their own vegetables. The cost of living was still low and the couple
were able to live adequately from Ellen's savings and the small fees Otten
earned for occasional articles. Otten was fascinated by the centuries-old
traditions of the local people, filling his notebook with records of the
conversations he conducted with them. One sketch, never published,
portrays the peasant who would stride the fields behind his horse-drawn
plough, loudly reciting Cervantes's *Don Quixote*.

The peace of Otten's life on Majorca was punctuated by short bursts
of political activity. During the next two and a half years, he spent some
months in Paris, also making short visits to the Saarland, then still under
French administration. Otten's French identity card gives his profession as 'journalist' and it was in this capacity that he travelled to the
Saarland where, like other émigrés, he was active in the campaign which
preceded the plebiscite on the future status of the area. Here he made
important contacts, two of whom were to play some part in his
subsequent life: the journalist Karl Gröhl and Max Sievers, editor of the

Antwerp-based newspaper *Freies Deutschland*. When, in January 1935, the Saar voted overwhelmingly in favour of rejoining the German Reich, Otten left in some haste, returning in disillusionment to Majorca.

However, even in the rural seclusion of Cala Ratjada, he was unable to escape the long arm of the Third Reich. German Foreign Office documents reveal that the Gestapo began proceedings to deprive him of his German citizenship as early as 1934, asking the German consul in Palma to report any evidence which might help to incriminate him. The consul reported back to his political masters that Otten had done nothing to draw attention to himself, but promised to keep him under surveillance. The consul did indeed have his spies in Cala Ratjada: Ellen Otten recalled that the manager of the village's only hotel was widely held to be a Nazi informer.

For the artists' colony in Cala Ratjada, the first shots of the Spanish Civil War signalled their expulsion from paradise and dispersal in the diaspora of exile. At least two other members of the artists' colony, Arthur Segal and Jack Bilbo, were, like Otten, to end up in London.

When fighting broke out on the island, Francoist supporters quickly gained the upper hand. Otten and other émigrés, probably denounced by the German consul, were arrested and held, together with Republican supporters, in the town hall. Otten was released the same day, following the intervention of a local doctor. The fighting on Majorca had culminated in mass executions. Fearing he would be re-arrested, Otten lost no time in leaving the island. He and Ellen fled to Palma, from where they were evacuated on British warships to Barcelona. One of Ellen's abiding memories of her husband is the picture of him boarding a British destroyer: a tall, slightly stooping figure, carrying a small suitcase, and a rucksack which contained his typewriter.

When Karl and Ellen Otten arrived in Britain in September 1936, they could hardly have imagined that they would stay there for the next twenty-two years. If their flight to Majorca had been carefully planned, their arrival in London was much more an improvisation. From Barcelona, they had travelled on to Marseilles, where they stopped to draw breath, sending out urgent appeals to fellow-exiles for help and money. They were virtually penniless, having left Majorca with only what they could carry in one suitcase.

Many of the refugees from Hitler's Germany experienced exile as a journey with no final destination, a restless itinerary arbitrarily determined by the historical currents of the moment. Marooned in Marseilles, the Ottens were confronted with the pressing question: where to go now? The obvious answer seemed to be Paris, where there was already a large German exile community, but although Otten knew the city well and had a good knowledge of French, he was reluctant to settle in France, deterred by the French authorities' growing hostility towards the émigrés. Furthermore, his premonition of impending war, sharpened by his experience in Spain, made him wary of settling in any country which bordered on Germany. Equally, there was no question of going to the USA; Otten had always disliked the American influence in Europe and rejected what he considered the facile American belief in material progress. Britain, as an island, seemed to offer a certain physical security. Moreover, there was no time for long deliberation. When they both received invitations from fellow-exiles in London – she from Anni Rosenblüth, a childhood friend from Berlin, now living in Hampstead Garden Suburb, he from Hans Wolfsohn, a journalist he had met during the plebiscite campaign in the Saar – the question of where to go was resolved.

Actually gaining entry to Britain was no easy matter, however. The aim of British immigration policy was to exclude any refugee who might become a charge on the public purse. Moreover, the granting of an entry visa was ultimately left to the discretion of the individual immigration officer, as the journalist Rudolf Olden emphasised in advising a fellow-writer:

> Whether or not you get in here is a matter of luck. On the boat or after landing you will meet the Immigration Officer and your fate depends on him. Show him a confirmation from your English publisher that you have money here, or can at least expect some. That's the best way of preventing the Immigration Officer from getting the idea that you could be a burden on the public purse or are even looking for a job. Best of all . . . show him confirmation from an English bank that you have an account here.[16]

Karl Otten had no English bank account, no English publisher, no English royalties – and no immediate prospect of any. That he was let in at all, was, he always maintained, purely 'a matter of luck'. Ellen Otten recalled that, though she had few problems in being admitted, in Karl's case it was 'a near thing'. Since he spoke no English and the immigration officer no German, the interview was conducted in French. The officer questioned him closely on his activities in Spain, his reasons for leaving the country and his work as a writer. What had he written recently? he asked, with what Otten took for professional suspicion. Otten listed several titles which elicited no response, the face opposite him remaining expressionless. Then, almost as an afterthought, he mentioned that he had written the script for the film *Kameradschaft*. There was a moment's silence, before the officer suddenly stood up, threw open the door to the adjoining room and called to his colleagues: 'Boys! Come and meet the man who wrote *Kameradschaft*.' Otten was granted the usual three-month visa, though he remained convinced that only *Kameradschaft* had provided his 'ticket of admission'.

When they arrived in Britain, the Ottens, though still unmarried, had been together for some six years. They had first met on 1 May 1930, when Otten had come into the antiquarian bookshop where Ellen had just started working. He was then forty, she only half his age, but this chance meeting made such a profound impression on them both that it proved the beginning of a relationship which was to last until his death in 1963.

During their early weeks in London, the couple were forced to live apart, he with Hans Wolfsohn in Rosebery Avenue, she in Hampstead with Anni Rosenblüth, who had come to London in 1933, renting a large house, where she took in paying guests. There were some half a dozen residents, all émigrés, prominent among them being the journalist Franz Borkenau, whose book *Spanish Cockpit* was later to became one of the best-known testimonies of the Spanish Civil War.[17] Ellen stayed there for several weeks before she and Karl were able to move into their first London home, a rather dingy furnished flat off Primrose Hill. With no income, and no obvious prospect of any, the couple might well have questioned their decision to come to London. Ellen at least had some knowledge of English, gained partly through her family connections with America, where her mother had been born, but Otten found himself in a totally alien environment. Educated at a German classical *Gymnasium*, he had never learned English, nor even set foot in Britain before.

Though in some ways an unpractical man, Otten was nothing if not resourceful. Within weeks of his arrival in Britain, he had signed a contract with European Books, a well-established literary agency, whose director, Elias Alexander, had first brought Robert Neumann to London in 1933. Faced with the immediate imperative of subsistence, Otten drew on his only capital, sending Alexander two radio plays he had written, as well as several ideas for film treatments. Both the radio scripts, as Otten was careful to point out, fortuitously dealt with 'British' subject-matter.[18] The first was *Stanley findet Livingstone* ('Stanley Finds Livingstone'), a play chronicling the American journalist's search for, and ultimate encounter with, the British explorer.[19] The second was *Nach Faschoda!* (English title: *Fashoda*),[20] dramatising an event in the colonial scramble for Africa, when a French officer, Captain Marchand, had hoisted the tricolour at Fashoda in the Sudan, causing a diplomatic incident which had brought Britain and France to the brink of war.

Although originally written in German, *Fashoda* had been devised for transmission in Paris, and therefore also existed in a French version. In October 1936, Otten's agent contacted Val Gielgud of the BBC Drama Department, and subsequently sent him copies of *Fashoda* and *Stanley findet Livingstone* in the original German versions.[21] The BBC later returned both manuscripts, requesting submission of the existing French translations – presumably because no one could read German. It was this version of *Fashoda* which was read and accepted by the BBC early in 1937, earning Otten sixteen guineas on acceptance, the first literary fee he had earned in London.

Even more than money, it offered Otten the lifeline of renewed hope, and he responded effusively (in French): 'I should like to thank you for accepting *Fashoda* – it was the first favourable moment, giving me a little courage to continue my work.'[22]

Radio, like theatre or film, is a medium which guarantees the writer little ultimate control over his own text or its interpretation. The writer in exile, for whom the inherent risks of the medium are compounded by differences of language and culture, was particularly vulnerable, often finding that, in the difficult process of adaptation, he did not even receive proper credit for his work. The fate of *Fashoda* provides very much a case in point.

While the French version of the play is a faithful translation of the German original which Otten himself had prepared with a French collaborator, the English adaptation is really an entirely new play. Otten's original script, written, it must be emphasised, with a French audience in mind, had focused on Marchand's expedition, and particularly on the journey of his fellow-officer Baratieri, who had led a small advance party across the hitherto impenetrable swamp of Bahr el Gazal, defying the dangers of hunger, sleeplessness and disease to establish the best route to the White Nile. Otten's script is a celebration of this heroic feat of courage and endurance, reaching its climax with Baratier's triumphant return from his mission and ending with the sound of the 'Marseillaise', signalling the ultimate success of the French expedition.

While the title and general theme of Otten's play survive into the English adaptation, little else remains. The broadcast script (still preserved in the BBC Play Library) is credited to Peter Creswell, and omits any reference to Otten. Creswell, already a veteran of BBC drama, adapted Otten's story line to the perceived requirements of British listeners. His script also portrays the heroic advance of Marchand's expedition, even using snatches of Otten's original dialogue. However, it deals above all with the diplomatic crisis caused by the Fashoda incident: a situation resolved when Marchand is instructed by his government to withdraw, thus returning control of the Sudan to the British. While the play was ostensibly adapted to suit the conventions of British broadcasting, its plot and structure endorse British success and prestige, in contrast to Otten's script which celebrates an epic deed – and the (French) patriotism which inspired it.

When the play was finally broadcast in January 1938, it was listed in the *Radio Times* as a 'dramatic chronicle, based on the French play of the same name by Karl Otten, written and produced by Peter Creswell'.[23] While Otten's role had thus effectively been marginalised, he was nonetheless grateful for the transmission fee: eighteen months after their arrival in England, he and Ellen were still desperately short of money. In a letter to European Books, Otten even asked if the agency would reduce its commission on the fee from 20 to 10 per cent. 'You can understand that every Schilling (*sic*) represents a fortune for me today. Quite apart from the disproportionate amount of work on the play in comparison to the fee.'[24] Alexander agreed. Following the acceptance of *Fashoda*, Otten bombarded the BBC with dramatic proposals, sample scenes and even finished scripts, but he was unable to repeat his initial success, at least two other radio plays of his being rejected.[25]

In December 1936, Otten was deprived of German nationality, his name appearing on the Nazis' fourth expatriation list, published in the official *Börsenblatt* under the headline 'Enemies of the People'. As was usual in such cases, expatriation proceedings had been conducted by the Ministry of the Interior at the instigation of the Gestapo. Otten's file, still carefully preserved in the archives of the Foreign Office in Bonn,[26] is now of interest only for the light it sheds on the Nazi agenda and the bureaucratic procedures which underpinned it. It shows that expatriation proceedings against him had in fact begun two years earlier, following the publication of his novel *Der letzte Zivilist* ('The Last Civilian'), 'in which he agitates against Germany in the most spiteful manner'. Although the novel had actually first appeared in Berlin in 1932, it had caught the attention of the Gestapo only in 1934, when it had been serialised in the Social Democratic newspaper *Volksstimme* in Saarbrücken. Thereafter, Gestapo spies had carefully monitored Otten's involvement in the Saar plebiscite campaign, providing evidence which Nazi bureaucrats regarded as damning: 'Otten has therefore violated his first and greatest duty, loyalty to the Fatherland, thus proving that he is not worthy to enjoy the rights of a German citizen.'[27] Bureaucracy, however, is a slow business and it was a further eighteen months before Otten's name appeared on the Nazis' fourth expatriation list, together with those of such notables as Thomas Mann, and two authors who had written recent exposés of Hitler: Rudolf Olden and Konrad Heiden.[28]

Otten received the news of his expatriation with equanimity and even satisfaction, considering it a mark of distinction. (The exile newspaper *Pariser Tageszeitung*, publishing the list, called it a 'roll of honour'.) However, the loss of his passport, and the consequent difficulties of travel and identification, undoubtedly added to the intrinsic uncertainties of life in exile.

Such uncertainties did not distract Otten from his vocation as a writer. His most pressing task was to record his recent experience on Majorca, which he felt was both an artistic and a political obligation – the two aspects are often inseparable with Otten, a committed writer who had always placed his pen at the service of freedom and, more recently, of the struggle against the tyranny of fascism. He had written a brief account of his experience immediately after leaving Spain, which had appeared in the *Pariser Tageszeitung*.[29] By then he was already working on the novel *Torquemadas Schatten* ('The Shadow of Torquemada'), a semi-fictional portrayal of events on Majorca in the weeks before and after the military *putsch*. The political focus of the novel was explicit: it was first published with the eloquent subtitle 'Roman aus dem spanischen Freiheitskampf' (Novel of the Spanish Struggle for Freedom). At a subjective level, the book was an attempt to exorcise his recent experience, but it also sought to place that experience firmly in a social and political context. Writing to the publisher Gottfried Bermann Fischer, Otten explained that he had tried to 'assimilate the quintessentially human to the political and factual background'.[30] The contemporary events of the novel are placed in an historical perspective through the explicit analogy with the Spanish Inquisition in which Torquemada had tortured and expelled the Jews in the fifteenth century.

Driven both by the intensity of his experience and his awareness of the book's fragile topicality, Otten wrote at great speed, completing the manuscript in some three months: by early December it was already in the hands of European Books, which lost no time in offering it to Victor Gollancz. When Gollancz rejected it, it was offered in turn to Methuen, Hutchinson and Knopf.[31] It was Otten's first experience of the British publishing world and he was dismayed by this rapid cycle of offer and rejection. 'I am rather concerned that we are having to wait so long with the book – it is unfortunately a topical book and the events it deals with are still at the centre of public interest. But how much longer will it be before I lose all chance?'[32] He eventually withdrew the book 'to stop it becoming an eternal boomerang'.[33] The epithet 'boomerang', applied to one or other of his books, was to become a private joke with his wife.

Otten was still determined to find a German-language publisher for

Torquemadas Schatten, but as he had foreseen, the book's very topicality now undermined its prospects. The conflict in Spain had already inspired a veritable flood of books and articles, inducing a certain war weariness among the reading public. The Swiss publisher Emil Oprecht doubted that such a book would sell, in view of the numerous books on Spain which had already appeared, while Walter Landauer of Allert de Lange observed that 'there is a certain weariness on the part of the public in reading books on Spain'.[34] Otten must frequently have despaired of ever seeing the book in print – until it was finally accepted for serialisation by the German-language weekly *Freies Deutschland* in Antwerp, appearing in fifty instalments from 23 September 1937 to 8 September 1938.

By this time, the manuscript was nearing the end of its long odyssey; in July it was submitted to the exile publisher Gottfried Bermann Fischer – and accepted. Bermann Fischer had now established himself in Stockholm, where *Torquemadas Schatten* was published before the end of the year. The reviews, though favourable, were limited to a handful of exile periodicals and the novel apparently made little impact, its reception undermined by the inexorable onward march of Nazism, which had once more dispersed and impoverished many of its potential readers. The book was printed in Holland, and despite Otten's express advice to the contrary, copies were also warehoused there: large stocks were consequently impounded and destroyed by the Nazis after the German occupation of the Netherlands.[35]

Otten's hopes that *Torquemadas Schatten* would help to solve the pressing problems of subsistence were of course also largely unrealised. He received an advance of five hundred Swedish kroner for the novel, though actual sales failed to cover even this small sum. However, he still hoped to publish the book in English, commissioning a young translator, Ethel Talbot Scheffauer, to produce an English version of three sample chapters. His correspondence with her plaintively acknowledges his difficulty in securing publication for his work:

> Straight after receiving your letter, I wrote to my agent about a
> translation of my new novel. He said it has nothing to do with me, it's
> the publisher's business. I understand nothing, absolutely nothing
> about English publishing. It seems to me that everything is settled on a

commercial basis, involving cliques about which I know even less. On the other hand, German publishers' readers – readers of books written in German – are also the authors of the publishers concerned . . . so that it is pure chance whether a German manuscript finds a publisher (i.e. isn't sabotaged). Furthermore, and this is the other side of the coin, German manuscripts provoke a storm of politeness so that I think it's definitely better to submit them immediately and only in English translation.[36]

Otten's inability to penetrate the somewhat arcane world of English publishing provides a classic example of the dislocation of exile. Arriving in London at the age of forty-seven, he was a writer who had achieved striking, if intermittent, success in Germany, but whose name was virtually unknown outside it. The London literary world was a far cry from Berlin. Literary agents, who secured publication for most manuscripts in Britain, were still virtually unknown in Germany. Otten had been used to dealing directly with editors and publishers, some of whom, such as the Munich publisher Heinrich Bachmair or Franz Pfemfert, had been close friends. In London he suddenly found himself in a situation in which publishers were remote and inaccessible, dealing with writers at arm's length.

Otten's difficulty in establishing himself as a writer in an alien environment meant that, like other émigrés, he and Ellen faced a constant struggle for survival during their early years in England. Home Office regulations officially prohibited refugees from working, though certain marginal activities were apparently tolerated. Ellen's friend Anni Rosenblüth was an agent for a toy manufacturer, whose products included the *Hampelmänner* (jumping jacks) known to every German child: Ellen attempted to sell these toys to department stores in central London, though with little success. She was later forced to take in homework, cutting out decorative motifs for leather goods. The couple's continuing financial difficulties are eloquently evoked in a letter Otten wrote to his wife in August 1937:

> Sievers *Freies Deutschland* wants to print my book for 1500FF. Better than nothing and a start. . . I've lived very economically. I can pay almost all the rent and will get something from the Quakers on Monday – then I'm getting 1500 francs (= about £13) so that we're getting some way out of the wood.[37]

Such financial problems were of course endemic to exile, as was the enforced resort to one of the bewildering number of relief organisations which had sprung up after 1933. The best-known of these was the Jewish Refugees Committee, housed in Woburn House, the newly-opened premises of the Board of Deputies of British Jews. As a non-Jew, Otten had been directed to the Germany Emergency Committee of the Society of Friends, which he had contacted shortly after his arrival in London. In the summer of 1937 he spent a holiday at a centre on the Isle of Wight, run by a Quaker charity called Christian Endeavour. As the above letter implies, Otten also received small but regular amounts of money. Otherwise he was thrown back on the generosity of sympathetic individuals, such as the journalist Wickham Steed, whom he had known since his early days in London.[38] Steed had numerous contacts amongst German émigrés, several of whom he seems to have helped with regular payments.

Otten's periodic depression at the struggle to make ends meet and his frustration at the apparent lack of understanding for the plight of the exiles are eloquently, if unidiomatically, expressed in a letter in English to his translator:

> The last two days I was busy to get a job – you know nothing about my conditions as an émigré – so I asked the Quakers, the only ones to get in touch with so odd a being as me. They gave me – like a cricket ball – to another Charity (God bless her) institution, the Basque Children Refugee Committee. They gave me on further to a charitable man (God bless him too) in Reading . . . and he let me wait firstly for two hours, for he had a car (all charitable people have cars) and his car had a breakdown.[39]

Despite the difficulties of a hand-to-mouth existence, Otten was astonishingly productive during his early years in London. He had always been a fluent and prolific writer, driven by a strong sense of vocation. His wife remembered him as 'enormously hard-working' (*ungeheuer fleißig*), capable of long bursts of intense concentration. He was also a systematic writer who followed a regular routine, settling to work each morning and continuing throughout the day, sustained by the 'inevitable cigarettes'. He would type most of his work directly, more rarely dictating it. During a period of some two years after his arrival in

London, he wrote two novels – *Torquemadas Schatten* (1936), and *Die Reise nach Deutschland* ('Journey to Germany') (1937-38) – a five-act play *Kein Held* ('No Hero') (1937), and also began studies for a major theoretical work – a 'sociology of National Socialism' – which would occupy him for the next three years. During 1938-39 he also worked on a further novel entitled *Das auserwählte Volk* ('The Chosen People') which was never completed, though a typescript of over 250 pages has survived.

Just as remarkable as the volume and variety of Otten's work are the strenuous efforts he made to get it published in Britain, a country whose language he did not yet speak, whose political culture he was unacquainted with and whose publishing conventions he did not understand. His attempts to secure publication of his work were recorded in a register kept by his wife which noted baldly but meticulously the dates on which manuscripts were sent to publishers, agents or translators – and those on which they were returned or, more rarely, accepted.

Among the works of Otten's which were never published is the novel *Die Reise nach Deutschland* ('Journey to Germany'),[40] in which Otten placed great hopes and invested much emotional capital. He continued to hope for its publication even after the end of the war, long after any realistic prospect of publication had vanished. Like *Torquemadas Schatten*, *Die Reise nach Deutschland* is a highly political novel, depicting Nazi Germany in the summer of 1938, ostensibly seen through the eyes of a young Englishman, James Taylor, who comes to Cologne to visit the family with whom his father had stayed, twenty years earlier, as a British officer in the army of occupation in the Rhineland. Otten sought to portray the divisions and antagonisms within Germany through the tensions within a single family. The Eilershovens are liberal opponents of Nazism, whose daughter Sybil has embraced the values of the 'national revolution'. So intense is the prevailing atmosphere of suspicion and mistrust that both parents fear their daughter will eventually denounce them: 'The rift running through the whole of Germany goes straight through this family.'

Margot Eilershoven has fled into 'inner emigration', retreating into her Catholic faith. She warns James, during their first meeting, that politics have increasingly invaded the sphere of personal relations:

'Everyone does and says only what he's ordered to. Everyone is afraid of the next man. A poisonous cloud hangs over the country. Till is suffering horribly.' Till Eilershoven, Professor of English History, opposes the regime from a perspective of liberal humanism. He deplores the loss of academic freedom, ridiculing the decision to prohibit German scholars from accepting the Nobel Prize. Germany, he warns, has been turned into a police state, a dangerous cocktail of 'bloody revenge, terror, balkanisation and cannibalism. And the prime cause of all wars in Europe.' He scathingly dismisses the 'national revolution' as 'the revolt of the petty bourgeois, of the NCOs, of the mentally and physically retarded' and denounces the ideology of Nazism as 'a mass lunacy which has taken hold of the entire people'. Eilershoven is a mouthpiece for many of Otten's own views, above all his certainty that the Nazi regime would plunge Europe into a new war:

Nothing's changed since 1914. That year is still, or once again, on the calendar. War will break out in the next two years. Treaties are no use. Paper against lunacy? War from inner necessity. because this regime is driving towards destruction.

The novel's personal significance for Otten is emphasised by its setting in his native Rhineland, allowing him to draw on his memories of Cologne, the topography of which is a leitmotif of the book. James Taylor is at first impressed with the new Germany. After meeting a group of young people representing various shades of Nazi youth, he is strongly drawn to their camaraderie and idealism. Above all, he is dazzled by the group's leader, Joseph (Jupp) Cremer. Otten was well aware of the seductive appeal of Nazism, particularly to the young, and Cremer is a fascinating embodiment of the new Germany: gifted and charming, but also unscrupulous and dangerously paranoid. He is above all a ruthless careerist, who does not hesitate to denounce former friends to further his ambition. Cremer arranges for James to go hiking in the Eifel with a group of young Nazis – a trip which finally confirms James's growing conviction of the evils of Nazism. The route chosen for the hike runs along the Franco-German border, skirting frontier defences and allowing James to witness military manoeuvres. Germany is revealed as a vast armed camp in which old and young alike are conscripted to a militaristic agenda, convincing James of the danger of an ideology whose internal momentum moves inevitably towards a new war.

Otten portrays his native Rhineland as the part of the Reich which is least susceptible to Nazism, stressing the region's diverse cultural and racial heritage. Even the Nazi Cremer is forced to acknowledge that 'the movement has its greatest problems in the Rhineland. Pressure from the West. Agitation by the Church. We are a mixed race.' Otten also portrays the Rhinelanders' endemic mistrust of the Prussians – exemplified by the peasant couple who give shelter to the group of walkers during a storm. Active resistance to the Nazis comes from elements within the Catholic Church: Edwin, the Eilershovens' son, is arrested, and ultimately murdered, as part of a Catholic resistance group. The chapter in which James meets the priest who leads the group is crucial both for the development of the plot and the delivery of Otten's message. Unfortunately, it also exemplifies the tendency of Otten's characters to converse in long speeches, delivered in the diction of the leading article. In a passage lasting several pages, the priest expounds the view that the freedom and moral integrity of the individual is threatened by the power of the state, resting on a highly developed industrial and technological complex. Moreover, this threat is not unique to Germany, but is a danger inherent in industrial society. The views which Otten expounds on the relationship between the individual, the masses and the state, anticipate the central thesis of his 'analysis of fascism', *Geplante Illusionen* (published in 1942 as *A Combine of Aggression*).

'Journey to Germany' is very much a 'Zeitroman', written both to reflect its time and to influence it. Otten completed the novel at the height of the political crisis in the summer of 1938. Writing to Gottfried Bermann Fischer, he called its subject 'an Anglo-German problem', suggesting that an English edition would have greater interest than a German one, since he had written the book 'totally with reference to English thinking'.[41] His comments confirm that his purpose was unashamedly didactic: to open British eyes to the true nature of National Socialism. The book's chilling prophecy that, within two years, the Nazis would plunge Europe into a new war, was distinctly at odds with the prevailing mood of appeasement in Britain which reached its peak with the signing of the Munich Agreement. That autumn Otten sent the manuscript of his book to the translator Claude Sykes, who was eventually to complete an English version.[42]

At the same time, however, he submitted the manuscript for a literary prize instituted by the American Guild for German Cultural Freedom. The Guild had been established by the emigré German aristocrat Hubertus, Prinz zu Löwenstein, as a means of aiding and supporting German writers and artists in exile. Löwenstein inaugurated the literary prize with the collaboration of the American publishers Little, Brown and Co., which had agreed to publish not only the winning manuscript, but possibly also others recommended by the judges. Though gratified to learn (unofficially) that the judges had placed *Die Reise nach Deutschland* on a shortlist of six, Otten grew increasingly impatient with their lack of urgency, writing to the Guild in terms which underline his intention in writing the book:

> It is all important to me to be able to throw this book into the struggle before the catastrophe. . . And how important it is to open the eyes of the English. To analyse away, to exorcise this inclination for the conference table, for humiliation to the point of self-destruction, for eating their hat and swinging their umbrella. I just hope we're not too late.[43]

The judges ultimately decided against awarding the prize to Otten's novel, though they did recommend it for publication, but by then he had long since submitted the novel to the London publishers Secker & Warburg, where the journalist Hans Lothar, an old acquaintance, was now working as an editor. Lothar read and enthusiastically recommended the manuscript, raising Otten's hopes that it would be published. A final decision, however, rested with Fredric Warburg himself, who, being unable to read German, requested an English version: it was at this point that Otten committed himself to an English translation.

Otten's high hopes that the novel would be published made his disappointment all the greater when Warburg ultimately rejected it. The latter's reasons were bluntly commercial: 'It is our belief that the book will not sell.' His critique of both style and content are a forceful reminder of the problems facing the exiled writer in the choice and treatment of his material.

We have come to this decision partly because of the somewhat compli-
cated way in which the book is written, making it rather difficult to
understand which character is speaking, but largely because the picture
it gives of Nazi Germany would, in our view, be almost incomprehensible to the average English reader and is likely to be understood only
by readers with a first-hand knowledge of the Nazi background. This
is why the book was so much enjoyed in the original German by Mr
Lothar and another German reader.[44]

Warburg's comments suggest the reluctance of the British reading
public to engage with political realities in Germany. Perhaps more
crucially, the outbreak of war had undermined the novel's topicality,
turning its powerful prophecy into accomplished fact. Otten considered *Die Reise nach Deutschland* to be one of his most important works,
but though he remained preoccupied with it for over fifteen years,
making repeated efforts to find a publisher, it was to remain unpublished in his lifetime: a literary casualty of exile.

ALFRED KERR: LIVING 'FROM MIRACLE TO MIRACLE'

Alfred Kerr's years of exile in London were marked by extreme
poverty, a humiliating descent from the easy luxury he had enjoyed as
Germany's foremost theatre critic. 'Economically we are living, so to
speak, from miracle to miracle, as we have for the last eight and a half
years,' he wrote in 1941 to Rudolf Kommer, the friend who had already
lent him money more than once.[45] Money (or the lack of it) is the
leitmotif of Kerr's letters from London, a constant undercurrent which
occasionally breaks surface in urgent cries for help.

Perhaps even more humiliating for Kerr than his new-found
poverty, was his lapse into literary anonymity. Few of his literary projects in London were realised, fewer still published. Kerr's difficulties
were largely those endemic to exile. He could transport neither his
column in the *Berliner Tageblatt*, nor his seat in the second row of the
stalls. Exile had effectively robbed him of his *métier*, making the critical
skills he had spent over thirty years refining suddenly redundant.

Nor could Kerr, the accomplished journalist, find a foothold in

Britain. In his early months in London he tried unsuccessfully to place work with papers like the *Observer* and the *Daily Telegraph*, the latter responding with a polite rejection:

> Many thanks for sending me the particulars of your career and of your writing. I think it may be rather difficult for us to take any articles from you in view of the fact that you are unable to write in English. This would involve, of course, the articles being arranged for – and received – some time in advance.[46]

While Kerr's early attempts to find a niche in journalism were frustrated by his lack of fluent English, a more persistent problem was the absence of any real equivalent to the literary feuilleton which had always been the main vehicle for his work in Berlin.[47]

Within weeks of their arrival in London, the Kerrs moved into a somewhat shabby boarding-house, run by a Swiss woman, at 12 Upper Bedford Place, which was to become their home for the next four years.[48] Occupied mainly by German refugees, the Foyer Suisse was very much a microcosm of exile, a Central European enclave in an implacably English Bloomsbury. As the Nazis advanced steadily across Europe, it gradually began to fill up with refugees of other nationalities: Austrians, Czechs and, after the outbreak of war, Poles.

The hotel was part of a terrace of four-storey houses, which Kerr described as a rabbit-warren of rooms and corridors, leading off stairs covered with world-weary carpet. The rooms on the upper floors of the hotel were cheaper, and as the family's stay in England had extended, they gradually moved up, until they finally arrived at the top floor. Kerr had a room of his own, which served as both bedroom and study, where he spent much of his time, sitting down to work each day, writing on a battered typewriter which, his daughter remembered, was always going wrong.

Little of what he wrote was ever published and yet in the years immediately following his arrival in London, he still hoped, even expected, to gain a literary foothold. His mind was rich with literary projects: over the next few years, he wrote much verse and literary journalism, and worked at different times on four separate books, only one of which was ever published, and that in Paris, not London.

Kerr's problems were perhaps partly of his own making. On his own admission, he lacked a practical turn of mind: 'What a shame that they drummed into us children in Silesia that the inability to earn money was a kind of idealism, instead of just inability.'[49] At his age, he also found the task of adjusting to a foreign culture too great. The only book he succeeded in publishing after 1935, the bitterly anti-Nazi verse anthology *Melodien*, is addressed almost exclusively to an audience of fellow-exiles. The published edition contains the note: 'The first fifty copies were signed by the author. The proceeds from these fifty signed copies are being donated by author and publisher for the support of political prisoners in Germany.'[50] Many of the poems evoke the stations of exile or pay tribute to the 'Verbannte' who shared Kerr's fate. While the overriding theme of the anthology is exile, Kerr also dwells on the question of Jewishness, with which so much of his work in exile is concerned. In his biography of Rathenau he had presented his subject as an instructive example of the failed German-Jewish symbiosis: a man who had devoted his whole life to Germany, only to become the victim of nationalist assassins. Kerr had accused Rathenau of anti-semitism, of the Jewish self-hatred so prevalent amongst assimilated Jews. Several of the poems published in *Melodien* return to the theme of anti-semitism, deriding its vicious stupidity. A satirical poem in Bavarian dialect, 'Vulksgenossen san schepferisch' ('Nazi Comrades are Creative'), stresses the outstanding contribution of Jews to German science and letters – and the Nazis' ignorant persecution of them.

While Kerr set great store by the publication of this volume, he had almost despaired of finding a publisher. In November 1937, after receiving what he termed 'the very very last rejection', he wrote to Kommer imploring him to see if there was any chance of placing such a book with a German-American publisher in New York.[51] There was not, but the anthology was finally accepted for publication in Paris in February 1938: 'I am very pleased about it,' he wrote to Kommer, confirming the volume's personal significance for him.[52] *Melodien* appeared later that year in an edition of 4,000 copies.

Kerr dedicated the volume to 'Rudolf Kommer – the best friend I ever met'. A German-speaking Romanian, Kommer was a larger than life figure who fascinated and mystified his contemporaries. He was a journalist, translator and literary agent, known above all for his association with the theatre impresario Max Reinhardt. Kommer was mysteriously well-connected, raising money from sources which have not always been identified, in ways which have often remained unexplained. His generosity is beyond doubt. He had been a benefactor to the Viennese critic Alfred Polgar long before befriending Kerr, whom he had met in 1934.[53] Kommer's unexplained affluence, especially in the straitened circumstances of exile, has given rise to speculation that he may have been a double agent, in the pay of the Gestapo. Such treachery was certainly among the ambiguities of exile, but in Kommer's case the available evidence is inconclusive.[54] Kerr himself had no reason to suspect his friend, remaining touchingly grateful for his generosity until Kommer's death in 1943.

Melodien was the last book of Kerr's to be published in his lifetime (he died in 1948). When it finally appeared, he was already writing a new book, with the working title *Zwei Männer in London* ('Two Men in London'), in which he intended to explore the question of Jewish identity. The work was originally conceived as a comparative biography of Disraeli and Marx, 'a book which will illuminate the continuing achievements of two modern Jews significant in world history'.[55] Kerr first mentions the book in June 1937, and worked on it spasmodically over the next few years, abandoning it after the outbreak of war, as chances of publication receded, only to revive it in 1943, as they once more improved. From the first, he had seen the book in a commercial perspective, having started it only after a careful study of American bestsellers in the lucrative market for historical biography, but though he discussed the proposal with London publishers such as Secker and Hamish Hamilton, he was unable to secure a contract.[56] As time passed, he entertained various schemes to finance the book, each more fanciful than the last: 'But wouldn't it be possible to find a group of five men who together could raise £25 a month for one year?', he asked Kommer.[57]

Though Kerr never completed the manuscript, he did publish some sections as individual essays; these were evidently to form the backbone of the proposed book, having survived among his unpublished papers under the title *Ein Jude spricht zu Juden* ('A Jew speaks to Jews').[58] Kerr had always readily acknowledged his Jewish descent. During his formative years in Imperial Germany, he had been all too aware of the 'eternal division' between Jews and non-Jews, 'but personally I have always felt my descent from this fabled people to be something enriching'. His visit to the Holy Land in 1903 had been a joyous and emotional occasion for him, but he had nonetheless concluded: 'Even in Jerusalem I always knew that I was a German.'[59] He was in fact a typical product of the German-Jewish symbiosis: a Jew steeped in German culture, indifferent to the Jewish religion, and, as he himself admitted, knowing barely ten words of Hebrew.

Although Kerr occasionally addressed the theme of Jewishness in his work before 1933, it was rarely mentioned in the Kerr household. His daughter Judith remembered that she and her brother were brought up entirely outside the precepts of the Jewish faith, even to the extent that the Kerrs celebrated a very German Christmas.[60] In exile, however, the question of Jewish identity acquired new relevance. Kerr's response to Nazi anti-semitism was to tell his children always to be proud of their Jewish heritage. What he had previously been content to internalise now became a matter for public assertion: he wished to emphasise the outstanding contribution which Jews had made to German culture and society. Thus the purpose of *Ein Jude spricht zu Juden* was 'not henceforth to refute idiotic accusations; but to stress all that the development of the world owes to this tribe'.[61] The surviving sections, which scarcely deserve the word manuscript, are disjointed and lacking in cohesion. The most coherent parts are the contrasting biographies of Disraeli and Marx, but even these lack any striking insight into the life of their subjects, or any particularly original thoughts on the role of the secular Jew.

Despite his sudden fall from fame, Kerr remained remarkably serene, even coming to regard exile as a blessing in disguise. In 1937 he summarised his experience nonchalantly in verse:

Manchmal fühlt das Herz sich sehr erheitert
(trotz der zugeschlagnen deutschen Tür):
Weil die Flucht den Horizont erweitert,
Ja, du dankst den Jägern fast dafür.

Sometimes my heart is full of cheer / (Despite the German door slammed shut): / Since exile widens the horizon, / You could almost thank your persecutors for it.[62]

Kerr was able to maintain his optimism even in the face of bitter poverty. During these pre-war years his only regular income was as 'London correspondent' of the German exile newspaper *Pariser Tageszeitung*, to which he contributed a weekly column. He was paid a fee of £6 a month, but even this pittance was not always paid promptly, or even regularly, being subject to the newspaper's frequent financial difficulties. Among Kerr's contributions to the paper were some of the sketches later incorporated into the book *Ich kam nach England* ('I Came to England').[63]

Kerr seems to have begun compiling his new work early in 1939, writing some months later to George Bernard Shaw: 'Now, after having lived for four years in London. . . I am preparing a book of my English impressions. . . I have just arrived in my book ("I Came to England") at the Shavian chapter and should be so glad to complete it.'[64] *Ich kam nach England* is an affectionate book, the diary of an often shrewd and always benign observer. It is both a record of Kerr's impressions of London during the previous four years, and the evocation of a social mood, a portrait of a nation moving unwittingly towards war.

Kerr outlined the theme and viewpoint of his book in a letter to a prospective publisher:

> The crux is very friendly to England. (Not without amusing criticism here and there.) The book portrays the impressions of a notable fellow-human and continental (namely me) here in England. It portrays, apart from the politically perceived era, other things which lie beyond it: customs, states of mind, society – amidst the constant, quiet suffering of the immigrant, who has no right to speak politically. And who knows more about political probabilities than the experts here.[65]

Kerr's book is a homage to the country in which he had found refuge, and which he had gradually learnt to love: 'The longer one lives in London, the greater the gratitude one feels for this country.' His portrait of England and the English is so favourable as to be almost indulgent: 'This people is, without the slightest doubt, the most considerate, most perceptive, and most reasonable in the world.' So great was his enthusiasm that at times he seemed ready to suspend his otherwise acute critical faculty, transforming even glaring faults into comparative virtues. The practice of flogging criminals in Britain is not approved, but any criticism is vitiated through an almost light-hearted comparison to Germany:

> I should warn the Third Reich not to use this custom to excuse its own brutalities. Because of this difference. In England the criminals are whipped. In Germany, the criminals do the whipping.

Kerr was also an uncritical admirer of the English public school system, sending his daughter to a girls' boarding school in Kent, while his son Michael attended the minor public school Aldenham in Hertfordshire. He notes the eccentricities of English schooling, such as the preoccupation with sports, but concludes: 'I think they learn more in England and swot less.'

His criticisms of England are mainly culinary. 'My main complaint about England is the sheep. They appear at mealtimes for years on end, for aeons. Too little wine, too much mutton. But don't let anyone say a word against the people – they're wonderful.' He conceded that, however much he admired England and the English, he found France more congenial, even confessing that he often thought of escaping there. He did in fact return to France twice during these pre-war years, once to take leave of his sister, who was travelling to Palestine.

It is striking that the noted theatre critic has little to say about the London theatre, which he found shallow and escapist, incapable of confronting contemporary problems. He commented after seeing a play by T. S. Eliot: 'Today, in 1939, before the new world war, the ultimate political truth can still not be pronounced in England.'

Kerr's almost unreserved admiration for England and the English is qualified by his despair at the prevailing political self-delusion. He was one of many prominent exiles who felt it their duty to enlighten the English as to the true nature of Nazism, but was too often met by disbelief and lack of interest. He reproached the English with an almost wilful refusal to face political reality, a tendency to trivialise unpleasant prospects:

> I sometimes feel that the English trivialise whatever they find unpleasant or awful. They called Napoleon by the nickname 'Napy' (really!). Perhaps they'll call Hitler, whom they find unpleasant, 'Dolfi'. Anything is possible. They find him threatening, and therefore make him cute.

The last, and by far the longest section of *Ich kam nach England* is called 'Tagebuch der Schmerzen' ('Diary of Sufferings'): a roughly chronological record of the political (and hence personal) crises of the years 1937–39. Kerr repeatedly complains that, as an outsider, he is unable to play any active role: 'The spring of 1937 is a grave time, and we ex-Germans, the spectators who are most deeply involved, are those who have to suffer most deeply – seeing . . . and yet obliged to be silent.' Kerr suffered at the alarming naivety of British attitudes to Germany, criticising a concert given in Berlin by Sir Thomas Beecham, who seemed quite unaware of how the occasion would be exploited for political purposes. He suffered increasingly from being an enforced spectator: 'We refugees see through Hitler's plans. But while we see through him, we can only look on. In our time, a whole country is playing cricket. Meanwhile Hitler is preparing.' He felt that even if people asked his opinion on Germany, it was simply so that he could tell them what they wanted to hear. British reactions to the annexation of Austria seemed to typify the country's political complacency and isolationism. When Kerr broached the topic to the son of an MP, the young man thought he was talking about a boxing match between Tommy Farr and Max Baer. Many Britons misunderstood the 'Anschluss' as simply a natural alliance between two German-speaking countries. Most felt untouched by such events: 'February 1938. While the brown rats burrow underground in the fields of Europe, the yeoman John Bull thinks himself immune to the plague.'

As the policy of appeasement reached its climax in the Munich crisis, Kerr, 'the mere onlooker', describes the incipient panic at the prospect of war – the rich transporting their possessions out of London to their bolt-holes in the country, airraid shelters and trenches for anti-aircraft batteries being dug in London parks and squares, the distribution of gasmasks: 'With the gravest fear of war, with hourly changes of unbearable tension, with the sight of trenches dug in every London square. (My gasmask lies in the cupboard.)'

With the passing of the crisis, Kerr nonetheless found it impossible to share the general relief that war had been averted; in the longer term, he considered war inevitable, even necessary: 'A German poet wrote: the tears and the sighs – they came afterwards. But in London people are saying: "How could we think there was going to be a war? How could anyone?"'

The most traumatic event in Kerr's 'Diary of Sufferings' came with the so-called *Reichskristallnacht* (Night of Broken Glass). On 9–10 November 1938 Jewish businesses throughout Germany were systematically attacked and plundered, while individual Jews were rounded up and transported to Dachau. Under the eloquent heading 'defeat for humanity', Kerr muses: 'I must apologise to myself. One feels ashamed in any case to be living in such an age.'

Appropriately for the former theatre critic, the London theatre was to provide the most striking sign of the times. Under the heading 'Gallows Humour', Kerr noted:

> We are marking the end of 1938. Dark times.
>
> In London a play (*Lot's Wife*) has been performed more than two hundred times which takes the destruction – of just a city, not of a whole continent – as its theme. Destruction. A symbol? The stalls are ... dying with laughter. Another symbol?

Alfred Kerr began 1939 just as he had begun each of the previous five years: in debt, but still in hope. He had once more been able to solve his most immediate problems through the generosity of Rudolf Kommer:

> Your letter came at one of the (not infrequent) critical moments, as though from heaven. Or: it was like the end of some melodrama in the cinema, when 'at the very worst moment'. . . etc. I haven't yet given up hope of a big hit in the cinema, and have just finished writing a film ('Das Erbe', 'The Patrimony'). I find it a bit stupid in its simplicity but perhaps its lack of intellectual complexity gives it a chance of being accepted.[66]

Kerr's money problems rumble on in his correspondence; the screenplay is never heard of again.

MAX HERRMANN-NEIßE: MONOLOGUE ON A FOREIGN STAGE

The year 1936 was one of growing resignation for Max Herrmann-Neiße, a feeling heightened by the realisation that exile had become permanent, a sentence from which there was no prospect of remission.

And yet it had begun well, seeming to promise the fulfilment of many of his literary hopes.

In April the Herrmanns and Sondheimer had moved once more, this time to a flat at Bryanston Court, George Street, where Herrmann-Neiße would spend the last five years of his life. The apartment block was newly built and indeed, as Herrmann-Neiße recorded in one of his poems, work on the building continued for several weeks after they moved in. Bryanston Court still stands, suggesting now, as then, the discreet but evident affluence it houses. The poet's beloved Hyde Park was still within easy walking distance.

May had seen the publication in Zurich of *Um uns die Fremde* ('Abroad All Around Us'), a collection comprising most of the poems Herrmann-Neiße had written during the first three years of exile. The theme of *Um uns die Fremde*, as of all Herrmann-Neiße's exile poetry, is exile itself. In a series of exquisitely musical short poems, he records the hopes and hardships, the sufferings and small joys of exile, evoking for an audience of refugees the day-to-day experience which united them. A decade earlier, Herrmann-Neiße had called his own work an attempt to express modern sensibility in traditional forms, to catch the finest nuance of experience in the simplest possible language, a description which equally applies to *Um uns die Fremde*. In a generous foreword, Thomas Mann had called it 'a sweet and lovely book', praising 'the classicism, emotional rationality and graceful clarity of the verses', adding that, virtually alone among exiled poets, Herrmann-Neiße had been able to evoke 'the painful situation of enforced exile, the tragedy of the refugee'.[67] A foreword by Thomas Mann naturally also helped to ensure that the volume was widely reviewed, particularly in Switzerland.

In the course of the year, three of Herrmann-Neiße's poems were even published in London, appearing in an anthology of *Modern German Verse*, edited by the Austrian writer Fritz Gross.[68] However, even such modest success was quickly soured. Though Gross was a fellow-exile, he and his co-editor were evidently concerned to be studiously impartial, including in their selection various poets who had earned approval in the Third Reich, such as Kolbenheyer, as well as exiles like Herrmann-Neiße and Berthold Viertel. The biographical notes on Herrmann-Neiße and Viertel stated blandly that they were 'now living in London', omitting to say why. Since the collection was intended for use in schools and colleges, the publishers evidently hoped to avoid any possibility of protest by the German Embassy. Even worse was the cavalier editorial treatment the poems received. Herrmann-Neiße was furious at the mutilation of his poem 'Ein deutscher Dichter bin ich einst gewesen' ('Once I was a German Poet'), published disingenuously under the title 'Der Dichter' ('The Poet') and with several lines printed in inferior variants which he disowned. Sadly, the three poems included in *Modern German Verse* represent the sum total of Herrmann-Neiße's work to be published in London during his lifetime.

More seriously, while *Um uns die Fremde* gained a certain *succès d'estime*, it achieved little financial success. In the first year after publication, the volume sold only 174 copies, failing to cover even the modest advance Herrmann-Neiße had received. In a letter to Paul Zech, he commented: 'My book of poems was read and praised by many people, naturally it didn't make any money,' adding wryly: 'Incorrigible as I am, I continue to write poems.'[69]

Artistic disappointment was matched by growing social isolation. His tiny circle of friends and acquaintances had shrunk even further as the German film and theatre colony in London moved on to New York and eventually Hollywood. Jessner and Graetz had left in 1935, Viertel and Toller the following year. One of Herrmann-Neiße's few friends to remain in London was the painter and graphic artist Martin Bloch, a fellow-native of Neiße. Bloch had first visited London in 1933, when he had made the acquaintance of the Australian painter Roy de Maistre. He had returned to London in October 1934 after fleeing from Germany with his family, securing an entry visa through the intervention of de Maistre, with whom he had established the School of Contemporary Painting in Ebury Street, Pimlico. Always at home in the company of artists, Herrmann-Neiße met Bloch regularly, sometimes visiting his studio in Ebury Street. Bloch executed one of only two surviving portraits of Herrmann-Neiße during his London years: a pencil drawing in semi-profile, presented on the occasion of the poet's fiftieth birthday party at Bryanston Court.

With no foreseeable alternative to economic dependence on Sondheimer, Herrmann-Neiße remained stranded in London. During 1936 he was denied even the respite of a return to his beloved Zurich, being unable to travel abroad because of passport difficulties. His work was now officially banned in Germany, having appeared on the Prohibition List (List 1 of Harmful and Undesirable Literature) issued by the Reichsschriftumskammer (Reich Chamber of Literature) in October 1935.[70] Strangely, Herrmann-Neiße himself seems to have remained unaware of this, asserting that 'whether one or other of my works has been banned is beyond my knowledge'.[71] When his passport expired in June 1936, his application for renewal was first deferred and finally refused by the Nazi authorities, forcing him to apply to the Home Office for the 'certificate of identity' which was issued to the growing number of those made stateless. He was superficially philosophical about such problems, acknowledging them as an inevitable consequence of exile.[72]

Herrmann-Neiße took no active part in exile politics and indeed viewed the fractious activities of political exiles with dismay. He was sickened by the show trials in Moscow, condemning such murderous sectarianism as 'left-wing Nazidom' (*linkes Nazitum*), with exactly the same inhuman methods, mendacious legal charades and cold-blooded orgies of revenge'.[73] Despite his distaste, he was all too aware of the emigrant's vulnerability to political events, watching them unfold with despairing fascination. He was haunted by a growing premonition of impending disaster, writing to Paul Zech that he could count himself lucky that he was far away from Europe 'and the terrible war which I think I feel drawing ever closer'. Once again, he acknowledged his feelings of isolation and emotional displacement, confessing that he felt 'rather lonely here and, so to speak, emotionally "out of place". The sheer extent of this city means that you can go months without seeing people.'[74]

He was happy to put 1936 behind him, recording in another of the poems which now read increasingly like daily diary entries:

Das vergangene Jahr sei ganz vergessen,
aus dem Buch des Lebens ausgerissen –

May the last year be quite forgotten, / eradicated from the book of life –[75]

The new year brought little relief from the defeats and disappointments of the old. Both he and Leni suffered illnesses which lingered on, he suffering from persistent conjunctivitis, the eye-drops which the doctor prescribed bringing little relief. Always something of a hypochondriac, he feared that his sight might be permanently affected.[76]

In February, Herrmann-Neiße learnt that his friend Paul Graetz had died suddenly in Hollywood, breaking his last surviving link with the Berlin cabaret, whose vitality and satirical irreverence had so appealed to him. He reacted with characteristic subjectivity: 'So do they vanish one after the other and it becomes emptier and emptier around us.'[77] In a funeral oration for Graetz in Hollywood, Ernst Toller said that he had died of a broken heart, caused by the enforced exile from his beloved Berlin. Herrmann-Neiße felt equally uprooted, but he was determined to survive.

> Ich wehre mich, ich will mich nicht ergeben,
> nicht eingestehen, dass ich am Ende bin –
>
> *I am resisting, will not surrender, / will not admit that I am finished* –[78]

He still took comfort from the small pleaures of his life and from the work which gave shape and purpose to it.[79]

By this time he had at least the satisfaction that his poems had begun to appear regularly in the major exile periodicals. The pattern of these publications charts the fortunes of the financially hard-pressed and often ephemeral journals in which they appeared. His first publication in exile appeared (in 1933) in the Paris-based periodical *Das neue Tage-Buch*, which also published his last (in 1940). *Das neue Tage-Buch*, the most enduring of the exile periodicals, published more poetry than any other – and Herrmann-Neiße, together with Walter Mehring, became the poet most frequently published in its pages. From 1933, his poems appeared in Klaus Mann's *Die Sammlung*, published in Amsterdam – until the journal's demise two years later. From 1935 they appeared occasionally in *Internationale Literatur*, a Moscow-published journal which began to open its columns to poetry, reflecting the emergence of the Popular Front policy. However, the most frequent outlets for his work were the exile daily *Pariser Tageszeitung* and the liberal *Basler Nationalzeitung*. In the three years following the publication of *Um uns die Fremde*, some twenty-five poems of Herrmann-Neiße's appeared in these two publications, helping to keep his name alive in the scattered community of German-speaking exiles. This steady trickle of publications slackened with the outbreak of war and dried up completely with the fall of France in 1940.

Superficially, Herrmann-Neiße seemed increasingly resigned to his situation, acknowledging his good fortune in being spared the constant struggle for mere subsistence which burdened so many of his fellow-exiles: 'Personally, I really can't complain about things. I have no illness worth mentioning, I have my wife with me, I have board and lodging guaranteed.'[80]

In fact, he felt increasingly isolated. In the same letter to Zech, he remarks that the only mutual acquaintances he still saw were Kerr and Zweig. Even these contacts were sometimes fleeting. On one occasion he accompanied Kerr to King's College, London, to hear a lecture by Stefan Zweig: 'Zweig spoke some fine words on Rilke, I understood him well, but Professor Rose afterwards less well.' It had all finished by seven o'clock and he walked back with Kerr to the latter's boarding-house in Bloomsbury, noting with evident regret that Kerr had no time to prolong the conversation: 'And so I went on home alone.'[81] Herrmann-Neiße always enjoyed the company of Kerr, with whom he could reminisce about Breslau and talk in Silesian dialect. Kerr, who had once championed his poetry in the now remote days of pre-war Berlin, continued to admire it. The admiration was mutual. Herrmann's regard for Kerr dated from his own days as a theatre critic in provincial Neiße, when he had eagerly awaited the arrival of the daily papers from the capital in order to read the latest *obiter dicta* of the 'king of critics'. He recorded his continuing admiration in a poem written for Kerr's seventieth birthday in 1937. He had hoped to arrange a reading in celebration of the event, but had abandoned the idea when the bookseller Hans Preiss had refused to stage it on the grounds that Kerr had far too many enemies in the exile community. Herrmann-Neiße commented bitterly on the 'disunity and mutual intolerance of emigrant writers, who have learned absolutely nothing from the experience of the last five years'.[82]

Stefan Zweig too thought highly of Herrmann-Neiße's work. Zweig had proved a loyal friend and mentor, concerned to alleviate

Herrmann-Neiße's artistic isolation and secure a limited measure of public access for his work. He arranged several private readings at his flat in Hallam Street for a small circle of friends, at which Herrmann-Neiße read his poems. These occasions were, as his wife later confirmed, of great importance to him.[83] He was grateful for any crumb of recognition, acknowledging Zweig as 'always the most helpful of comrades'.[84]

For his part, Zweig seems to have felt a warm affection for Herrmann-Neiße, addressing him in their occasional correspondence as 'mein lieber Macke' (my dear Macke) and asserting that 'from the very beginning we have always understood each other in all important things'.[85] He admired the poet's moral steadfastness and his unswerving devotion to his art. They were in fact near neighbours, and Zweig, when walking in Hyde Park, would occasionally see him, lost in thought on a park bench, insulated from immediate reality:

> Always when I saw him like that . . . in his great loneliness, I had a feeling of respect, or even pride, that there was one among us who remained pure, unconcerned, committed to the cause of poetry in the midst of a catastrophic world.[86]

In the course of 1937, Max and Leni made two extended trips to Switzerland, the first in May and June, visiting Berne, where they had celebrated their twentieth wedding anniversary, Spiez on Lake Thun and finally his beloved Zurich. Once more, the trip was paid for by Sondheimer, to whom Herrmann-Neiße wrote, thanking him effusively for 'this wonderful May journey. . . It was really the finest birthday present I've ever had.'[87]

During the summer, Herrmann-Neiße suffered from an intestinal complaint, causing digestive problems. He lost over ten pounds, his weight falling to a mere six stone five pounds. He was still convalescing when he and Leni returned to Switzerland in September. On this occasion, Sondheimer accompanied them as far as Paris, where they stayed for a week, mainly to visit the World Exhibition, an experience which Herrmann-Neiße described as 'an indescribable pleasure for me'.[88] Sondheimer then returned to London, while the Herrmanns travelled on to Switzerland, spending the next three weeks (9–30 September) in Lugano.

Noted as a nature poet, Herrmann was transported by the beauties of the Ticinese countryside, which he evoked in a cycle of poems ('Bilderbogen Lugano'). He was unable to manage the long walks he and Leni had taken during their last stay in Zurich. His health was still shaky and although he had put on weight, he still weighed only 44 kilos (6 stone 13 lbs.) He still complained of digestive problems and loss of appetite. But nothing could mar his enjoyment; he wrote again to Sondheimer thanking him for 'all these wonderful experiences'.[89] During their stay in Lugano, the couple paid a visit to Hermann Hesse in Montagnola. Hesse was an author whose work Herrmann-Neiße had long admired and publicly lauded in a series of reviews before 1933. In conclusion, the couple stayed a week in Zurich, where Herrmann-Neiße read a selection of poems on the radio: the occasion providing welcome reassurance that he was not forgotten in the German-speaking world. It was perhaps the most stimulating and satisfying of all his visits to Switzerland and certainly the last in which he could briefly forget his fears of the future. When he returned to the country the following year, his pleasure was already overshadowed by the storm clouds of international crisis.

The worsening international situation in 1938 was reflected in a further deterioration in the personal circumstances of the refugees from Nazism. For Max Herrmann-Neiße, this inevitable conjunction of the personal and the political was particularly distressing. The annexation of Austria coincided with the official announcement that he had been deprived of his German nationality, his name appearing on the Expatriation List (Ausbürgerungsliste) in the official *Deutscher Reichsanzeiger* on 9 March 1938, one of twenty-eight names on the thirty-fourth such list, which included those of the playwright Bruno Frank and the leading exile publisher Fritz Landshoff.[90] As his wife, Leni automatically suffered the same fate.

The physically deformed poet, whose main inspirations were the beauty of nature and the memory of his native Neiße, was thus declared an enemy of the Third Reich. The office of the Reichsführer SS, monitoring the German exile press, had scrupulously catalogued all Herrmann's contributions to *Das neue Tage-Buch*, also noting the appearance of *Um uns die Fremde*.[91] Though his expatriation came as no surprise, Herrmann-Neiße nonetheless found it traumatic. He felt as though 'something had collapsed within him . . . as though he had received a blow on the head'.[92] Friends too noted the effect: Alfred Kerr recalled that he appeared deeply shaken.[93] He could cope with this blow only by turning it into poetry. In a poem pointedly prefaced by the official announcement of his expatriation, he reasserted his German identity and his love of his homeland which would withstand the administrative theft of his nationality:

> Wer mich zu entehren glaubte
> wenn mit frevelndem Befehle
> er das Heimatrecht mir raubte
> ahnt die ewig lenzbelaubte
> Heimat nicht in meiner Seele.

He who seeks to dishonour me / with a criminal decree which / robs me of the right to my homeland / does not know the eternal springtime / of the homeland within my soul.[94]

Such public defiance was only half convincing. Privately, he confessed that, over three months after the announcement, he was still in turmoil:

> In the meantime, we have been officially expatriated. I had been expecting it for a long time, but when it actually became a clear and undeniable fact, it really hurt me, I felt a spiritual soreness. I felt deeply hurt and treated inhumanly. . . I tried to defend and console myself with the poem which I have also written out for you, but between you and me: I'm afraid that, precisely in my case, this consolation seems to lack any lasting or permanent effect.[95]

Herrmann-Neiße was all too aware that the Germany invoked in his verse had long ceased to exist, that (in Kerr's striking phrase) 'he was longing for a land which was no more the land of his longing'.[96] He was increasingly convinced that he had wasted his life in a series of half measures and missed opportunities, feelings summarised in a poem composed for his fifty-second birthday:

> Je mehr ich altre, desto böser muß
> Verfehltes das Gewissen mir verstören.[97]

The older I grow, the sharper does / my conscience prick at what I have left undone.

The sense of failure is a constant undertone in his work in 1938; he felt that he no longer had the strength to resist the turbulence of the times:

Ich bin zu schwach, ich werde mitgerissen
und wage keine letzte Gegenwehr,
ganz wider bessres Wissen und Gewissen:
so hat mein Dasein keinen Segen mehr.
Es bleibt mir nichts als reuig abzudanken:
fruchtlos war alles, was ich sang und tat.

I am too weak, I am swept along / And do not even dare a last defence, / Quite against my conscience and my better instinct / My being has no blessing any more. / There is nothing left but to depart ruefully: / Everything was fruitless that I sang or did.[98]

In an increasingly hostile world, his only remaining refuge was poetry:

Mir bleibt mein Lied, was auch geschieht.
Mein Reich ist nicht von dieser Welt.

I still have my song, whatever happens / My kingdom is not of this world.[99]

This declaration of faith was published in the *Basler Nationalzeitung* in July 1938, though it would still have reached few of his fellow-exiles. However, even more than public access for his work, Herrmann-Neiße needed the endorsement of his fellow-writers. One of the rare occasions when he was able to share his work with his peers was a meeting in June 1938 at the Hallam Street home of Stefan Zweig, who invited his compatriots Berthold Viertel and Franz Werfel to join Herrmann-Neiße in reading from their own recent work. Herrmann-Neiße was greatly heartened by the occasion, which he called 'an unforgettable afternoon'.[100] Werfel, who had left Vienna in the immediate aftermath of the Anschluss, was deeply moved by Herrmann-Neiße's poems evoking the alien metropolis whose swirling activity was clearly audible outside the windows. He later confided to Herrmann-Neiße that he felt a great affinity with him, a feeling which returned whenever he came across one of his poems in an exile journal.

In the following months, Leni was haunted once more by Cassandra-like dreams of disaster. Her premonitions seemed to be fulfilled as international tension rose sharply during the summer. Herrmann-Neiße felt stifled by the tense atmosphere in London as the Sudeten crisis unfolded. As one who had always opposed militarism, who had even refused to share the patriotic enthusiasm of August 1914, he felt despair at the renewed preparations for war: slit trenches were being dug in his beloved Hyde Park, and anti-aircraft defences erected in the square not fifty yards from the entrance to Bryanston Court. An event which, in 1918, he had firmly believed he would never see again, suddenly seemed inevitable. 'One can sense war in close proximity,' he wrote to Paul Zech. 'My wife has the most awful premonitions, I myself am very depressed. I almost envy you for being so far away from Europe.'[101] So strong were Leni's forebodings that, at the last moment, the couple cancelled plans to return to Switzerland that summer, not wishing to be caught away from London at such a time. As ever, Herrmann-Neiße transposed his feelings into verse, enclosing a poem with his letter to Zech.[102]

As the political crisis momentarily receded, Max and Leni did finally return to Switzerland, but it was a short and uneasy visit. While in Zurich, Herrmann-Neiße renewed discussions with Emil Oprecht about the publication of a second volume of poems. The publisher was quick to point out that 'the difficulties of selling German books, particularly poetry, outside Germany have increased considerably since we published your last volume'.[103] He finally agreed to publish the new collection only on a subscription basis, postponing a final decision until July in order to give Herrmann-Neiße time to collect 'at least 200–250 subscribers'. Though he actually opened a subscription list, which included distinguished names like Kerr and Heinrich Mann, he was still well short of the required number by July, and the project finally foundered with the outbreak of war. Such were the vicissitudes of publishing poetry in exile.[104]

In October 1938, having completed the necessary five years residence, Herrmann-Neiße applied for British nationality, an ironic (if expedient) step for one who had always felt so out of place in Britain. Though he stressed, in his letter to the Home Office, that he was 'always loyal to this country as the keeper and defender of my own democratic ideals', he remained no less a cultural outsider. His application for naturalisation was supported by such distinguished sponsors as H. G. Wells, Hermon Ould and William Rose, Professor of German at

London University, who enjoyed contacts with a number of literary exiles. For reasons which are unclear, his application was not proceeded with. 'I have never heard another word from the Home Office from that day to this,' he wrote indignantly two years later.[105] He would remain stateless until his death.

His application for naturalisation did not imply any emotional rapprochement with England, where he felt as out of place as ever. He continued to live in the cultural limbo of the émigré, uncertain in his command of English, but apprehensive that his native language was atrophying. One of the prerequisites for naturalisation was an adequate command of English; Herrmann-Neiße's application, with its evidence of considerable interference from German, served only to underline his linguistic shortcomings.

In the last two years of his life, Herrmann-Neiße's poems gradually assume the character of an intimate journal, a relief-map tracing the shifting contours of his thoughts and feelings. He took refuge increasingly in books – old friends with whom he could converse in the language of the past – or in the private world of his poetry. But even this was ultimately not a safe retreat, for reality was always apt to intrude. He describes one such occasion in Hyde Park, when, deep in the composition of a poem, he was suddenly addressed by a passer-by, an intrusion which so disrupted his train of thought that he was left literally speechless.

Ganz vergebens such' ich mich zu sammeln,
Meine gute Stunde ist zerstört.
Hilflos werde ich Verfehltes stammeln,
weil mir keine Sprache mehr gehört.

Quite in vain, I try to compose myself, / my good hour is destroyed. / Helplessly, I stammer something inappropriate, / because I no longer command any language.[106]

Suddenly estranged from even his native tongue, he feels the threat of the complete disintegration of language and, with it, of identity.

In truth, he never adjusted to living in London, never really considered the option of adapting to an English environment. The sights and sounds and smells of the city served only to prompt his memories of Germany, and particularly of his native Neiße.

Der Nelkenduft, den meine Mutter liebte,
weht jetzt mir zu aus diesen fremden Beeten.
Wer dachte einst, ich müßte je betreten
dies ferne graue Land, das ungeliebte.

The scent of carnations, which my mother loved / blows over to me from
these foreign beds. / Who would once have thought that I should ever come /
to this distant grey country which I do not love.[107]

He not only summons up remembrance of things past, but defends his
attachment to them, insisting that memory was his lifeline. 'How
otherwise could I bear my fate?' he asks in the poem 'Rechtfertigung
eines Emigranten' ('Justification of an Emigré').

His feelings of homesickness sometimes threatened to engulf him,
feelings he could cope with only by transposing them into verse, as in
the poem with the plaintive, childlike title 'Ich möchte heim' (I Want to
Go Home'):

Das Gastland kann die Heimat nie ersetzen,
hat mich sein Frieden freundlich auch bedacht.
Gefangen fühl' ich mich in fremden Netzen
und um das Lebenselement gebracht.

My host country can never replace my home country, / though I too have
received its peace. / I feel trapped in alien nets / and deprived of my natural
element.[108]

During the early months of 1939, he was still troubled by ill health,
taking several weeks to recover from a severe attack of flu. He saw little
of his compatriots: 'Recently, I've seen hardly any of our main
acquaintances,' he wrote to Heinrich Mann, though adding that Stefan
Zweig, newly returned from America, was due to visit him that evening.
He expressed the hope that he would be able to visit Mann in Paris that
summer, 'if everything remains peaceful in the world'.[109]

The more intimate discourse of his poetry offered no such hope; even
the coming of spring held a scarcely-concealed threat.

Was morgens sich die Lüfte sagen,
enthüllt am Abend einen schlimmen Sinn.
So gehe ich durch den Lenz in Unbehagen,
ist bei mir noch herbstlich grau zumut,

und auch was kommt mit holden Sommertagen,
ist voll Gewaltsamkeit und riecht nach Blut.

*What breezes whisper to each other in the morning, / reveals by evening a
wicked meaning. / So I walk uneasily through spring, / my feelings are still
grey and autumnal, / and what the balmy days of summer will bring / is full
of violence and smells of blood.*[110]

THE END OF AUSTRIA

Despite its strategic position in Central Europe, Austria had not been
a major focus of British foreign policy in the thirties. Austrian independence was guaranteed by the Versailles Treaty, and reaffirmed by the
Geneva Treaty of 1922. The introduction of an authoritarian constitution and the establishment of a corporate state (*Ständestaat*), in which
political power was monopolised by the Patriotic Front, were therefore
viewed tolerantly in Whitehall and the Quai d'Orsay. While Chancellor
Dollfuß could count on the continued support of Britain and France,
the main guarantor of Austria's independence after 1933 was Mussolini, anxious to contain German ambitions in Central Europe.

The assertion of Austrian independence in the face of determined
Nazi efforts to undermine it was the overriding concern of the *Ständestaat* throughout the four years of its existence. The most serious threat
to it was the attempted Nazi coup of 1934 in which Dollfuß was
murdered by Nazis who broke into the Chancellery. The coup itself was
quickly suppressed, but served to emphasise the extent of Austria's
vulnerability. Mussolini moved troops up to the Brenner Pass and sent a
telegram promising his support in defence of Austria.

Against the background of Hitler's reintroduction of conscription in
Germany in 1935, the British, French and Italians, meeting in Stresa,
reiterated their support for Austrian independence. However, the
following year saw a conclusive shift in the international balance of
power. The premise on which an independent Austria largely rested,
namely the unity of Italy, France and Britain, and their superior power
vis-à-vis Germany, was radically changed by Hitler's reoccupation of
the Rhineland and the tacit condoning of his action by Britain and

France. The new Austrian Chancellor Kurt Schuschnigg, acknowledging this change in the balance of power, hastened to negotiate an Austro-German agreement. Signed on 11 July 1936 the agreement was ostensibly designed to improve relations between the two countries. Hitler was to recognise Austria's full sovereignty and promise non-intervention in Austrian affairs, while Austria was to acknowledge that it was a 'German state' and conduct its foreign policy accordingly. In fact, the Germans exploited the treaty to undermine Austrian independence, infiltrating leading Nazis into positions of influence and bringing pressure to bear on Schuschnigg.

Mussolini's support for Austria was meanwhile increasingly contingent. In October 1936 Italy signed a secret agreement with Germany which outlined a common policy for the two countries in foreign affairs. The Rome–Berlin 'Axis' (as Mussolini termed it) was to prove fateful for Austria. Hitler was free to bring further pressure to bear on Schuschnigg, culminating in the humiliating summons to Berchtesgaden in February 1938 which preceded the Anschluss. Returning to Vienna, Schuschnigg had announced a plebiscite as a mechanism to endorse Austrian independence. Before it could be held, German troops crossed the border, annexing the country.

The consequences of the Nazi takeover in Austria were more immediate and far-reaching than they had been in Germany. Jews were subjected to brutality and humiliation, deprived of their rights as citizens, and in some cases of their freedom. The scenes of anti-semitic excess in Vienna far outstripped anything which had been seen in Germany. Day after day, Jews were forced to scrub the city's pavements, while crowds of onlookers gathered to jeer and taunt them. Political opponents of the regime were arrested and sent to concentration camps, often on spurious or trifling charges. The writer Raoul Auernheimer, for example, spent five months in the harsh regime of Dachau because one of his books, in which he had written a personal dedication, was found in the library of the deposed Chancellor. Schuschnigg himself was placed under house arrest and subjected to consistent humiliation, before being finally consigned to Dachau.

The atmosphere of sadistic repression caused considerable panic amongst Jews. Men and women who had lived their whole lives in

Austria were abruptly forced to prepare for an emigration which few of them had hitherto even remotely considered. Foreign embassies in Vienna were besieged by would-be emigrants, desperate to find a foreign country – any country – which would offer them refugee status.

While these scenes evoked much public sympathy in Britain, the official reaction was more sanguine. Diplomatic observers played down the Anschluss as no more than a disagreement between neighbours in their own back yard. The British government evinced little alarm, hastening to recognise the new status quo. Before the end of March, the Austrian embassy in London had been handed over to the German authorities.[111] The long-serving ambassador, Baron Georg Franckenstein, who refused to work for the Germans, left his post and effectively became an exile, albeit a privileged one. Few other Austrian exiles were so fortunate. Austrian refugees who left the country immediately after the Anchluss were still able to travel on Austrian passports. Those who left later were issued with new-style German documents, prominently stamped – if they were Jewish – with the letter 'J'. The British, like other European governments, further condoned the new regime by recognising such passports. Refugees who used them to enter Britain were of course registered as Germans, and later subsumed into the category of 'enemy aliens'. By the same token, Austrians already living in Britain automatically became citizens of the Reich. Those who protested their Austrian identity, refusing to claim their new passport, were forced to apply for stateless persons' papers. Austria had vanished from the map of Europe, its right to exist remaining unacknowledged until the Allies' Moscow Declaration of 1943. Despite shifts of policy during the war, the British government consistently refused to countenance an Austrian government in exile.

The first refugees began to arrive in London shortly after the Anschluss. Robert Neumann recalled the scenes at Victoria Station, as trains 'full to bursting' with refugees disgorged their unhappy cargo.

> If I close my eyes, I still see these refugees of 1938 in front of me. Their shoes were new, their clothes, their hats were new, their suitcases were new, only their expressions were not. I am a lawyer, stood inscribed on one such face, I am a bank manager, a businessman, a doctor. I've always led an honest life and now they have destroyed me.[112]

The consequences of the Nazi takeover for publishing in Austria were also more immediate than they had been in Germany. Gottfried Bermann Fischer, who had reluctantly decided to quit Germany in 1936 to re-establish his business in Vienna, left Austria overnight. His firm, along with other Jewish-owned businesses, including that of Zweig's publisher Herbert Reichner, was put in the hands of Nazi 'administrators' who transferred the assets to so-called 'trustees' as part of the process of 'Aryanisation'.

The consequences for exile publishing houses were no less severe. The Querido Verlag in Amsterdam found that warehouse stocks of their books in Austria were impounded; their distributor was arrested and committed to Dachau, where he died the following year.[113] The loss of the Austrian market altered at a stroke the economics of publishing, reducing print runs, wiping out economies of scale, and destroying the economic viability of German-language publishing outside Germany. That, however, was only half the story. The Nazi annexation of Austria also caused serious problems of distribution in neighbouring countries such as Czechoslovakia. The problem was even worse in countries like Hungary, Poland and Romania, where German political influence was strengthened and the book trade grew more and more anxious to placate an increasingly implacable Reich.

In 1933 it had been a courageous experiment to publish German books with no access to the German market; in 1938 it became a gesture of defiance in which normal commercial considerations played little part. There were attempts at this time by Querido Verlag and others to realise the potential for German-language books in the United States, but these largely failed: the returns from American sales were certainly never able to compensate for the virtual loss of every market in Central and Eastern Europe.

STEFAN ZWEIG: THE BURDEN OF SUCCESS

Stefan Zweig was always an unusually fluent and prolific writer, and despite the adversities of exile he remained astonishingly productive during his years in London, writing a book a year and rarely even allowing himself to pause between works. In the six years to the outbreak of war, he published *Erasmus* (1934), *Maria Stuart* (*The Queen of Scots*) (1935), *Castellio gegen Calvin* (*The Right to Heresy*) (1936), *Der begrabene Leuchter* (*The Buried Candelabrum*) (1937), the miscellany *Begegnungen mit Menschen, Büchern, Städten* (*Encounters with People, Books, Cities*) (1937), *Magellan* (1938), and *Ungeduld des Herzens* (*Beware of Pity*) (1939). Each of these books, with the exception of the last, was published first in German by Reichner, appearing later the same year in English translation with Cassells, a pattern confirming Zweig's emergence as a bestselling author in Britain in parallel to the disappearance of his German-speaking readership.

On 7 August 1936, Zweig boarded the liner *Alcantara* in Southampton, bound for Brazil, where he was to make an extensive lecture tour at the invitation of the Brazilian government. He was also to attend the congress of the International PEN in Buenos Aires. The journey came at a very opportune moment for Zweig, enabling him to defer difficult personal decisions and escape a continent which seemed bent on war. The difficult personal decisions concerned his marriage, which had now broken down irreparably. Zweig's literary work had always offered escape from the dark depression which increasingly haunted him – he even acknowledged that he wrote best in periods of depression.[114] But he now found himself between books and was therefore more than glad to escape into his other great palliative, foreign travel.

Zweig's reception in Brazil was nothing short of remarkable, more fitting for a head of state than for a writer, even one of Zweig's standing. He was received by the Brazilian President, fêted in high places, his movements widely reported in the press, his picture on virtually every front page. His progress through the country was almost triumphal, his enthusiasm for it boundless. (It is a measure of Zweig's political naivety that his enthusiasm seemed to blind him to the autocratic and repressive nature of the regime which honoured him.) The Brazil which he perceived was a country of warmth, beauty and racial harmony: he had found 'the land of the future', the country to which he would return to spend the last months of his life.

Back in London in October, Zweig was abruptly reclaimed by a less happy reality. The ensuing months were a time of frequent unhappiness, soured by the discord and bitterness of his final separation from Friderike. Early in 1937 he instructed her to sell the house in Salzburg and dispose of the remaining books and manuscripts. He bequeathed a large part of his manuscript collection to the National Library in Vienna, a further part was auctioned, and he retained for himself only a limited collection, consisting mainly of musical manuscripts. Desmond Flower, also an avid collector, with a particular interest in Voltaire, remembers telling Zweig that he would have liked to possess every manuscript Voltaire had ever written. Why everything? Zweig asked in gentle reproof. It was better to have just a few choice pieces: he himself had reduced his collection to a few outstanding items fitting into a small suitcase, which he could take anywhere with him.[115] Only after his move to Bath in 1939 did Zweig once more begin to gather books and possessions, even buying new manuscripts.

From the time he had moved into Hallam Street, Zweig had become more reclusive: 'I seldom go out and see virtually nobody,' he told Rolland in March 1936. A year later he reported to the same correspondent: 'I am living a completely secluded life and music is my only companion.'[116] His separation from Friderike was finalised in 1937. In a farewell letter to her, he admitted that exile had changed him, that he was no longer the man he had been. He had become 'afraid of people' (*menschenscheu*) and had withdrawn completely into himself, now finding pleasure only in his work.[117] He had of course first come to London in search of the creative concentration which he felt was disrupted in Austria: 'I fled here precisely in order to cling to my writing-desk, the only thing we can hold on to,' he told Joseph Roth.[118] Work had increasingly become an emotional necessity, an antidote to the long periods of depression. In April, he completed his book on Magellan, which Reichner published the following year, the last book of Zweig's to appear in Austria. By then he was already engaged in a new work – *Ungeduld des Herzens* (*Beware of Pity*) – the only novel of his to be published during his lifetime. He did not want even to leave a pause between books, 'because one's writing is the best way of not hearing the adversities of the present'.[119]

In fact, Zweig found it increasingly difficult to reconcile himself to the political and psychological pressures of exile. In 1933 he had professed 'the strongest possible disinclination to become an émigré',[120] but by 1937 that is precisely what he had become. His house in Salzburg was no longer a home to him, and despite his decision to stay in London, his flat in Hallam Street had not become one. He was forced to admit that he had 'no talent for being an emigré'.[121] In fact, he found exile an increasingly disheartening experience, resulting in a gradual erosion of personality. 'Emigration undermines and slowly kills you,' he wrote gloomily to Rolland, 'it renders you powerless.'[122] He later defined exile as 'a loss of equilibrium, a displacement in which the individual suddenly finds he no longer has the weight and standing he once enjoyed'.[123] Above all, he was aware that exile had severed his literary work from its cultural roots, that he lacked the intellectual nourishment of German language and culture.

Despite his estrangement from Austria he had remained emotionally involved in its fate, watching the death throes of the Republic with sombre fascination. 'I am very depressed,' he wrote to his compatriot Joseph Roth in 1936. 'My nose for political disaster tortures me like an inflamed nerve. I fear for Austria and the fall of Austria would also mean our spiritual destruction.'[124] A month or two later came the Austro-German agreement which, while ostensibly safeguarding the integrity of Austria, in fact fatally undermined it. Zweig now took a more jaundiced view of Britain's non-engagement in Europe: 'In England they still nurture the illusion that the next war will be "a war of other people". It's a torture to have to hold your tongue here.'[125]

As time passed, his political pessimism deepened: 'We have strained our eyes looking for the notorious silver lining on the horizon. Instead it becomes darker and darker,' he wrote to Schickele.[126] He worked harder than ever, travelled more frequently. He had once more become a nomad, he told Rolland. His view of the future was extraordinarily bleak, but – as he always insisted to those who reproached him with it – realistic. He was convinced that, because of the pusillanimity of Britain and France, European war was inevitable: 'The fascist powers have more drive than the others,' he commented succinctly.[127] He could see no independent future for Austria, especially now that Britain had manifested its indifference and pursued its traditional policy of preventing the emergence of a dominant power in Europe. At the end of

1937 he travelled to Vienna to visit his mother and – as he wrote to Rolland – 'to take perhaps my final leave of the city where I was born'.[128] Three months later came the Anschluss.

Though the annexation of Austria was an event which Zweig had long feared, its actual arrival pushed him into unknown territory, depriving him at a stroke of his nationality and his passport, transforming him into a refugee: his native land inaccessible, his property confiscated, his books proscribed. He remembered the weeks following the Anschluss as the most terrible of his life. 'Perhaps the most philosophical response was Egon Friedell's,' he told Felix Braun, referring to the writer who, shortly after the Nazis' arrival in Vienna, had thrown himself out of a window to his death. 'Never have I better understood the phrase "taedium vitae". Happy the dead! There will be no new dawn for us. This night will be infinitely long and only the flames of war will perhaps illuminate it in some devilish way.'[129] His mother remained in Vienna and the violent outburst of anti-semitism there gave him great cause for concern, the more so because it was now impossible for him even to visit her. When she died in September, not a single member of the family was there; Zweig admitted that her death gave him almost a sense of relief.

It is clear that the loss of his nationality and his consequent reduction to the status of refugee was a severe blow to his self-esteem, undermining his confidence and even seeming to alienate him from his own identity. He felt overwhelmed by the day-to-day problems of exile, many of which he was forced to confront for the first time: 'The perpetual starting again, one's head bespattered with a thousand filthy formalities, passports, nationality, family problems, living problems. I sometimes get very tired.'[130] Thus the loss of his passport was a more traumatic experience than he could have imagined. He and Lotte were obliged to join the long queues outside the Home Office in order to apply for a stateless person's certificate of identity, a document which seemed to symbolise the provisional and precarious nature of their situation: he was all too aware that it could be withdrawn at any time and for any reason. The couple were finally granted identity papers in August.

The annexation of Austria had not only robbed Zweig of his

homeland but of the remnants of his German-speaking readership. He wrote to Schickele:

> Forgive the pessimism audible in these lines but the Austrian business has greatly affected me. Not only is my mother still there and many friends, not only will all my work be pulped once again . . . it also means the loss of our only remaining sphere of influence, the drop into the void.[131]

He was only too aware that the loss of the Austrian market rendered German-language publishing virtually uneconomic. In letters to one of his oldest friends, Victor Fleischer, he acknowledged his deep pessimism and fears for the future:

> It's practically all up with German books, because if the Sudetenland goes the same way, publishing just isn't viable. The one million Swiss aren't a big enough market and the German emigrants are overstretched and impoverished.

With a somewhat histrionic flourish, he signed the letter: 'Stefan, ex-Austriacus'.[132] He was obliged to consider whether he should adapt the style and content of his work to tastes in his adopted country, but felt incapable of doing so.[133]

He was dismayed by the loss of his German reading public. Though he continued work on the novel *Ungeduld des Herzens* he could not throw off the feeling that he no longer had an audience, that he was 'writing German into thin air'.[134] He was depressed at the prospect of being read only through the mediation of the translator and dismayed by the loss of a readership with whom he shared a common language and cultural heritage. 'What is life worth now?' he asked the Hungarian writer Ferenc Körmendi. 'We are condemned to write in the German language – and therefore finished in a world which effectively belongs to that other Germany.'[135]

Beware of Pity is a very Austrian book. Set, like many of his earlier *Novellen*, in the twilight of the Austro-Hungarian Empire, it is an elegy for the society which had borne and nurtured him. He felt that it would have little interest or meaning for the English reader, but in fact it was to be one of his greatest successes in the English-speaking world. The British edition appeared in May, and sold so quickly that Cassells reprinted it four times before the end of the month. 'Strangely, my novel is a great success here,' he told Felix Braun. 'It has been a best-seller for six weeks, nobody is more astonished than I am.'[136] It was the last book of his to appear in Britain in his lifetime.

The Anschluss forced Zweig to seek a new German publisher. Herbert Reichner had initially stayed in Vienna, paralysed by indecision, but had finally fled to Zurich, leaving his business in the hands of an 'Aryan' administrator. He subsequently emigrated to the United States, but there is no record that he and Zweig ever met again. Zweig had been dissatisfied with their business relationship for some time, but nonetheless found it inconceivable that his books should not be published in the language in which he had written them. He hastened to reach an agreement with Gottfried Bermann Fischer, who had succeeded in re-establishing his publishing-house in Stockholm and whom Zweig summoned to London for negotiations.

As the Nazis tightened their hold on Austria, institutionalising anti-semitic persecution and provoking a new stream of refugees, Zweig found himself inundated with requests for help. Friends, acquaintances, and others he hardly knew, wrote asking for money or favours, such as introductions to publishers or intercession with the visa authorities. He had never felt so keenly the burden imposed by his own fame. He attempted to help where he could, with advice or money (many witnesses have confirmed his personal generosity to fellow-exiles) but he often felt helpless, complaining that people completely overestimated his influence.

For more than three months, these concerns monopolised his time and attention. 'I hardly have any work of my own any more, so totally am I preoccupied with the cares of my compatriots,' he wrote to his old friend Felix Braun.[137] He confided to Rolland that he was so over-whelmed by these pressures that he was considering leaving London to escape them. Whereas he had once written approvingly of English isolation from the affairs of the Continent, he now complained that the English were indifferent to the Austrian problem: 'They are concerned with sport and society news, and the ordinary people just don't realise the danger.' He confessed that he felt like leaving England, but did not know where to go, 'and so I stay with a feeling of ingratitude, because I feel more isolated here than anywhere else in the world. . .'[138]

1 Stefan Zweig in Alexandra Palace
  television studio, London 1937

2 Stefan Zweig in the garden of his
  house in Bath, 1940

3, 4 Alfred Kerr in 1941 and *above* with
     his daughter Judith and his wife Julia
     c. 1941

5 Max Herrmann-Neiße,
   drawing by Martin
   Bloch, 1936

6 Max Herrmann-Neiße
   in Hyde Park, 1935

7 Karl Otten, drawing by
   Egon Schiele, 1914

8 Karl Otten in the garden
   of 58 Hampstead Way,
   Golders Green, 1939

9   Robert Neumann in 1936

10 Robert Neumann in the garden
    of the 'Plague House',
    Cranbrook, Kent, after 1948

Like all his fellow-exiles, Zweig felt increasingly at the mercy of international events. During the summer of 1938, there was growing international tension, as Germany, emboldened by the Anschluss, precipitated the Sudeten crisis. If Zweig was previously a spectator in British society, he now became a participant, a shift of perspective which can be inferred from his own account in *The World of Yesterday*. His memories of London, hitherto bloodless and sketchy, suddenly became vivid and concrete. He became increasingly alarmed as the prospects for peace receded. While other exiles longed for a war which they felt was the only way of removing Hitler, Zweig prayed fervently for peace. Franz Werfel, who met him in London at this time, acknowledged his genuine pacifism, calling him 'a man without anger' and remembering that, when others in his company called for war, Zweig would go pale and turn away.[139]

He regarded the Munich agreement with very mixed feelings. In his memoirs, he recalls the crowds who cheered Chamberlain on his return, sharing their relief that war had been averted, but he was also aware of the new wave of refugees displaced by the agreement. On a card to an old friend, Guido Fuchs, by then also in exile in London, he wrote:

My dear fellow, one has almost already forgotten that Austria ever existed, so quickly and turbulently does time pass. One wave overtakes the other. We are no longer really alive, but consigned to the coffin of history.[140]

In December 1938, having completed the necessary five years' residence, Zweig took the considerable step of applying for British naturalisation, naming as his sponsors Archibald G. Russell, whose monograph on William Blake he had translated over thirty years ago, Newman Flower, Professor William Rose and Viscount Carlow, to whom he had recently been introduced by the author Louis Golding.

Zweig's attitude to naturalisation was, and would remain, highly ambivalent. Only six months earlier, he had denied even contemplating such a move:

I am not even thinking of becoming an English citizen. And I find all the formalities revolting. . . I don't like living in London. I feel lost here. I don't want to become an Englishman as long as I can avoid it. I dream of perhaps going to South America.[141]

In the meantime, the question of nationality had become more pressing. His Austrian passport had expired, leaving him stateless, with all the difficulties of residence and travel which that implied. Paradoxically, the prospect of acquiring British nationality only heightened his awareness of his Austro-German heritage. He was forced once more to acknowledge that his cultural identity was inextricably involved with the language in which he thought and wrote: it was at this time that he first began to plan *The World of Yesterday*, the memoirs which would celebrate the now vanished world in which he had come to maturity. In his memoirs, Zweig significantly fails to mention that he even applied for naturalisation, still less that he actually acquired it. He failed to reconcile himself to his new nationality, privately admitting the ambivalence of his position as 'a German writer without books, an Englishman who is not really English'[142] – and, he might have added, who would never be able to write in the language.

Shortly after applying for naturalisation, Zweig left Britain for a lecture tour of the USA, which he agreed to for financial reasons. He was plunged into a whirlwind schedule which entailed giving some twenty-five lectures across the entire country.[143] In New York, he saw a number of fellow-exiles, including his brother Alfred, Hermann Broch and Raoul Auernheimer, who had just been released from a concentration camp. He was also able to attend a performance of his *Jeremias* by the Theatre Guild on 18 February. He sailed back to Europe on 3 March: 'Probably the most stupid thing I can do,' he commented bitterly.[144] He arrived back in London as Hitler's armies annexed what remained of Czechoslovakia. He was increasingly certain of the inevitability of European war: 'Hitler is now drunk with success and wants a war,' he commented wearily to Felix Braun.[145]

Whatever his premonition of impending disaster, he had returned to London determined to start work on the book he had dreamed of since his youth: a study of Balzac which would record his lifelong admiration. International developments once more frustrated his plans. The occupation of Bohemia and Moravia had released a new flood of refugees, many of whom were fleeing for the second time. In the next couple of months they began to pour into London: every day, Zweig's post brought new appeals for help. Zweig was distressed by the suffering he saw, but his dominant feeling was one of self-pity. With the egotism of the artist, he resented the growing demands on his time and the distraction from his work which they entailed.

> I have a great desire . . . to retreat to the country for some time. It is impossible to cope any more with the onslaught of people from Austria, Germany, Czechoslovakia and Hungary. I no longer have time to see my actual friends . . . and feel utterly exhausted by constant conversations about permits, affidavits, Home Office, guarantees – all those things which now control life instead of the spiritual things.[146]

He went on to mention that he was doing preliminary work for his Balzac study: 'Anything which distracts you from the present helps to give you some inner stability.'

ROBERT NEUMANN: AN EXPERT IN SURVIVAL

The arms manufacturer and financier Sir Basil Zaharoff died on 27 November 1936. For Robert Neumann it proved a very timely death, curtailing the legal proceedings against him and creating renewed interest in his biography of 'the armaments king'. Early in 1937, Neumann applied for a permanent residence permit in Britain. Aware of the criteria guiding British immigration policy, he went to some lengths to demonstrate that he was an author of international standing, stressing that his earnings were not confined to Britain and that he was actually spending money there which he had earned elsewhere.[147] His application marked a further step towards a new cultural identity: two years later he would apply for British naturalisation.

Up to 1936 he had still been able to maintain a precarious foothold in the German-speaking market. Although his books were banned in Germany, his publisher Engelhorn still had large stocks of previous titles and continued to sell a handful of copies abroad. However, attempts to pay Neumann his outstanding royalties in 1936 were blocked by the currency-control authorities inside Germany. Publication of his work in Austria was also hindered by growing censorship. In 1934 his Viennese publisher Zsolnay, mindful of the growing political dangers, had established a small company (The Library of Contemporary Books) in Zurich to publish some of his more 'leftish' authors. Both *Zaharoff* and the short novel *Die blinden Passagiere* ('The Stowaways') appeared under this imprint. However, the Nazi threat of boycott effectively intimidated much of the book trade in Switzerland, fatally undermining Zsolnay's Swiss venture and forcing it into bankruptcy, leaving Neumann stranded without a German-language publisher.

In the remaining three years before the outbreak of war, Neumann wrote two further novels, whose publishing history exemplifies the growing frustrations and difficulties facing the exiled writer. His next novel, *Eine Frau hat geschrien* (*A Woman Screamed*), though also written in German, was actually first published in English translation. Like its predecessor, *The Queen's Doctor*, it was an historical novel, with which Neumann hoped to consolidate his literary reputation in Britain and solve his continuing financial problems. The conflict between the desire for artistic recognition and the need for material reward was, as Neumann cheerfully admitted, always present in his calculations. The book is set against the background of the Hungarian struggle for independence in 1848, under the leadership of Lajos Kossuth, though Kossuth himself plays only a minor role. The central figure is a fictional character, Rosza Sandor, an idealist morally committed to the struggle against oppression and injustice. Although the rebellion fails, betrayed by the compromise and collusion of its leaders, Sandor remains true to his ideal of freedom.

Neumann completed the novel under the working title *Rosza Sandor. Räuberhauptmann* ('Rosza Sandor. Robber Chieftain') by the end of 1936. Although he had only a German manuscript, he immediately offered the book to Victor Gollancz, who almost as immediately rejected it: 'I've had a very good report on it, but I find these translations more and more difficult to handle.'[148] Gollancz's comment was something of a polite evasion — it was undoubtedly Neumann himself whom he found difficult to handle. Moreover, he was now deeply involved in the burgeoning Left Book Club, which claimed more and more of his time and attention. Six weeks later the book was accepted by Cassells, whom Neumann approached through his agent Curtis Brown. It was Cassells who suggested the book's final title *A Woman Screamed*: 'a stroke of genius', Neumann commented sarcastically.

Still concerned to have the novel published in German, Neumann approached Stefan Zweig's Austrian publisher Herbert Reichner, whose initial response was positive, if cautious. Reichner, always sensitive to the political climate, called it 'an unusually interesting book', but added that 'we, as publishers in Vienna, would find it impossible to publish a book which evinced a negative attitude to the old Austria'.[149] Reichner was also aware of the economic realities of a dwindling market. Having read the complete manuscript, he called the book 'quite splendid', but nonetheless felt unable to publish it, 'in view of the restricted sales area and the considerable costs of production for a book of such length'.[150] The political difficulties in Austria forced Neumann to turn once more to Switzerland. He was finally able to secure publication through a small, and only recently-established publisher in Zurich, Humanitas Verlag, the edition appearing some four months after the English translation.

The sobering experience of these few months served to impress on Neumann the full extent of his dependence on the English-speaking market. Even worse was the feeling that he, the acknowledged German stylist, the gifted parodist, the 'magician of words', was now forced to depend on the mediation of the translator. At his own request, the task of translating *A Woman Screamed* was assigned once more to the Muirs, but he was unhappy with their first draft, writing 'some frank words' to Edwin Muir which far transcend the normal conventions of correspondence between author and translator:

> You are aware of the extremely difficult situation in which we exiles find ourselves. We have lost our German readership – and our material and spiritual existence now depends on finding an English one to replace it. Even in normal circumstances, the task of the translator is not one which finds any real equivalent in the usually very modest fee. In todays's special circumstances translation becomes not merely a literary task but also a moral one, entailing a sense of responsibility and solidarity.[151]

The vulnerability of the exiled author and his excessive expectations of the translator have rarely been more intensely stated.

The novel elicited the praise of Neumann's fellow-exiles, notably Stefan Zweig, who called it 'a model of how to hold a balance between the tension, the excitement which must carry the reader along, and the higher sense of tragedy inherent in the fate of a deeply honourable man fighting for the pure principle of justice'.[152]

Publication in Britain was followed by an American edition, but the novel was not widely reviewed. Neumann, with characteristic exaggeration, called it 'a resounding failure',[153] but this is a commercial, not a literary, judgement. Cassells had paid him an advance of £300 on the novel, which, though a respectable sum at a time when the company's advance on a first novel was never more than £150, was much less than Neumann had received for either of his previous books in Britain. Sales of the novel failed to cover even this modest advance and Neumann did not publish with Cassells again.

Up to this time Neumann probably still considered himself a German writer, who was also published in English, an emphasis which shifted abruptly under the impact of political events in 1938. The experience of exile had already forced him to reappraise his literary identity. Neumann's family belonged to the highly-assimilated Jewish middle class in Vienna and he had consequently always felt more Viennese than Jewish, but the cultural pressures of exile and, above all, the growth of anti-semitism, had heightened his awareness of his Jewish heritage. For the first time in his literary career, he now turned to the theme of Jewish identity.

In August 1937 Neumann sent the outline of an ambitious new novel to his friend and fellow-novelist Hermann Broch; by the end of the year he was working intensively on the book which would become one of his most accomplished and successful novels: *An den Wassern von Babylon* (*By the Waters of Babylon*). The novel consists of ten episodes recounting the individual stories of ten Jewish exiles, whose lives converge when they meet as passengers on a bus seeking to enter Palestine. Exile is portrayed as the essence of the Jewish experience, the individual characters being a cross-section of the Jewish diaspora: the refugee from the pogroms of Eastern Europe, the Viennese financier, the New York boxer, the well-born Englishman and the exiled German writer Marcus. The Marcus chapter itself is a paradigm of German literary exile, including a wealth of autobiographical details.

In March 1938 Neumann travelled to Switzerland to offer the novel, then only half-written, to his Swiss publisher, Humanitas Verlag, a tiny concern which the owner, Simon Menzel, ran from two rooms in his private flat. Visiting Menzel, Neumann read him parts of the manuscript, only to find the book rejected, apparently because Menzel (himself a Jew) felt that the specifically Jewish theme was currently too problematical for a German-language publisher to handle. Neumann had intended to travel on to Vienna to vote in the plebiscite called by the Schuschnigg government on Austrian independence, but his plans – and Schuschnigg's – were abruptly pre-empted by the Anschluss. The event finally cut Neumann off from his native country.

Now an exile in earnest, Neumann returned to Basel to meet Rolly Becker, the couple then travelling on to France. Their destination was Sanary-sur-Mer, a small fishing-village near Toulon which had become a centre for German literary émigrés. Lion Feuchtwanger had settled there in 1933, shortly followed by the literary critic Ludwig Marcuse. Their presence attracted a stream of prominent visitors, such as Bertolt Brecht, Ernst Toller, Hermann Kesten and Friedrich Wolf, briefly transforming Sanary into what Marcuse called 'the capital of German literature'.[154]

The interlude in Sanary was only a temporary escape. Once back in London, Neumann was forced to confront the bitter realities of exile. With the incorporation of Austria into the Third Reich, he had become stateless, ceasing to be an émigré and becoming a refugee. While his own situation was worrying, it was almost comfortable compared to the fate of Jews and other opponents of the new order in Austria. Neumann's own family faced a desperate situation. His mother, then aged seventy-five, was evicted from the house she had lived in for many years under new laws restricting Jewish residence. His sister suffered a similar fate. In 1939 Neumann was able to bring them both to Britain, where his mother finally died during the war.

The personal consequences of the Austrian tragedy were soon swamped by its wider implications. From the autumn of 1938 Neumann became deeply involved in the campaign run by the English PEN Club to rescue Austrian and Czech writers from the threat of arrest and persecution. Neumann had joined the English PEN shortly after settling in London, enjoying friendly relations with several of its leading figures, notably Storm Jameson, Henrietta Leslie and H. G. Wells –

although Wells would turn his back on Neumann when the latter was interned in 1940, claiming he knew too little about him to make a statement on his behalf.

Early in 1938 Storm Jameson had become President of the English PEN Centre, increasing PEN's involvement in political affairs. She had begun her presidency by writing a letter to the *Manchester Guardian* on the duty of the writer to denounce racial intolerance: 'a most worthy letter' she commented with retrospective self-irony.[155]

In the wake of the Anschluss and the anti-semitic excesses it unleashed, a new stream of refugees tried to leave Austria. Partly at Neumann's instigation, English PEN mounted a relief campaign, establishing an Austrian Writers Fund, primarily intended to offer financial support to writers and journalists once they had been able to reach Britain. The level of assistance was small, amounting to about £3 a week for some six to eight weeks.[156]

The cries for help from Austria were shortly echoed by those from Czechoslovakia, as the Sudeten crisis reached its climax. On 29 September, the British, French and German governments signed the Munich Agreement, acceding to Hitler's claim to the Sudetenland. German occupation of the Sudeten areas, in accordance with the terms of the treaty, left Czechoslovakia within frontiers which were no longer secure, exposing it to the threat of invasion. In the ensuing weeks the Czech government made various moves intended to ease its relations with Nazi Germany. On 20 October it banned the Czech Communist Party, ordering police to occupy the party's headquarters in Prague, and summarily closed four Communist newspapers – two Czech and two German-language. Such measures only increased the sense of panic among German and Austrian émigrés in Prague, setting in train a mass exodus of artists and intellectuals, many of whom were being forced into exile for the second time.

The PEN Club launched an immediate appeal on behalf of Czech writers, signed by Storm Jameson and PEN Secretary Hermon Ould, as well as past PEN Presidents Henry W. Nevinson, H. G. Wells and J. B. Priestley.[157] Storm Jameson was firmly convinced that 'PEN should do anything it can, bring all possible pressure to bear through any influential persons'.[158] By the end of the year she and Hermon Ould were engaged in an energetic campaign to rescue writers and journalists whose lives were threatened by the Nazis. They both worked tirelessly, writing letters, seeking sponsors, lobbying persons of influence and raising money: 'From one source or another, we raised almost three thousand pounds, not a great sum.'[159] PEN could offer only modest financial assistance, consisting of a small weekly living allowance for the first three months, but for many it offered a lifeline.

Neumann became one of the key figures in this campaign. In January 1939, challenging the disappearance of Austria from the political map, he established an Austrian Exile PEN Group, with Franz Werfel (who had already fled from Vienna) as Honorary President and himself as Secretary. What he may initially have seen as a symbolic step rapidly became a vehicle for practical assistance. Neumann's correspondence for 1938–39 contains numerous letters from writers and journalists, pleading for help and advice. He set out to help as many as possible, issuing membership of the Austrian PEN to even the most occasional writer, later recalling that some who lacked passports were able to use their membership cards as identity documents.

By far the most essential task was to secure entry visas from the Home Office. In the face of this new wave of refugees, the British government had reintroduced a visa requirement, but had also eased immigration restrictions, enabling many refugees to reach London, some with visas permitting them to stay in Britain, some only with transit visas to other countries like the USA. Working from PEN's cramped and dingy office in New Oxford Street, Neumann performed the task of procuring visas with considerable energy and great success; by June 1939 he was able to boast of 'a properly functioning visa office in the PEN'.[160] It was not his only achievement. Under the auspices of PEN, he was able to offer professional advice, putting authors and translators in contact with publishers, and journalists with newspapers, the whole process being eventually formalised into what he described as 'a sort of labour exchange for the refugees'.[161]

Among writers for whom he was able to secure visas were Hermann Broch, Felix Braun and the polyglot Elias Canetti. Although Broch stayed only briefly in Britain before moving on to the USA, both Braun and Canetti were to remain in London for many years. PEN's efforts to bring Robert Musil, then living in great poverty in Switzerland, to London, had to be abandoned on the outbreak of war: Musil remained in Switzerland until his death in 1942.

Neumann became so deeply involved in this work that for many months he did little else. Storm Jameson paid generous tribute to his commitment and self-sacrifice at a time when he himself was stateless and his own right of residence in Britain was far from certain.

> Day after day he sat in what was then the very small shabby office [of the London PEN] and tried to solve or mitigate the (largely insoluble) problems of the exiles, himself an exile, with all the anxieties that was beginning to imply for him. I can still hear him talking in a soft steady voice to a man broken down into tears, and sending him away encouraged and comforted. This work of his should not be forgotten.[162]

The friendship between Jameson and Neumann was based on a mutual respect which was no less sincere for the tacit reservations which existed on both sides. She sensed that Neumann's surface charm concealed a sharp and sometimes malicious observation:

> I knew the amiable side of a complex character. I suspected that in private he used his witty tongue, sharpened in the literary café society of Vienna, on his English friends, whom he found provincial, but I believed him to be kind.[163]

Her suspicions were not unfounded. Neumann later described her, with ironical affection, as 'overburdened with work, doubting herself, basically fearing people, short of money, not exactly fond of strangers, foreigners, Jews – she threw herself in self-chastisement into this hated activity, with great courage, energy and immense success'.[164]

Despite the anxieties of his personal situation in 1938, Neumann continued to work on *By the Waters of Babylon*, which he completed by the autumn. Faced with the dwindling opportunities for German-language publishing, he submitted the manuscript, under the working title *Aber deine Kinder werden nicht untergehen* ('But Your Children Shall Not Perish'), for the literary prize inaugurated by the American Guild for German Cultural Freedom. Like Karl Otten, he quickly became impatient at the slow deliberations of the adjudicating panel, writing in January 1939: 'I'm afraid I can't wait very much longer on the result of the competition. My financial situation is strained and I can't afford withholding my book

from the open market indefinitely.'[165] Just how strained his financial
situation was is made clear in a letter to Richard A. Bermann:

> I simply can't wait any longer. I worked on the book for two years, now
> it's been in the competition for a further eight months. At the moment I
> have seven people to support and another couple to contribute to – in
> short, I have to turn the book into money, now, without waiting even
> another week.[166]

When the jury finally pronounced judgement, *By the Waters of
Babylon* did not receive the prize, but was especially recommended for
publication. By then, Neumann had already sold the British rights to
Dent, who published it that autumn in a translation by Anthony Dent.
Neumann was still undecided as to a German edition, but such indecision was soon resolved by the outbreak of war. The book was not
published in Germany until 1954.

In contrast to Neumann's previous work, *By the Waters of Babylon*
was widely acclaimed in Britain and the USA. H. G. Wells pronounced
it 'well done, in places brilliantly done', calling it 'a vivid contribution to
the perennial problem of the Jewish mentality'.[167] In all, the novel was
reviewed in over twenty British papers and periodicals, from *Reynolds
News* to the *Sunday Times*, and from *The Times Literary Supplement* to
the *New Statesman*. The critics were almost unanimous in their praise,
stressing the timeliness of the theme. In November, the book was
named the *Evening Standard* Book of the Month. Neumann had finally
consolidated his literary reputation in Britain at the very moment when
any prospect of publication in German had virtually disappeared. He
had little time to savour his success.

PEACE IN OUR TIME

Hitler's seizure of the rump of Czechoslovakia in March 1939 finally
shattered the illusions of even the most fervent advocates of appeasement. In the same month, Britain made a solemn promise to support
Poland in the event of a German invasion. This declaration marked a
pronounced shift in government policy – away from appeasement and
towards reluctant preparations for war.

Plans were laid for large-scale evacuation from major cities in the event of war. In May, the government introduced limited conscription, a move unprecedented in Britain in peace-time. Plans for the establishment of the Ministry of Information, which for some time had existed as a 'shadow ministry', began to take definite shape. Great public institutions also made preparations for war. The British Museum began to remove its collections from London. The National Gallery did likewise, consigning its pictures to a disused quarry in North Wales, the last consignment leaving London on the Saturday before war broke out.

The BBC laid plans to disperse its various departments, locating its main centre at Evesham. Changes in government policy also impinged on foreign broadcasting. The German and Italian news services, which had been inaugurated at the time of the Munich crisis, were maintained and, from March 1939, expanded. From mid-March the political content of broadcasts to Germany was increased, and 'contributors were able to permit themselves a far greater measure of plain speaking'.[168] Between spring and summer 1939, the BBC conducted intensive research into German propaganda techniques in press and radio.

Changes in government policy were matched by a corresponding shift in public mood. It is estimated that from the end of June to the first week of September 1939 some three and a half million people moved from areas thought vulnerable to enemy bombing to those considered safe. Among the signs of impending war were the greatly increased numbers of refugees fleeing countries annexed by the German Reich. Estimates of the number of German-speaking refugees who arrived in Britain vary. However, at the beginning of 1938, there were probably no more than 5,500 living in Britain; by September 1939, this number had swollen to some 60,000.[169]

The guiding precept of British immigration policy up to 1938 had been that Britain was a country of temporary refuge, not of permanent settlement. Faced with the vast increase in the number of refugees, the British government sought to control the flow. In July 1938 it re-introduced the visa requirement for Germans and Austrians wishing to enter Britain. This measure was accompanied by more stringent entry regulations, requiring those wishing to enter Britain to show either sufficient financial resources or definite guarantees of maintenance.[170]

In November, the horrors of the 'Kristallnacht' pogrom triggered a further flood of Jewish emigration from Germany and Austria. The British government responded to pressure from various groups representing refugees by relaxing the entry regulations – for instance, by granting work permits for domestic servants or for transmigrants, and most notably by waiving the visa requirement for children up to the age of 17.[171] In the following months some 10,000 Jewish children left Greater Germany on special trains: the so-called 'Kindertransporte'. As the pace of emigration from Germany and Austria accelerated, Hitler's seizure of Czechoslovakia set off a new wave of refugees, some of whom were fleeing for the second or third time. Under considerable public pressure, the government agreed to admit some 6,000 Czech refugees up to September 1939, also providing funds (originally part of a gift to the Czech government in compensation for the Munich Agreement) for the relief of refugees, setting up the Czech Refugee Trust Fund to administer them.

The greatest concentration of refugees was in London, remaining there despite the best efforts of the authorities to disperse them. Their growing numbers were matched by a proliferation of organisations working on their behalf. Bloomsbury House (in Bloomsbury Street) became the location of the main agencies – the Jewish Refugees Committee, the Church of England Committee for non-aryan Christians and the Quakers' Germany Emergency Committee. There were however a host of other organisations which dealt with refugees: a list compiled by the German Emergency Committee in 1939 enumerates nearly seventy such agencies. While the new arrivals inevitably looked to those already living there, the situation of the latter had also deteriorated. The new influx of refugees had had a levelling effect. Personal biographies began to converge, their individual contours progressively reduced to the common denominators of exile. This levelling process would reach its climax with the mass internment of 'enemy aliens' in 1940.

In his autobiography *The World of Yesterday* Stefan Zweig records the changing public mood in that last pre-war summer: 'A bitter awakening had swept over England. . . Everywhere one could sense the preparations for the coming war.' The signs of the times were almost impossible to overlook. The normally reserved English suddenly began to speak to total strangers. More belligerent tones were heard in Parliament. Barrage balloons hovered once more in the sky, trenches were being dug again in city parks and squares.

Exile had begun to take a heavy toll amongst Zweig's fellow-writers. In May, the dramatist Ernst Toller, whom he had met only a few weeks before in New York, committed suicide. Shortly after, Zweig's much-loved friend Joseph Roth, on whom he had lavished help and money, finally drank himself to death. Zweig was deeply affected: 'I loved him like a brother,' he told Rolland.[172] He was persuaded to give a valediction for Roth at a memorial service arranged by Wickham Steed at Conway Hall.[173]

It was only the obligation of friendship which persuaded him to break silence: in general he shunned public appearances more than ever, feeling a growing need for seclusion and detachment. He did his best to ignore radio and newspapers: all news was now bad news. He and Lotte left London on several weekends. In fact, Zweig found the city increasingly intolerable and in the course of the summer finally turned his back on it altogether.

Zweig's reasons for escaping from London do him little credit. He had begun to find his fame increasingly burdensome. As the tide of refugees reaching London began to swell, and the distractions from his work increased, so his efforts to help his less fortunate compatriots began to decline; even a desperate appeal for help from an old friend like Albert Ehrenstein fell on deaf ears. The note of self-pity in his letters grew stronger. Indeed, in a curious reversal of perspective, he began to see himself as the victim of the desperate refugees who begged his aid. Writing to Romain Rolland, he complained:

> I haven't been able to work for months. I'm the victim of an avalanche of refugees. Since November, the flood has swelled to an alarming degree and the whole tide is now surging towards London. Yes, one gives advice and money, but one's brain and heart can no longer bear these painful stories. And how to help these writers who even in their country were only small fry?[174]

In May and June he and Lotte spent several weekends in Bath and in July Zweig finally decided to buy a small house there. Situated on Lyncombe Hill on the southern slopes of the city, 'Rosemount' had a panoramic view of Bath which reminded him of his former home on the

Kapuzinerberg. If he had left London 'in order to escape this century and to regain my composure', he had chosen Bath because its architecture and literary associations 'reflected more than any other in England a past, more peaceful century, the eighteenth'.[175] Zweig was equally attracted by the surrounding countryside. During the unusually warm summer of 1939 he began to take long country walks, resuming a habit he had once cultivated in Salzburg, where he had walked regularly in the surrounding mountains of the Salzkammergut.

The purchase of the house in Bath was Zweig's first real attempt to make a home for himself since leaving Austria. Throughout his six years of exile in London, Zweig had travelled light, his life a provisional arrangement on which he could turn his back at any moment. Even the flat in Hallam Street had been little more than a base for his extensive travel. Bath represented the peace and serenity he craved:

> I'm very happy with Bath. I feel extraordinarily well here . . . and hope you keep your promise to come by. You will find the most remarkable and most English city in England.[176]

He went on to tell Frischauer, who had moved out of London to Buckinghamshire earlier that year, that he intended 'to become your pupil in country life and to emigrate from the emigration.' 'Rosemount' was therefore intended as a place of refuge, where he could work undisturbed on the grand design of his Balzac and where he and Lotte could build their life together. In fact, they would live there for less than a year.

With his inherently nervous disposition, Max Herrmann-Neiße was especially apprehensive of the impending conflict. 'For the rest, I live in some seclusion here and rather in fear of the approaching war,' he wrote to Hermann Hesse.[177] Writing shortly after to his friend Fritz Grieger, he referred to 'the awful storm clouds' and 'the eve-of-war atmosphere' which banished all other thoughts or plans:

> One loses the courage or inclination to make holiday plans or to venture on a journey. Even so, Zurich seems particularly attractive this year – the Swiss exhibition there is supposed to be very good. In the absence of the real thing, I tried at least to summon up a vision of it in a poem.[178]

He enclosed the short poem 'Zürcher Verzauberung' ('Zurich Enchantment'), the last such poem he was able to send to his friend.

Though he continued to return to Zurich in his imagination, he would never see the city again.

Herrmann-Neiße continued to pray that war could be averted, long after it had actually become inevitable. His 'Gebet um Frieden' ('Prayer for Peace'), written on 24 August, affirms:

> Auf alles will ich gern verzichten
> wird unserer Welt der Mord erspart.
>
> *I will gladly renounce everything / if our world is spared this slaughter.*[179]

In the following days, even after the British ultimatum to Germany, he continued to hope for a miracle:

> Laß uns von deinen Engeln retten,
> mach durch ein Wunder alles gut.[180]
>
> *Let your angels come to our rescue / Perform a miracle to make everything good*

When the miracle did not happen, he fell momentarily silent, failing to find consolation even in poetry.

Alfred Kerr longed for war sooner rather than later. Convinced of the necessity to resist Hitler, he deplored Britain's lack of military preparation, 'The beginning of 1939 – and still no conscription. A German almost despairs when he hears what some of the English are saying.'[181]

So great was his frustration at the policy of appeasement, that he had again considered emigration to the United States, making a renewed appeal to Albert Einstein at the end of 1938:

> Is there no possibility for me and mine to come over? The people in England are (outside politics) law-abiding, helpful, conscientious, in a word: splendid; but slow. In the struggle against the resurgent Stone Age they will arrive too late. . . I am crying out for activity, but in tame England I have little chance. I think America, with its get-up-and-go attitude, offers much better possibilities.[182]

Kerr's fierce defiance of Nazism also influenced his reaction to two illustrious literary compatriots in 1939. On meeting the Communist novelist Ludwig Renn, who was passing through London on the way to America, he noted in *Ich kam nach England*: 'Encounter with a man, such as we shall need in the coming struggle.' In June he attended a memorial service for Ernst Toller. In Weimar Germany he had been a great admirer of Toller's early works, rating him more highly as a dramatist than Bertolt Brecht. In the face of his suicide, he was indulgent but resolute: 'Peace be with Ernst Toller, his action is almost beyond discussion. But we who remain . . . we are not there to give Hitler reason to rejoice by eliminating ourselves.'

Despite the 'gathering storm-clouds', Kerr once more travelled to Nice to bid farewell to his sister, who was about to leave for Palestine, going in the almost certain knowledge that he would never see her again. 'Once more I have come to draw breath in the South of France. It is May 1939. One can feel the mood of a humanity living in the interim.' The gathering crisis at the beginning of the summer forced him to return to London: he had now discarded all thoughts of leaving for America.

As war approached, and more and more anti-Nazi refugees began to look towards America, Karl Otten turned even more emphatically towards his adopted country. Increasingly certain that the war he had prophesied in *Die Reise nach Deutschland* was imminent, he began to take what precautions he could against it. On 8 April he and Ellen Kroner were married at Hendon Registry Office. A highly independent man, who had been scarred by the misfortunes of his first marriage, Otten had always hesitated to marry again. Now it seemed a prudent step to forestall the possibility of enforced separation. Shortly before their marriage, the couple had moved into a three-bedroomed house at 58 Hampstead Way, Golders Green. The house was unfurnished, but Ellen succeeded in getting furniture she had inherited from her parents shipped from Berlin, where it had been in storage for almost a decade. Two or three of the pieces survived in her apartment until her death.

During 1938 Otten had tried strenuously to persuade his first wife Mizi to leave Vienna, where she was still living with their son, Julian, then aged nineteen. Otten had maintained contact with her in the years after their divorce, though making little attempt to get to know his son, who seems to have resented his father's absence. Born and raised in Vienna, Mizi Otten was, like most Viennese Jews, greatly attached to her native city and highly reluctant to leave it: only the deteriorating situation finally convinced her of the force of Otten's arguments. Late in 1938, she and Julian arrived in London, spending several weeks with the Ottens in their new home before finally leaving for the USA. Mizi ultimately settled in New York, where she continued her career as a textile designer and enameller.

Mizi and Julian were not the Ottens' only long-term guests during these months. As many Jews became increasingly desperate to escape from Germany, the number of countries willing to accept them declined. Switzerland, a traditional land of asylum, had closed its borders to refugees, officially declaring that 'the boat was full'. France too was reluctant to admit more refugees. While the British government had relaxed some entry regulations, admission for adults of working age was in practice available only to those prepared to enter domestic service. Even then, 'domestic' permits were granted only against guaranteed offers of employment and required much paper-work. The Ottens nonetheless applied successfully for a permit on behalf of a cousin of Ellen's, who stayed with them for several months before leaving for the USA. Likewise, a sister of Ellen's closest friend in Berlin also arrived on a 'domestic permit', leaving Germany shortly before war broke out and staying with the Ottens until she was able to find a regular job.

Despite such personal preoccupations, and the domestic disruption they entailed, Otten did not neglect his literary work. Convinced of the importance of his novel *Die Reise nach Deutschland*, he made further efforts to secure its publication, commissioning the translator Claude W. Sykes to prepare an English version. Aware as always of his dependence on the translator, he requested Sykes to be as faithful as possible to the style and spirit of the original text. He had, he wrote, striven for a unity of style, adopting, even in the dialogue, a 'poetic', 'visionary' language which he implored Sykes not to 'flatten out'. Above all, he asked Sykes not to render this poetic diction into the prosaic language of colloquial English. 'It is preferable that the book should appear unmodern than that it should be flat and unpoetic, that is – modern.'[183]

Sykes was familiar with the problems of Otten's style, having already made an English translation of his play *Kein Held* (*No Hero*) during 1938. The play, a five-acter, was based loosely on newspaper reports of a man who loses his memory and is unable to remember his identity, is apparently reunited with his wife and family, only to be confronted with a second woman claiming that he is in fact *her* husband. Otten described

No Hero laconically as 'a play waiting for a theatre'.[184] It was indeed
offered to more than one London theatre, but without success. Finally
deciding to cut his losses, Otten sent *No Hero* to the BBC, suggesting it
could be adapted for radio. He was prepared, even anxious, to stress the
play's political dimension: in a letter to Val Gielgud, Head of BBC
Drama, he described its theme as 'the struggle of the individual against
the totalitarian principle'. Gielgud, however, rejected the play as unsuitable for radio treatment.[185] A year later, Otten was to join the
Corporation's staff as a member of the German Service, writing features
for wartime propaganda broadcasts to Germany.

Robert Neumann made equally determined efforts to reorientate his life
towards Britain. In February he brought his mother and sister to
London; shortly after he brought over his wife and son, though continuing to live apart from them. In April, he and Rolly moved out
of London, renting a cottage in the Buckinghamshire village of Long
Crendon, near Thame. The cottage itself was somewhat primitive,
lacking mains water, but the village and its surroundings were idyllic.

In March, having completed the required five years residence in
Britain, Neumann applied for naturalisation, naming as his sponsors D.
N. Pritt, Hermon Ould, Professor William Rose and Jeffrey Marston, a
retired army major. He was told that, because of a technicality, his
application could not be considered before 20 September – by which
time the war had intervened. He did not finally acquire British nationality until 1947.

He wrote little during these months, devoting himself principally to
his relief work for PEN. It was in his capacity as President of Austrian
PEN that (with Rudolf Olden) he wrote a letter to the *Manchester
Guardian* in which both men reaffirmed their 'irreconcilable opposition
to the Nazi regime', asserting that the battle lines for the impending
conflict were not so much national as ideological.[186] In this respect
Neumann misjudged the public mood, unable to see that few of the
British viewed the war as a crusade against fascism and apparently
unaware of the latent xenophobia, which surfaced only nine months
later with the internment of 'enemy aliens'.

Part Four

Enemy Aliens

1939–1941

THE PHONEY WAR AND INTERNMENT

In the final paragraph of his book *Ich kam nach England*, Alfred Kerr greeted the outbreak of war with unconcealed satisfaction and even relief: 'The long overdue headline: "Hitler attacks Poland. French and British ultimatum to Berlin." At last. So it's war.' Kerr's enemies might have pointed out that he had greeted the war with equal enthusiasm in 1914, albeit for entirely different reasons. This time, however, Kerr's feelings were mingled with an evident sense of paradox: 'That one can wish for a misfortune, because another misfortune is even more terrible.'

Most of the German-speaking refugees who listened to Neville Chamberlain's announcement that Britain was now at war with Germany must have heard the news with very mixed feelings. This was not a consequence of divided loyalty. Most of them welcomed the war as the only means of removing Hitler and thereby restoring their native countries to some degree of normality. However, their feelings were qualified by understandable unease about the anomaly of their own situation: under the terms of the Aliens Act, the outbreak of hostilities had transformed all German and Austrian refugees overnight into 'enemy aliens', subject, under the Aliens Order, to curfew and travel restrictions, and required to register with the police. By the same token, German had now become the language of the enemy, lending the mere act of speaking or writing their native language a new and sinister dimension.

Even before the outbreak of war, refugees from Germany and

Austria who passed through Bloomsbury House in 1938–39 were given an information booklet containing thirteen Do's and Don'ts: it advised them not to draw attention to themselves through noisy behaviour, not to talk loudly and above all not to speak German in public.[1] This advice was warmly endorsed by Neville Laski, Chairman of the Board of Deputies of British Jews. Certainly there had always been prejudice against foreigners, particularly foreign Jews. In fact, the Anglo-Jewish establishment had long been concerned to regulate the flow of refugees arriving in Britain for fear of stirring up latent anti-semitism. The outbreak of war brought such feelings into the open, resulting in an upsurge of xenophobia. Angus Calder records that foreign refugees, many of whom were now stateless, became 'the most obvious targets for hatred and suspicion'.[2] Foreign employees were abruptly sacked simply because they were of foreign origin. Many refugees who had entered Britain as domestic servants – often the only means of gaining entry – now found that they had lost both work and the only home they had. Organisations like the Austrian Centre found themselves dealing with a stream of refugees who had once more become destitute.

Robert Neumann was greatly distressed by the prevailing climate of suspicion. Eager to contribute to the British war effort, he had offered his services to a variety of official, and less official organisations, including the British Council and the BBC. He had written to the latter, suggesting the introduction of a special news service for Austria, but had received no more than a polite acknowledgement. He was also in touch with the Friends of Europe, run by the former Labour MP Rennie Smith, offering to help with 'the dissemination of ideas and be active in various ways'.[3] He felt particularly well suited to the task of writing propaganda and also offered his services to the newly-formed Ministry of Information, then provisionally housed at London University's Senate House, but despite the intervention of D. N. Pritt he was given little to do apart from translating a short pamphlet, entitled *Who Hitler is.*

Neumann was disheartened by these successive rebuffs, complaining to Pritt:

I feel greatly grieved by being registered as an 'enemy alien' in this country, in spite of my record and in spite of my willingness . . . to be of some help in what I do not regard as a war in the ordinary sense, but as a crusade against Nazi ideology.[4]

All his letters make clear that he felt the war was *his* war, in a way that the British could neither share nor even fully appreciate.

Stefan Zweig, the inveterate pacifist, was altogether more ambivalent. He admitted that his 'heart was heavy'. With the outbreak of war, he had resumed the habit of keeping a diary. His entry for 3 September notes with characteristic egocentricity: 'Now begins another life for me, being no more free and independent.'[5] He was aware that his own situation had once more been transformed. No longer the famous foreign author, nor even a refugee, he was now subject to petty restrictions which he found 'shameful' and 'humiliating'. He briefly entertained 'a secret hope' that war would not start in earnest (10 September 1939), a hope which is eloquent of Zweig's capacity for self-delusion. Six weeks later he was forced to concede that 'this (i.e. the war) will go on against my expectations, my hopes, my dispair' (*sic*) (16 October 1939). He was apprehensive of the atmosphere of growing mistrust, complaining that the British simply lumped the Austrians together with the Germans.

Such feelings were widely shared. Max Herrmann-Neiße too found it shameful to be equated with the very enemy from whom he had fled to take refuge in Britain. He greatly feared the introduction of internment, and the inevitable separation from his wife Leni, on whose care he had come to rely, both physically and morally.

Karl Otten, who had prophesied the inevitability of war two years earlier in *Die Reise nach Deutschland*, took some grim satisfaction from the realisation of his prophecy. He was, moreover, in no doubt where his loyalties lay. 'We must act now. There is no going back and the existence of every one of us, the existence of Europe, depends on the victory of the Allies,' he wrote to Gottfried Bermann Fischer.[6] Otten was certainly determined to be 'of use to the common cause'.[7] Even before the outbreak of war, he had apparently been working for British intelligence services. During 1939 he seems to have been recruited by the Department for Enemy Propaganda, Electra House, a secret government organisation which operated under the cover of the non-secret Political Intelligence Department of the Foreign Office. Electra House had been set up during 1938, assuming responsibility for propaganda to enemy countries. In 1942, both Electra House and its counterpart Special Operations I were consolidated into the Political Warfare Executive, through which the government controlled all propaganda output, including the transmissions of the BBC.

It is impossible to establish how Otten's association with Electra House began, though he may well have been recommended by Wickham Steed. Nor is it possible to ascertain the precise nature of his work there: even today, the activities of the Political Warfare Executive remain shadowy and mysterious. Its records, particularly those of its predecessor organisations, are only partially open for examination. For his part, Otten never wrote or talked about these activities, even to his wife, insisting that there were some things it was better she knew nothing about. Otten's unpublished papers give some idea of the work he undertook for the intelligence services. During the early months of the war, for example, he was engaged in writing propaganda material, such as stickers and leaflets bearing resistance messages, which were dropped over Germany. Though many such documents have survived, it is, by their very nature, impossible to ascribe their authorship with any certainty. Much more certain is that Otten's main use to British intelligence was his intimate knowledge of the Rhineland: during 1940 he recorded two 'Messages to the Rhinelanders', in which he called on the population to refuse to support a 'Prussian' war.[8] Though they were clearly intended for transmission to Germany, it is impossible to say whether they were ever actually broadcast. Otten also had long-standing contacts with anti-Nazi journalists such as Max Sievers in Belgium and Karl Gröhl in France. Gröhl (later known as Karl Retzlaw) had been working for British intelligence since 1937.[9]

In 1939–40 Otten also involved the unsuspecting Gottfried Bermann Fischer, whose base in a neutral country and extensive mailing-list represented a possible conduit for introducing illegal propaganda into Germany. At Otten's instigation, Bermann was contacted by a man called Alfred Rickman, who was a British intelligence agent – and was consequently arrested and briefly imprisoned by the Swedish authorities.[10] Otten's usefulness to British intelligence seems to have dwindled with the loss of his contacts in mainland Europe after the fall of France. In any case, his correspondence suggests that he had no further dealings with them after the end of 1940. While the full extent of his work for the intelligence services may never be known, it was clearly considered to be vital to the war effort: sufficiently vital, for example, to exempt him from the internment which shortly befell so many of his compatriots.

Even before the outbreak of war, many German-speaking refugees had feared the possibility of internment, the threat of which was always implicit. British policy during the First World War had been disastrously simple – the indiscriminate internment of all enemy aliens between the ages of seventeen and fifty-five. A post-war review of the policy had concluded its essential futility and in 1939, when the government had considered possible contingency measures in the event of war, it had rejected the option of general internment.

On the day after war was declared, the new Home Secretary, Sir John Anderson – whose name was to become a household word with the adoption of the Anderson shelter – rose to make a short statement to the House of Commons. He reported that the government had moved rapidly and decisively to detain some three hundred German nationals in Britain, such as journalists, businessmen and a sprinkling of merchant seamen whose vessels had put into British ports at the wrong moment. However, the government did not wish to resort to general internment, opting instead for a policy of review, under which all 'enemy aliens' were to appear before specially constituted tribunals, to be chaired by members of the legal profession. The tribunals were required to place aliens, according to Home Office criteria, into one of three categories: 'A' (to be interned), 'B' (exempt from internment, but subject to restrictions) and 'C' (exempt from internment and restrictions). The mere enunciation of these administrative measures conveys none of the resentment or uncertainty they induced amongst refugees. There was particular apprehension as to how the tribunals would work: their proceedings were to be held in secret, aliens would not be allowed legal representation, though they could bring a friend.

The Aliens Tribunals began work in the first week of October 1939 and before the end of the month had considered over 13,000 cases. Historians have generally concluded that their proceedings were conducted fairly. In fact, their decisions were inconsistent and often arbitrary, depending almost entirely on the whim of the tribunal chairman. Max Herrmann-Neiße was summoned to appear before a tribunal in London on 6 October, being placed in the 'safe' category 'C', and thus entitled to have the prized designation 'refugee from Nazi oppression' stamped in his police registration book. Though undoubtedly relieved at the outcome, Herrmann-Neiße remained apprehensive as to how long he would be left at liberty, a fear later encapsulated in the title of his poem 'Wie lange noch?' ('How Much Longer?').[11] For his part, Stefan Zweig anticipated 'the cross-fire (*Fegefeuer*) of the tribunal' with some apprehension.[12] His fears were not misplaced. The tribunal at Bath inexplicably chose to place Zweig in the category 'B', denying him the status of a 'friendly enemy alien', even though his application for British naturalisation was by then well advanced.

Even more extraordinary was the case of Robert Neumann who was summoned to appear on 17 October before a tribunal at Aylesbury, which placed him too in the category 'B'. The tribunal chairman gave three reasons for this classification. Firstly Neumann's book on the arms manufacturer Sir Basil Zaharoff was adjudged to be hostile to the armaments industry and therefore also anti-British. Secondly, he was told he could hardly be a genuine refugee, since he had left Austria long before the Anschluss. Thirdly, and most damningly, there were 'the most peculiar circumstances' of his private life, namely his relationship with Rolly Becker.[13] Rolly later appeared before the same tribunal, and was placed in the same 'B' category because she was living with Neumann: a clear case of guilt by cohabitation.

The combative Neumann immediately appealed against the decision; he was frustrated by the ideological myopia which took no account of his record and resented the petty travel restrictions which prohibited the use of his car and virtually isolated him in Long Crendon. He wrote to anyone of influence who could vouch for him, including the poet Humbert Wolfe, then a civil servant in the Ministry of Labour, who promised to intervene with the Home Office.[14] The Home Office, still pursuing a relatively liberal policy, actually agreed to review all 'B' category cases once the tribunals had completed their work, but the review had barely started before it was spectacularly overtaken by events.

'CONCENTRATION CAMP, ENGLISH STYLE': ROBERT NEUMANN'S
INTERNMENT DIARY

In May 1940, in the atmosphere of near panic following the German invasion of Holland and Belgium, the British government hastily introduced a policy of wholesale internment. On 15 May it ordered the arrest of all 'B' category men. The arrests were carried out in conditions of secrecy, often at night, adding greatly to the uncertainty and anxiety of the victims. Neumann was arrested at home at five o'clock in the morning and given time only to pack a small suitcase before being transported to Cowley Barracks, Oxford, where the authorities had set up a makeshift internment camp.

In the following days, Rolly made frantic attempts to get him released, appealing to anyone he knew who might have influence – including his publishers, Victor Gollancz and Stanley Unwin, and fellow-writers H. G. Wells and Storm Jameson. With Anna Mahler, the Austrian sculptor, daughter of the composer, Rolly tried to persuade Stefan Zweig to intervene on Neumann's behalf, but Zweig, perhaps apprehensive of his own position as a British subject of only two months standing, refused:

> I am afraid there is in the present situation nothing to do. . . perhaps he is safer now than anywhere else – better in an English concentration camp than to be in France or Belgium or Holland – I wish I could share his hardship and I am ashamed that a simple chance has given me a respite.[15]

Zweig's phlegmatic judgement may well have been correct, but Neumann, to whom the reply was forwarded in his internment camp, never forgave him. Zweig later tried to make amends, offering to use his connections to secure Neumann a visa for Cuba – but by then they were on different sides of the Atlantic and nothing came of it.

Neumann spent the first two weeks of his internment at Cowley, before being transferred to a transit camp at Huyton and finally to the Isle of Man. In his book of memoirs, written some twenty years after the events, Neumann portrays internment – under the title 'Concentration Camp – English Style' – as an irksome but amusing episode, distancing the events through irony.[16] The diary he kept at the time tells a very different story, revealing that he suffered greatly from the physical and mental pressures of confinement. Neumann's diary, written in German, is a highly personal document, which was not written for publication.[17] He began it as a substitute for dialogue with Rolly Becker, though it also undoubtedly acted as a safety-valve for feelings of frustration and depression which sometimes bordered on despair. (The word 'despair' is a leitmotif running through the whole diary.) As an intimate record of internment, the diary is also an oblique account of an historical episode which historians have not yet fully illuminated. Even now, some sixty years after the events, historical research is handicapped by the government's continuing reluctance to release all the relevant Home Office documents for public scrutiny.[18]

In the initial chaos of internment, conditions at the Cowley camp rapidly deteriorated. The camp was severely overcrowded, so that many prisoners had to sleep on the floor and the conditions were made worse by torrential rain which turned the ground outside into a morass. Food was poor, hygiene primitive. Close confinement had a coarsening effect, rapidly reducing the men to the sum of their basic physical functions. The main topics of conversation were defecation, food and washing. Neumann commented: 'How this community reduces men to the most animal level' (22 May).

Two days after his arrest, Neumann began a hunger strike in protest against internment. On 22 May, his forty-third birthday, he noted:

Fourth day of fasting. 6: woke, determined to have a good birthday. Heavy rain. 7: escorted to washroom. (Corporal to sentry: Is your gun loaded? Alright.) Breakfast for the others. No hunger, no temptation (22 May).

During these early days of internment, prisoners were held in virtual isolation from the outside world: they were forbidden newspapers and although they were allowed to listen to the radio, news of the war merely emphasised their isolation and vulnerability. There was particular anxiety about the threat of an imminent German invasion: the internees feared that, in this event, they would become sitting ducks. Neumann's feelings are recorded in a further diary entry made on his birthday:

Radio-News: Germans in Amiens-Arras. Instruction to keep identity cards with you at all times. . . Looked at my face in mirror. Face of a much older man, with grey-white and red stubble. If the Nazis come, we shall have to know how to die (22 May).

Internees at Cowley were initially unable to send letters, except for simple messages requesting clothes or other necessities. Later communications were limited to a postcard, or to the infamous twenty-four lines. Neumann commented: 'Permission to write reduced once more . . . how much one can write on a postcard. What an education for a writer' (26 May). Internees' anxiety was further heightened by the lack of news of family and friends. Incoming post was subject to censorship and hence to considerable delay. It was eleven days before Neumann finally received a letter from Rolly, but even then his pleasure was short-lived: 'Your letter, my love – and then straight after, the great horror : radio announcement that women are to be interned! I feel such despair that I simply can't express it' (27 May).

Against a background of military defeat and growing fear of invasion, the policy of internment was gaining a momentum of its own: on 26 May the government ordered the arrest of all remaining 'B' category aliens, mainly women. Rolly was arrested the same day and held overnight in Oxford before being transferred to the Isle of Man. The island had been used for internment during the First World War, and the government now requisitioned all hotels and boarding-houses at Ramsey in the north-east of the island, and at Onchan, near Douglas, surrounding them with barbed wire and thus transforming them into internment camps. Similarly a women's camp was quickly established at Port Erin, on the southernmost tip of the island, where Rolly was brought on 28 May. She sent a postcard to a neighbour in Long Crendon, bearing the address Hotel Bay View and the wry comment: 'Doesn't it sound nice?'[19]

On 1 June, after days of speculation, Neumann and his fellow-internees at Cowley heard that they were being transferred to Liverpool, the news producing a mood of temporary euphoria which lent their departure from Cowley an air almost of elation and celebration. They were bound for the transit camp at Huyton, where the government had requisitioned an unfinished housing estate. Here, amid scenes of complete disorganisation, they found the conditions far worse than at Cowley: the regime more military, the guards more hostile, the atmosphere that of a prison camp. In common with other anti-Nazi internees, Neumann also suffered the indignity of being herded together with Nazi civilian prisoners. The houses in Huyton had neither furniture nor beds, but they were at least dry: because of the severe overcrowding, new arrivals such as Neumann had to be housed in tents which, after frequent rain, quickly became waterlogged. Neumann later described his days at Huyton ironically as 'an unparalleled chaos'; at the time he called it 'hell on earth' (5 June).

Neumann had by now learned that Rolly was in Port Erin and he successfully volunteered to be in the first convoy to be transferred from Huyton to the Isle of Man. Disembarking on the island under the gaze of a silent and hostile local population, the internees faced a long march to the Mooragh camp at Ramsey, where the government had commandeered groups of hotels and boarding-houses along the seafront and surrounded them with a double line of barbed wire which, to Neumann's eyes, seemed more friendly than that at Huyton. He noted 'neglected buildings, ancient dirty mattresses in a completely empty filthy room', but also the sea-view and the luxury of sharing a room with only one other person (5 June).

Neumann's diary is in many ways an exemplary text: a highly personal account which is nonetheless representative of a much wider experience. Most internees suffered from feelings of frustration and anxiety, the trauma of arrest and detention being heightened by uncertainty as to its duration, and concern for the fate of family and friends. Neumann notes these uncertainties and their effect on the internees' physical and mental well-being, not least his own. He records, sometimes involuntarily, the growth of prison psychosis.

On 13 June, at the height of the battle for France, Neumann noted: 'Argument with room-mate about trivialities. Moving furniture etc. Nervous outburst, first symptoms of prison psychosis in this camp' (13 June). From this point on, 'prison psychosis' (*Haftpsychose*) and 'barbed wire' are words repeated with alarming frequency in the diary. The paramount fear was of German invasion. The following day Neumann recorded: 'Paris is supposed to have fallen. Went down to the sea for a couple of minutes and looked for mussels. Full of colours and secrets. Race with death. And death always ahead by a whisker' (14 June). He chafed increasingly at his confinement, feeling that time was slipping through his fingers, while outside the fate of the world was being decided.

Throughout these weeks, the internees were cut off from contact with the outside world: newspapers and radios were banned, turning the whole camp into a hotbed of rumour and counter-rumour. One of Neumann's diary entries reads: 'Days of great agitation. Collapse of France. Ban on newspapers – and inferno of rumours' (20 June). While the danger of invasion gradually receded, it continued to dominate the thoughts of internees. On 7 August Neumann records: 'With no apparent pretext, several people dreamt tonight that the Nazis were occupying the island' (7 August). There were frequent rumours of German peace overtures to Britain, increasing the internees' fear that they might simply be handed over to the Nazis. In fact, such overtures had been rejected.

At the height of internment, Mooragh camp held some 1,200 prisoners, representing a cross-section of German-speaking exiles: Austrian monarchists, German Jews, Social Democrats of all shades and Communists, between whom there was a constant and not always very friendly rivalry. Neumann records on one occasion

> a court of arbitration between the Socialist Friedrich and the Communist Metzig, concerning some important triviality, enabling both to burnish their proletarian honour. The arbitrators were a director of the German Mortgage Bank, the Chairman of an insurance company who had been a volunteer in the German Freikorps – and me.

The material conditions of internment undoubtedly improved on the Isle of Man. The internees were allowed a degree of autonomy which enabled them to arrange various cultural activities, which the authorities encouraged as a means of alleviating boredom and improving morale. Despite the best efforts of historians, many such events have gone unrecorded, largely because of their ephemeral nature.[20]

Neumann's diary mentions several such events in the Mooragh camp, his descriptions evoking both their fleeting nature and their essential incongruity: 'An evening of Schubert, strangely serious, solemn and moving behind the barbed wire' (28 June). There was also cabaret:

From there straight on to the world premiere (and perhaps final performance) of the cabaret 'Rose-tinted Spectacles'. The splendid Becker, who has already performed cabaret with Fritz Grünbaum in a Nazi concentration camp; the female impersonator 'Mitzi' Turteltaub, an over-genuine (Jewish) Viennese folk singer. Transfigured faces in the audience.

Neumann himself held a writing course, in which he invited participants to write on the theme of 'Huyton Camp'. Those present listened to a series of contributions, factual and fictional, 'until everyone, under the dark star of this subject-matter, found themselves greatly agitated, tired, churned up'.

Neumann also gave a reading from his novel *By the Waters of Babylon*, choosing the semi-autobiographical episode of Marcus, the exiled German writer. 'Read 'Marcus' to 180 people in a basement room. Gruesomely untopical, hyper-topical' (30 June). He read the same chapter a fortnight later, and also attended readings by other writers:

Jesse Thor, poetry reading, not bad at all, a dash of Villon, a lot of honesty, some vividness, hardly any literary affectation – on the whole, a touching and likeable figure (16 July).[21]

Neumann was well aware of the possibilities of literary exploitation of his experience. Though certainly not written for publication, his diary frequently betrays the eye of the writer, containing – alongside personal reflections – a series of anecdotes and thumbnail character sketches which are very much jottings from a writer's notebook:

A lecture by Max Freyhahn on Literature and History . . . delivered immaculately and with great intellectuality, with commitment, somewhat boringly and yet movingly, while, behind the excited speaker, a smiling figure stands asleep, leaning on the mantelpiece, snoring, half waking, obliterating the effects of the intellect – ah, what a symbol!

In fact, the physical conditions of internment hindered sustained concentration, making writing often impossible. Nevertheless, the later pages of the diary contain passing references to 'work on the novel', probably an allusion to the novel *Scene in Passing*[22] which he completed the following year.

There was also a camp newspaper. In the hope of improving morale, the authorities had sanctioned camp newspapers from the end of July and several camps on the Isle of Man produced duplicated news-sheets which generally dealt with matters such as conditions within the camp, the status of internees – and the burning question of release.

François Lafitte, in his contemporary polemic *The Internment of Aliens*, wrote: 'The Mooragh Camp reads the *Mooragh Times*, contributors to which include Robert Neumann and Bruno Heilig.'[23] Lafitte could not have known that there was only one issue of the paper, which appeared on 12 August, edited by the Austrian journalist Joseph Kalmus. The front page carried an introductory article by Neumann, which was evidently written from the heart, since he transcribed the first paragraph in its entirety in his diary:

> We wish this paper a short life. May it die shortly, together with the cause of its publication. But after its demise, let it not just be interred among the bibliophiles' collection of curios. It should remain alive for us, the prisoners, as a document of shame. And for our prison warders, as a testimony of how a great nation, for the first time in the centuries of its heroic history, found it right to begin its campaign to liberate Western culture by imprisoning its most loyal friends, its enemies' most bitter enemies (16 August).

If camp newspapers were generally written for internal consumption, Neumann's words are obviously addressed to an audience outside the camp. He indeed wrote to the editors of various newspapers – including *The Times*, *Daily Herald*, and *News Chronicle* – enclosing a copy of the camp newspaper, giving brief pen portraits of the main contributors, not least himself, and emphasising their anti-Nazi credentials, not least his own.[24]

The camp commandant had given his official blessing to the *Mooragh Times*, even contributing a few words of his own, but Neumann's diary records his surprise and anger at the first issue:

> He makes me stand in front of his desk and tells me off like a schoolboy. These words in the camp newspaper. Whom do they help? There is an official channel for complaints – to him. From now on, all the newspaper can contain is 'something to make people laugh'. . . Went away tremendously angry. The newspaper refuses 'to make people laugh' and stops publication (16 August).

The thought which dominated the minds of all internees was that of release. Richard Friedenthal reported that such was the disturbing power of the word that he even suggested banning its use.[25] Neumann made repeated applications for release, which were almost routinely rejected. He records an official announcement that those believing they had good grounds could apply for release – and the commandant's unofficial comment that there was no point in doing so, because no one had time to process such applications.

Neumann himself was considering ways of escaping not only internment – but also a Britain increasingly threatened by invasion. While still at Cowley he had mobilised friends such as Storm Jameson and Anna Mahler to help him secure a screen-writing contract in Hollywood.

The fall of France had forced emergency rescue committees in the USA to intensify their efforts to rescue German intellectuals from occupied Europe. It was in this context that the European Film Fund persuaded the major film studios to offer refugee writers one-year contracts, intended principally to enable them to secure an immigration visa. Among the prominent writers engaged by the studios were Heinrich Mann, Alfred Döblin, Leonhard Frank, Alfred Polgar and Walter Mehring. They were paid a modest salary of $100 a month; few of them were expected to do any serious work. Unlike them, Neumann had actually sought a Hollywood contract as early as 1936, though without success.

His intermediaries enlisted the aid of the playwright Bruno Frank, then at the height of his success in Hollywood, who succeeded in gaining a contract from MGM covering both Neumann and Rolly Becker. After considerable efforts, the contract was finally lodged in London at the beginning of August, but the US consulate refused to grant the couple visas and the contract finally lapsed.

In Mooragh, Neumann had received further letters from Rolly, which he was at first unable to answer. Internees were allowed to write only two letters a week, which had to be restricted to matters of urgency. Because of censorship, letters often took as long as a fortnight to reach their destination – even if it was only the other side of the island. After making repeated requests, he was finally permitted to see her, being taken under military escort to the women's camp, where they were allowed half an hour together. 'It broke my heart when I saw her there for half an hour, so distant, so composed, she was just like herself, only more so.'[26] All requests for a further meeting were refused.

At the height of the invasion scare following the fall of France, the government had ordered the internment of even 'C' category aliens, deciding – to use Churchill's brutal shorthand – to 'collar the lot'. At the same time, it had inaugurated, in great secrecy, the mass deportation of internees. The policy of deportation had been devised in such panic that it was initially far from clear where internees should be deported to. Churchill, doubtless inspired by historical precedent, suggested the island of St Helena. The first ship carrying deportees left on 21 June, bound for Canada.

Many internees were subjected to considerable moral pressure to persuade them to 'volunteer' for deportation. Neumann records the repeated assurances given to married men that their interned wives would be allowed to accompany them in the same convoy. He himself agreed to join a deportation convoy, only to change his mind. On 1 August he noted:

> The Australian transport, organised with lies, deceits, bribes and black-mail has been cancelled at the last minute without any reasons being given. How they've crushed these people, dissipated their nervous capital.

The reason for the cancellation – unknown to Neumann and his fellow-internees – was that the government had suspended the policy of deportation.

Public opinion had begun to move strongly against internment, following the sinking of the liner *Arandora Star*. The luxury cruise liner, commandeered for war duties, had set sail from Liverpool on 1 July, carrying some 1,200 internees – Germans, Austrians and Italians – who were being deported to Canada. The ship was torpedoed off the coast of Ireland, sinking with the loss of 700 lives. Public concern at the incident caused the government to think again, reversing its internment policy so rapidly that, less than a month after ordering the internment of 'C' category aliens, the Home Secretary was announcing in the Commons that they could now apply for release. The first fifty walked free from internment on the Isle of Man on 5 August 1940.

Neumann's memoirs, *Ein leichtes Leben*, contain a partly fictionalised account of his internment, in which some incidents can be authenticated from his contemporary diary, but details are often heightened or even invented for narrative effect. This is exemplified in the account he gives of his release. He tells us that, increasingly impatient with the official channels of application, he finally wrote a letter to Winston Churchill in person. The letter itself can be authenticated from his diary to which he confided it in full on 1 August: 'Sir, my name may have escaped your attention, but the Information Minister should be in a position to tell you who I am, and the Home Secretary will certainly find no difficulty in furnishing you with the full particulars of my case.' However, Neumann then portrays his release as a direct consequence of the letter, citing the incident as a notable example of democracy in action: 'A week later I was free. A worn-out, devalued currency, hardly accepted any more: democracy.'[27] The truth is more prosaic. Although he *was* released some three weeks later, it was actually at the recommendation of the camp doctor on the grounds of ill-health.

As internment drew on, Neumann had begun to show symptoms of stress, suffering from sleeplessness and violent bouts of angina. The first attack had occurred on 7 July, the very day that he had first agreed to join the next shipload of deportees – and then suddenly changed his mind:

> Much excitement, haste, hunger today, severe headaches which wouldn't go away, but even so I went to bed feeling calm. . . Then it started, about three or four hours after I went to sleep. . . Woke up and felt I couldn't breathe. . . My God, what a tight feeling round my chest. . . the next moment, I came out in a cold sweat, sweat of death all over . . . it's simply been too much for me recently, and I've also lost eighteen pounds in eight weeks . . . woke up in the morning as though dead (7 July).

The stress, briefly contained, finally broke surface again on 12 August:

> I can't go on. Suddenly woke shortly before dawn, absolutely freezing. Margaret's letter means that the Americans wont let me over there, I'm suddenly sure, I can't go on any more (12 August).

Neumann's agitation becomes evident in his handwriting, which suddenly changes in size and slope, becoming in places almost illegible: '14th. Awful days: sleep, doctors. Can't breathe this air any more.

ENEMY ALIENS - 1939-1941

They've destroyed me here, these people in whose hospitality and uprightness I'd trusted.' In fact, he had already been examined by the camp doctor, who made an official recommendation for his release. Ten days later he was free. The final entry in the diary is addressed directly to Rolly Becker. Written in a hand rendered almost illegible by emotion, it reads: 'Released. Released. Telegraph Storm (i.e. Storm Jameson) to have you set free.'

The diary ends here, but resumes on 29 August, after Neumann's return to London, detailing his attempts to hasten the release of Rolly Becker. In fact, she remained interned for a further six weeks. So protracted was the process of her release that Neumann applied for permission to visit her, actually returning to the Isle of Man on 10 October, an experience on which he never commented, even in the privacy of his diary. When Rolly finally did return, he found her visibly changed by her experience: 'Taut, on edge, reticent and, in an embittered way, purposeful.'[28]

Though Neumann may have intended to write a factual account of internment, using his contemporary diary notes (such a plan is mentioned in a letter Neumann wrote to a deportee in Canada) – he never actually did so, apparently finding the episode too disturbing. Instead, he transposed the experience into fiction, firstly in the novel *The Inquest*, written in 1943, and later into the light comedy of his memoirs. In both these versions, memory is mitigated by imagination; his contemporary diary remains more immediate, a less polished but more honest account of what internment was actually like.

THE WORLD OF YESTERDAY

Though professing detachment from political events, Stefan Zweig had always been unusually acute in predicting them. As the war which he had long foreseen approached, he attempted to put his personal affairs into order. Fearing the introduction of internment, he took steps to expedite his naturalisation, appealing to H. G. Wells and Desmond Flower to help him, though their intercession seems to have had no noticeable effect. Lotte, as a former German citizen, seemed particularly vulnerable to the threat of internment. Concerned at the risk of being separated from her, Zweig also hastened to fix a date for their marriage. By chance, he was discussing this with the registrar when a clerk burst into the office with the news that Germany had invaded Poland, thus making war inevitable. To Zweig's astonishment, the registrar scarcely bothered to look up: 'The magistrate (*sic*) continues to explain to us what he will do in our case, as if nothing had happened . . . everyone remains self-possessed and sure.'[29]

Zweig was amazed at the calm with which the British received the news of war: 'The way they go off to the army. As though they were going to a match – it's splendid and yet I shudder, for with this calm determination the war can last ten years.'[30] While nothing in the town seemed to have changed, he knew that his own situation had once more been transformed: on 4 September, he and Lotte duly presented them-selves at the police station to register as 'enemy aliens'. He wrote to Sigmund Freud (recently established in London) that he now needed a permit to travel anywhere more than five miles from the centre of Bath, commenting: 'Sic transit gloria mundi. Thus does literary standing melt away before a police regulation.'[31] A week later he heard the announcement on the radio (now more than ever the bearer of bad news) that Freud had died at the age of eighty-three. The death of the man who had so profoundly influenced his work, and whom he had formally celebrated in his book *Mental Healers*, caused Zweig to reflect sombrely on his own situation: 'I feel once more my isolation in this country. . . I have no newspaper in which I can write a few words, no opportunity to say something, and this after six years in England' (*Diary*, 24 September).

He applied for a permit to attend Freud's funeral, arriving in London after an adventurous journey through the blackout, waiting for three hours on the darkened station at Salisbury for a connection. On the following day he delivered the funeral oration at Golders Green crem-atorium in what was to be his last public appearance in England. He found it a sombre experience: barely three months after the death of Joseph Roth, he was once more called upon to give the funeral oration for a dear friend. He felt that Freud's death symbolised the end of an era.

Never had he felt his linguistic isolation so keenly. With the outbreak of war he had begun a regular diary, which he had felt it necessary to keep in English, though regretting the need to resort to a language which he was unable to use with any ease. Above all, he was aware of being a German-speaking Jew, fated to be 'a living anomaly, speaking and thinking in a language which has been taken away from us, living in a country to whose fate we are tied, to which we are not completely attached, and in which we are only tolerated. Jews without religious faith and the will to be Jews.'[32]

Zweig had always been fond of quoting Rilke's aphorism: 'Wer spricht von Siegen? Überstehen ist alles' ('What is victory? Survival is everything'). During these early months of the war, he was intent on survival, comforted by Lotte's companionship and the beauty of his surroundings. He had quickly become attached to 'Rosemount', completing the purchase of the house by the end of the year. 'I have never felt more at home anywhere,' he wrote to Fleischer in January 1940. He was enjoying a new sense of permanence, happy to have his books and papers around him once more. It was a feeling which persisted even into the crisis of the following summer, when he maintained that 'for the first time for years I have a feeling of being at home, I'm happy to have my books and papers around me'.[33]

The house had become a refuge, in which he tried to insulate himself from external events, turning his back on the war and refusing to read newspapers or listen to the radio. He had ceased writing his diary, working intensively on his Balzac, transforming the notes and jottings of half a lifetime into the fluent narrative which was his professional trademark. He was afraid that the book might never appear, conscious of the almost insuperable difficulty of sending any manuscript, let alone a German manuscript, abroad in time of war. But he also knew that he was committed to writing in German, though he was increasingly aware of the danger of 'loss of language' (*Sprachverlust*). He told Felix Braun – a friend of more than thirty years' standing – that he had given up reading or speaking English, fearing that it was eroding his command of his native language.[34] Though German had now become the language of the enemy, it was still the tongue in which he wrote, thought and felt: 'I cannot and will not learn to write in another language, we cannot escape our fate of writing in the very language which disowns us.'[35] Ironically, it was later that month that his application for British nationality was finally approved; Lotte, as his wife, received her naturalisation papers three days later.[36]

In April 1940 Zweig made his last visit to Paris, following an invitation to lecture there. The subject he chose was 'The Vienna of Yesterday', a theme very much in his mind, since he had recently begun work on the autobiography which was to evoke the now-vanished world which had borne and nurtured him. He was astonished at the interest his theme aroused: when he rose to speak in the Théâtre Marigny, the hall was already packed with an audience of 1,600, while many more stood outside, unable to gain admission. There was no time to repeat the lecture, but Zweig did broadcast three times over Radio Paris. He also saw old friends like Masereel and Paul Valéry. He was very much in his element, relishing a nostalgic return to the city which he had always regarded as his second home. 'It was like a return of old times,' he wrote to Max Herrmann-Neiße after arriving back in Bath. 'One forgot one's sorrows for a moment.'[37] But events would rapidly overtake him: within two months Paris was in German hands.

Zweig's decision to settle in Bath had signalled his commitment to Europe; he had put aside any thoughts of further emigration to America. In January 1940 he wrote to Hermann Kesten that he would stay in Europe, because anyone who left it now would never return. 'And we must stay, even if it's all a lost cause. Here we can fulfil a duty through our very presence. America would swallow us up.'[38] When the two men met again in Paris, Zweig became even more emphatic, saying that any writer who left Europe now was guilty of intellectual treason.[39] However, the German breakthrough in France plunged him into renewed indecision.

From 20 May, as the Germans captured Amiens and began to advance inexorably towards the Channel coast, Zweig resumed the diary he had abandoned in October. Almost the first entry records difficulties concerning the film rights for *Volpone*, ending with the wry reflection: 'How strange to be bothering about personal and private matters, when the whole of existence is at stake' (*Diary*, 23 May 1940). The German breakthrough had plunged him into sudden panic, confronting him with the danger of an invasion which he had previously thought impossible: 'Perhaps it will still be possible to get to America, but it may already be too late even for that' (24 May 1940).

As the situation deteriorated, he felt increasingly isolated. An official announcement exhorted the population to be vigilant in dealings with former Austrians and Germans, forcing Zweig to reflect '. . .that will certainly be the case for the rest of my life, given my name which the English can never pronounce. The only question is actually whether one will be more hated as a German or as a Jew' (*Diary*, 30 May 1940). He could no longer even take refuge in his work: 'The thought that my books no longer exist at all is simply shattering. . . Much worse that you remain for ever condemned to write in the very language which is spoken by those who are forbidden to read you . . . that for my generation it is already too late' (29 May 1940). The seeds of despair which led to his suicide had already been sown.

Shortly after returning from Paris, Zweig received an invitation to make a further lecture tour of Brazil. Despite his affection for the country, Zweig hesitated to accept, doing so only after weeks of characteristic indecision. He told Emil Ludwig that it was not the dangers of the sea journey which gave him pause for thought, but the feeling that he could not, as he had in the First World War, merely observe events from afar.[40] But as the prospect of invasion began to seem imminent, he became more and more alarmed: 'It's unthinkable! And yet I think of nothing else,' he confided to his diary on 10 June. By now he had made up his mind to accept the invitation from Brazil, and he spent much of the following week in London, attempting to arrange tickets and visas for the journey.

He had invited Desmond Flower and his wife to Bath for the following weekend to discuss the publication of *The Tide of Fortune*, the latest volume in the series *Sternstunden der Menschheit* ('Great Moments in Human History'). Events in France had moved quickly. The announcement of the fall of Paris threw Zweig into complete despair. Flower recalled that he seemed stunned by the news: 'I have never seen anyone so completely shattered, he was speechless, shrunk into himself, like a mummy.'[41] Zweig's diary confirms his despair, which surpassed anything he had felt even at the fate of Austria: 'Total depression.

France lost, ruined for centuries, this most endearing of all European countries. Who should one write for?' (17 June). The fall of France represented the disappearance of the Europe which was his spiritual home, for he clearly did not feel that England was part of that Europe. The situation in France also had a personal dimension. He waited anxiously for news of Friderike, who had established herself in Paris after the annexation of Austria.

The situation in Britain was increasingly tense: despite his naturalisation, Zweig felt 'a complete outsider' (June 17). As the rumours of imminent invasion spread, he became more and more apprehensive. He was now prepared for the worst: 'The Nazis will not catch me alive,' he wrote to Victor Fleischer.[42]

Zweig had by now completed arrangements for his trip to Brazil. Despite his fear of invasion, he was reluctant to travel, knowing that he was leaving behind his house, his books and his work. He certainly intended to return, writing in a farewell letter to Max Herrmann-Neiße that he would be back by the end of October or the beginning of November, since he neither wanted nor was able to stay in America.[43] At the beginning of July, Zweig and Lotte left Liverpool on the Cunard liner *Scythia*, bound for New York.

'QUIETLY AND INCONSPICUOUSLY'

For Max Herrmann-Neiße himself there was no such escape. He was doomed to live out his life 'in this London dark and under threat', as he had described it during the first Christmas of the war. London had learned to live with the blackout and had already suffered its first airraids; anti-aircraft defences disfigured Herrmann-Neiße's beloved Hyde Park. His poems during these last eighteen months of his life record the impact of wartime contingencies on a sensitive temperament. The outbreak of war had underlined the absolute finality of his exile:

War mir auch längst die Stätte schon verboten,
wo meine beste Lebenszeit verrann,
so ist sie mir erst jetzt ein Reich der Toten,
aus dem kein Hauch zu mir mehr kommen kann.

If I have long been excluded from the place / where my best years were spent, / It has now become a kingdom of the dead, / From which no breath of air can ever reach me.[44]

Though grateful for Sondheimer's continuing hospitality − where else could he and Leni have gone? − he still felt uneasy with his position as permanent guest:

Bitter ist es, das Brot der Fremde zu essen
bittrer noch das Gnadenbrot,
und dem nächsten eine Last zu sein.

It is bitter to eat the bread of exile / more bitter still to eat the bread of charity / and to be a burden to one's neighbour.[45]

The dispositions of wartime had only reinforced his personal isolation: 'I am now living an even more secluded life than before, I am still writing poetry, which seems to be my fate,' he wrote, in what proved to be his last letter to Paul Zech.[46] He saw even fewer of his fellow-exiles now that Zweig had left London for Bath, though the latter responded with unfeigned appreciation when Herrmann-Neiße sent him some of his recent poems:

I found your poems deeply moving. What a consolation you possess in being able to portray your immediate world stripped of all its meanness. Seldom have you written more beautiful verses. . . I consider them the purest document of our times I have seen up to now.[47]

He saw Herrmann-Neiße as a kindred spirit ('one of the very few people with whom I can speak now') and was anxious to reaffirm their friendship: 'How good it would be to have a frank conversation with you now. From the first, we have always understood each other in all crucial matters.'[48] In the same letter, he invited Herrmann-Neiße to stay in Bath, assuring him that 'a guest room will always be ready' − but in fact the two men were never to meet again.

Though he continued to write with his customary regularity, Herrmann-Neiße was forced to question the value of poetry, conscious of the apparent irrelevance of artistic creation at a time when Europe stood on the brink of mass destruction.

Ist es nicht eitel, jetzt noch nachzusinnen,
wie sich die Dinge gut beschreiben lassen,

Gedichte wieder kunstvoll zu beginnen,
in eine Form Unsagbares zu fassen,
wenn rings im schwersten Kampf, die Welten wanken . . .

*Is it not vain now to consider / how best things can be described, how poems
can be artistically begun, / how to find the form to grasp the unspeakable /
when all around in bitter struggle worlds are shaking.*[49]

Only with reservations could he justify the moral ambiguity of his
continuing concern with metre and rhyme. It was, in Brecht's telling
phrase, a 'bad time for poetry'. The world had stopped listening,
attuned to words on a different frequency.

London was already subjected to a night-time blackout, a city from
which most children had been evacuated. The parks and playgrounds,
which had echoed to the cries of children, were now 'as deserted as
Hamlin after the Pied Piper's revenge'.[50] The city lived in daily
anticipation of German airraids. Herrmann's nervous disposition made
him particularly apprehensive, aware of the irony that death might be
inflicted on him by his own compatriots:

Noch gestern konnte ich ruhig schlafen gehen
dem Weltenschlummer friedlich eingeschmiegt;
heut fürcht' ich mich, die Nacht zu überstehen,
durch die das mordende Geschwader fliegt.

*Even yesterday I could go to sleep / peacefully bedded in the slumber of the
world; / today I fear I may not survive the night / through which the
murdering squadron flies.*[51]

The new dispositions of war were so terrifyingly immediate as to render
past reality unreal – 'as if things past never really were' ('als sei Vergang-
enes nicht wahr gewesen'). In October, reflecting on his last visit to
Zurich a year earlier, he found that his memories now seemed
fantastical:

Heut ist das alles wie ein Traum gewesen.
Gefangen fühl' ich mich in fremdem Haus,
ein Friedlicher, der nicht hierher gehört.

*Today it all seems as though a dream. / I feel trapped in a strange house,
A man of peace who has no business here.*[52]

The images of imprisonment began to multiply in his poetry: he wished himself anywhere but London. He struggled to summon up hope for the New Year, but conceded that hope flew in the face of all logic: 'To begin the New Year full of hope / demands an almost foolish trust.'[53]

Among the few people he saw at this time was the British Germanist Jethro Bithell who, swimming courageously against the tide of public hostility to all things German, chose 1940 to compile an anthology of modern German poetry. Introduced to Herrmann-Neiße by Stefan Zweig, Bithell took a great liking to him, thanking 'this most beloved of London poets for all help out of the fullness of his knowledge of books and men'.[54] No fewer than eight of Herrmann-Neiße's poems were included in the anthology, though he did not live to see their eventual publication.

During these turbulent months Herrmann-Neiße could find consolation only in a nostalgic evocation of the past. He had transformed one corner of his tiny bedroom into a study, with a writing-desk and a shelf of books: familiar friends with whom he could continue the dialogue of his past life. During 1939–40 he worked regularly on a novel entitled *Unglückliche Liebe 1931* ('Unhappy Love 1931'), a depiction of a long-lost Berlin in which old friends like Heinrich Zille and Alfred Kerr appear, thinly disguised. He told his wife how much he enjoyed these excursions into the past, plundering his memory for many details of the narrative. He continued to work on the novel until his death, but it remained unfinished.

In one of his short poems, he evoked an elegiac picture of his native Neiße, retracing his steps through its streets in stanzas which lament a long-lost friendship of his youth. Although this friendship, apparently so permanent in its youthful intensity, had proved only transitory, it prompted strong feelings of nostalgia:

> Wenn eins vom andern Abschied nahm
> am Brunnen auf dem Rathausplatze,
> die Stadt lag still in ihrem Schlaf,
> nur eine herrenlose Katze
> mit mir sich auf dem Heimweg traf. . .
> obgleich ich heimlich längst erkannte
> was falsch an dieser Freundschaft war!

Heut' wünscht sich dennoch der Verbannte
zurück in jedes Jugendjahr. . .

When, each from the other we took our leave / at the fountain on the town
hall square / the town lay still in slumber, / and only a stray cat / kept me
company on the way home. . .
Although I have long secretly known / what was false in this friendship, /
the exile still wishes nonetheless / that he could return to every year of his
youth. . .[55]

As a 'C' category alien, Herrmann-Neiße was exempted from
personal restrictions, but such categories were swept away in the panic
caused by the invasion of Holland and the hysteria about a fifth column.
In early July, two plain-clothes policemen called at Bryanston Court to
take him away for internment. Their attitude softened perceptibly once
they saw the 'dangerous' poet. At the insistence of Sondheimer who,
Herrmann-Neiße said, 'spoke with angels' tongues', the two policemen
phoned the doctor who was treating the poet and after consultation
agreed to exempt him from the order on grounds of ill health.[56] Despite
this reprieve, Herrmann-Neiße was deeply hurt and embittered by the
experience, complaining that he had turned his back on Germany:

Um hier nun in der Freiheit Mutterlande,
in dem ich mich in Freundesland gemeint,
zu meiner und der ganzen Menschheit Schande
mißtrauisch gleichgesetzt zu sein dem Feind.

In order that in the motherland of freedom / where I thought I was in a
friendly country, / to my shame and that of all humanity / I am mistrust-
fully equated with the enemy.[57]

He also wrote an angry letter to the Home Office demanding to know
why he, 'the only firm and true, no Jewish, no communistic, anti-Hitler
poet of the German emigration' should be 'treated in such groundless
distrustfull (*sic*) and degrading manner'.[58]

The incident spurred him into perfunctory attempts to escape London: the draft of a letter to Thomas Mann, requesting the latter's help in
securing an emergency visa for the USA, is preserved among his papers,
though it is doubtful the letter was ever sent. Stefan Zweig attempted to
get Hermann Kesten to take up his case, but to no avail. German airraids

were now a daily occurrence, every meal, every night's sleep likely to be disrupted by 'the diabolical sound of the sirens'.[59]

In the last year of his life, his health deteriorated rapidly and he suffered from stomach pains which the doctor believed were 'partly caused by pressure on the abdomen owing to his stature'.[60] When the doctor finally prescribed a milk diet, Herrmann-Neiße commented to his wife that there were three things he had always vowed to avoid: living in England, living through another war and drinking milk. And now he was stranded in London, in wartime, condemned to a milk diet. It was really too much.

The premonition of death, an undertone in much of his earlier work, now became its dominant motif. Even at the start of the war, he had still been able to speculate whether he would be 'one of the few who would survive the great slaughter', but the effect of the blitz on his nervous disposition was to place him 'under the spell of death', feeling that every hour might be his last.[61] As life outside his room began to recede, death became the only certainty: 'Death alone is true, which lies in wait for me.'[62] Finally, in one of his last poems, he reproaches Leni and Sondheimer with failing to realise that he was dying:

Ihr merkt es nicht: es geht mit mir zu Ende;
halt ich mich aufrecht heut – wie lange noch?
Das Sterben steht an jeder Wegeswende
und findet den auch, der sich feig verkroch.

You don't notice: my end is drawing near; / even if I walk upright today – for how much longer? / Death waits at every turning of the way / and finds the coward in his hiding- place.[63]

He carried on writing regularly almost to the end, working every evening and night that was not disrupted by air raids. He would sit wrapped in his dressing-gown, his feet – which always felt cold – resting on a hot-water bottle. In daylight hours he would try to get some fresh air, often leaving the house in the aftermath of a raid to witness the destruction it had wrought. Fleeting impressions are woven into his verse. The sight of a mirror, still hanging on the only surviving wall of an otherwise ruined house, prompted his last poem, written on 18 March 1941 and ending, in pointed parody of the fairy story:

Spieglein, Spieglein an der Wand,
Wann kommt der Friede diesem Land?

Mirror, mirror on the wall, / when will peace come to one and all?[64]

During his last few months, Herrmann-Neiße worked stubbornly on a lyric cycle called 'Die Zwischenzeit' ('The Interval'), a title eloquently evoking the transitory nature of exile. He read extracts from the cycle to his wife, sitting up in bed to read 'in a beautiful, calm, clear voice', only two days before his death.[65] The cycle was still unfinished when he died from a heart attack on 8 April, six weeks short of his fifty-fifth birthday.

Max Herrmann-Neiße died as he had lived, 'quietly and inconspicuously',[66] but his death did not pass unnoticed in the German exile community. The bookseller Hans Preiss arranged a commemoration at which the critic Monty Jacobs gave the funeral oration and the actor Peter Ihle read some of the poet's final verses. Alfred Kerr wrote an epitaph, in which he called Herrmann-Neiße's London poems 'a lasting symbol, a monument to exile'.[67]

Herrmann-Neiße had written his own epitaph two years earlier, after a visit to a London cemetery, in lines which encapsulate the whole tragedy of exile:

In fremder Sprache schweigt mir jeder Stein,
und stürbe ich und würde hier begraben,
die Seele könnte keine Ruhe haben
und fühlte sich in Ewigkeit allein.

In a foreign language every stone is silent / and if I were to die and be buried here, / my soul would have no rest / and would feel alone for all eternity.[68]

He is buried in Marylebone cemetery, East Finchley.

'DOING THEIR BIT' – GERMAN WRITERS AT THE BBC

One of the most fascinating stories of German-speaking exile in Britain is the contribution made by German and Austrian exiles to the wartime propaganda output of the BBC. When war broke out, German-language broadcasting by the BBC was still in its infancy. The German

Service had been established almost by accident, its initial broadcast having been a hasty improvisation. The immediate pretext for it was a speech delivered by Neville Chamberlain at the height of the Sudeten crisis in September 1938, which the BBC was instructed to broadcast in German, French and Italian. Robert Lucas, then London correspondent of the Austrian newspaper *Neue Freie Presse*, received an unexpected phone call asking him to come into the studio in order to translate the speech. Lucas's account of the proceedings emphasises their chaotic, improvised nature. Inside the studio, he translated the speech as it was actually being made, working from the text which was coming through on the telex machine. His German version was broadcast from another studio by the artist Walter Goetz, who was then working as a cartoonist for the *Daily Express*. There were often long pauses, as Lucas waited for the telex machine to continue transmission.[69]

Daily broadcasts in German were continued for the duration of the Sudeten crisis, creating a de facto German Service, of which Lucas and the former lawyer Carl Brinitzer became the first members. In April 1939 the German Service was inaugurated as a permanent section of the BBC's foreign language broadcasting, transmitting some five hours a week, its programme consisting of news bulletins supplemented by special reports.

This pattern survived the outbreak of war, remaining virtually unchanged until the autumn of 1940, when it was decided to increase German-language broadcasting in order to counter the Germans' intensive propaganda output. Hugh Carleton Greene (younger brother of Graham Greene), who had been the *Daily Telegraph* Berlin correspondent from 1934 to 1939 and went on to become Director-General of the BBC, was named Head of the German Service. He began a period of reorganisation and expansion. One significant development was the emergence of the feature programme, which soon became a major constitutive element of German programming. Features consisted of regular or occasional series, intended to provide colour and variety to the staple diet of news bulletins and commentary. At the end of 1940 a small editorial group was formed with responsibility for producing feature programmes. The Head of the new department was the film

actor and director Walter Rilla and among the initial team of collab-
orators were Robert Lucas, and Julius Gellner, once the artistic director
of the famous Kammerspiele in Munich and later of the German
Theatre in Prague. It was this team which Karl Otten joined early in
1941.

'MARCHING ON': KARL OTTEN AS SCRIPTWRITER

In December 1940 Otten had applied to Lindley Fraser, Head of BBC
Foreign Broadcasts, and was subsequently employed as a programme
assistant in the German Features Department, initially for two months,
though his contract was later extended to the end of the year.[70] His
appointment may have been recommended by Walter Rilla whom he
had known since 1919, when he had contributed articles to the Expressionist periodical *Die Erde*, which Rilla had edited in Breslau. Like
Otten, Rilla was a practised survivor. A prominent actor and film
director in the Weimar Republic, he had left Germany in 1936, partly
on account of his Jewish wife, and settled in London. Despite roles in
films such as *Victoria the Great* (1937), in which he played Prince Ernst
to Anton Walbrook's Prince Albert, he had always struggled with language difficulties as an actor, gradually turning to writing and directing.
At the time of his appointment as Head of Features at the German
Service in 1940, he was the only German to hold a post of responsibility
in the BBC. He would produce many of the features which Otten wrote
for the Corporation. Otten had only limited experience of writing for
radio, but he quickly proved to be a prolific and versatile scriptwriter.
His unpublished papers contain some 180 radio scripts written between
1941 and 1946, though the actual total he wrote is probably even
higher.[71]

London was then experiencing the rigours of the blitz, with the BBC
a major target. Broadcasting House had been hit by a bomb in October
1940, forcing the relocation of various services, and the new German
Features Department had found a temporary home in Bedford College
in Regent's Park. The department's first production was a weekly series
called 'Vormarsch der Freiheit' ('Advance of Freedom'), designed to

report facts and war stories from the battle-fronts. The programme was first transmitted on 9 November 1940 and thereafter broadcast regularly. In his amusing account of these hectic and sometimes chaotic early days, Robert Lucas remembered that the title of the series was something of an anachronism, 'as there was more *Rückmarsch* at the time than *Vormarsch*', the news consisting almost entirely of Nazi victories.[72] After joining the Features Department, Otten became one of its most prolific contributors. His first programme, a fifteen-minute feature, 'Zum Tage der Machtergreifung', commenting on the anniversary of Hitler's seizure of power, was broadcast on 30 January 1941. Thereafter he wrote some twenty features for 'Vormarsch der Freiheit' (only half of which seem to have been broadcast), as well as almost eighty other scripts.

Among the most interesting and remarkable of these are the satirical sketches and song lyrics which were incorporated into the cabaret programme 'Stacheldraht' ('Barbed Wire'). Though explicitly drawing on the German cabaret tradition exemplified by Wedekind, Tucholsky, Mehring and others, Otten's lyrics were consciously adapted to wartime propaganda purposes. Some were an incitement to resistance, such as the 'Song vom Dreh' ('Song of the Lathe'):

Wenn ich an diesem Knoppe drehen tu
Oder 'ne Handvoll Sand in det Jetriebe schmeisse
Steht die janze Scheisse
Dann hat die liebe Seele Ruh –
Mir machste keen X vor'n U
Hitler Adolf Du Oberammergauner,
Mir nich!

If I just turn this knob / Or chuck some sand in the drive / The whole bloody lot stops. / Then my soul can rest in peace – / You can't fool me / Hitler Adolf, you crook from Oberammergau, / Not me.[73]

Other texts clearly aimed at undermining German morale, such as the 'Deutsches Fliegerlied' ('German Airman's Song'):

Wir fliegen England entgegen
Gespenstisch leuchtet die Nacht
Wir fliegen dem Tode entgegen
Die Jäger halten Wacht.

Viel Tausend deutsche Piloten,
Sie stürzen zum Ozean,
O England, das wir bedrohten,
Du bist unser Massengrab.

We fly towards England / The night is ghostly bright. / We fly towards death / The fighters lie in wait.
Many thousand German pilots / Crash into the sea, / O England which we threatened / You are our mass grave.

This text, set to music by Mischa Spoliansky and sung by Walter Rilla, was one of three recorded by the BBC in June 1941 and probably broadcast about the same time.[74]

Shortly after Otten's arrival, there was another new recruit to the Features Department, the young Austrian Martin Esslin, who had previously been working for the Monitoring Service in Evesham. Esslin, who was to rise to become the BBC's Head of Radio Drama, was then only twenty-two and very much the junior member of the department. He still remembers Otten's personal kindness towards him:

Otten was extremely kind to me. He was a man of great charm. The difficulty he had came from the fact that his eyesight was going and he tended to approach our English bosses too closely, peering at them from a few inches away; he also (often justifiedly) showed some contempt of the knowledge of Germany and German conditions and culture some of them displayed. And that did not make him too popular.[75]

Esslin's comments confirm that Otten was not always an easy person to work with; a man of wide knowledge and strong convictions, he sometimes lacked tact, failing to suffer fools gladly.

In fact, Otten's work with the German Service lasted less than a year, his contract being terminated at the end of 1941. During 1940 the BBC had lost its fragile independence, coming increasingly under the control of the Foreign Office which began to determine the tenor of broadcasting. In particular, broadcasting to enemy countries was subject to the control of the Foreign Office's Political Intelligence Department, led by the former Oxford don Richard Crossman. Like the rest of the BBC, the German Service received a weekly political directive which Crossman would elaborate in regular meetings. The Features Department also received a daily digest of the German press to be used as a basis for counter-propaganda. During the summer of 1941 there was a dramatic shift in policy, resulting in a much tougher propaganda line. Crossman was critical of the output of the German Service, including the Features Department. In a thorough reorganisation of the department, Walter Rilla was removed as Head of Features and replaced by the English actor Marius Goring. Karl Otten, one of Rilla's appointees, was also a victim of these sweeping changes, his contract being terminated at the end of 1941.

Otten's dismissal actually worked in his favour: following the termination of his contract, he was immediately re-engaged by the BBC as an outside writer. As a programme assistant he had received a fixed salary of £640 per annum, but freelance work was better paid and his numerous contributions ensured that for the first time since their arrival in Britain he and Ellen found themselves comfortably off.

In January 1942, the BBC broadcast a feature programme called 'Czechoslovakia Protected', which was written by Otten: the first of many English-language scripts he was to write for the BBC. He was commissioned to write the programme, apparently on the recommendation of Walter Rilla. He made the most of the opportunity. The programme producer, John Glyn-Jones, a mainstay of BBC feature programmes, was evidently impressed with Otten's work. Shortly after, in March, he invited Otten to join the team writing the new weekly series 'Marching On', which became one of the BBC's most popular and successful programmes. First broadcast on 30 April 1942, 'Marching On' was based on the American newsreel programme 'The March of Time', reconstructing the week's most newsworthy events in dramatic form. Broadcast on Thursday evenings, the programme took half a dozen items from the week's news and turned them into 'tense little dramas', using dialogue, sound effects and incidental music, which were underscored by brief editorial commentary. 'The whole thing is an intelligent and discerning use of sound and voice to achieve an impression no less vivid than the one the cinema gets with the extra aid of image.'[76] Such was the popularity of the programme that its running time was eventually extended from thirty minutes to a full hour. Otten was one of a team of writers, which included the journalists Gordon

Boshell, Donald Stokes and the Australian news commentator Colin Wills, working under the direction of the Programme Editor Robert Barr, and producer John Glyn-Jones. Otten himself records that he contributed thirty-five items to the series in a period of eight months – a rate of roughly one a week.[77] Scriptwriting for news and feature programmes required rapidity of conception, as well as the ability to write under pressure, and often to order, qualities which Otten evidently possessed in ample measure. After the fitful progress of his career since 1933, he had clearly once more found his *métier*.

While the sheer quantity of work Otten produced for the BBC confirms that he was a prolific scriptwriter, the wide range of programmes for which he wrote indicates that he was also a versatile one. While writing regularly for 'Marching On', he was also contributing to other well-known series such as 'Europe in Chains' and 'It Might Happen Here'. The latter series consisted of dramatised accounts of Nazi war crimes in the occupied countries, transposing the events, for dramatic effect, into a British context. This device was not original, having already been used by Douglas Brown and Christopher Serpell in their book *If Hitler Comes*, but it quickly became an effective means of mass propaganda.[78] Among Otten's credits was the opening programme of the series, 'The Miners', broadcast on 3 May 1942, which translated the repression of Belgian miners under Nazi occupation to a coalfield in South Wales, ending with the warning which was repeated after every programme: 'It can, will happen here . . . if we allow the Germans to win this war.' Otten's script was highly praised by reviewers, including Tom Harrisson.[79] The series was broadcast regularly at peak listening hours, being widely regarded as evidence of a new policy by the BBC to 'get tough' with the enemy.

The obvious element of propaganda was even more direct in 'The Black Gallery', a series of weekly broadcasts featuring portraits of Nazi leaders, to which Otten contributed a script on Hermann Goering ('General Field Marshal: Bully, Buffoon and Big Business Man'). Among other writers who contributed to the series were Arthur Koestler and the poet Louis MacNiece, all the programmes being produced by Walter Rilla, who had previously produced Otten's features for the German Service. Otten also contributed to other series such as 'Fighters for France and Freedom', or 'They Shall Rise Again', a series devoted to major cities under Nazi rule. It is notable that virtually all these features were broadcast, not in the German Service, but in the BBC's two main channels, the Home Service and the Forces Programme. Indeed, while the frequency and variety of Otten's contributions is remarkable, it is even more remarkable that, after the end of 1941, most of them were written in English, a language he had scarcely spoken five years earlier.

In autumn 1942, at the height of his involvement with 'Marching On', Otten was invited by the Ministry of Information to prepare a film treatment portraying the contribution made by refugees to the British war effort.[80] He spent many weeks devising an extended scenario, even contacting various refugees working in British factories, who were to appear in the film. The surviving synopsis begins with the wholesale arrest of refugees for internment, continues with a series of montages showing refugees in the Pioneer Corps or working in armaments factories, and culminates with scenes from a factory producing tanks for Russia. The film was evidently intended also for distribution in Russia, but eventually fell victim to the changing priorities of wartime propaganda, being abandoned early in 1943.[81]

By this time Otten had found a new focus for his scriptwriting talents, starting work for the BBC's London Transcription Service, which sent out recordings to overseas broadcasters for transmission from local stations and was regarded as an important part of the BBC's propaganda output. Between August 1943 and January 1945 he contributed numerous scripts to the Near East Section of the Transcription Service. During these eighteen months he wrote, according to his own estimates, a total of sixty-four talks on European countries, the British Empire and the Far East, all of which were broadcast in Arabic by Station Teheran. During the last winter of the war Otten became blind, a handicap which virtually ended his association with the BBC: the last scripts he contributed, broadcast in the European Service in spring 1945, were written in collaboration with Walter Rilla.

'SERVING THE CAUSE': ALFRED KERR AND THE BBC

In the first four years of his exile in London, Kerr had enjoyed little success. With the outbreak of war, he was anxious to 'do his bit', feeling that there was at last a worthwhile outlet for his talents. In October 1940, he made the first of several approaches to the BBC, submitting a radio play called *The Judgement on Nazis*.[82] The play was considered unsuitable for broadcasting, but while returning the script to Kerr, Duckworth Barker of European Services also wrote that he had noted his name for a future broadcasting test as an announcer.[83] There is however no record of any such test and it seems unlikely that one ever took place. Unlike speakers on the French Service, prominent Germans, such as Kerr, were not allowed to appear on air as themselves. From the start of its broadcasts to Germany, the BBC policy had been not to use identified exile speakers, presumably in order not to compromise the credibility essential to a propaganda broadcast. Commentaries were always delivered by a native English speaker.[84]

However, Kerr had not been entirely forgotten. With the decision at the end of 1940 to expand the BBC German Service to counter the Germans' intensive propaganda output, Walter Rilla, the new head of Features, wrote asking Kerr to meet him in order to discuss 'certain questions of our German programme which I think will interest you'.[85] There is no record of what was discussed at this meeting, but Kerr wrote shortly after to propose a daily series of short commentaries on the news. 'I'd like to give a daily, purely satirical, compressed commentary, lasting two minutes, on the news events of that morning. Mainly humorous, but also propagandistic. To some extent telegraphic. (Much as I used to illuminate topical events in Berlin.)'[86]

Kerr clearly hoped to recreate the 'Tagesglossen' for which he had once been well known on Radio Berlin. Rilla's reply hints at the constraints of wartime broadcasting and particularly the limited role assigned to German staff. Kerr's suggestion, he wrote, was not possible, because of a corporation directive that news broadcasts could only be made by British-born members of staff.[87]

The surviving correspondence in the BBC Written Archives makes it possible to document some of Kerr's early contributions to the

German Service, consisting of satirical songs with political comment. They were submitted through Rilla, who also produced them. While the correspondence confirms that several songs were recorded and broadcast, neither the recordings nor the original manuscripts have survived. This is particularly regrettable in the case of the 'Ballad of Belgrade' ('Ballade von Belgrade') for which Kerr not only wrote both words and music but which he also sang. Rilla remembered that the song was a great success, being broadcast several times on the German Service.[88]

Few of Kerr's efforts were so successful, indeed his correspondence with Rilla reveals his evident frustration at the slow progress of his collaboration with the German Service. He complained bitterly that many of the items he submitted were not used: 'Today is the 1st of March. My so-called collaboration began in January. The four contributions I sent you since January (with today's it's five) have neither been broadcast nor discussed.'[89] He was particularly upset that consideration of some items was delayed until they were no longer topical: it could not, he complained on one occasion, take so long to rehearse and record a short song.[90]

Kerr's frustration during these months frequently breaks surface. While he continued to submit proposals to Rilla, they were now accompanied by injunctions not to delay. 'These verses are quite topical. If the situation changes, they've once again been written for nothing.'[91] Rilla had his own problems, pointing out that many programming decisions were subject to propaganda directives and therefore largely outside his control. While prepared to acknowledge Rilla's difficulties, Kerr could not escape the feeling of 'storming a fortress', adding that he would be glad if Rilla 'were more inclined to lower the drawbridge'.[92] Kerr remained determined to rise above his own feelings of frustration:

> If this war of nerves continues, England's splendid endurance (on a far bigger stage) will be my model. I know that I can serve the cause – and that it's a waste of resources not to use capable helpers.[93]

It is a tribute to his determination that he continued to submit items.

The reasons for the rejection of Kerr's material were both technical and political. For example, a parody of the Horst Wessel song, which

Rilla had particularly liked, was rejected on the grounds that· the problems of reception made it likely that clandestine listeners would hear the tune rather than Kerr's new lyrics.[94] Other items fell foul of political propaganda directives.

His 'Rudolf-Hess-Lied', written after the latter's flight to Scotland, was not used following a BBC directive to programme producers 'to stick strictly to facts and straight news' in reporting the incident.[95] However, it has also been suggested that Kerr was the victim of personal animosities.[96] In over thirty years as an influential theatre critic, with strong opinions, he had made a number of enemies, notable amongst them being the critic and satirist Karl Kraus, with whom Kerr had conducted a notorious feud during the twenties. Kraus had died in 1934, but among those who had found employment in the German Service was his friend and literary executor Heinrich Fischer, whose unyielding hostility to Kerr is alleged to have influenced other members of the German Service to reject much of the material he submitted. While it may seem astonishing that the personal and professional animosities of German writers in the twenties should be pursued so vehemently two decades later in wartime London, and in such a quintessentially British institution as the BBC, it is unfortunately only one example of the factional infighting amongst German exiles.

Kerr's correspondence with Rilla reveals evident tensions between the two men, but it seems likely that Rilla was something of a sponsor, able to mitigate much of the hostility to Kerr within the German Service. Significantly, Kerr's contributions to the German Service ended abruptly when Rilla was replaced as Head of Features by Marius Goring at the end of 1941.

This was not however the end of Kerr's work for the BBC. 'I am now working mostly in the European Department,' he wrote some months later to Leonard Miall, Talks Editor of the German Service, to whom he sent a proposal for a short dramatic feature.[97] Apparently through Rilla's mediation Kerr had been invited by Gibson Parker, Head of the European Service, to write a number of short talks. What Kerr proposed was a series of five-minute features, consisting of biographical sketches of famous Austrians and Germans, all of whom he knew personally and all of whom were now in exile – Heinrich and Thomas Mann, Bruno

Walter, Albert Einstein, Marlene Dietrich, Max Reinhardt, Stefan Zweig, and his own former editor at the *Berliner Tageblatt*, Theodor Wolff. These features, which Kerr actually wrote in French, were broadcast in 1942 in the Spanish programme of the European Service.

French was also the language in which Kerr wrote a series of features, mainly during the last year of the war, which were broadcast by the Latin American Service of the BBC. It is one of the many ironies of exile that a distinguished German theatre critic should contribute to British war propaganda by writing talks in French to be translated into Spanish for transmission to Latin America. Kerr himself was not unaware of the intrinsic absurdity of the situation, writing laconically to George Bernard Shaw that nobody had wanted to publish any of his manuscripts: 'Only the BBC asked me to write many broadcasts . . . which I wrote in French.'[98]

According to Kerr's own records, some twenty-six of his talks were broadcast by the Latin-American Service, each lasting about fifteen minutes. An internal BBC memo gives an indication of how the talks were planned and devised: 'Dr Kerr has been in the habit of coming to see me from time to time with subjects for talks for my approval. He then writes the talks selected and sends them on. We build them in as we may.'[99] The talks covered a variety of cultural and historical questions, ranging from 'Hitler is not the "product of Versailles"' to 'Dualism in the German Mind' and 'How to deal with German artists who supported Hitler'. While the earliest of these programmes date from 1942–43, most of them were transmitted in quick succession during the last year of the war. Kerr received a standard fee of £10 for each of these broadcasts, thus securing a relatively regular income for the first and indeed the only time in his thirteen years in London. However, even this modest success was short-lived, falling victim to the changed priorities of broadcasting in peacetime. The Head of the Latin American Service wrote to Kerr in June 1945: 'Unfortunately some of the scripts you sent in round about VE-Day are now unsuitable for our programmes and there is a growing feeling at the moment that German subjects should not be overdone.' Kerr's own records confirm that his last talk was broadcast in November 1945; his offer to contribute further material to the Latin-American Service was never taken up.[100]

Part Five

No Man's Land

1941–1945

WRITERS WITHOUT LANGUAGE

War and internment helped to focus the minds of exiles ever more clearly on the existential question confronting them: whether to try to maintain their German identity or to assimilate as best they could to their host society. For literary exiles this question was intimately concerned with the very language in which they wrote.

Many writers undoubtedly still considered themselves the custodians of a literary tradition which had been disrupted, but as the opportunities for German-language publishing shrank and finally vanished with the advance of Nazism across Europe, even authors of international reputation, such as Thomas Mann and Lion Feuchtwanger or Stefan Zweig were effectively reduced to writing for the translator. Their reputation enabled them to continue writing in German and even to deal with Austro-German themes. Less famous authors were not so fortunate, being progressively forced to adapt the theme and content of their work to the conventions and requirements of their host country, and even, in some cases, to take the final step of writing in the language of that country.

In September 1941, the International PEN held its Congress in wartime London. This, the Seventeenth International Congress, was probably the most remarkable ever held, bringing together representatives of some thirty-five countries. The decision to hold the conference in London had been made in the early part of the summer, when there were still frequent and heavy airraids on the city; the PEN Secretary Hermon Ould described the decision to hold the Congress at all as 'an act of faith'. The Congress, held in the building of the French Institute, lasted four days, taking as its main theme the future of literature after the war. Those taking part included such literary notables as E. M. Forster, J. B. Priestley and Rebecca West from Britain, and John dos Passos and Thornton Wilder from the United States. Many of the delegates were refugees, whom the tide of war had washed up in London, including the Catholic philosopher Jacques Maritain, representing France, the playwright Frantisek Langer for Czechoslovakia, and Alfred Kerr for Germany. It was very much in their name that the young novelist Peter de Mendelssohn gave a paper entitled 'Writers Without Language', which became one of the talking-points of the Congress.[1]

De Mendelssohn argued that there were two distinct kinds of creative writer, one whose main concern was with subject-matter, for whom 'the thing they want to say is of more immediate importance than the manner in which they say it' – and the other for whom 'the art of saying the thing is of more importance than the actual thing itself'. In each case, he argued, the relationship of form and content, and hence the function of language itself, was quite different. As examples of these respective categories, he cited J. B. Priestley and Virginia Woolf. For the former, language was concrete and denotative, a means of exposition and argument, for the latter, it was evocative and connotative, a means of conveying the finer nuances of mood and sensibility. If they had been driven into exile, he argued, they would have reacted in completely different ways. Priestley would not have hesitated to learn a new language as the necessary medium of communication with a new public. Woolf would have retreated into herself to preserve her native language from the interference of an alien culture. The former would have adapted language and subject-matter to his new circumstances, the latter would simply have continued writing as before.

His argument might equally have been applied to his two Austrian contemporaries, Robert Neumann and Stefan Zweig. The latter, who had found a last refuge in Brazil, was then writing the final draft of his 'autobiography' *The World of Yesterday*, the true subject of which was the lost world which had nurtured him. Neumann, who was among those listening to Peter de Mendelssohn's paper, had become increasingly preoccupied with the contemporary Jewish diaspora as a paradigm of persecution and exile. Zweig had sought a final refuge in the German language which he had long regarded as his 'only true homeland'; Neumann was just completing his first novel in English.

DEATH OF A EUROPEAN

Sailing from England in 1940, Stefan Zweig had left behind books, papers and work in progress, including – perhaps as an earnest of his intention to return – the already half-completed manuscript of his study of Balzac. All his early letters from the New World stressed his intention to return to Britain. Thus he told Thomas Mann that he was 'actually determined to return to England, unless Mosley becomes dictator there',[2] writing a few weeks later to Desmond Flower: 'I am longing to be back in England and to write my books.'[3]

He and Lotte had disembarked in New York, where they stayed for four weeks. There he learned, to his relief, that Friderike, together with her two daughters, had succeeded in escaping from Paris to the un-occupied zone of France. Three months later they were to arrive in New York, but by then Zweig had long since left for Brazil. Though his reception in Rio was more muted than on his previous visit four years earlier, his enthusiasm for the country was undiminished. After a short time in Rio, he set off on extended lecture tours which took in not only Brazil but also Argentina and Uruguay. He apparently hoped to return to England at the end of the tour, but was forced to acknowledge that U-Boat attacks on British shipping convoys made it unwise, indeed unsafe to travel. In the circumstances, he undertook a further tour of Brazil, giving lectures in the north of the country.

Throughout his life, Zweig had been a regular, almost compulsive correspondent, and despite the difficulties of wartime communication, he continued to write to old friends still in Britain, such as Felix Braun, Fleischer or Friedenthal, as well as Alfredo Cahn, his Argentinian translator – and Friderike, with whom he had been able to re-establish contact in New York.

Frustrated by his enforced separation from Europe, Zweig abandoned himself to deep pessimism. He wrote to Friderike that he did not believe he would ever again return to Europe – 'and everything I have there, my books and above all my Balzac (three quarters of which is written and prepared) is lost.'[4] The fear that his house and possessions – particularly the Balzac manuscript – were lost, continued to haunt him, heightened by the news that autumn that the entire warehouse stock of the volume *Tide of Fortune* had been lost when Cassells' London warehouse had suffered a direct hit in a German bombing raid. If he had once been fond of quoting Rilke's aphorism 'Survival is everything', he now felt obliged to qualify even that. 'Survival could be everything,' he wrote to Paul Zech, adding ominously, 'but will one summon up the patience for it?'[5]

In January 1941 he finally returned to New York. He wrote to Victor Fleischer that he intended to return to England but was still unable to do so because no passage was to be had for weeks or months ahead.[6] He had been apprehensive of returning to New York, imploring Friderike to tell no one of his impending arrival, fearing the demands that would be made on his time: he knew at least three hundred people in New York, all of whom would be mortally offended if he did not visit them. Characteristically, he did not even tell Friderike when he was arriving: during a chance visit to the British Consulate, she was astonished suddenly to see him waiting for the lift she was just leaving.

Unable to tolerate the empty bustle of New York, he rapidly moved on to New Haven, where he hoped to find materials in the Yale University Library for a short study on Amerigo Vespucci. During the next six months he threw himself into his work. In a period of intense creative activity, he completed his homage to Brazil: *Brasilien – Land der Zukunft* (*Brazil. Land of the Future*), his study of Vespucci, and also the greater part of his autobiography, *The World of Yesterday*. During the summer months he moved to Ossining, a small town on the Hudson, renting a villa close to Friderike's temporary home, so that he could consult her on various details of the autobiography. He had worked intermittently on the book for two years, but he now began to write feverishly, writing nine hours a day, as though working towards some private deadline. By August he had finished the first draft, but the effort had left him physically and mentally exhausted, prompting the sombre reflection that the book might perhaps be his last. He felt that his life had been curtailed by the war: 'We with our sixty years will be too old for the new world to come', he wrote to Victor Fleischer, adding: 'I live in the past.'[7] Working intensively on his memoirs, he was indeed reinhabiting the world of yesterday, the only world in which he now felt remotely happy.

As so often after the completion of a major work, Zweig relapsed once more into depression. In a letter to his old friend Felix Braun, he wrote that his book on Brazil was about to be published, adding:

> But nothing can satisfy or relieve me – I am so frightfully depressed by the present as well as by the future and feel superfluous – what is a writer without its (*sic*) own language, without a country, without its past, without its future? . . . I feel very alone in this 'new world' and if there would be a possibility I would return to Bath where my Balzac work waits for me, where my books are and all my personal manuscripts.[8]

In reality, he had now abandoned any such hope. On 15 August he and Lotte sailed once more for Brazil, returning to the 'land of the future', in which they were to spend their remaining months. He had always felt out of his element in America and initially he was happy to be back in Brazil. He hoped that the mild climate would alleviate Lotte's asthma, which was increasingly troublesome, and that the restful atmosphere would help him to rediscover his inner calm. He wrote to Friderike:

> On the whole, I cannot praise highly enough my decision to leave America. Here you live closer to yourself and in the midst of nature, you hear nothing about politics, and however egotistical that may be, it is self-preservation in the physical and spiritual sense.[9]

His initial concern was simply with survival. He was grateful for the seclusion from the problems of Europe: 'The news from France reminds you that eating and sleeping peacefully are now astonishing achievements.' Brazil, he said, would be a veritable paradise, if only he had access to a first-class library.[10]

Shortly after, he and Lotte took a house on the outskirts of Petropolis, a summer health resort some thirty miles from Rio. The house itself was a bungalow, consisting of living-room, kitchen and two small bedrooms. Here Zweig sought, and seemed briefly to find 'the trace of a settled existence'.[11] Since leaving England he and Lotte had led an increasingly nomadic life, living in a succession of hotel rooms, hardly able to unpack their cases. Successive lecture tours had left him feeling exhausted with the constant change of climate, culture and language. (In Argentina he had lectured not only in German and English but also in Spanish, a task he had accomplished only by taking lessons in the language.)

In his new surroundings, Zweig's spirits seemed to lift, soothed by the beauties of the landscape. Petropolis, set in idyllic mountain scenery, might almost have been translated from his native Austria:

> At this time of year it is cool and wonderfully deserted, like Ischl in
> October. . . If I succeed in forgetting Europe, in considering all my
> possessions – house, books – as lost, in remaining indifferent to 'fame'
> and success, and merely being thankful to live in a divine landscape,
> while Europe is devastated by famine and misery, I shall be content.[12]

Before long, he had begun to sink back into depression. His letters to Friderike, now more than ever the confidante of his private thoughts, chart the long downward curve of his last six months, revealing the recurrent obsessions which were ultimately to drive him to suicide: his preoccupation with old age, his feelings of rootlessness, of estrangement from his own language and culture and his conviction that the war had scarcely yet begun.

> We are still only at the start or in the middle of this war. . . I feel hamp-
> ered in my work in every sense. What can old age bring that is any good?
> I am already very despondent. . . If only I could start a large-scale new
> work, things would be much better, but the lack of reference material
> stands in the way of any such work.

He had begun to read Montaigne, whom he perceived as another (better) Erasmus and was attracted by the idea of writing a biography: 'but there is next to nothing about him here'. He talked of surviving the war, but complained that even then it would be 'two, three or four years before I can settle anywhere, and then the material guarantees have gone. I think this war will destroy everything the previous generation had built up.'[13]

For the moment, he could still turn to his work, which had always been his last refuge. Seated on the large veranda at the back of the bungalow, a feature which had first made him decide to take the house, he carried out the final revisions to *The World of Yesterday*, despatching the manuscript to his publisher Bermann Fischer in New York in November.

He was increasingly uncertain of his command of German which – for all his aspirations to be a 'European' – remained the language in which he thought and wrote. During the autumn he had begun to read widely, reimmersing himself in the German idiom. 'Continually speaking in foreign languages secretly tires the brain,' he confided to Felix Braun, 'I am constantly afraid of forgetting my own language.'[14]

In fact, he now felt increasingly rootless, robbed of his German reading public and unable to adjust to any other. 'I still write on, but without the old pleasure in my work. I feel even as I write that I no longer have the proper readership, as I always used to. And occasionally I become a bit slipshod, because I am writing for the translator,' he wrote to Richard Friedenthal, writing in English to comply with the requirements of British censorship.[15] Reverting to German in a letter written on the same day to Alfredo Cahn, he expressed himself more vividly, confessing that he could no longer identify with the individual shown in his passport. He felt neither fish nor fowl, a German writer without books, an Englishman who was not really English. 'It is not only plants and teeth which cannot survive without roots, human beings are no different.'[16]

However, even his feelings towards his native language were ambivalent: in the same letter, he called himself 'a Coriolanus who hates the country in whose language he writes and expresses himself'. German had become the language of the oppressor. 'What a curse to have to read, think, write in that very language,' he wrote to Victor Wittkowski, a young writer whom he had befriended in Rio, adding: 'Unfortunately, I shall never be able to master a foreign language completely, that is for literary purposes – least of all Portuguese.'[17] Estranged from his mother tongue, Zweig seemed to see little future for himself, complaining that he would never see Europe again.

In November he finally finished the revision of his autobiography. Completed just before his sixtieth birthday, *The World of Yesterday* is perhaps Zweig's most characteristic book. Critics have long recognised that it is not an autobiography in the conventional sense, but the evocation of a vanished world. He had been forced to write the book without access to the personal papers and correspondence which he had left behind in Bath, but – in keeping with his natural reserve – he had always intended to portray not himself, but the era through which he had lived. At one time he had wanted to call the book *My Three Lives*, because he felt that he had lived through three different periods, separated by the historical turning-points of 1914 and 1933.

The World of Yesterday has little value as a biographical source, containing only the most general allusions to Zweig's personal life. He rarely dwells on his own thoughts and feelings, says little or nothing about his personal relationships and makes no real comment on his own literary works. What comes vibrantly to life, giving *The World of Yesterday* its charm and originality, is the atmosphere of a vanished epoch, particularly that of *fin-de-siècle* Vienna and Europe in the years preceding the First World War. The names occurring in the narrative are those of individuals he had met, like Theodor Herzl, Sigmund Freud or Frans Masereel, who had helped to shape the world he sought to evoke. On the other hand, lifelong friends like Victor Fleischer or Felix Braun do not appear. Even more astonishingly, Friderike is nowhere mentioned and the uninformed reader would be completely unaware that Zweig's first marriage had ever taken place. Lotte fares no better, for though there is a reference to their marriage, she remains anonymous. *The World of Yesterday* ends abruptly in 1939 with the outbreak of war, an event signifying the end of the Europe which Zweig had loved and lived for – and which is the only real subject of the book. The volume is subtitled 'Erinnerungen eines Europäers' ('Memories of a European'). *The World of Yesterday* would have made a fitting climax to Zweig's career, but he was in fact to write one more book, the short novel *Schachnovelle* (*The Royal Game*), which shows him still at the height of his creative powers. The finished manuscript, neatly typed by Lotte, reached his American publisher Ben Huebsch after its author was already dead.

Zweig was increasingly obsessed with the thought of growing old. As his sixtieth birthday approached, he wrote to Friderike imploring her not to remind anyone of the event, subsequently writing that he had 'happily survived the dismal day'.[18]

His depression was becoming more acute, affecting him so badly that he found it impossible to concentrate. He was deeply disturbed by the attack on Pearl Harbour and America's enforced entry into the war. From then on, he wrote all his letters to Friderike in English, a step which he apparently thought wartime regulations made necessary but which merely underlined his lack of ease in the language and the anomaly of his own situation.

Life continues in a quiet and monotonous way, reading, writing, walking, without interruptions by concerts, theatre and society. . . We have to be prepared that this war will be a very long and exhausting one. For me it becomes more and more sure that I will never see my house again and will remain everywhere but a travelling guest; happy those who could begin a new life where ever. I'm depressed by the prospect that the real decision and the final victory will not come this year.[19]

The following month he and Lotte visited the annual carnival in Rio, a spectacle whose colour and vivacity would once have enchanted him: 'But my mind is far away from festivities and more distressed than ever. There will be never return to all bygone things (*sic*). . . I am continuing my work but with a quarter of my strength; it is more continuing an old habit than really creating.'[20]

Four days later he and Lotte committed suicide by taking an overdose of the sedative veronal. It was a conscious step, meticulously prepared, the reasons elaborated in a handwritten note he left behind: he loved 'this wonderful land of Brazil', and would have liked to make a new start there, 'but after one's sixtieth year unusual powers are needed in order to make another wholly new beginning'. In a farewell letter to Friderike, he wrote of the lack of the books he needed, of the impossibility of finishing his 'central work, the Balzac', and of his conviction that the war had not yet reached its climax, concluding: 'I was too tired for all that.'[21]

There was widespread shock in the literary world at the suicide of an author who enjoyed both literary success and material security. His compatriot Franz Werfel was one of many who paid tribute to Zweig's gentle humanism, but in the exile community there were also more critical voices. Emil Ludwig found his action 'inconceivable'; Thomas Mann called it tantamount to desertion, an action which could only

succour the enemy. Close friends like Felix Braun struck a more personal note, regretting that he should 'throw his life away without
thinking what this life meant to us'.[22]

In truth, Zweig had always lived a self-centred life, subordinating
everything to his own artistic needs. It was his artistic persona which
had suffered from the corrosive effect of exile: the successive loss of his
country, his language, and the cultural environment in which he had
flourished. 'Old trees wither when they are transplanted,' he had once
confided to Max Herrmann-Neiße.[23] His will to live had finally been
undermined by the realisation that he was too old to adjust to a new
homeland – or ever to regain his former one. Above all, he was stricken
by the virtual loss of an audience in his native language. At a memorial
service in London later that year, Robert Neumann recounted that
Zweig had written to him only days before his suicide, lamenting that he
had 'no other language to write' but German, 'which makes me feel
useless'.[24] Neumann's reference was no mere chance. He, by contrast,
was in the throes of reinventing himself as an English novelist.

METAMORPHOSIS: THE MAKING OF AN 'ENGLISH' AUTHOR

Robert Neumann and Rolly Becker were finally married on 30 May
1941. Shortly after Rolly's release from internment, the couple had left
their cottage in Long Crendon and moved back to London. The screen-
writing contract with MGM had long since lapsed and Neumann had
made no effort to renew it, deterred by the dangers to shipping in the
Atlantic. These had been vividly affirmed by the fate of Rudolf Olden,
who had associated so closely with Neumann in the PEN Club. Olden
had been released from internment to take up an appointment with the
New School for Social Research in New York. In September 1940, he
and his wife Ika had sailed for New York on the liner *City of Benares*;
both had been drowned when the vessel was torpedoed and sunk in the
Atlantic. Writing to Arnold Zweig, Neumann admitted that the
Oldens' death had greatly affected him. Only the delay in Rolly's release
from internment had prevented them from sailing on the same ship: 'So
we are still here and still alive.'[25]

He and Rolly had moved back to London at the beginning of 1941. They had taken a two-roomed flat in Finchley Road which Neumann would later remember as 'that cramped flat in that émigré street . . . where everyone looked like a second cousin whose name you couldn't quite remember'.[26] Their overriding concern was subsistence. Fortunately, Rolly was able to find work with surprising ease: 'Rolly (whom I was finally able to marry) has been accepted as the first "enemy alien" into the Civil Service and is working in the Ministry of Labour, finding jobs for Germans and Austrians.'[27] Neumann himself was not so lucky: though he applied for various jobs, from publisher's reader to night-watchman, he was always turned down. He found it difficult to sell anything he wrote. Even the German manuscripts he submitted to the BBC were mostly rejected. 'I sat there and did nothing, earned in 1940 eight pounds and eleven shillings, in 1941 twenty-two pounds and in 1942 –'[28] Their only regular income was Rolly's modest salary, without which, Neumann acknowledged, they would both have starved.

It was during these difficult months that Neumann completed the novel *Scene in Passing*, which he wrote entirely in English.[29] He had begun writing in English shortly after the outbreak of war, sending an early sample of his work to Storm Jameson, who responded with enthusiasm and encouragement: 'I do so admire Robert's courage in writing in English – as much as I admire the manner in which he has begun writing it. . . I am longing to see the finished book.'[30] What he had sent her seems to have been a draft chapter or chapters from *Scene in Passing*. His correspondence confirms that he continued to work on the novel over the next two years, persisting even in adverse personal circumstances.[31] His foreword to the novel records that parts of it were 'written, destroyed and lost in British internment camps'. Certainly, the diary he kept during internment contains several references to 'work on the novel'. The diary entries are all brief, but suffice to suggest the intrinsic difficulties of writing in a second language: 'Dogged work on the novel. Will it ever amount to anything?' (5 August 1940) and three days later: 'Worked on novel. Completely unsure about it' (8 August).

Neumann always considered himself a writer who enjoyed exper-imentation and he later portrayed his decision to write in English as simply one more experiment: 'a new beginning with a self-invented idiom . . . a second linguistic virginity.'[32] The truth is much more complex. In his foreword to *Scene in Passing*, Neumann stated that he had considered it 'a matter of dignity' to drop his native language in favour of that of his adopted country, and that he, the exile, also 'hoped to escape the curse of otherness, to throw bridges over the abyss of loneliness'. Such phrases merely hint at the enormous psychological pressures which exiles suffered in the closeted atmosphere of wartime Britain. German had become the language of the enemy. Like all his compatriots, Neumann was acutely aware that even speaking or writing his native language could be deemed suspect. There were also considerable economic pressures: there was little prospect that his work would be published in German, while growing paper shortages and mounting costs made even translation a diminishing possibility. These pressures must have been heightened by the trauma of internment and the siege atmosphere into which he emerged after his release: he and Rolly returned to London at the very height of the blitz.

Dedicated 'to my friend Margaret Storm Jameson', *Scene in Passing* is a short novel recounting the arrival of Mr Tibbs and his family in an unnamed village, as refugees from an unnamed war. Tibbs is a gentle and dignified man, the third generation of a crumbling industrial dynasty. He is characterised by 'a peculiar detachment . . . a detachment from the so-called realities, a tendency to blot out the borderline between them and the unreal that lay beyond'. He and his family are adrift on the tide of war, his daughter reflecting that 'his life, her mother's life had been adrift for long, as far back as she could remember, torn off their moorings, rudderless.' The book has a melancholy, elegiac quality which doubtless reflects Neumann's mood during the period of its composition.

In retrospect, Neumann was inclined to disparage his own linguistic achievement, observing that *Scene in Passing* 'was written in a language which non-English speakers consider to be English. . . In reality it was an attempt to write English with German means of expression – stiff, struggling with every metaphor, groping for every word.'[33] In fact, when the novel was finally published in 1942, it was precisely Neumann's use of his adopted language which interested and impressed the critics most. Philip Toynbee called Neumann's achievement 'heroic, linguistically on a par with Conrad's',[34] while the novelist and critic Frank Swinnerton praised 'a mastery of words which should shock English writers into emulation'.[35] The language of the novel is indeed often striking and even original; as the following extract illustrates, it is also sometimes faintly archaic: English which has been read rather than heard.

> That night the frost came. It rode on a grey horse of fog, a slow, sad rider. It had been cold before, the water froze, and snow, and all that. But this frost's riding was different. Perhaps the fog made it so very cold; perhaps the wind. It was not the wind we used to know up there where our village is, with those whiffs and floating tokens of far-off parts. It blew right over from the freezing stars – out of the empty space between them; it blew out of death's own house. Brave it not, or your bones turn into brittle glass; you just touch them, they crumble to icy dust. Yes, it was death's own brother riding in silence.

Philip Toynbee claimed that 'there is no internal evidence to suggest that *Scene in Passing* was not written by an Englishman'. In fact, the use of English idiom is sometimes uncertain. 'Brave it not, or your bones turn into brittle glass', for example, is not a sentence an English author would have written.

However, despite Neumann's impressive linguistic achievement, the novel has considerable weaknesses of structure and conception: there is a lack of coherent narrative, characters appear only to vanish again and there is an uncertain sense of place, Neumann's English village being more akin to Central Europe.

Neumann's correspondence at this time was also conducted almost entirely in English. The evidence of his letters suggests that his English was still prone to minor errors of syntax and vocabulary and it seems likely that the published version of *Scene in Passing* owed something to careful editing. Neumann certainly sent some sections of the novel to Anthony Dent, who had translated *By the Waters of Babylon*, but it is impossible to assess the extent of editorial intervention, since no manuscript version has survived. Among Neumann's English friends was the novelist Henrietta Leslie, whose address he occasionally used and who, according to Hilde Spiel, actually typed some of his manuscripts.[36] If she typed the manuscript of *Scene in Passing*, she may also have corrected it, but this too must remain a matter for conjecture.

Despite sympathetic reviews, *Scene in Passing* sold few copies, doing little to alleviate Neumann's financial difficulties, but it nonetheless helped him to transform his fortunes in London. In 1943 he was invited by Walter Hutchinson to become executive editor of a new series, Hutchinson International Authors, also being offered fifteen per cent of the profits of the venture. Hutchinson's was then Britain's largest publisher, with a list ranging from serious literature to romantic novels, from scientific and philosophical works to coffee-table books on royalty – a total of some twelve thousand volumes a year. Despite this success, Walter Hutchinson remained a social outsider, excluded from the magic circle of English publishing. His offer to Neumann was the gesture of one outsider to another. At the same time, Hutchinson's took an option on Neumann's next five books, giving him an advance on the first, which, he recalled, 'was precisely ten times as much as my solid and conservative publisher Dent had given me. . . In all the years of exile, I had not earned as much as I got here for a single, as yet unwritten, book.'37

This book, completed in January 1944 and published later that year, was *The Inquest*, arguably one of Neumann's best novels and certainly one of the most translated. Consistent with its title, the novel takes the form of an investigation. At an Austrian exile theatre, The Flare (an obvious allusion to the Austrian Centre's Laterndl – in English, the Lantern), the English author Shilling meets a woman called Bibiana Santis, with whom he subsequently spends the night. On leaving her the following morning, he gives her his address. He soon receives a visit from the police, telling him that the woman has committed suicide and requiring him to attend the inquest. If the inquest seeks to establish the circumstances of the woman's death, Shilling attempts, in the intervening forty-eight hours, to reconstruct her life, uncovering an odyssey of political struggle, emigration and exile. Her biography is an account of the hopes and failures of the political left in the thirties and ultimately a paradigm of exile itself.

The Inquest is a structurally complex novel, maintaining its narrative tension and confirming Neumann's considerable skill as a storyteller. It is also a stylistic *tour de force*, demonstrating Neumann's remarkable command of idiomatic English, and his ability to move easily between the formal and the colloquial, as the following passage illustrates:

As to that sparse little old Miss Lee, she lost her fiancé in the Boer War. Being chiselled of a tougher wood than other wartime losers of fiancés, she became a fighting mad pacifist, struggled for women's suffrage against the Herculean arms of six-foot members of the Metropolitan Police, nursed through yesterday's world war in France; saved children in Versailles Europe, went as a Moral and Social Hygienic League of Nations White Slave Traffic Investigator first to fascist Poland, second to democratic Hong Kong; and was well fitted, when called upon, to deal with the drafting of middle-aged middle-class middle European ladies into the domestic services of the British Isles.

The novel received generally favourable reviews, critics being once more impressed by Neumann's linguistic achievement, though one reviewer did express reservations about his liberties with English syntax: 'Would it be impertinent to remind so skilful a writer that even the English sentence, that lithest of literary instruments, will crack under a cartload of adjectives? Or that though it is indeed effective to omit all commas, it gives a certain flexibility to use one now and then?'[38]

The Inquest marks a further stage in Neumann's transition from successful German author to successful English author, a metamorphosis which was completed by the success of his post-war novel *The Children of Vienna* (1946), which was translated into twenty-five languages. The phenomenon of German-speaking authors writing in English has received only scant attention from critics in either Britain or Germany, and yet Neumann was only one of a number of writers who were able to make the transition to writing and publishing in English.

The decision to write in a second language is a daunting one for any author, posing crucial questions of cultural identity. It presupposes not only complete fluency in the second language but also considerable familiarity with another culture. The linguistic problems involved undoubtedly vary with the genre in which the author is working. It is certainly easier for the author of non-fiction to adopt a second language than for the novelist or poet, for whom the intrinsic pitfalls of style and register are greater. Many of those who switched languages most successfully were journalists or writers of non-fiction, such as Franz Borkenau, Willi Frischauer, Heinrich Fraenkel or Sebastian Haffner. Nonetheless, there were a surprising number of creative writers who succeeded in writing in English, including the novelist Hilde Spiel and her husband Peter de Mendelssohn, Elisabeth Castonier, who made a name as a children's author, and the remarkable case of Ernest Borneman, whose novel *The Face on the Cutting Room Floor* (1937) remains a considerable literary feat: published under the pseudonym Cameron McCabe, it was widely accepted as the work of a native speaker. The novel which made the greatest impact on English literary circles, Arthur Koestler's *Darkness at Noon*, was translated from German, but Koestler's subsequent novels were written directly in English.

Hilde Spiel had come to London after the publication of her first novel; Borneman, arriving in London at the age of eighteen, had actually begun his literary career there. At the time of their arrival in London, Spiel was ten years, Borneman fifteen years younger than Neumann, a fact which makes the latter's achievement in his adopted language all the more remarkable. The reasons for Neumann's success, like Borneman's, undoubtedly lay in his gift for literary impersonation. It is no accident that he had first become known, as a German author, with a book of parodies in which he convincingly (and amusingly) impersonated a range of contemporary authors and styles. Much of his writing in English was also a form of impersonation.

Hilde Spiel suggested that Neumann simply transposed his highly idiosyncratic German style into English, an argument which is difficult to sustain. In the post-war years, Neumann wrote for a time exclusively in English, becoming widely accepted as an 'English' author, whose work was translated into German. It was only later, in the mid-fifties, that he undertook the translation himself, though he stressed that, in preparing German editions of his 'English' books, he was not able simply to translate them, but was obliged to write two different versions, emphasising his unusual position as a writer between two languages. For all Neumann's apparent fluency in English, it must be stressed that his is a distinctly alien voice. His English-language novels remain relentlessly un-English in style, subject-matter and focus, rapidly forcing the reader to conclude that none of them could conceivably have been written by an English writer.

For some fifteen years, Neumann was an established figure on the British literary scene, a respected, if highly individual voice. Although his work was widely reviewed when first published, it has long been out of print, and has since been almost totally forgotten, a fate shared by most other exiles who wrote in English. Some, like Neumann, eventually resumed writing in German and were able partially to re-establish themselves in the German-speaking world. Even then, the enforced migration between languages has restricted recognition of their work. The books which they wrote in English are now forgotten, barely acknowledged as English literature, because they were written by German-speaking authors, and yet ignored in Germany precisely be-cause they were written in English. Nothing better illustrates the cultural dilemma of German-speaking literary exiles, caught (even posthumously) in the no man's land between languages.

ALFRED KERR: THE LIMITS OF CULTURAL MOBILITY

Also among the audience for Peter de Mendelssohn's paper on 'Writers Without Language' was Alfred Kerr, who must have listened as intently as anyone. Kerr was an acknowledged stylist in his own language, who in his moments of more sublime vanity even claimed to have reinvented German, 'shortening those incredibly long periods that weave about like rain worms, putting clarity into its fogginess',[39] but was never able to use English for more than purposes of everyday communication.

Kerr was all too aware of the material and intellectual constraints of exile, of the difficulties of communication with a host society which remained largely ignorant of or even indifferent to the exiles' problems. Most refugees in London had remained completely unassimilated, as he noted in 1940:

> If I am walking down a street in London, I can recognise refugees, singly or in groups, from a distance of several yards. This is no accom-plishment. They stand out sharply from those around them. Not only because a German suit has a different cut. But because they are recog-nisable from the invisible martyr's halo of woe which surrounds them. From their look of being at their wits' end. From their complete differ-ence to the average English muddling calm. From the involuntary air of heroic misery which shines through.[40]

Part of the problem, Kerr concluded, was that people had seen all too many refugees, so that custom had dulled their initial feelings of sympathy.

Kerr's miniature of life in exile was part of an ongoing debate amongst exiles as to whether they should eventually return to Germany or adapt to a new environment, a debate which intensified after the outbreak of war.[41] Kerr was among the most fervent advocates of integration; ironically, he was also among those least able to adapt. However, he recognised the logic of assimilation for his children, both of whom had long since discarded their German identity. His son had won a scholarship to Cambridge to study law, and had joined the RAF in 1941 after his release from internment; his daughter, wavering between a stage career or training as an artist, was engaged in war work.

Inevitably, the Kerrs were once more beset by financial problems. Julia's brother Gert Weismann, who had sent them money on previous occasions, now faced financial problems of his own, and Kerr was obliged to send one of his periodic appeals to Rudolf Kommer. Like so many such requests it was touchingly unrealistic:

Dear Friend,

can you mobilise something for us in New York? Things are going terribly for us. I am drawing £2 a month from a French periodical (*Aux Écoutes*) and should also get £2 from an American journal *Aufbau*. These £4 are all we have. . . Isn't it possible for you to ask a couple of American Jews for help? Show them the chapter 'Juda' in the book of verse. Or the chapter 'Jeruschalajim' in *Die Welt im Licht*. I'm told that in Palestine my picture is included in cigarette packets. Israel can't allow one of its sons to starve – not if he's in cigarette packets. Nor let him get thrown out of his hotel, in his seventy-third year.[42]

In fact, the Kerrs were not thrown out, continuing to live at the Foyer Suisse, until the misfortunes of war disrupted even this semblance of stability. In October 1940 the hotel was severely damaged in an airraid, when a direct hit on the house next door brought down the ceilings. Kerr himself was thrown out of bed and briefly buried beneath the ceiling plaster, but though shaken was otherwise unhurt. The building was no longer habitable and the hotel moved to Putney (Lytton Hall, Lytton Grove, London SW15), which remained Kerr's home for the rest of his life.

The experience of being bombed out gave Kerr an odd sense of 'belonging': 'Personally, it gives me almost a feeling of satisfaction that I've been bombed out, that I've shared a fraction of the general suffering. A duty demanded by decency.'[43] In one of his letters to Kommer he had expressed grim satisfaction that he and his family had officially been declared 'stateless persons', thus severing any remaining formal links with Nazi Germany. He also expressed the fervent hope that within a year they would be 'native Britons'.[44] In the event, he was unable to pursue this application, since, with the exception of special cases, all applications for naturalisation were suspended in 1940 for the duration of the war.

Kerr's desire to pursue British naturalisation rested on far more than an appreciation of the pragmatic advantages of a British passport. His correspondence reveals a strong, at times almost touching aspiration to 'belong'. In Berlin he had always been something of an outsider, a man of many acquaintances but few friends, marooned in his own fame. In London he had found himself unknown and unsung, and as though to compensate for his almost complete isolation, he became increasingly eager to claim recognition and a place in society.

Two sets of autobiographical notes which Kerr drafted at this time are eloquent of his self-perception. Writing to the Home Office early in 1940,[45] he understandably sought to stress his anti-Nazi credentials, recording proudly that the Nazis had declared him 'an enemy of the state' and put a price on his head. He also sought to portray himself as a man whose literary reputation had preceded him: 'my books are to be found in the libraries of the British Museum and the English universities.' Always something of a social snob, he found it important to record that his son Michael 'has been educated at an English public school, won a major open scholarship for Cambridge'. While he had almost inevitably failed to penetrate English social networks, Kerr was obviously fascinated by the English preoccupation with rank and title, his pretensions sometimes cruelly underlined by the shortcomings of his idiomatic English:

> I enclose three letters from English friends: Admiral Hall; Lady
> Bonham-Carter; Captain Gardner, justice of the peace – whose wife
> is Mrs Kerr's best friend. (Apart of these we have many prominent

English friends.) . . . My wife was social secretary of Viscountess Wimborn until Lord Wimborn's death and is now working with Colonel A. M. Grenfell, D.S.O., and Mrs Grenfell, President of the Y.W.C.A.[46] Kerr's reference to his wife suggests that she was better integrated than he. Always an Anglophile, Julia undoubtedly shared her husband's aspiration to 'belong'. Exile had probably treated her more cruelly than her husband. It was she who had had to support the family throughout their early years in England, working long hours in poorly-paid secretarial jobs and thereby sacrificing any chance of achieving her artistic and musical ambitions.

Even the episode of internment had failed to destroy Kerr's admiration for the English. He himself was able to escape internment because of his age, but his son Michael was among the earliest internees, plucked from a Cambridge college in May 1940 and released only five months later. Despite his son's internment, Kerr had publicly defended the government's policy as 'appropriate' since 'the Nazis often disguise their spies as émigrés, so the whole lot must be filtered'.[47] Kerr's statement, echoing the official justification for government policy, was perhaps another example of his benevolent indulgence towards the English. He soon revised his opinion, writing to H. G. Wells to endorse the latter's sweeping criticism of 'the scandalous mistreatment of anti-Nazi aliens who are only too eager to fight'.[48]

The outbreak of war had inevitably also impinged on Kerr's literary plans. 'I have begun writing French again, which is a joy but brings in next to nothing. The "Two Men in London" have been put on ice and will only thaw out in a peaceful spring,' he wrote to Rudolf Kommer, also noting that he had just finished the manuscript of *Ich kam nach England*: 'The light and entertaining book . . . is ready.'[49]

Ich kam nach England in fact ends with the announcement of the outbreak of war, 'the redeeming conclusion', as Kerr called it. Although (or perhaps because) war had thrown a new light on the years of appeasement, Kerr hastened to offer the book to several publishers, including Macmillans and the newly-founded Lincolns Prager, whose director Eugen Prager was a German-speaking Czech. It was Prager who showed most immediate interest, concluding an agreement to publish a German edition within twelve months and an 'Anglo-

American' edition thereafter. Kerr was to receive an advance of £350 against royalties.[50] It seemed that he had belatedly made the literary breakthrough he had so long sought, but the book was to encounter the ill fortune which attended all his enterprises in London. Publication was first delayed, and then abandoned, apparently because of the growing paper shortage, and the contract was finally dissolved by mutual consent.[51] Kerr was bitterly disappointed, convinced that, apart from the book's intrinsic interest, it represented a genre unprecedented in English writing: 'The book is, neutrally viewed, also capable of being a success.'[52] He subsequently offered the book to another publisher, Nicholson and Watson, who also rejected it in the light of the current paper shortage; Kerr, ever philosophical, called it 'an enthusiastic refusal' – but it was a refusal nonetheless.[53] In February 1944, evidently hoping that the intervening years had endowed the book with a certain historical interest, Kerr offered it to other publishers, including Lindsay Drummond, and the newly-launched Hutchinson's International Authors. Drummond, a small publisher with a keen interest in German matters, apparently gave serious consideration to publishing the manuscript, but ultimately felt that he had other (more topical) priorities. Hutchinson's too declined. In the immediate post-war years, Kerr attempted to find a German publisher for the book, but the difficulties proved too great. *Ich kam nach England* did not finally appear in Germany until more than thirty years after Kerr's death; it has never been published in English.

Kerr also made perfunctory attempts to find a publisher for *Ein Jude spricht zu Juden*, offering the manuscript to Lincolns Prager, and later to Victor Gollancz, whom he clearly addressed as a *Jewish* publisher.[54] There is no record of Gollancz's response, if any.

Undeterred by this accumulation of failure, Kerr continued to write, still hoping to shape an uncooperative future. In *The Other Way Round*, part of the autobiographical trilogy she wrote in the nineteen seventies, Judith Kerr remembered her father in the tiny room to which he retired each morning:

> In her mind she saw him in his poky room with his typewriter that kept
> going wrong and his writings that no one wanted to publish, in a
> country whose language he did not speak.[55]

In fact, Kerr's command of English was more than adequate for everyday purposes, but he nonetheless remained frustrated by his limitations
in the language. An acknowledged stylist in German, who could use
quite ordinary words to convey a quite extraordinary meaning, he was
never able to use English as more than a language of practical communication.

Kerr's frustration at his inability to write in English was undoubtedly
heightened by the fluency his children had acquired. After 1940 he
wrote letters to his son in English, but he would often comment on his
own ineptitude in the language: 'I even prefer to torture you with my
awful English than to be always silent.'[56] He later referred to himself as
'your pidgin-speaking father'.[57]

Kerr's last work in exile was the short novel *Der Dichter und die Meerschweinchen* ('The Writer and the Guinea-Pigs').[58] The plot is somewhat contrived. The writer Clemens Teck sets out to conduct a literary
experiment, studying his environment and its inhabitants, like so many
guinea-pigs in the laboratory of exile. Speaking through his protagonist, Kerr registers his own feelings of marginalisation in wartime
London: 'I, Clemens Teck, had no echo here in England.'

The story starts well enough, containing some lively and amusing
descriptions of the boarding-house and its inhabitants:

> Downstairs in the lounge, or 'drawing-room' of the boarding-house,
> the guests were able to relax after dinner. They would read, usually
> the *Evening Standard*, or listen to the radio, or drink coffee, or do the
> crossword, and they chatted – mostly in very restrained tones; exer-
> cising caution, for you never knew who might be listening. . . One
> group normally played bridge on a table with a threadbare green-baize
> cloth. . . Only these four people were sometimes noisy.

Teck proposes not merely to portray his fellow-exiles but, as author, to
intervene in their lives, to provoke a reaction which will reveal their
innermost selves. However, his guinea-pigs do not respond as expected,
forcing their author to react; it is he who becomes the guinea-pig, the
object of his own experiment.

As a coda to Kerr's distinguished literary career, *The Writer and the
Guinea-Pigs* is disappointing. Despite a few striking vignettes, the plot
does not develop, indeed little actually happens at all. The novel

remains unpublished – and probably unpublishable. It is even uncertain how far Kerr intended it for publication, for although he prepared a revised and corrected version of the manuscript, he made little apparent attempt to find a publisher, as though it really *were* a scientific experiment, in which the guinea-pig was himself.

At first sight it seems surprising that Kerr, distinguished theatre critic, master of the short essay and accomplished broadcaster, should fail so completely to make any mark in Britain. His lack of resonance is in fact a classic example of the limits of cultural mobility, of the writer whose skills were too rooted in German language and culture to be transferred. His critical role was lost in transit, his attempts to find a foothold in journalism were frustrated by his lack of English which made direct comment on current events impossible. Though his English eventually became much better than he pretended, it remained inadequate for use as a literary language. Even translation posed considerable problems. Kerr was a consummate stylist in German, but his very style – pithy, epigrammatic and idiosyncratic – really defied translation. The typical Kerr sentence is a short one in which quite ordinary words are sometimes assigned quite extraordinary meanings.

Kerr himself was only too aware of the problems, but his efforts to adapt his work, or to find a new medium for it, were unsuccessful, attended by ill luck – or ill will. His attempts to write for the cinema coincided with a slump in the British film industry; his relations with the BBC were haunted by the ghosts of former literary feuds. Throughout his years in England he remained trapped in the inexorable contradiction of exile, unable to write in English and equally unable to publish in German.

'AFTER THE WAR IS OVER. . .'

Wartime London was full of governments which had no country to rule, or whose country had even ceased to exist. Free French and Free Poles rubbed shoulders with Norwegians and Czechs, Hungarians and Catalans. The city was also home to thousands of refugees of different nationalities, most of whom resisted the best efforts of the authorities to disperse them to the provinces.

The first half of 1942 marked the absolute low point of the war, with a succession of serious reverses: in February the surrender of Singapore, in June the fall of Tobruk followed by retreat in North Africa, in August the ill-conceived raid on Dieppe. But 1942 was also the year which marked the turning-point of the war. The British recapture of Tobruk and the defeat of the Afrika Korps at El Alamein in November – the first military reverses inflicted on the hitherto invincible German Army – were followed by the Anglo-American landings in French North Africa. Even more significantly, the German advance on the eastern front had been halted and the grimly symbolic battle for Stalingrad had begun; on 2 February 1943, the remnants of the German Sixth Army surrendered.

One consequence of the progress of the war was the gradual integration of refugees into the British war effort, first into war production, then into the armed forces. From the beginning of 1941, the Ministry of Labour set up a Foreign Department to facilitate the employment of refugees in war industries. For some time, German and Austrian refugees had been allowed to serve in the Pioneer Corps, indeed some had volunteered for service as the only means of securing their release from internment. Only in June 1943 were they finally allowed to enlist in other regiments of the British Army, an announcement which was soon answered by a wave of volunteers. Within weeks over three thousand Austrians had volunteered to join the British Army.

One sign of the changing fortunes of war was the end of the blitz, the last major German raid on London taking place on 10 May 1941. Between 1942 and 1944 London was largely free of air raids. This changing situation helped to bring about a change of perspective, as preoccupation with survival began to give way to consideration of the future. The British writer Mollie Panter-Downes noted in the *New Yorker*, at the end of 1942, that the phrase 'after the war' was coming back into circulation.[59]

The experience of the war, and the far-reaching measures it had necessitated, had also profoundly changed public attitudes, challenging the premisses which buttressed the pre-war social order. The publication of the Beveridge report in December 1942 initiated widespread discussion of the form of society which would prevail after the war. A new political agenda emerged: meetings were held on many national and international issues, at which a generation of distinguished academics, such as Julian Huxley, J. B. S. Haldane, J. D. Bernal, Richard Tawney and Harold Laski began to disseminate their ideas.

Discussion of the post-war political order in Europe inevitably focused on the crucial question of what was to be done with Germany, and its corollary, what was to happen to Austria. Not unnaturally, such questions increasingly preoccupied German and Austrian exiles.

THOUGHTS ON GERMANY

The debate about the post-war political order in Europe was equally lively in exile circles, particularly among the politically committed, most of whom intended to return to their native countries to take part in political reconstruction. Various plans for post-war Germany and Austria were expounded, some within the narrow confines of German exile groups, others in the growing number of books which appeared with British publishing houses.

Paradoxically, it was only after the outbreak of war that German-speaking authors began to gain a firm foothold in the lists of English publishers. These were straitened times for the publishing business, in which chronic paper shortages restricted the publication of new titles, forcing publishers to rely increasingly on their back-lists.[60] At a time when fewer new titles were published, it is remarkable how many of these were by German-speaking authors, some appearing in translation, others actually written in English.

One reason for this increasing acceptance of German-speaking authors was their ability to address one of the burning political questions affecting the conduct of the war, namely: whether the German population bore collective responsibility for Nazism, and whether any effective political opposition therefore existed inside the Reich, questions addressed at the outset of the war by the journalist

Heinrich Fraenkel in *The German People versus Hitler* (1940).[61] The
stated aim of Fraenkel's book was 'to help to destroy the fallacies
rampant throughout the civilised world regarding the Third Reich.
The foremost of these fallacies is the identification of Germany and the
Third Reich, Germanism and Nazism, the German people and the Nazi
Party.' The distinction between the German people and the Nazis had
an important corollary: the existence of a sizeable and dedicated political opposition within Germany, embracing a wide political spectrum.
British reviewers of the book were sceptical, the *New Statesman*'s
reviewer calling it 'an example of the gross over-optimism of the Left'.[62]
Similar scepticism greeted Willi Frischauer's *The Nazis at War*.[63]

During 1940 the debate as to whether the German population bore
collective responsibility for Nazism was dominated by the views of Sir
Robert Vansittart, which became an automatic point of reference for all
subsequent discourse. Vansittart, formerly Permanent Under-Secre-
tary at the Foreign Office, had been a determined opponent of appeasement in the thirties, finding himself increasingly in opposition to the
government he was serving. During 1940 he made a series of seven
broadcasts in which he dismissed the distinction between 'good' and
'bad' Germans, expounding the view of collective German responsibility for the war and the post-war need for permanent demilitarisation.
Vansittart's views gained wide currency with the publication of his talks
under the title *Black Record. Germans Past and Present*.[64] The most
immediate response to Vansittart had been that of Heinrich Fraenkel,
whose emphatic rebuttal was issued as a Fabian Society tract.[65]

As the tide of war turned against Germany, there was an increasing
number of books by German authors which sought to influence the
debate as to how Germany should be treated by the soon-to-be-victor-
ious Allies. Julius Braunthal's *Need Germany Survive?*, published in
1943, was also in part a reaction to Vansittartism.[66] Braunthal asserted
the existence of the 'Other Germany', setting out to disprove the idea
that the emergence of Nazism was the inevitable result of the German
mentality and national character. (cf. Chapter 4, entitled 'The Lost
Battle of "the Other Germany"'.) His book received the endorsement of
a foreword by Harold Laski. Similarly, the essays contained in the
anthology *In Tyrannos* (1944) sought to give an historical account of

Germany's democratic traditions.[67] Austrians too were eager to influence the fate of their own country, perhaps the most notable work being Emil Müller-Sturmheim's *What to do about Austria?*[68]

Other exiles, including Alfred Kerr and his fellow-critic Otto Zarek, advanced an opposing point of view, influenced in varying degrees by Vansittart. Zarek's book *German Kultur. The Proper Perspective* (1942)[69] was a sceptical review of Germany's political and intellectual traditions. This pessimistic critique was, as we shall see, largely echoed by Kerr, whose discourse increasingly showed the influence of Vansittart. A similar, though more subtle exposition of the social and intellectual roots of Nazism was formulated by Karl Otten in his weighty, at times even ponderous work, *A Combine of Aggression*, which like Fraenkel's *The German People versus Hitler* was published by Allen & Unwin.

In the years 1939–40, there was a sudden flourishing of German cultural activity in London. Prior to 1939, there had been no organisation in Britain to fulfil the cultural needs of refugees, simply because they were not sufficiently numerous to warrant it. The situation changed dramatically with the huge influx of refugees into Britain in 1938–39, resulting in the emergence of important cultural and social organisations. The two largest and most influential of these were the Freie Deutsche Kulturbund (Free German League of Culture) and its Austrian counterpart, the Austrian Centre.

Because of restrictions placed by the British authorities on overt political activity by 'enemy aliens', cultural organisations came to be seen as a means of promoting political aims. The Freie Deutsche Kulturbund (FDKB), founded in the hope of uniting all Germans in exile,[70] occupied a house in Belsize Park, placed at its disposal by the Church Commissioners through the good offices of George Bell, Bishop of Chichester. It enjoyed the backing of prominent British sympathisers like Sybil Thorndike, Wickham Steed, J. B. Priestley and the scholar Gilbert Murray, whose support helped to establish the League's credibility. However, although it always remained a broad-front organisation, the FDKB came increasingly under the influence of the German Communist party, alienating a number of unaligned left-wing intellectuals. The next three years saw the emergence of various literary and cultural groups, often with lofty aspirations (and even loftier titles), but each usually comprising only a few members. Among the first of these was the Gruppe Unabhängiger Deutscher Autoren (Group of Independent German Authors – GUDA), created by the writer Kurt Hiller as a cross-party organisation.[71] Hiller, a diligent creator of groups – particularly those in which he was the leading intellectual light – conceived of GUDA as a counterweight to the FDKB, which he accused of being a Soviet-run front organisation. GUDA met regularly for political and literary discussion during the war years, organising some forty lecture and discussion evenings, usually held in the Austrian Labour Club, near Finchley Road underground station. Though its actual membership probably never exceeded fifteen, its meetings were often well attended, producing lively discussion, and at least one notable publication devoted to the question of post-war Germany.[72]

Probably the best-known group to separate from the FDKB was Club 1943 which broke away in that year following political disagreements. Founded as a forum for cultural discussion, Club 1943 still exists today. However, the broadest spectrum of unaligned socialist intellectuals was to be found in the Klub Konstruktivisten, formed in September 1942 and comprising some 35 members, including journalists Wilhelm Sternfeld, Bernhard Menne and Hans Jaeger, Professor Hermann Friedmann, and Otto Lehmann-Rußbüldt. Like other such organisations, the Konstruktivisten were kept under surveillance by the intelligence services, whose reports, dutifully preserved in the Public Record Office, make suitably unintelligent reading.[73] According to Karl Retzlaw, who drafted the group's founding declaration, the Konstruktivisten were opposed by both KPD and SPD as 'pro-Vansittart' – and consequently boycotted.

Despite this proliferation of political groups and programmes, the FDKB remained, throughout the seven years of its existence, by far the largest organisation of German refugees. At its inaugural meeting in 1938 Alfred Kerr was elected as one of the League's Presidents, together with Berthold Viertel, Stefan Zweig and Oskar Kokoschka. Kerr thus achieved the unusual distinction of being the only German among the four presidents of the Free German League of Culture, the others being a Czech (Kokoschka) and two Austrians. In common with his colleagues Kerr was very much a figurehead, whose name and prestige provided democratic legitimation for the FDKB, helping to give it the appearance of a 'broad church'. At the League's first public meeting, held at the Friends House on 28 March 1939, and attended by some 250 people, both Kerr and Viertel read from their work. This occasion probably marked the peak of Kerr's involvement with the FDKB, though he continued to play an active role until his resignation in November 1939.

The FDKB was a broad-front organisation, in which political rivalries became increasingly intense as the Communist Party gradually extended its influence, a process culminating in the split in the organisation and the formation of Club 1943. Kerr had genuinely hoped that the FDKB might be able to transcend its political differences in support of the war effort. In practice, such hopes fell victim to the Nazi–Soviet Pact and the ideological line consequently adopted by the Communists.

In his letter of resignation from the FDKB Kerr emphasised his differences with the Communist functionary Alfred Meusel, voicing his frustration at the latter's insistence on procedural niceties and on discussing 'peace aims' at a time when the war had hardly begun. Above all, he complained of Meusel's election 'in highly debatable circumstances' to the post of vice-president, complaining that he represented only a small group. He concluded his letter with the hope that 'we are following different paths – to the same destination'.[74]

For his part, Kerr remained actively involved in the fight against fascism, an involvement all the more remarkable in a man who was then well into his seventies. During the war years, his energies were mainly channelled into rebuilding the German exile PEN Group, whose President he became in 1941. The Group had virtually ceased to exist in 1940 with the emigration and tragic death of its secretary, Rudolf Olden. In order to revive it, Hermon Ould, the International PEN Secretary, turned to Kerr, whom he persuaded to become President. He was an apparently obvious choice, having been the last President of the German PEN Centre in Berlin before its suppression by the Nazis.

When Kerr assumed his office early in 1941, the German Exile PEN Centre existed in name only, as the new secretary, Friedrich Burschell, was quick to concede: 'Our club is at present more of an illusion than a reality. The other exile Centres have official backing, official rooms for functions and they have funds. We have nothing of the kind, quite apart from the fact that most of our more famous colleagues are in America.'[75] Burschell, Kerr and Richard Friedenthal set about rebuilding the organisation, a task which proceeded slowly, and not without difficulty, over the next twelve months.

The new group (officially known as the PEN-Club, Deutsche Gruppe, London) was finally approved at the International PEN Congress in September 1941. During 1941-2, the Group's activities were severely limited by the difficulty of finding suitable meeting rooms, a problem made worse by the hazards of German bombing. Inevitably, there were also financial problems. The new committee could not even afford the postage for the necessary letters to potential members, and Friedenthal felt obliged to ask the English Centre for a loan of £5 to be repaid once they had been able to collect membership subscriptions.[76]

Kerr's inaugural address expressed the hope that, for all its literary credentials, the group would not divorce itself from the political situation: 'We, the German PEN Group, are not a political association . . . but we have a common political aim in the fight against fascism.'[77] Unfortunately, the history of the German Exile PEN after its reconstitution in 1941 was marred by the private feuding which seems endemic to any exile organisation. Kerr himself had always been a controversial figure, inspiring admiration and opposition in roughly equal measure. The new PEN Group had hardly been established before he was involved in furious arguments with other exiled writers, among them the notoriously disputatious Kurt Hiller. Kerr tried to make light of this feud, describing Hiller as 'a professional non-conformist' and 'trained querreller' (sic), commenting ironically that there were eleven associations of exiled German writers in London: 'Hiller is 'leading' only two of them, each composed of about two and a half members.'[78] Hiller was rapidly excluded from the organisation for his intemperate comments – though some members contended that he could not be excluded as he had never joined, having refused to pay the members' subscription.

There were however more serious disagreements, occasioned by Kerr's opinions on post-war Germany. He had originally pronounced his views – with his usual mixture of polemic and stylistic aplomb – in a speech to the International PEN Congress in London in September 1941. Speaking on 'Germany Today and Tomorrow', he asserted that 'the fall of Hitler will not be simultaneously the fall of Hitlerism'. He argued that, in order to instil democracy, and eradicate Nazism, one would have to resort to undemocratic methods. For a short time after the war, literature would have to be primarily 'educational'.

The German mind, so rich in qualities, and yet so irrational, can only be ploughed up, transformed, educated, if this is carried out with an iron-like, an inexorable coercion . . . otherwise something may easily happen which, in the terminology of Nietzsche, is called 'the repetition of the same' (*der Wiederkehr des Gleichen*).[79]

Kerr's opinions on Germany caused a furore amongst German exiles. The journalist Heinrich Fraenkel accused him of supporting the views of the recently ennobled Lord Vansittart, published the previous year in his *Black Record*. The particular object of Fraenkel's outrage was a letter Kerr had written to the *Spectator*, affirming that the Germans had 'an innate urge' to conquest and concluding that there was only one solution: 'the iron hand from outside'.[80] Kerr hastened to repeat his views in an article in the *Central European Observer*,[81] sending copies of both publications to Vansittart, as though to acknowledge their intellectual provenance.[82] At a later date he actually met Vansittart, subsequently confirming 'the pleasure of meeting you in flesh and blood after having met you in the spirit'.[83]

Fraenkel, the author of a polemical response to Vansittart, was so incensed by what he called Kerr's 'ill-judged political outbursts' that he attempted to force his resignation as PEN President. However, it was Fraenkel who was finally forced to resign, commenting: 'In any case, I do not wish to remain another hour as a member of a German writers' association which has Alfred Kerr as its chairman.'[84] For his part, Kerr continued to stand by his views on Germany. He was also in contact with other disciples of Vansittart, such as Walter Loeb of the group 'Fight for Freedom', for whom he wrote an article tracing the influence of fascism on German film and theatre of the twenties.[85]

In a post-war report to the International PEN Secretary Hermon Ould, Kerr identified two conflicting strands of opinion within the

German Exile PEN Group. 'One group wanted to make distinctions between the Nazis and the German people; whereas the other group, especially Alfred Kerr . . . advocated the following view with regard to the bulk of the misled Germans: "Force is the only way with them. Force is the only way to improve them. This task has to be performed from outside." '[86]

Kerr wished to be more than merely a titular head of the PEN Group, aspiring to be its intellectual guide and mentor. His addresses to the Group have survived for the most part only in note form, but among the topics he suggested for discussion were: promoting younger authors, establishing an editorial committee to read and review their work, discussions of recent non-German works, a lecture on the changing role of film, and the prospects for naturalisation.

It was under his tutelage that the Group finally started to function as what it ostensibly always had been – an association of writers. It began to hold regular meetings at the National Liberal Club, inaugurating a pro-gramme of talks and lectures which far exceeded anything undertaken in the pre-war years. During 1942, for example, Kerr spoke on 'The Art of Translating', Richard Friedenthal read a paper on 'Poetry in Two Languages', and several members read from their work, including the journalist Gabriele Tergit and the theatre critic Monty Jacobs, once Kerr's arch-rival in the Berlin of the twenties. There were invitations from and to other PEN groups – the Czechs, the Poles and the Catalans. Wartime conditions made it necessary to restrict membership to German writers who were actually living in Britain but despite this the Group soon mustered some thirty members. Even this modest success could not have been accomplished without the support of the English PEN which provided help in various ways, including occasional facilities for meetings. Kerr's daughter recorded her impressions of one such gathering, noting 'a collection of the usual intelligent refugee faces and the usual frayed refugee collars and cuffs'.[87] Though one or two tried hard to hold themselves back, most of them fell voraciously on the tea which was provided after the meeting.

As President of the German Exile PEN, Kerr undoubtedly saw himself as the custodian of a German language increasingly contamin-ated by the idiom of Nazism, reclaiming a culture which had presumed to exclude him. In a retrospective account of the wartime activities of the Group, he and Friedenthal reported that it had held over thirty meetings and lectures, and had grown steadily to number forty two members by the end of the war. As writers, the adverse circumstances had condemned them largely to silence.[88]

In the tense summer of 1940, Karl Otten was acutely aware of the vulnerability of his own situation. As a German who had enlisted in the war against Germany, he knew he could expect short shrift in the event of an invasion. His apprehension was not misplaced. Though he could not have known it, his name was among those on the *Fahndungsliste* of the Gestapo, a list of persons – mainly leading figures in British public life – who were to be arrested immediately following a successful invasion of Britain. The inclusion of Otten's name and current address, along with those of other prominent German exiles, confirms the excellence of the Gestapo's pre-war sources of information in Britain.

Otten was all too aware of the situation in France, where the Vichy government had interned German exiles, and was preparing to hand them over to Germany. It was at Otten's instigation that the journalist Karl Gröhl was eventually rescued by British intelligence from Lisbon, where he had taken refuge after an adventurous escape from France. Fleeing before the German advance on a bicycle, Gröhl had managed to reach the small town of Montauban, near Toulouse, where he acquired false papers in the name of Retzlaw, a name he was later to adopt permanently. From Montauban on 24 July he sent Otten a letter containing the optimistic message: 'It's necessary to get down to work. Germany won't win the war. Despite all the idiocies of the English.'[89] Retzlaw, as he was now known, was finally able to reach Lisbon, where he was obliged to wait for a British visa which was being arranged through Otten's contacts. Never a discreet man, Retzlaw wrote urging Otten to expedite matters, stressing that he had no money and was in difficult circumstances in a city teeming with Gestapo agents. Further letters followed, complaining of Otten's failure to reply.[90] Otten had in fact left London to escape German airraids, and was staying near friends in Grange-over-Sands, Morecambe Bay in Cumbria. Retzlaw was eventually flown out of Lisbon, arriving in London to be questioned by British intelligence experts on conditions in France. Retzlaw later records several meetings he and Otten had with their intelligence masters.[91]

During his first few weeks in London, Retzlaw stayed with the Ottens in Hampstead Way – the last in a succession of house-guests there. He remembered Otten as 'a nervous man', who at the first sound of the airraid siren would drop everything and rush for shelter. Although the house in Hampstead Way had a small garden, it had no airraid shelter, and the Ottens had to go several hundred yards to the nearest public shelter in Finchley Road. During the winter of 1940–41, when German airraids were a nightly occurrence, the Ottens spent almost every night in the shelter, leaving home when the sirens sounded around six o'clock, carrying blankets and pillows, and returning only the following morning. Ellen Otten remembered that conditions in the shelter were somewhat primitive, the long nights often boring, alleviated only by humour and the solidarity engendered by a sense of mutual danger. Like many other refugees, she also remarked on the absence of any apparent resentment against them. Even though their accent betrayed their origin as clearly as any passport, the prevailing feeling was that everyone was 'in the same boat'.

In June 1940, with the fear of invasion in the air, Otten finished writing a major study of the origins of Nazism, sending the literary agent L. Mohrenwitz a chapter-by-chapter synopsis of what he described as a manuscript of one hundred thousand words.[92] Completion of the manuscript was the end of a protracted and painful process of research and gestation. Otten had begun work on the book in the autumn of 1937 under the working title *Geplante Illusionen* ('Planned Illusions'), describing it as a 'psychology of fascism, the attempt at an analysis, which is concerned with current problems of mass psychology, and thus a medical-sociological book'.[93] From the first he stressed that the book was an attempt to make a scientific investigation of the phenomenon of fascism and, more specifically, its social and psychological roots in Germany. In researching it, he had made systematic readings in psychology and sociology, recording the titles meticulously in an exercise book.

The main premise of the book, finally published under the title *A*

Combine of Aggression, is the massification of society: the collapse of traditional communities and the absorption of the individual into the mass. Although this process was intrinsic to all industrial societies, it had reached its apogee in Germany, in which the military, industrial and technological elite had controlled the play of forces in order to mould and direct the masses for their own aggressive purposes. Otten defined the Third Reich as the most complete attempt yet 'to guide all life within the state technologically'. In an analysis of the mass media which remains strikingly current, Otten asserted that local and national cultures were yielding to the penetration of mass media: mass-film, mass-sport, mass-emotionalism. Otten analysed the origins and psychology of German militarism, before turning, in a final chapter of great interest, to Hitler himself, whom he described as the archetypal petty bourgeois, governed by a hypnotic and paranoic egotism. Surveying Hitler's life, Otten concluded that he was 'hypnotised by his own experience' and 'equipped with this rich store of traumatic hypnosis', he 'hypnotises the German masses and subjects them to the condition of a medium's spiritual oppression, similar to that which formerly was, and probably still is, his own condition'. Otten insisted that Hitler was no more than the tool by which the General Staff hoped to realise its 'great plan'. With considerable prescience, he predicted that, if Germany faced the threat of imminent military defeat, the real elites would depose him, taking power back into their own hands. The 20 July plot to assassinate Hitler was still more than two years away.

The substance of Otten's argument, partly sociological, partly psychological, reflects the influence of anarchist thinkers such as the philosopher Max Stirner and the maverick psychoanalyst Otto Gross (whom Otten had known during his student days in Munich), but also of the existentialist philosopher Karl Jaspers. Written in dense, occasionally impenetrable prose, *A Combine of Aggression* was not an easy book to read. Otten had written it partly to clarify his own perception of the tensions between the modern state and the individual, but also with the purpose of enlightening the British as to the true nature of the adversary confronting them, a purpose which acquired greater urgency with the book's completion at the very height of the political crisis in June 1940. He addressed an urgent plea to Wickham Steed to help him to get the book published: 'I don't want a literary success; I want this book to be my war effort for this country in the sphere of political knowledge.'[94]

Mohrenwitz offered the book initially to Jonathan Cape, who rejected it,[95] but within three months it was accepted for publication by Allen & Unwin. Stanley Unwin must have felt that the book was an important one, or he would scarcely have agreed to publish it in the light of the prevailing paper shortage. However, in order to minimise the financial risk, he originally made the proviso that an American co-publisher should take part of the edition, because, he added presciently, 'books of this character seldom have a sufficiently large sale over here to cover the complete cost of their production'.[96] Unwin also stipulated the condition that Otten himself should pay for the translation. Otten assented, but was anxious to ensure that the translation was as faithful as possible to the original.

Publication was, from the first, beset by problems which illustrate the difficulties inherent in translation for author, translator and publisher. These began with the title. Unwin rejected Otten's original title *Planned Illusions* and it was some months before they could agree on the new title *A Combine of Aggression*, a suggestion which particularly pleased Otten because 'this phrase has been used by Mr Churchill in his latest speech'.[97] Even more contentious was the translation, which was assigned to the experienced Eden Paul, who with his wife Cedar had translated much of Stefan Zweig's work into English. The translation was delayed, first by Paul's illness and then by Otten's dissatisfaction with the English version he produced. The correspondence between writer, translator and publisher confirms that Otten was a 'difficult' author, often impatient and even irascible, sometimes pedantic in defence of a particular formulation. Paul, who met Otten several times in the course of translating *A Combine of Aggression*, commented that he was 'an able man and I like him, but he is not very easy to deal with', later adding euphemistically: 'He is keen on his terminology and I shall have to keep closer to his text than I was doing. . .'[98] Terminology was far from being the only problem. In one letter to Unwin, Paul noted Otten's blazing hatred of many aspects of his native country, calling him 'more anti-German even than Vansittart'.[99]

Perhaps tactlessly, Otten had by then appointed a second translator, a fellow-émigré called Field, who, working under Otten's 'supervision', basically rewrote the parts of Paul's English text which Otten was dissatisfied with.[100] This step abruptly alienated Eden Paul, who wrote plaintively to Unwin: 'I am working hard on Otten's book, and am doing my best with it. Never again will I "collaborate" with a German author. The more English he thinks he knows, the worse he is.'[101] Part of the problem may have been that Paul, while an able literary translator, was unfamiliar with the terminology of sociology or psychology.

These problems persisted even into the page proofs, which Otten returned with a large number of corrections, insisting that he was merely correcting changes which Paul had made to a version which he (Otten) had already approved. Otten eventually got his way, but Unwin had long since come to regret their collaboration. It had proved impossible to find an American co-publisher and Unwin feared 'that the venture will involve us in very heavy loss'.[102] Because of paper shortages, there was a delay of six months before the book finally appeared.

The reviews were largely uncomprehending, reviewers complaining that, although the argument was sometimes grandiose, the language was often less than lucid. The historian A. J. P. Taylor, reviewing the book for the *Manchester Guardian*, observed sarcastically:

> One cannot but confirm the author's statement that the British reader is confronted less with 'reading matter' than with a 'task' – and what a task! A high reward should be offered for its performance.[103]

The reviewer in *The Times Literary Supplement* was scarcely more generous:

> One would have wished to be able to say appreciative things of this book, which is more than earnest and possibly better than informed. Unhappily, it is less than readable. The author's ponderosity of thought and style is German ponderosity at its most forbidding.[104]

Sales of the book were slow. A number of copies were destroyed by enemy action, but even so, at the end of 1944 well over half the original printing was still in stock and as late as 1947 over 400 copies still remained unsold.

In April 1941 the Ottens had moved into a flat in Grove End Road, St John's Wood so that he could be closer to his job at the BBC. It was this work which increasingly monopolised his time and attention, leaving little margin for independent writing. In contrast to his pre-war productivity, there are no major literary projects dating from these years, no record of any contributions to the exile newspapers which flourished in wartime London, such as *Die Zeitung* or *Zeitspiegel*. Otten had in any case little inclination to become part of the exile scene, though many of his friends were exiles.

The flat in St John's Wood consisted of only three rooms, leaving little space for guests, but there were a number of regular visitors, particularly fellow-exiles who shared Otten's political views. Prominent among these were his BBC colleague and near neighbour, Walter Rilla. Others included the artist Arthur Segal, who had shared the Ottens' exile on Majorca, the art historian Kurt Badt and the Austrian writer Fritz Gross, whose stance as an independent socialist matched Otten's own. It was Gross, whose lending library in Regent Square, off Gray's Inn Road, had long been a meeting-place of German-speaking émigrés and sympathisers, who had introduced the Ottens to Louise Haworth, a schoolteacher with literary aspirations, who became their closest English friend; on several occasions they stayed near her family home in Arnside, Grange-over-Sands.

However, the two most frequent visitors were the journalists Bernhard Menne and Hans Jaeger, who were Otten's closest political associates. Menne, who like Rilla lived near the Ottens in St John's Wood, was a former Communist, who at one time had edited the party's newspaper *Rote Fahne*. During the war years, he was to complete the ideological journey from left to right, by espousing Vansittartism. In London, he was a member of the small Fight for Freedom Group which believed that Hitler was no chance phenomenon but had been brought to power by the largest mass movement in German history. Menne was a signatory to the Group's declaration to this effect in January 1942.

Jaeger too was a former Communist, who in the twenties had been Director of the Marx-Engels archive in Frankfurt. He was a long-standing opponent of militarism and nationalism, who had some claims to being an original thinker. In such publications as *No More German Nationalism* and *A New Form of Democracy*, he expounded a German People's Socialism, based on a more direct democracy.[105] Jaeger too acknowledged the wide popular base of Nazism. His programme called for the extirpation of what he termed German *Volksimperialismus* (popular imperialism); an Allied victory was to be followed by thorough political re-education and spiritual renewal. Jaeger's ideas represented merely one of many blueprints for a future Germany. Their interest in the present discussion lies in their similarity with many of the ideas Otten had advanced in *A Combine of Aggression*.

While Menne and Jaeger were both leading actors on the German exile scene, Otten seems to have been content to remain a bit player. Partly for reasons of political discretion, he shunned the main exile organisations, such as the Free German League of Culture, cautious of the predominantly Communist influence within it. However, he also kept his distance from other smaller groups to which like-minded friends belonged.

Both Menne and Jaeger were prominent members of Kurt Hiller's Group of Independent German Authors, which met regularly during the war to discuss questions of political and literary importance. According to one source,[106] Otten was also a member, but if he was, he attended their meetings rarely, if at all. Jaeger was a leading light in Club 1943, but significantly Otten had little to do with the Club until long after the war. Similarly, both Menne and Jaeger were founder members of the Klub Konstruktivisten, which met (usually on a Sunday afternoon) 'to discuss questions of a future Germany in a positive sense'.[107] Although the Konstruktivisten represented a broad spectrum of unaligned socialist intellectuals in London exile, Otten conspicuously did not join them.[108] He was by temperament an *Einzelgänger*, a lone wolf, who even before 1914 had adopted the position of a non-aligned socialist, scrupulously avoiding all party (though not political) involvement. In London, he remained a lone voice in the Babel of political discourse amongst exiles.

In the course of 1942, Otten also made the acquaintance of the young writer and teacher Stanley Godman, who had written one of the few positive reviews of *Combine of Aggression* in the Christian *New English Weekly*.[109] Godman was sufficiently impressed by Otten's work to make contact with him, becoming a regular visitor at the flat in Grove End Road. It was he who introduced Otten to socially concerned members of the Anglican Church, notably Philip Mairet, editor of the *New English Weekly*, to which Otten later contributed various articles between 1944 and 1948. The tendency of these pieces documents the gradual shift in Otten's opinions during the war, a process which led him back towards the spiritual precepts of his Catholic childhood, though not, it must be emphasised, to Catholicism itself.

Otten's intense hatred of some aspects of his native country, noted by Eden Paul, was matched by a deep local patriotism. While detesting Prussia, he remained deeply attached to his native Rhineland. The ambivalence of his feelings emerges most clearly in his response to the progressive destruction of German cities, particularly Cologne, where he had spent much of his childhood. Cologne had been selected as the target of the first thousand-bomber raid by the RAF in May 1942. In subsequent months Otten could hear, and often see, the British bombers flying overhead on their way to assembly points over the South Coast before setting off against Germany.

Otten had spent the first fifteen years of his life in Cologne, and his memories of the city remained so vivid that on his first return visit to Germany in 1957, he had been able – although by then completely blind – to guide his wife unerringly around the inner city. However, Cologne was more than the scene of his childhood memories; with its rich architectural and artistic heritage, it was also a cradle of European civilisation. The Ottens' home had been close to the Romanesque church of St Severin, which he had attended as a child. Even after losing his sight, Otten retained a strong visual memory of the paintings of Stefan Lochner, the master of the Cologne School.

Otten's sorrow at the destruction of his native city and its priceless cultural heritage was inevitably compounded by feelings of guilt. He was, after all, no neutral; his wartime propaganda work had contributed to the destruction of his native city as surely as if he had been aboard one of the planes which had bombed it. His remorse grew as the full extent of Germany's degradation and the scale of physical destruction became clear, finding expression in the *Londoner Elegien*, a lyric cycle written during the war years. The final poem in the cycle is an elegy for his native land, whose destruction is seen as total and irreparable:

Was soll das, wie soll das weiterleben,
Das Land, das einmal unsere Heimat war,
Und ist nun ganz und gar zerstört
Für immerdar, für immerdar.

What shall it be, how shall it live on, / The land that was once our homeland / And now is utterly destroyed, / For evermore, for evermore.[110]

Otten was ultimately dissatisfied with the cycle which remains unpublished, but the theme continued to preoccupy him.

During the last winter of the war Otten became blind, something he had long feared. Always short-sighted, he had virtually lost the use of his left eye as the result of a childhood accident. During 1943–44 his remaining eye gradually deteriorated and despite consulting an eminent specialist, he finally became completely blind in December 1944. Despite two operations, at Moorfields and at St Mary's, Paddington, he remained blind for the rest of his life.

In the course of a turbulent career, Otten had become practised in the art of new beginnings – in Vienna in 1919, in Berlin in 1923, in Majorca in 1933, in London in 1936 – but the painful struggle to resume his writing career after 1945 was undoubtedly the most difficult new beginning of all. That he was able to succeed was a tribute not only to his own determination but also to the support of his wife. Though he learned to touch-type, he relied completely on her to read his work aloud to him for purposes of revision, and then retype the corrected version. Her patience and collaboration became even more indispensable in the extensive editorial work he undertook during the late fifties.

FREE AUSTRIA

Robert Neumann's adoption of English as a literary language did not mean that he had repudiated German. On the contrary, he continued to use his native language both domestically and professionally. Moreover, after his return to London early in 1941, he began to play an increasingly active role in the main Austrian exile organisations – the Austrian Centre, and its political counterpart, the Free Austrian Movement.

In fact, Neumann had thrown himself heart and soul into this political work, his enthusiasm audible in a letter to Stefan Zweig, written the day before Zweig's suicide.

> Rolly and I are leading intensely active lives. She is working on economic and labour matters, both for her Ministry and for the Free Austrian Movement, and I am doing a lot of cultural political and propaganda work.
>
> The emigrants here are no longer depressed, they almost all have work, many intellectuals are in factories and terribly proud of it. . . You may smile when you read this, dear friend. You wouldn't if you were here and saw the people.[111]

The Austrian Centre was the biggest of the various self-help organisations which emerged in London in 1938–39, as more and more refugees began to arrive from the newly-Nazified Austria. Established in two adjacent terraced houses in Paddington, the Centre aimed to provide a social and cultural meeting-place for Austrians in London, and to represent their interests in dealings with the British authorities. Its activities soon comprised a library, a weekly newspaper, a theatre and a coffee-house and restaurant.

Neumann's first contacts with the Austrian Centre dated from 1939, when it had opened a small theatre, the Laterndl, intended to recreate a typically Viennese theatrical tradition, that of the *Kleinkunstbühne*, or small cabaret theatre, offering satirical comment on political events, which had flourished under the *Ständestaat*, only to be ruthlessly suppressed by the Nazis in 1938. The Laterndl had turned to Neumann, as a figure of some standing in the London literary scene, to persuade the PEN Club to act as patron of the fledgling theatre. It was also largely due to his efforts that English literary notables, such as Wells and Priestley, were in the audience for its first production.[112]

With the internment of many of its leading performers, and much of its audience, the Laterndl was forced to close in May 1940. After reopening in September 1941, it offered a mixture of classic and contemporary Austrian plays, alternating with political cabaret, a programme which documents a wider dichotomy. Neumann was one of the leading spokesmen in a debate on the role and function of exile theatre, conducted in the columns of *Zeitspiegel*, in which other participants included Oskar Kokoschka, and the writer Bruno Heilig. The controversy centred on a short play, written for the Laterndl by Franz Hartl, the brutal realism of which had shocked and upset part of its audience. Neumann was unequivocal: 'The play is by far the best thing that Hartl has written up to now, in fact it is the best thing produced by an Austrian exile up to now.'[113] Exile theatre, he affirmed, was not merely an excuse for nostalgic entertainment, but also a forum for moral and political debate, a view he repeated a year later in an open letter to *Zeitspiegel*, chiding his compatriots for their failure to support the Laterndl production of *Thunder Rock*. Written by the American author Robert Ardrey, *Thunder Rock* dealt with the very problem of racism which had indirectly created the Laterndl and its audience. Praising the production as a risky but successful experiment, Neumann compared it favourably with its West End counterparts: 'It is a long time since I spent such an interesting and exciting evening. But I spent it in a room in which there were roughly thirty people. The rest was empty.' Emphasising the important role which theatre could play in the common struggle against fascism, he concluded by asking caustically when *Zeitspiegel* would bring its readers on a conducted tour of the Laterndl.[114] Neumann's spirited intervention confirms his still passionate involvement in Austrian cultural affairs in spring 1943 – more than a year after the publication of his first novel in English. He remained a regular visitor to the Laterndl which he actually chose as the setting for the opening scene of his next novel, *The Inquest*.

While the Austrian Centre was primarily a social and cultural organisation, Neumann was also prominent in its political counterpart, the Free Austrian Movement (FAM), founded on 3 December 1941 to pursue 'the right of self-determination of the Austrian people'. The very name of the organisation was naturally intended to invite comparison with the Free French, the Free Czechs and the other national resistance movements based in London. There was, however, one difference which it was impossible to overlook. While Austria, like Czechoslovakia, had been annexed to the Reich, the British government had given this annexation de facto recognition, so that Austria no longer officially existed as a political entity, whereas Czechoslovakia continued to be recognised, even enjoying the status of an allied country. The immediate objective of the FAM was to secure British recognition of Austria as the first victim of Nazi aggression. and the acceptance of 'free Austrians' as wartime allies. There was of course a post-war correlative: the re-establishment of an independent Austria, and the explicit adoption of this goal as an Allied war aim.

The FAM was an umbrella organisation to which virtually all the main Austrian exile groups were affiliated. Political adversity had created some unlikely bedfellows, uniting the Austrian Communists in Great Britain, the Association of Austrian Social Democrats and the predominantly monarchist Austrian League. Only the London 'Büro österreichischer Sozialisten' (representing the dominant group of Social Democrats) stood aside, refusing to affiliate on the grounds that they opposed the aim of an independent Austria. Despite the Anschluss, the 'Büro' still adhered to the party's pre-1934 policy that Austria should be part of a greater Germany.

Neumann was one of several well-known Austrians who publicly declared their support for the FAM, others including Anna Mahler (whose reputation as a sculptress had transcended even her fame as Gustav Mahler's daughter), Elias Canetti and Oskar Kokoschka. In the following months Neumann played a prominent, if largely decorative role in the FAM. At the Movement's first mass rally on 24 January 1942, when over 1,500 Austrians packed the Porchester Hall, it was Neumann who opened the proceedings by reading a message from the Free Austrians to Winston Churchill, thanking the Prime Minister for his statement that Austria had been the first victim of Nazi aggression, and declaring total support for the struggle of Great Britain and her allies. In a subsequent keynote speech to the meeting, Neumann recalled the dark days of 1938, when destitute and bewildered refugees had begun to arrive in London. Going on to apostrophise Free Austria as part of the great coalition of allied nations opposing Germany, he ended his speech with the rhetorical slogan: 'We are no longer alone.'[115]

Neumann also presided over a gradual but inexorable politicisation of the Austrian Exile PEN Group.[116] The Group was among the first organisations to affiliate to the Free Austrian Movement, even changing its name to Free Austrian PEN to make the collaboration more visible. In subsequent discussions it was agreed to draw up an action plan to develop a cultural programme, under the auspices of Austrian PEN, which would unite all Austrian writers and artists living in Britain in one single organisation, and bring them together at artistic and literary events.

The first of these events, held in August 1942, was the Austrian Cultural Conference (*Kulturkonferenz*), convened by Austrian PEN and chaired by Neumann.[117] The aim of the Conference was twofold: to raise awareness of Austrian culture amongst refugees and the British public, and to assert Austria's distinct cultural identity. The demonstration of an independent cultural tradition had of course a political corollary, namely: the political independence of Austria and the post-war re-establishment of an independent Austrian state. Indeed, the need to assert an independent *cultural* identity in the pursuit of political independence goes far to explain the extraordinary range and vitality of Austrian cultural activity which flourished in London during the war.

Four years earlier, Neumann had established the Austrian Exile PEN as a quixotic gesture of opposition to the Anschluss; now it seemed an appropriate vehicle for cultural self-assertion. The Group's annual report for 1942 outlines a plan to publish a series of books and pamphlets, beginning with a collection of verse by Theodor Kramer, an exile poet whose Austrian credentials needed no emphasis.[118] Though this slim volume did eventually appear under the title *Verbannt aus Österreich* ('Expelled from Austria'),[119] it was much delayed and the project soon lost momentum. Only two further titles appeared under the PEN imprint, an outcome certainly reflecting financial difficulties, but perhaps also Neumann's gradual political disillusionment.

At the outbreak of war, Neumann had written to the BBC, proposing the creation of a separate service to broadcast to Austria. The BBC was cautious. In the light of the British government's lack of any clear policy towards Austria (a legacy of the over-hasty acceptance of the Anschluss in 1938) it had made no provision for separate broadcasting to Austria. It was spring 1941 before the BBC finally introduced a specifically Austrian news bulletin within the framework of the German Service, though even then it amounted to only fifteen minutes out of a total of four hours' broadcasting. Austrian exiles were quick to criticise these broadcasts, and their lack of any clear political focus. In a letter to Richard Crossman, Neumann asserted that the broadcasts spoke to a patriotic middle-class audience, ignoring the workers and peasants. A stronger political line was necessary to reach this audience, he claimed, suggesting that 'a straightforward Socialism could work'.[120]

It was clearly this constituency Neumann hoped to address in a series of manuscripts, written in 1942–43, which have survived amongst his unpublished papers. These were written for the Austrian Talks Section which the BBC belatedly introduced early in 1942 in order to improve the quality of broadcasting to Austria.[121] One of the most interesting manuscripts, of which there are three variants, is entitled 'Austrian Brains Trust', following the format of the BBC's hugely successful 'Brains Trust' programme, which had already become a weekly listening landmark in most British households. Written in May/June 1942,[122] the manuscript outlines a discussion between a Tyrolean peasant farmer and a Viennese industrial worker about Austria's postwar future: 'What should happen to Austria – that's a great and burning question, now that Nazi Germany is approaching its end.' Clearly premissed on the political agenda of the FAM, the discussion ends on a note of exclamatory apotheosis: 'A free Austria!' – 'That's right. In a free Europe!'

The script is a rather pedestrian piece, lacking Neumann's customary wit and élan, and suggesting he was probably unsuited to the crudities of propaganda, but precisely its lack of subtlety underlines his commitment to the cause of Austrian independence. Neumann subsequently remarked that few of his manuscripts were accepted by the BBC and this was certainly not among them, its rejection owing less to its stylistic crudities than to its espousal of a political agenda which did not conform to official British policy towards Austria.

It was not until March 1943 that a fully independent Austrian Programme was finally introduced and by then Neumann had turned his attention to other matters. During that year he was commissioned by the Ministry of Information to write two short films. For the first of these, *Those were the Men*, he provided an outline scenario which was scripted by Dylan Thomas.[123] He also submitted an outline for a film on 'Free Austrians and Free Germans in Great Britain', though this was never made.

During the same year Neumann also made occasional contributions to the BBC's regular English programmes, among them a short feature called 'Nietzsche's Zarathustra', dealing with the perversion of Nietzsche's philosophy by the Nazis, which was broadcast in the series 'Books and People'.[124]

On 1 November 1943 the three Allied Powers issued the Moscow Declaration, which included the statement that a free, independent Austria was among Allied war aims. With the achievement of its main political objective, the FAM was in celebratory mood. It held a large rally at the Porchester Hall to mark the twenty-fifth anniversary of the founding of the Austrian Republic, at which Neumann was again one of the main speakers.[125] Six weeks later (on 16 December 1943) the Home Secretary announced that all those who could prove that they had been Austrian citizens before the Anschluss could re-register as Austrians.

In retrospect, Neumann was inclined to belittle his own involvement with Austrian exile organisations. His memoirs devote little space to it, even the few sparse references being marked by irony, not least against himself. He recounts, for example that his speech to the Porchester Hall meeting had been adjudged too flippant for so grave an occasion. On the following day he had received 'an official protest letter, signed jointly, shoulder to shoulder, by representatives of both the Austrian Communists and Monarchists'.[126] Communists and Monarchists were soon to turn against each other, and both were to turn against the Social Democrats.

This fragmentation, and the relentless politicking which accompanied it, may have persuaded Neumann to withdraw from exile political activity. More probably he had already decided not to return to Austria and to apply for British naturalisation after the war. His desire to assimilate to British society, foreshadowed in his switch to English as a literary language, was reinforced in 1943–44 by his editorial involvement with Hutchinson's, and the success of his second 'English' novel, developments which linked his literary career more firmly to Britain, and made an early return to Austria even more unlikely.

However, the event which finally determined his break with exile circles was neither political nor professional, but personal: the death of his son, Heinrich, in the spring of 1944. Despite his divorce from his first wife, Neumann had maintained a close relationship with his son.

Interned shortly after his father in 1940, Heini had managed to gain his release by volunteering for the Pioneer Corps, subsequently joining another army unit. Outside his army service, he had shown considerable promise as a writer, having already published one or two short pieces. He died suddenly and unexpectedly as the result of a mysterious kidney complaint. The death of his son was an emotional blow from which Neumann took many months to recover. The diary he kept during these months reveals the depth of his grief and incomprehension at a tragedy for which neither literary success nor personal affection would ever console him. It ends on a note of resignation: 'They were the three most terrible months I have ever experienced. But I live on. I am still alive.'[127]

Part Six

Return Journey

'ONCE AN EMIGRÉ, ALWAYS AN EMIGRÉ':
THE RECEPTION OF EXILE LITERATURE IN POST-WAR
GERMANY

When the war came to an end in 1945, exile did not suddenly end with it. Both Germany and Austria lay in ruins, occupied countries to which few were inclined, or even allowed, to return. In the immediate post-war years, nobody could travel to Germany or Austria without the permission of the military authorities in the specific zone of occupation. While certain political refugees, such as leading SPD politicians, were allowed to return to Germany almost immediately, many other political refugees were not, so that some were only able to return long after the crucial political decisions had been made.

Most refugees had little initial incentive to return. Many had, after desperate struggles, succeeded in making a new life in their adopted countries and saw little advantage in exchanging this precarious security for the uncertainties of Germany or Austria. Those who had found refuge in Britain also felt a debt of gratitude, which many discharged by becoming British citizens. The revelation of German war crimes, encapsulated in British eyes by pictures taken at the liberation of Belsen, had made Germany a moral leper. Nor did the nascent West German state make any effort to welcome back the refugees.

Many of the refugees who had come to Britain had made great efforts to assimilate to English language and culture – and were surprised to find how little the English accepted them. The novelist Hilde Spiel and her husband Peter de Mendelssohn had made a determined and superficially successful attempt to assimilate to English language and culture. Both had secured a foothold in London literary circles, contributing regularly to the *New Statesman*. Spiel recalls a conversation with the journal's editor Kingsley Martin, which had been interrupted by the radio announcement that the Americans had dropped an atomic bomb on Hiroshima. 'That's the end of the war,' Martin commented, and turning to Spiel and her husband: 'I suppose you'll be going back home now?' Only then had she realised that their strenuous efforts to assimilate over the previous decade had been largely in vain.[1]

In the immediate post-war years, there were particular problems confronting exiled writers who wished to re-establish themselves in the German-speaking world. Book publishers faced chronic paper short-ages and were also subject to indirect censorship through the system of publishing licences issued by the military authorities in the respective occupation zones. The handful of German-language publishers outside occupied territory, such as Bermann Fischer in Stockholm or Emil Oprecht in Zurich, faced considerable obstacles to the sale and distrib-ution of books in Germany and Austria. Alfred Kerr was among those who blithely assumed that he could reclaim his reading public in Germany. His correspondence with Gottfried Bermann Fischer in 1946–47 vividly documents the tenacity of this illusion, and the logistic difficulties facing the publisher.[2]

As the technical difficulties of the early occupation years receded, they were replaced by ideological problems. Many exiled writers had seen themselves as the curators of German culture, attempting to preserve the literary tradition which Nazism had intended to destroy. But cultural continuity was not reasserted in post-war Germany. The exiles who returned to West Germany were mostly unable to re-estab-lish themselves, finding the spirit of the times inimical. Their pre-occupation with the experience of exile was intrinsically backward-looking, and was widely perceived as irrelevant or even threatening, in a country concerned to forget the past and forge a new identity. The work they had written in exile met with indifference or often even downright opposition. They were viewed critically by writers who had remained in Germany, including those who had opportunely withdrawn into 'inner emigration'. In 1945 Walter von Molo called on Thomas Mann to return from exile, a summons to which the latter responded with a sweeping condemnation of all books published in

Germany between 1933 and 1945: 'A smell of blood and shame clings to them. They should all be pulped.' The author Frank Thieß, who had remained in the Third Reich, thereupon published his 'Goodbye to Thomas Mann', whom he accused of leading a well-upholstered life in America and of being ignorant of the realities of Germany, which only those who had stayed on, suffering the tortures of 'inner emigration', were competent to speak of.[3] Such disputes were symptomatic of a wider social schism.

A younger generation of writers, if not hostile, had little time for literature written in exile: their literary subject-matter was to be their own experience of war and its aftermath. In particular, the younger writers associating in the Gruppe 47, which came to dominate the literary scene in post-war Germany, perceived exile literature as backward-looking in style and subject-matter. Many exiled writers – not least Robert Neumann – felt marginalised by the Group and its claim to represent post-war German literature. In an open letter to the critic Marcel Reich-Ranicki, but addressed no less to the Gruppe 47, Neumann commented scathingly: 'Here in this country, they've forgiven and forgotten our exile, our life in purgatory, in the misery of foreign climes and now just wish tactfully not to be reminded of it any more.'[4]

Many of the exiled writers had begun their literary careers in a period dominated by Expressionism, a movement whose works the Nazis had pursued with particular vigour and which the post-war literary establishment in both West and East Germany treated with almost contemptuous disregard. Much of the writing of this period had survived the war only fragmentarily. That the best of it is still accessible today is due to the devotion of a handful of dedicated editors, most notably Karl Otten, whose anthologies of Expressionist verse and prose, selected and edited with the indispensable assistance of his wife, were published after 1957.[5]

With the emergence of the Cold War, in which Germany constituted the front line, the exiles and their work encountered growing suspicion. In a cultural agenda increasingly dominated by the political Right, they became, in Hans-Albert Walter's telling phrase, 'the victims of a political situation for the second time'.[6] Even some of those who had elected to return to Germany in the early fifties, such as the poet Hans Sahl, found the atmosphere so hostile that they felt obliged to re-emigrate.[7]

Few of the writers who had sought refuge in Britain chose to return to Germany or Austria. Most of those who did were committed Communists like Jan Petersen, Max Zimmering or Kurt Barthel (KuBa), who returned to the Soviet zone of occupation; and for those who settled in what became the German Democratic Republic, the prospects initially seemed much brighter. There was a genuine attempt to reclaim the literary tradition which the Nazis had disrupted, but which had continued to be cultivated in exile. Famous writers such as Johannes R. Becher, Anna Seghers, Arnold Zweig and Bertolt Brecht received public honours and official positions in the new state. As attitudes hardened in the Cold War, they found themselves as cultural figureheads for the new political regime, their work conscripted to a political agenda they could only partly endorse. Even the works they had written in exile were reread and reassessed with the hindsight of a new ideological orthodoxy.

The exigencies of the Cold War delayed any serious consideration of exile literature in West Germany or Austria for more than twenty years. Not until the early seventies did academic interest in different aspects of exile begin to emerge. Exile Studies became established as an academic discipline with the emergence of research centres in Frankfurt, Hamburg and Munich. As the decade progressed, exiled writers were 'rediscovered', unpublished manuscripts rescued and long-forgotten works reissued. Many of those who had survived the rigours of exile and post-war indifference were already dead; more were to die in the course of a decade which finally offered them the recognition they had so long been denied. This interest peaked during the eighties and has apparently begun to decline in the wake of German reunification, as the search for a new national identity dictates a different cultural agenda.

Alfred Kerr lived on in Putney, an impoverished and increasingly lonely figure, vividly remembered by his daughter. Returning after his death to look at the boarding-house which had been his last home, she found that it had been demolished:

The only thing that had been the same was the bench at the end of the street where Papa had sometimes sat in the sun with his pipe. He had eked out the tobacco with dried leaves and rose petals and for lunch he had eaten bread toasted over the gas ring and spread with exactly one seventh of a jar of fish paste.[8]

Early in 1947, Kerr's wife Julia had returned to Germany to work as an interpreter for the Americans at the war crimes tribunal in Nuremberg. Kerr's children had both grown up during the war. His son Michael had served in the Royal Air Force before resuming his study of law; he was to become a distinguished QC and later a judge. His daughter Judith won an art school scholarship and became an illustrator and author of children's books. Her autobiographical novel *When Hitler Stole Pink Rabbit* was to become a children's classic in both Britain and Germany. The novel was the first of an autobiographical trilogy, which Judith Kerr wrote as part of the process of defining her own identity.

Kerr himself – who at the end of the war was in his seventy-eighth year – acknowledged that he could not return to Germany – and was not interested in doing so. At the first opportunity, he applied for British naturalisation, asking George Bernard Shaw to act as one of his sponsors. He finally became a British citizen in May 1947, six months short of his eightieth birthday.[9] His application for naturalisation was both a practical step, acknowledging the impossibility of returning permanently to Germany, and a gesture of loyalty, demonstrating his feelings of affinity with Britain, despite his realisation that he could never really become British. Above all, it was an endorsement of his children, both of whom had assimilated to British society.

When Kerr finally returned to Germany, it was therefore, ironically, as a British citizen. In July 1947 he went to Switzerland to attend the International PEN Congress and from there travelled to see his wife in Nuremberg, the first time he had set foot on German soil for fourteen years. He was shocked by the total devastation he saw, finding the whole experience profoundly disturbing:

> Today I am, for the first time in fourteen years, once more in the country of my youth, my love, my agony. And of my language. . . How does one feel, after all that has happened? Not like an unforgiving enemy – truly not. But like a shattered companion. Shattered, but mistrustful.[10]

Kerr made a further trip to Germany in September 1948, at the invitation of the British Council, flying to Hamburg for a lecture tour. On his first evening there, he went to the theatre, where he was acclaimed by the audience: once more the king of critics appearing to his people. But the excitement proved too much for him. That same evening he suffered a stroke, which left him paralysed on his right side. He was taken to the British Military Hospital in Hamburg where, on 12 October, he took an overdose of sleeping tablets to end his life. In a final letter to his son Michael, he wrote: 'I loved life very much, but ended it when it became a torture.'[11] A month later, the German community in London met to honour his memory, aware that it had lost its most emblematic figure.[12]

Kerr was buried in the cemetery at Ohlsdorf, outside Hamburg, but though his remains lie in German soil, Germany has received him back only hesitantly. For fifty years after his death, there was still no Kerr biography, no complete edition of his works. Now at last a biography is in progress and the publication of his collected works, a project abandoned in the early nineties after the withdrawal of a publishing subsidy, has been resumed.[13] Such occurrences confirm the recent revival of interest in the 'Kritikerpapst', prompted by the publication in 1997 of his letters from *fin-de-siècle* Berlin, which became a surprising bestseller. Time will tell whether the success of this volume is evidence of a Kerr renaissance or merely a token of the renewed interest in Berlin as the old/new cultural capital of Germany. Berlin also houses Kerr's literary estate, including the manuscripts he wrote in exile in Britain: significantly, these remain largely unpublished and unknown.

Robert Neumann played a leading part in re-establishing the Austrian PEN Centre in post-war Vienna, becoming its Honorary President, though he himself elected not to return to Austria. He settled after the war in the village of Cranbrook in Kent, living in a house which had formerly been an isolation hospital for plague victims. He later described his life there in the informal memoir, *The Plague House Papers*. In 1947 he acquired British nationality and, in one of the feats of literary impersonation which had first made him famous, became an 'English' writer, publishing a total of seven novels in his adopted language.

The critical acclaim which had greeted *The Inquest* in 1944 was followed by commercial success for *Children of Vienna* in which Neumann sought to draw attention to the post-war suffering of his native city.[14] His publisher, Victor Gollancz, was at first sceptical about the book's prospects, believing that people wished to forget the sufferings of war, but the book rapidly progressed from a modest first printing to become an international bestseller, the topical theme contributing greatly to its success.

In the immediate post-war years Neumann was also an energetic General Editor of the Hutchinson's International Authors series, in which he published numerous works by fellow-exiles, as well as re-issuing his own novel *A Woman Screamed* under the title *Failure of a Hero*. He finally severed his connection with the firm in 1948 after the suicide of Walter Hutchinson. Neumann's marriage to Rolly Becker did not endure: they separated in 1952, and divorced the following year. Neumann married for a third time, but on the sudden death of his new wife in 1958 he decided to leave England, abandoning his house in Kent and making a new home in Switzerland with his young son, Michael. There he married for the fourth time, relinquishing his British persona, though not his British nationality, and reverting once more to writing in his native language. Speaking German in his private life, he had little occasion to use English – 'and you can write in a foreign language only if you live in it'.[15]

Neumann was always conscious of his position as a writer between two languages. He later asserted that he used to end up writing two versions of any new work, one for the German and another for the English publisher: two essentially different texts, their differences dictated by the rhythms of language and the cultural cues that prompt them.

In post-war Germany, he was never really able to regain the stature he had achieved before 1933. In 1960 he described himself, with typical exaggeration, as 'unknown – in the country which discovered me'.[16] In fact, in one of the oddities of post-war cultural relations, he was re-introduced to the German reading public during the fifties through the translations of the very novels he had written in English. But his career in Germany was dogged by publishing misfortunes. His first post-war publisher, Curt Weller, announced plans to republish his pre-war oeuvre, but this project collapsed almost immediately with the insolvency of the Weller Verlag. From 1950 Neumann's work was published in Germany and Austria under the imprint of the Kurt Desch Verlag, which in 1959 began to issue an edition of his collected works in single volumes. Interest in this project was certainly stimulated by the appearance of his memoirs, *Ein leichtes Leben* (1963), a dazzling and witty entertainment which reconstructed his own life, sometimes subordinating biographical fact to the requirements of a good story. The success of this, and a subsequent volume, seemed to have re-established Neumann's reputation, but misfortune once more intervened. Desch went into liquidation in 1973, resulting in the disappearance of many Neumann titles from the market. Neumann himself died shortly after and in the twenty-five years since his death his literary reputation has suffered the same eclipse as that of so many of his contemporaries. In the German-speaking world, he is still remembered – but mainly as the brilliant parodist of the twenties. Only three of his many books are now in print in Germany, two of which are the collections of parodies which first made him famous.

Karl Otten was another who chose not to return to Germany. Both he and his wife became British citizens in 1947, his wartime work entitling him to make a priority application. Ellen was by then working full-time for the BBC and the possibility of returning to Germany was made more remote by Otten's blindness. In the early post-war years, Otten wrote extensively in English, trying to establish himself as a journalist, though with limited success. The poems he wrote in English, mainly about the English countryside (Westmoreland) were never published.

Like many exiles, Otten was sceptical of the willingness of the emergent Federal Republic to come to terms with Germany's immediate past. He was particularly embittered by the new state's failure to invite the exiles to return or even to reinstate the German nationality of which the Third Reich had robbed them, the formal response of the federal government being that those who had been deprived of German nationality could reapply for it if they wished.

Otten finally left England in 1958. His increasingly delicate health required a warmer climate, while his creative work demanded greater proximity to the German-speaking world. By then he had been able partly to re-establish his literary reputation in Germany, enjoying at least one tangible success with the novel *Die Botschaft*, which was awarded the Albert Schweitzer prize in 1957.[17] Among his later publications were the verse collection *Herbstgesang* (1961) and the autobiographical novel *Wurzeln* (1963).[18] But Otten's own writing was largely eclipsed by his work as an editor. In 1954 he also began plans to compile an anthology of Expressionist writing, a project which inevitably drew him back into a German-speaking context. The anthology was to be a work of conservation and reparation, intended to save the best writing of his generation from the ravages of historical neglect. The Nazis had banned Expressionist writing as decadent, consigning it to oblivion for over twenty years. Otten saw it as a moral duty to rescue it and make it available to a new generation. It was in order to prepare the publication of this anthology that Otten finally revisited Germany in 1957, after an absence of almost twenty five years.

The anthology *Ahnung und Aufbruch*[19] provoked great literary interest, its surprising success convincing Otten of the need to continue his editorial work – and finally persuading him to leave Britain, though not to return to Germany. Instead, he chose to move to Switzerland, settling with his wife in Minusio, near Locarno. They had first visited the region in 1952, staying in Ascona, which they visited every year afterwards. One attraction was the climate, another the literary associations of Ascona, where a number of German exiles already lived. At the end of 1957, Ellen gave up her job at the BBC and the couple moved to Switzerland, living first in Ascona before settling in Minusio early the following year.

Otten's editorial work dominated the final years of his life, during which he edited no less than five anthologies of Expressionist writing, as well as two of Jewish prose and poetry, the last of which appeared only shortly before his death. It was these anthologies which made his name known to a new generation in Germany and which today represent his most lasting monument.[20] Otten died in 1963 from bronchial cancer. He is buried in Minusio, where Ellen Otten continued to live until her death in 1999.

Max Herrmann-Neiße's application for British naturalisation was never processed: at the time of his death he was stateless, and in the sixty years which have since passed, Germany has done almost as little to reclaim him as England did to accept him. In post-war Germany he was a forgotten figure, despite the efforts of his friend Friedrich Grieger, who published a short selection from his work in 1951. Occasionally one of his poems would appear in an anthology, but much of what he wrote in exile remained unpublished for more than forty years. In the eighties an edition of his complete works was finally published,[21] but though obviously a labour of love, it occasioned only modest interest. A wall plaque with a relief portrait marks the house where the poet once lived on Berlin's Kurfürstendamm: perhaps symbolically, the plaque is invisible from street level. Sixty years after his death, Max Herrmann-Neiße remains firmly in exile.

Stefan Zweig, by contrast, has become part of the literary canon of the early twentieth century. Following a brief period of relative neglect after the war, his work was republished and has since remained widely available in Germany and Austria. In addition, his work has continued to attract scholarly interest, both in and outside Germany, and has become the subject of a thriving academic industry. In his native Vienna, a plaque marks the house where he lived for many years; a memorial tablet stands at the approach to his house on the Kapuzinerberg in Salzburg.

What of Britain now? What legacy, if any, have German-speaking exiles left to English literature? In the last decade there has been a rapid growth of interest in German-speaking exile, and an increasing recognition of the influence of exiles on British culture in such areas as opera production (Carl Ebert and Fritz Busch), film (Emeric Pressburger), graphic art (Berthold Wolpe and Hans Schmoller) and publishing – George Weidenfeld and Nicolson, Phaidon, Thames and Hudson and Paul Hamlyn were among notable publishing houses founded by émigrés. Yet German-speaking writers have had no comparable influence on the English literary scene, indeed, with the exception of Koestler, and possibly Canetti, they are no longer even remembered, except by a small circle of scholars of German.

None of the authors discussed in this book has made any lasting mark on English literature. Even those who attempted to assimilate by switching to English as a literary language, have been long forgotten. For a decade and a half Robert Neumann was a distinguished, if distinctly alien voice on the English literary scene, only to vanish from it almost as soon as he left the country. His work has been out of print in English for thirty-five years.

Despite early naturalisation, Karl Otten felt that the British wished to keep the exiles at arm's length; his efforts to break into the English literary market were unsuccessful. His children's story *Pilgrimage of a Donkey*, though first written in English, was published only in German, finally appearing in Switzerland. The BBC archives record the rejection of several works for radio, including the verse drama, *They Shake the Pillars of the Earth*: rejections which hastened Otten's eventual return to a German-speaking environment.

Stefan Zweig, always the most readable of authors, has fared rather better in that several of his stories, including *Amok*, *Letter from an Unknown Woman* and *The Royal Game*, have remained in print or been republished. However, his once-fashionable biographies have fallen out of favour. Even *The Queen of Scots*, which once consolidated his fame in Britain, is long out of print. Moreover, in an interesting echo of the 1930s, his work has far less resonance in Britain than in neighbouring European countries. In France, no less than three biographies of Zweig have appeared in recent years, while virtually all his work has been republished, including a new translation of *Die Welt von Gestern*. By contrast, the only edition of *The World of Yesterday* available in Britain is that published by an American university press, reprinting Benjamin Huebsch's contemporary (and now often dated) translation. Only Zweig's extra-literary activity has assured him a minor place in British cultural history. The British Library still holds the collection of musical manuscripts which he bequeathed to the British Museum. Zweig, the discerning collector, whose happiest hours in London were spent in the Museum's Reading Room, would have been quietly pleased. The only other tangible sign of his eight years in Britain is the newly-erected plaque outside Rosemount, his former house in Bath, recording his brief residence there.

What of general attitudes to foreign (and particularly German) literature? In an era of information technology and globalisation, it might be assumed that British cultural horizons have widened since the thirties. While this assumption is true, it is a very specific truth. The possession of a common language has made British culture more vulnerable than any other to American influence, but precisely for this reason it has remained strikingly monolingual.

In the last decade British publishing has witnessed unprecedented 'rationalisation'. Many of those whose names figured prominently in the preceding pages – Gollancz or Hamish Hamilton, Hutchinson or Jonathan Cape – have either vanished or become local imprints of global media businesses, such as Pearson, Reed or Bertelsmann. One of the seeming paradoxes of globalisation is that translation still accounts for roughly the same proportion of the output of British publishing, some three per cent, as it did in the thirties.

There are, however, more encouraging signs of change, notably in the emergence of several outstanding translators from German. German and Austrian exiles have played an important role in cultural reconciliation between Britain and the German-speaking world, representing a tangible benefit of German exile in Britain. The Austrian poet Erich Fried, like the nineteenth-century exile Ferdinand Freiligrath, made a notable contribution to German understanding of British culture with his translations of contemporary poets like Dylan Thomas and Sylvia Plath. Conversely, Michael Hamburger's translations have deeply affected English perceptions of German poetry. By 1980 there was hardly a contemporary German poet of any standing who did not owe his or her reception in English to Hamburger. More recently, the work of talented younger translators such as Michael Hulse and Michael Hofmann has helped to secure an international reputation for authors like W. G. Sebald, or in Hofmann's case, his father, Gert Hofmann. There is now even a journal, *New Books in German*, which exists to stimulate the interest of British publishers in new writing in German. The fact that it exists is a hopeful sign; the fact that it *needs* to exist is a measure of the still hesitant nature of Anglo-German literary relations.

Notes

NOTES TO THE INTRODUCTION

1. See for example, Hans-Albert Walter's multi-volume survey *Deutsche Literatur im Exil 1933–50 in sieben Bändern*, Stuttgart 1978ff.

2. A. J. Sherman, *Island Refuge. Britain and Refugees from the Third Reich 1933–39*, London 1973; Peter and Leni Gillman, *Collar the Lot*, London 1980; Werner Röder, *Die deutschen sozialistischen Exilgruppen in Großbritannien* (1968); Helene Maimann, *Politik im Wartesaal. Österreichische Exilpolitik in Großbritannien 1938–1945*, Vienna/Cologne/Graz 1975.

3. Cf. the volume *Exile in Great Britain*, published by the London German Historical Institute in 1982, in which significantly only a single chapter is devoted to 'The Arts in Exile'. There is an excellent documentary compilation in Wolfgang Muchitsch (ed.), *Österreicher im Exil. Großbritannien 1938–1945*, Vienna 1992.

4. Marion Berghahn, *Continental Britons. German-Jewish Refugees from Nazi Germany*, Oxford/New York/Hamburg 1988; Werner E. Mosse (ed.), *Second Chance. German-speaking Jews in the United Kingdom*, Cambridge 1991.

5. See, for example, Günther Berghaus, *Theatre and Film in Exile*, Oxford/New York/Munich 1989; *Kunst im Exil in Großbritannien 1933–1945*, edited by Neue Gesellschaft für Bildende Kunst Berlin, Berlin 1986.

6. Sylvia Patsch, *Österreichische Schriftsteller im Exil in Großbritannien: ein Kapitel vergessene österreichische Literatur*, Vienna/Munich 1985.

7. See Richard Dove, *He was a German. A Biography of Ernst Toller*, London 1990.

8. Will Schaber, *Profile der Zeit*, Eggingen 1992.

9. Theodor Kramer, 'Es mögen andere eine Heimat suchen', written in British exile in September 1941, in *Gesammelte Gedichte 2*, edited by Erwin Chvojka, Vienna 1985.

10. Christopher Isherwood, *Prater Violet*, London 1961, p. 20.

NOTES TO PART ONE

1. Fritz H. Landshoff, *Amsterdam, Keizersgracht 333. Querido Verlag*, Berlin 1991, p. 34.

2. Kurt R. Grossmann, *Ossietzky. Ein deutscher Patriot*, Munich 1973, p. 258 f.

3. *Alfred Kerr. Lesebuch zu Leben und Werk*, ed. Herrmann Haarmann and Klaus Siebenhaar, Thomas Wölk, Berlin 1987, p. 9.

4. *Die Welt im Licht*, Berlin 1920 and *New York und London*, Berlin 1923.

5. *Lesebuch*, op. cit., p. 33

6. ibid., p. 10.

7. Kerr, *Die Diktatur des Hausknechts*, Frankfurt 1983, p. 13.

8. Max Herrmann-Neiße, 'Autobiographisches', autobiographical notes orig-
inally written in about 1925; quoted according to typescript in William Rose Papers,
Institute of Germanic Studies, London (IGS). The typescript was given to William
Rose by Leni Herrmann.

9. *Verbannung. Ein Buch Gedichte*, Berlin 1919; *Der Flüchtling. Roman*, Potsdam
1921.

10. 'Autobiographisches', see note 8. The same in 'Max Herrmann-Neiße über
Max Herrmann-Neiße', *Die neue Bücherschau*, VI (1928).

11. 'Zuversicht' ('Confidence'),written 24 February 1933. See Max Herrmann-
Neiße, *Gesammelte Werke in zehn Bänden*, ed. Klaus Völker, Frankfurt 1986–8, Vol.
II ('Gedichte II'), p. 263 (cited throughout as *Gedichte II*).

12. Cf. autobiographical notes (1939). He also calls himself a 'Rheinländer' in his
application to the BBC, 1940. Both documents in Otten Estate.

13. The critic Kasimir Edschmid would praise the book (in 1917) as an early
example of Expressionist prose.

14. The sketches are reproduced in *Die rheinischen Expressionisten*, Reckling-
hausen 1979.

15. '1914 – Sommer ohne Herbst', in Paul Raabe (ed.) *Expressionismus*, Olten/
Freiburg 1965, p. 153; originally broadcast by Nordwestdeutscher Rundfunk, 15
February 1955.

16. *Karl Otten. Werk und Leben*, ed. Bernhard Zeller and Ellen Otten, p. 9, citing
notes contained in the Otten Estate.

17. Cited by Kurt Pinthus in his Afterword to the anthology
Menschheitsdämmerung, Berlin 1920, p. 295ff.

18. 'Organisiert den Widerstand des Geistes', *Berliner Tageblatt*, 31 July 1932,
Beilage 'Die Brücke', p. 1.

19. Neumann, *Ein leichtes Leben* ('An Easy Life'), Munich/Vienna/Basel 1963,
p. 20. Neumann's memoirs, written long after the events they describe, are a
dazzling entertainment, in which narrative sometimes takes precedence over
historical accuracy.

20. ibid., p. 21.

21. ibid., p. 23.

22. ibid., p. 505.

23. Zweig, *Die Welt von Gestern. Erinnerungen eines Europäers*, Frankfurt: Fischer
Taschenbuch 1970, pp. 367–68 (cited as *WvG*). Although written in German,
Zweig's memoirs were first published in English: *The World of Yesterday. An
Autobiography by Stefan Zweig*, New York: Viking Press 1943, also London: Cassell
1943. The Viking Press edition was reprinted, with an introduction by Harry Zohn
(Lincoln and London: University of Nebraska Press, 1964. Page references are to
this edition, which is still in print (cited as *WoY*, here p. 321). However, the
language of the translation is now somewhat dated, and I have consequently
preferred to use my own version of the original German.

24. *WvG*, p. 321; *WoY*, p. 280.

25. *WvG*, p. 373; *WoY*, p. 326.

26. Zweig to Frans Masereel, 15 April 1933, Zweig, *Briefe an Freunde*, ed. Richard Friedenthal, Frankfurt 1984, p. 227.

27. ibid.

28. Zweig to Romain Rolland, 10 April 1933, *Romain Rolland: Stefan Zweig. Briefwechsel 1910–40*, Vol. 2, Berlin 1987, p. 506.

29. Zweig to Franz Servaes, 11 May 1933 (StB, Vienna).

30. Zweig to Erich Ebermayer, 4 June 1932 (DLA).

31. Zweig to Ebermayer, January 1934, *Briefe an Freunde*, op. cit., p. 244.

32. *WvG*, p. 434; *WoY*, p. 382.

33. Zweig to Romain Rolland, *Briefwechsel*, Vol. 2, p. 561.

34. 'Concerning the Label Emigrant', translated by Stephen Spender, Brecht, *Poems 1913–1956*, London 1976.

35. 'Information compiled by League of Nations High Commission for Refugees' – Public Record Office (PRO): Foreign Office 371/17700/178.

36. Gerhard Hirschfeld, 'Great Britain and the Emigration from Nazi Germany: an Overview', in *Theatre and Film in Exile*, ed. Günter Berghaus, Oxford/New York/Munich 1989.

37. Rudolf and Ika Olden, *In tiefem Dunkel liegt Deutschland*, ed. Charmian Brinson and Marian Malet, Berlin 1994, p. 76. The original manuscript dates from 1933–34.

NOTES TO PART TWO

1. See Ariela Halkin, *The Enemy Reviewed. German Popular Literature through British Eyes between the Two World Wars*, London 1995.

2. Zweig to Romain Rolland, 18 March 1934, *Romain Rolland: Stefan Zweig. Briefwechsel 1910–40*, Vol. II, p. 563 (cited as *RR/SZ*). Zweig's letters to Rolland, with whom he corresponded regularly for thirty years, were (with the exception of the period 1914–17) written in French. His original letters are held in the Bibliothèque Nationale, Paris, but I have chosen – for reasons of accessibility – to quote from the German translations in the edition cited above; the English translations (which have been checked against the French originals) are my own.

3. *The Times Literary Supplement*, 10 July 1930, p. 567.

4. The title of Warburg's autobiography, *An Occupation for Gentlemen*, London 1959.

5. Cf. F. R. Leavis, *New Bearings in English Poetry* (1932) and *Revaluations* (1936), a collection of essays originally published in *Scrutiny*.

6. Among the French authors cited in *The Unquiet Grave* are Montaigne, Molière, Sainte-Beuve, Gide, Proust, Mallarmé, Valéry, etc. The only Germans quoted are Kant, Nietzsche, Schopenhauer, Karl Marx and Goethe (while even the latter is considered an 'artist-philosopher').

7. *New Statesman*, 2 March 1935, p. 284.

8. Zweig to Cassells, 25 January 1932, Österreichische Nationalbibliothek, Handschriftensammlung (NB), Ser. n. 1183/40–1.

9. *WvG*, p. 443; *WoY*, p. 390.

10. *WvG*, pp. 444–45; *WoY*, pp. 391–92.

11. See D. A. Prater, *European of Yesterday. A Biography of Stefan Zweig*, Oxford 1972, p. 271. Prater's biography was later published in a revised and expanded version: *Stefan Zweig. Das Leben eines Ungeduldigen*, Frankfurt 1984, here p. 281.

12. *WvG*, p. 442; *WoY*, p. 389.

13. Zweig to Romain Rolland, 5 May 1934, *RR/SZ* II, p. 567.

14. Huebsch to Zweig, 3 November 1933: quoted in Jeffrey B. Berlin, 'Stefan Zweig's Exile in Great Britain', *England? Aber wo liegt es? Deutsche und österreichische Emigranten in Großbritannien 1933–1945*, ed. Charmian Brinson et al., London 1996, p. 145.

15. Huebsch to Zweig, 21 March 1934, Berlin, op. cit., p. 151.

16. Zweig to Erich Ebermeyer, January 1934, Zweig, *Briefe an Freunde*, op. cit., p. 244. The figure of $3,000 a week is mentioned by Huebsch.

17. Friderike Zweig to Leonhard Adelt, 20 July 1934, quoted in Prater, op. cit. p. 238.

18. Zweig to Hans Carossa, 9 March 1934, *Briefe an Freunde*, op. cit., p. 245.

19. Zweig to Anton Kippenberg, 31 March 1934, Deutsches Literaturarchiv (DLA).

20. Zweig to Rolland, 10 June 1934, *RR/SZ* II, pp. 568–9.

21. Stefan to Friderike Zweig, 8 October 1935, *Stefan Zweig/Friderike Zweig: Briefwechsel 1912–1942 (SZ/FZ: Briefwechsel)*, Bern 1951, p. 287.

22. Zweig to Kippenberg, 20 December 1934 (DLA).

23. Zweig to Rolland 26 April 1933, *RR/SZ* II, pp. 510–11.

24. *WvG*, p. 441; *WoY*, p. 387.

25. Mann to Zweig, 15 September 1933, Klaus Mann, *Briefe und Antworten*, Vol. I, Munich 1975, p. 135.

26. Zweig to Rudolf Kaiser, 30 November 1933, *Stefan Zweig: Spiegelungen einer schöpferischen Persönlichkeit*, ed. Erich Fitzbauer, Vienna 1959, p. 75.

27. Zweig to Romain Rolland, 26 April 1933, *RR/SZ*, II, p. 510.

28. ibid., 18 December 1933, *RR/SZ*, II, p. 551.

29. Zweig to René Schickele, 2 August 1934 (DLA).

30. Zweig to Rolland 10 June 1934, *RR/SZ* II, pp. 568–69.

31. Zweig to Richard Strauss, 17 June 1934, *Richard Strauss /Stefan Zweig: Briefwechsel*, ed. Willi Schuh, Frankfurt 1957, p. 66.

32. Strauss to Zweig, 24 June 1932, ibid., p. 18.

33. ibid., 24 January 1933, p. 41.

34. ibid., 17 June 1935, p. 141.

35. Cf. Thomas Koebner, 'Militant Humanism: a Concept of the Third Way in Exile 1933–45' in *German Writers and Politics*, ed. Richard Dove/Stephen Lamb, London 1992, pp. 121–48.

36. *WvG*, p. 434; *WoY*, pp. 381–82.

37. Zweig to Joseph Roth, undated (autumn 1937), *Briefe an Freunde*, op. cit., p. 286.

38. Feuchtwanger to Zweig, 29 May 1936 (Zweig Estate, Atrium Verlag, London).

39. Zweig to Hermann Kesten, 15 January 1942, *Deutsche Literatur im Exil. Briefe europäischer Autoren 1933–1949*, ed. Hermann Kesten, Frankfurt 1973, p. 155.

40. Zweig to Cassells, 25 January 1932, Österreichische Nationalbibliothek, Handschriftensammlung (ÖNB), Ser. n. 1183/40–1.

41. See Prater, *European of Yesterday*, pp. 225–27; German edition, pp. 238–40.

42. Cf. *Briefe an Freunde*, op. cit., p. 254.

43. Zweig to Huebsch, 29 March 1934, Berlin, op. cit., p. 151.

44. Zweig to Kippenberg, 31 March 1934 (DLA).

45. Zweig to Rolland, 14 February 1934, *RR/SZ* II p. 558.

46. ibid., 4 October 1934, pp. 582–3.

47. Zweig to René Schickele, 26 September 1934, *Briefe an Freunde*, op. cit., p. 259.

48. Zweig, 'Tagebuch' – *Gesammelte Werke*, Frankfurt 1984, pp. 379–80.

49. Zweig to Kippenberg, 5 April 1935 (DLA).

50. A. L. Rowse, *Spectator*, 18 October 1935, p. 618; J. E. Neale, *Saturday Review of Literature* (New York), 31 August 1935.

51. Cf. Stefan to Friderike Zweig, 2 October 1935, *SZ/FZ: Briefwechsel*, p. 286.

52. Zweig to Rolland, 28 October 1935, *RR/SZ* II, p. 608.

53. ibid., 27 March 1936, p. 625.

54. *SZ/FZ: Briefwechsel*, p. 289.

55. Zweig to Ebermayer, 6 June 1934 (DLA).

56. Emil Ludwig on Zweig, *Aufbau* (New York), 27 February 1942.

57. *WvG*, p. 446; *WoY*, p. 393.

58. Zweig to Huebsch, 4 December 1933, *Briefe an Freunde*, op. cit., p. 148.

59. Author's interview with Desmond Flower, 14 December 1990.

60. Zweig to Desmond Flower, 29 November 1934, ÖNB Ser. n. 1183/40–12.

61. Zweig to Rolland, 31 October 1933, *RR/SZ* II, p. 537.

62. Cf. Zweig to Carossa, 2 August 1936, *Briefe an Freunde*, op. cit., p. 275.

63. 'Das Haus der tausend Schicksale', in *Begegnungen mit Menschen, Büchern, Städten*, Vienna 1937, pp. 230–33. The English version of Zweig's address, *House of a Thousand Destinies*, was published as a pamphlet, a copy of which is held at the Tower Hamlets Local History Library, London E1.

64. Cf. Fritz H. Landshoff, *Amsterdam. Keizersgracht 333*, Berlin 1991.

65. Cf. Landshoff, op. cit., p. 77.

66. See Charmian Brinson, *The Strange Case of Dora Fabian and Mathilde Wurm. A Study of German Political Exiles in London during the 1930's*, Berne 1997, particularly Chapter 5.

67. Desmond Flower, *Fellows in Foolscap*, London 1991, p. 107.

68. See Gloria Fromm, *Dorothy Richardson. A Biography*, Urbana/London 1977, pp. 266–8.

69. See handwritten manuscript, *Young Man of 1944. The Journal and Memoirs of*

Henry Herbert Neumann edited by his Father, p. 11 (ÖNB, Ser. n. 20.892). The manuscript is not only edited but also largely written by Neumann himself.

70. Reader's report by R. T. Clark, the eventual translator of the book (Allen & Unwin Archive, Reading).

71. See letters from Neumann's solicitors, Rubinstein and Nash, to Gerald Barry, editor of the *News Chronicle* (ÖNB, Ser. n. 22.471).

72. Neumann to Unwin, January 1935 and Furth to Neumann, 5 January 1935 (Allen & Unwin Archive, Reading).

73. *New Statesman*, 21 September 1935 and *The Times Literary Supplement*, 17 October 1935.

74. Furth to Neumann, 21 October 1935 (Allen & Unwin Archive, Reading).

75. Reader's report by Edward Crankshaw (Allen & Unwin Archive, Reading).

76. Neumann to Muir, 3 August 1935 (Gollancz Archive).

77. Muir to Gollancz, 11 September 1935 (Gollancz Archive).

78. Gollancz to Muir, 30 March 1936 (Gollancz Archive).

79. Muir to Gollancz, 4 April 1936 (Gollancz Archive).

80. *Ein leichtes Leben*, p. 54.

81. ibid.

82. Fromm, *Dorothy Richardson*, p. 268.

83. *Ein leichtes Leben*, pp. 114–15.

84. *Ein leichtes Leben*, p. 45. See also Fritz Kortner, *Aller Tage Abend*, Munich 1959, pp. 427–37.

85. Ronald A. Button to Neumann, 20 January 1937, ÖNB, Ser. n. 21.801.

86. *Ein leichtes Leben*, pp. 117–18.

87. Ronald A. Button to Neumann, 20 January 1937, cf. note 85.

88. *Ein leichtes Leben*, p. 35.

89. Hilde Spiel, *Die hellen und die finsteren Zeiten*, Munich 1989, p. 103.

90. Letter to PEN International Executive Committee, 28 December 1933 (DEA, 75/175–1). (PEN stands for Poets/Playwrights, Editors/Essayists, Novelists.)

91. *Das Wort* (Moscow), I/2 (1936).

92. Max to Leni Herrmann, 12 May 1933 (DLA).

93. Herrmann-Neiße to Friedrich Grieger, 22 September 1933 in *Max Herrmann-Neiße. Eine Einführung in sein Werk*, ed. Friedrich Grieger, Wiesbaden 1951, p. 76.

94. Herrmann-Neiße to Friedrich Grieger, 30 November 1934, Grieger, op. cit., p. 83.

95. First published in *Letzte Gedichte* 1941, reprinted in *Gedichte II*, Frankfurt 1986, p. 639.

96. Herrmann-Neiße to Klaus Pinkus, 23 May 1935 (DLA).

97. 'Herbstliches London' ('Autumnal London'), *Gedichte II*, p. 300

98. 'Herbst im Hydepark' ('Autumn in Hyde Park'), *Gedichte II*, p. 303. Byron's statue is near Hyde Park Corner.

99. 'Fremd ist die Welt und leer' ('The World is Alien and Empty'), *Gedichte II*, p. 347.

100. The novel was published for the first time in *Gesammelte Werke, Prosa I*, Frankfurt, 1986.

101. *Prosa I*, p. 437.

102. ibid., p. 442.

103. Max to Leni Herrmann, 27 July 1934 (DLA).

104. Herrmann-Neiße to Alphonse Sondheimer, 12 August 1934 (DLA).

105. Herrmann-Neiße to Friedrich Grieger, 8 August 1933, Grieger, op. cit. p. 74.

106. Herrmann-Neiße to George Grosz, 29 May 1934, quoted in *Max Herrmann-Neiße. Künstler, Kneipen, Kabaretts – Schlesien, Berlin, im Exil*, ed. Klaus Völker, Berlin 1992, pp. 175–6.

107. Herrmann-Neiße to Friedrich Grieger, 26 March 1934, quoted in *Gedichte II*, p. 750.

108. *Gedichte II*, p. 746.

109. Herrmann-Neiße to George Grosz, 29 May 1934, see note 106.

110. 'Untergang' ('Doom'), written March 1934, *Gedichte II*, p. 316. The version quoted is that sent to Friedrich Grieger, 26 March 1934, quoted in *Gedichte II*, p. 749.

111. 'Immer leerer wird mein Leben' ('My Life Grows Ever Emptier'), poem dated 23 May 1934, *Gedichte II*, p. 326.

112. Herrmann-Neiße to Alfred Wolfenstein, 20 December 1934 (DLA).

113. Herrmann-Neiße to Paul Zech, 27 January 1935 (DLA).

114. 'Erinnerung an Zürich' ('Memory of Zurich'), *Gedichte II*, p. 318. Written April 1934 in Marlowe, Bucks.

115. Herrmann-Neiße to Klaus Pinkus, 24 May 1934 (DLA).

116. 'Niemals werden wir dazu gehören' ('We Shall Never Belong Here') (1936), *Gedichte II*, p. 437.

117. 'Klage und Trost' ('Lament and Consolation'), *Gedichte II*, p. 385.

118. 'Die Mörder' ('The Murderers'), *Gedichte II*, p. 331.

119. 'Die geliebte Stadt' ('The Beloved City'), *Gedichte II*, p. 349.

120. Herrmann-Neiße's unpublished papers are held in the Deutsches Literaturarchiv, Marbach. For details of their contents and how they were acquired, see Bernhard Zeller, *Marbacher Memorabilien*, Marbach 1995, pp. 133–4.

121. Max to Leni Herrmann, 9 January 1936, (DLA).

122. ibid., 4 January 1935 (DLA).

123. ibid., 7 March 1934, (DLA).

124. 'Nacht in der Emigration' ('Night in Emigration'), *Gedichte II*, p. 377.

125. 'das was meine Sendung ist' – 'Die Zimmer' ('The Rooms'), *Gedichte II*, p. 643.

126. Herrmann-Neiße to Sondheimer, 12 August 1934 (DLA).

127. Cf. Herrmann-Neiße to Paul Zech, 2 June 1936 (DLA).

128. ibid., 2 June 1936 (DLA).

129. ibid., 13 August 1936 (DLA).

130. Herrmann-Neiße to Friedrich Grieger, 4 June 1936, quoted in Völker, op. cit., p. 198.

131. Zweig, Afterword to Max Herrmann-Neiße, *Erinnerung und Exil*, Zurich 1946, p. 145.

132. Herrmann-Neiße to Thomas Mann, 4 June 1936, quoted in Völker, op. cit., p. 198.

133. 'Nach dem Fest' ('After the Party'), *Gedichte II*, p. 427.

134. Herrmann-Neiße to Klaus Pinkus, 8 September 1936 (DLA).

135. Kerr, *Die Diktatur des Hausknechts*, Frankfurt 1983, p. 28.

136. Kerr, *Ich kam nach England*, ed. Walter Huder and Thomas Koebner, Bonn 1979, p. 181.

137. Kerr to Albert Einstein, 15 May 1934 (SAdK).

138. Cf. Kerr to Rudolf Kommer 26 August 1934, and 2 October 1935 (SAdK).

139. Kerr to Rudolf Kommer, 20 December 1934 (SAdK).

140. Kerr, *Walter Rathenau: Erinnerungen eines Freundes*, Amsterdam 1935.

141. Kerr to Kommer, 26 August 1934 (SAdK).

142. Kerr to Einstein, 4 August 1935 (SAdK).

143. Kerr to Kommer, 21 July 1934 (SAdK).

144. Kerr to Johann Plesch, 14 June 1934 (DEA 307).

145. Kerr to Klaus Mann, 24 May 1934 (SAdK).

146. Author's interview with Judith Kerr, 30 January 1990.

147. Kerr to Kommer, 19 August 1934 (SAdK).

148. Kerr to Johann Plesch, 14 June 1934 (DEA 307).

149. Kerr to Kommer, 28 January 1935, Kerr to George Bernard Shaw, 26 February 1935 (SAdK).

150. Kerr to Kommer, 21 July 1934 (SAdK).

151. ibid., 6 August 1935 (SAdK).

152. ibid., 17 August 1935 (SAdK).

153. London Film Productions to Kerr, 9 January 1936 (SAdK).

154. Kerr, *New York and London. Stätten des Geschicks*, Berlin 1923, prologue.

155. Kerr to George Bernard Shaw, 1 December 1935 (SAdK).

156. Extension of residence permit, issued by Home Office, 16 December 1935 (SAdK).

157. *Seine Mutter Letizia*, Typescript (SAdK).

158. The surviving typescripts are part of the Kerr Archive held in the Academy of Arts, Berlin SAdK. I have dated the scripts according to the copyright dates on the manuscripts.

159. Kerr later published an exposé, containing dialogue for some scenes, in *Das Wort*, September 1938.

NOTES TO PART THREE

1. Fred Uhlman, *The Making of an Englishman*, London 1960, p. 201.

2. Otto Lehmann-Russbüldt, 'Aufrüstung?', *Sozialistische Warte*, X, 7 (1 May 1936), p. 172.

3. Zweig to Gisela Selden-Goth, 21 December 1935: Selden-Goth, *Stefan*

Zweig: Unbekannte Briefe aus der Emigration an eine Freundin, Vienna 1964, p. 12.

4. Cf. Olden to Hilde Walter, 9 December 1936, quoted in C. Brinson and M. Malet, 'Die Friedensnobelpreiskampagne in Großbritannien', in *Carl von Ossietzky und die politische Kultur der Weimarer Republik*, ed. Gerhard Kraiker and Dirk Grathoff, Oldenburg 1991, p. 338.

5. Moritz Bonn, *Wandering Scholar*, London 1949, p. 358.

6. From the unfinished cycle 'Die Zwischenzeit' ('The Interval'), *Gedichte* II, p. 715.

7. Martin Gilbert, *The Roots of Appeasement*, New York 1966, p. 143.

8. 'I do my utmost, night after night, to keep out of the paper anything that might hurt their [German] sensibilities,' Dawson wrote in 1937. Cf. William Shirer, *Rise and Fall of the Third Reich*, New York 1962, p. 396n.

9. Olden to Berthold Jacob, 28 July 1934, Brinson and Malet, op. cit., p. 326.

10. Angus Calder, *The People's War*, Pimlico edition, London 1996, p. 23.

11. Lothian, 'Germany and France: the British Task', *The Times*, 1 February 1935.

12. Uhlman, op. cit., p. 201.

13. Christiane Grautoff, *Die Göttin und ihr Sozialist*, Bonn 1996, p. 66.

14. Many of the details in this and later sections on Karl Otten come from the author's interviews with Ellen Otten, recorded in April 1994, September 1996 and December 1997.

15. Otten, *Torquemadas Schatten*, Hamburg 1980, p. 11.

16. Rudolf Olden to Oskar Maria Graf, 1 April 1938 (DEA 75–175).

17. Borkenau, *The Spanish Cockpit. An Eye-Witness Account of the Political and Social Conflicts of the Spanish Civil War*, London 1937.

18. Karl Otten to European Books (Elias Alexander), 30 and 31 October 1936 (Otten Estate).

19. *Stanley findet Livingstone*, Typescript, 45 pp. ('Nachlaß', which also contains a French version: *À la recherche de Livingstone*.)

20. *Nach Faschoda! Der Wettlauf zwischen Kitchener und Marchand zum Nil*. Hörspiel. The Estate also contains a French version of the script.

21. Elias Alexander to Van (*sic*) Gielgud, 14 October 1936 and 2 November 1936, BBC Written Archives Centre (WAC).

22. 'Enfin je voudrais bien vous remercier que vous avez retenu ma pièce "Fachoda" – c'était le premier moment favorable me donnant un peu de courage d'avancer dans mon travail.' Otten to BBC, 16 March 1937 (BBC WAC).

23. *Daily Telegraph*, 14 January 1938; see also *Radio Times*, 12 January 1938.

24. Otten to European Books, 28 December 1937 (Otten Estate).

25. There is correspondence regarding two other scripts, *Der Amokläufer* and *The Girl from Botany Bay* in BBC Written Archives. Neither script was accepted; neither has survived.

26. Politisches Archiv des Auswärtigen Amtes, Bonn, 1934–36, Bestand Inland II, A/B, 132/1 (Aktenzeichen (file number) 8.3–76).

27. The official grounds for expatriation, listed in Otten's file, p. 21 (see note 26).

28. The list was published in *Deutscher Reichsanzeiger und Preußischer Staats-anzeiger*, No. 282, 3 December 1936.

29. *Pariser Tageszeitung*, 21 and 22 September 1936.

30. Otten to Gottfried Bermann Fischer, 9 July 1938. This correspondence is part of the S. Fischer Verlag Papers, held in the Manuscripts Department, Lilly Library, Indiana University, Bloomington/Indiana.

31. Cf. European Books to Otten, 22 December 1936 and 12 April 1937 (Otten Estate).

32. Otten to European Books, 11 February 1937 (Otten Estate).

33. ibid., 1 April 1937 (Otten Estate).

34. Walter Landauer to Otten, 15 July 1937 (Otten Estate).

35. Otten to Bermann Fischer, 17 December 1938 (Otten Estate).

36. Otten to Talbot Scheffauer, 11 November 1937 (DLA).

37. Karl to Ellen Otten, 20-22 August 1937 (Otten Estate).

38. Cf. Wickham Steed to Otten, 3 August and 1 November 1939, also 19 December 1945 (Otten Estate).

39. Otten to Ethel Talbot Scheffauer, 17 December 1937 (DLA).

40. *Die Reise nach Deutschland*, typescript 235 pp. – later title *Themse und Rhein* (Otten Estate); now published as *Die Reise nach Deutschland*, edited with an Afterword by Richard Dove, Bern/Frankfurt 2000.

41. Otten to Bermann Fischer, 4 August 1938 (Otten Estate).

42. *Thames and Rhine*, translated by Claude Sykes, typescript (Otten Estate).

43. Otten to American Guild for German Cultural Freedom, 16 April 1939 (DEA 70/117). For details of the literary prize, see *Deutsche Intellektuelle im Exil. Ihre Akademie und die 'American Guild for German Cultural Freedom'*, Munich/London/New York 1993, pp. 370–99.

44. Frederic Warburg to Otten, 1 November 1939 (Otten Estate).

45. Kerr to Rudolf Kommer, 19 August 1941 (SAdK). Cf. also Kerr to Kommer 26 August 1934 and 2 October 1935. The unpublished correspondence between Kerr and Kommer held in the Akademie der Künste comprises over 70 letters, written between 1934 and 1942. For details on Kommer, see Deborah Vietor-Engländer, '"The Mysteries of Rudolfo" – Rudolf Kommer from Czernowitz . . . a Puller of Strings on the Exile Scene', *German Life and Letters* 51/2, April 1998, pp. 165–84.

46. *Daily Telegraph* to Kerr, 29 November 1935 (SAdK).

47. Cf. Kerr to Johann Plesch, 18 November 1935 (DEA – 307).

48. The name Upper Bedford Place was changed to Bedford Way in October 1939. The house itself no longer exists; it suffered bomb damage and was subsequently demolished.

49. Kerr to Kommer, 23 January 1939 (SAdK).

50. Quoted by Walter Huder in his Afterword to the reprint of *Melodien*, Frankfurt 1983, p. 262.

51. Kerr to Kommer, 22 November 1937 (SAdK).

52. Kerr to Kommer, 9 February 1938 (SAdK).

53. See Ulrich Weinzierl, *Alfred Polgar. Eine Biographie*, Frankfurt (Fischer Taschenbuch Verlag) 1995. See also Deborah Vietor-Engländer, 'The Mysteries of Rudolfo' (note 45 above).

54. The accusation is made by Walter Huder, Afterword to the reprint of *Melodien* (see note 50 above), p. 263. See also Vietor-Engländer, 'The Mysteries of Rudolfo'.

55. Kerr to Kommer, 24 January 1938 (SAdK). According to an article of Kerr's, it was in fact Kommer who suggested the idea for the book; cf. *Die neue Weltbühne* 11/24 (1938), pp. 751–2.

56. Cf. Kerr to Kommer, 21 October 1937 (SAdK).

57. Kerr to Kommer, 24 January 1938 (SAdK).

58. The manuscript is among Kerr's papers in the Akademie der Künste, Berlin. The essays appeared in *Die neue Weltbühne* during 1938: 'Mordechai Levi (Der Großvater von Karl Marx)', *DNW* VI/12, pp. 371–4; 'Zwei Männer in London', *DNW*, VI/24, pp. 751–8; 'Lord Beaconsfields Großvater', *DNW*, VI/33, pp. 1035–40.

59. Kerr, *Die Welt im Licht*, Vol. II, Berlin 1920, p. 177.

60. Judith Kerr, *Eine eingeweckte Kindheit*, Berlin 1990.

61. Kerr to Victor Gollancz, 28 November 1943 (SAdK).

62. 'Exil', *Die neue Weltbühne*, V/45 (1937), p. 1423.

63. Alfred Kerr, *Ich kam nach England*, edited by Walter Huder and Thomas Koebner, Bonn 1979.

64. Kerr to George Bernard Shaw, 8 July 1939 (SAdK).

65. Kerr to Lincolns Prager, 6 July 1941 (SAdK). The original letter was written in German.

66. Kerr to Kommer, 23 January 1939 (SAdK).

67. Max Herrmann-Neiße, *Um uns die Fremde. Gedichte*, Foreword by Thomas Mann, Zurich 1936.

68. *Modern German Verse. An Anthology*, edited by A. Weiner and Fritz Gross, London: Gregg Publishing, 1936. For further details on Fritz Gross, see Charmian Brinson and Marian Malet, 'Fritz Gross: An Exile in England', *German Life and Letters*, XLIX No. 3, July 1996, pp. 339–57.

69. Herrmann-Neiße to Zech, 24 November 1937 (DLA).

70. See *Der deutsche PEN-Club im Exil*, Frankfurt 1980, p. 49.

71. Reply to a questionnaire from the American Guild for German Cultural Freedom, published in the journal *Das Wort*, in 1937 (DLA).

72. Herrmann-Neiße to Heinrich Mann, 20 December 1936 (DLA).

73. Herrmann-Neiße to George Grosz, 8 September 1936.

74. Herrmann-Neiße to Paul Zech, December 1936 (DLA).

75. 'Absage an das vergangene Jahr' ('Rejection of the Year Past'), *Gedichte II*, p. 456.

76. Herrmann-Neiße to Friedrich Grieger, 17 March 1937, quoted in Völker, op. cit., p. 204.

77. Herrmann-Neiße to Paul Zech, 19 February 1937 (DLA).

78. 'Letztes Widerstreben' ('Final Reluctance'), *Gedichte II*, p. 460.

79. 'Genugtuung' ('Satisfaction'), *Gedichte II*, p. 469.

80. Herrmann-Neiße to Paul Zech, 24 November 1937 (DLA).

81. Max to Leni Herrmann, 28 October 1937 (DLA).

82. Herrmann-Neiße to Rudolf Olden, 8 November 1937 (DEA 75/175/403); Herrmann-Neiße to Paul Zech, 24 November 1937 (DLA).

83. Rosemarie Lorenz, *Max Herrmann-Neiße*, Stuttgart 1966, p. 52.

84. Herrmann-Neiße to Paul Zech, 13 August 1936 (DLA).

85. Zweig to Herrmann-Neiße, 29 September 1939, *Briefe an Freunde*, p. 303.

86. Zweig, 'Nachruf für Max Herrmann-Neiße', in *Erinnerung und Exil*, Zurich 1946, p. 145.

87. Herrmann-Neiße to Alphonse Sondheimer, 25 May 1937 (DLA).

88. Herrmann-Neiße to Friedrich Grieger, 16 September 1937, Grieger, op. cit., p. 85.

89. Herrmann-Neiße to Alphonse Sondheimer, no date (DLA).

90. 'Ausbürgerungsliste 34', 8 March 1938, published in *Deutscher Reichsanzeiger*, 9 March 1938 – see Landshoff, op. cit., pp. 134, 476.

91. 'Leitheft Emigrantenpresse und Schrifttum', March 1939, Nr. 59, pp. 21 and 33, Berlin Document Centre – see *Der Dichter und seine Stadt*, ed. Yvonne-Patricia Alefeld, Düsseldorf 1991, p. 74.

92. Lorenz, op. cit., p. 54.

93. Alfred Kerr, 'Epitaph on Max Herrmann-Neiße', *PEN News* (London), April 1941, pp. 4–5.

94. 'Ewige Heimat' ('Eternal Home'), *Gedichte II*, p. 513.

95. Herrmann-Neiße to Hermann Hesse, 30 June 1938, quoted in Völker, op. cit., p. 220.

96. Kerr, 'Epitaph', *PEN News*, April 1941.

97. 'Versäumtes Leben' ('Wasted Life'), *Gedichte IV*, p. 492.

98. 'Katastrophe' ('Catastrophe'), *Gedichte II*, p. 508.

99. 'Mir bleibt mein Lied', *Gedichte II*, p. 509.

100. Herrmann-Neiße to Hermann Hesse, 30 June 1938, in Völker, op. cit., p. 220.

101. Herrmann-Neiße to Paul Zech in Argentina, 14 September 1938 (DLA).

102. 'Das sind die Tage der Gefahr' ('These are Days of Danger'), *Gedichte II*, p. 524.

103. Herrmann-Neiße to Klaus Pinkus, 12 February 1939 (DLA).

104. The author actually made a selection of poems, which corresponds to the first part ('Erinnerung und Exil') of the posthumously published *Letzte Gedichte*.

105. Herrmann-Neiße to Home Office, 24 July 1940 (DLA).

106. 'Dichter im Exil' ('Poet in Exile'), *Gedichte II*, p. 575.

107. 'Die Nelken' ('Carnations'), *Gedichte II*, p. 530.

108. 'Ich möchte heim' ('I Want to Go Home'), *Gedichte IV*, p. 500.

109. Herrmann-Neiße to Heinrich Mann, 23 March 1939 (DLA).

110. 'Unseliger Frühling' ('Ill-starred Spring'), *Gedichte II*, p. 554.

111. Cf. *Österreicher im Exil*, ed. Wolfgang Muchitsch. Preface by Herbert Steiner, p. x).

112. Robert Neumann, 'Wir sind nicht mehr allein', Rede auf der Kundgebung der FAM in der Porchester Hall, *Zeitspiegel*, 7 February 1942.

113. Fritz H. Landshoff, op. cit., p. 291.

114. Zweig an Felix Braun, 21 June 1937, *Briefe an Freunde*, p. 281.

115. Author's interview with Desmond Flower, 14 December 1990.

116. Zweig to Romain Rolland, 1 May 1937, *RR/SZ* II, pp. 652–3.

117. Stefan to Friderike Zweig, 12 May 1937, *Briefwechsel*, p. 313.

118. Zweig to Joseph Roth, *Joseph Roth. Briefe 1911–1939*, Cologne and Berlin 1970, pp. 512–13.

119. Zweig to René Schickele 28 April 1937, *Briefe an Freunde*, p. 278.

120. Zweig to Frans Masereel, 15 April 1933, *Briefe an Freunde*, p. 227.

121. 'Zum Emigranten habe ich kein Talent' – Zweig to Hermann Hesse, 30 January 1935, *Briefe an Freunde*, p. 264.

122. Zweig to Romain Rolland, 28 September 1936, *RR/SZ* II, p. 637.

123. Zweig to Thomas Mann, 29 July 1940, *Briefe an Freunde*, p. 317. Cf. *WvG*, p. 467, where he uses almost the same formulation.

124. Zweig to Joseph Roth, undated (1936), *Roth: Briefe*, p. 467.

125. Zweig to Romain Rolland, 4 May 1936, *SZ/RR* II, p. 628.

126. Zweig to René Schickele, 28 April 1937, *Briefe an Freunde*, p. 278.

127. Zweig to Romain Rolland, 1 May 1937, *RR/SZ* II, pp. 652–3.

128. ibid., 7 December 1937, *RR/SZ* II, pp. 667–8.

129. Zweig to Felix Braun, 21 March 1938, St.Bib.

130. Zweig to René Schickele, 22 April 1938, *Briefe an Freunde*, p. 290.

131. ibid., 22 April 1938 (DLA).

132. Zweig to Victor Fleischer, 28 March 1938 (DLA).

133. Cf. Zweig to Schickele, *Briefe an Freunde*, p. 289.

134. Zweig to Lavinia Mazzuchetti, his Italian translator, quoted in Prater, *Das Leben eines Ungeduldigen*, p. 277.

135. Prater, *European of Yesterday*, pp. 280–1; German edition, p. 290.

136. Zweig to Felix Braun, June 1939, St.Bib.

137. ibid., 23 June 1938, St.Bib.

138. Zweig to Romain Rolland, 21 June 1938, *RR/SZ* II, p. 683.

139. *Der große Europäer Stefan Zweig*, ed. Hanns Arens, Frankfurt 1981, p. 154.

140. Zweig to Guido Fuchs, 8 October 1938, St.Bib.

141. Zweig to Romain Rolland, 2 May 1938, *RR/SZ* II, pp. 677–8.

142. Zweig to Alfredo Cahn, 19 September 1941 (see Donald Prater, 'Stefan Zweig in England', *German Life and Letters*, October 1962).

143. Zweig to Raoul Auernheimer, undated, St.Bib.

144. Zweig to Gisela Selden-Goth, 9 February 1939, *Unbekannte Briefe*, p. 64.

145. Zweig to Felix Braun, *Briefe an Freunde*, p. 292.

146. ibid., 27 April 1939, St.Bib.

147. Neumann to Home Office (Aliens Dept), 2 February 1937 (ÖNB, Ser. n. 22.472).

148. Gollancz to Neumann, 11 January 1937 (ÖNB, Ser. n. 22.472).

149. Herbert Reichner to Neumann, 7 May 1937 (ÖNB, Ser, n. 22.472).

150. ibid., 4 June 1937 and 30 June 1937 (ÖNB, Ser. n. 22.472).

151. Neumann to Edwin Muir, 7 October 1937 (ÖNB, Ser.n. 21.817).

152. Stefan Zweig to Neumann, 28 September 1937 (DÖW: 11548/3).

153. *Ein leichtes Leben*, pp. 54–5.

154. Cf. Ludwig Marcuse, *Mein zwanzigstes Jahrhundert*, Zurich 1975, pp. 180–203.

155. Jameson, *Journey from the North. The Autobiography of Storm Jameson*, London 1969/1970, Vol. II, p. 18.

156. Hermon Ould to Rudolf Olden, 18 November 1938, *Der deutsche PEN-Klub im Exil*, Frankfurt 1980, p. 230. For details of the Refugee Writers' Fund, see *PEN News*, London, June 1939.

157. Cf. *New Statesman*, 22 October 1938.

158. Storm Jameson to Rudolf Olden, 28 November 1938, DEA 75/175.

159. Jameson, op. cit., p. 19.

160. Neumann to Rudolf Olden, 29 June 1939 (DEA 75/175).

161. ibid., 15 February 1939 (DEA 75/175).

162. Jameson to H. J. Mundt, 8 January 1957 (ÖNB, Ser. n. 21.824).

163. *Journey from the North*, II, London 1969/1970, p. 53.

164. *Ein leichtes Leben*, p. 108.

165. Neumann to American Guild for German Cultural Freedom, 31 January 1939, DEA 70/117.

166. Neumann to Richard A. Bermann, 2 May 1939, DEA 78/15.

167. H. G. Wells to Neumann, 24 September and 6 October 1939 (ÖNB Ser. n. 21.825).

168. Asa Briggs, *The History of Broadcasting in the United Kingdom*, Vol. II (revised edition), Oxford/New York 1995, pp. 601–2.

169. See A. J. Sherman, *Island Refuge. Britain and Refugees from the Third Reich 1933–1939*, London 1973, pp. 264–5; also Gerhard Hirschfeld, 'The Emigration from Nazi Germany' in *Theatre and Film in Exile*, ed. Günter Berghaus, Oxford/New York/Munich 1989, pp. 1–13 and Bernard Wasserstein, *Britain and the Jews of Europe 1939–1945*, Oxford/New York 1988, p. 7.

170. Marion Berghahn, *Continental Britons. German-Jewish Refugees from Nazi Germany*, Oxford/New York/Hamburg 1988, p. 77.

171. Berghahn, op. cit., p. 77.

172. Zweig to Romain Rolland, 27 May 1939, *RR/SZ* II, p. 706.

173. *Daily Worker*, 24 June 1939.

174. Zweig to Rolland, 27 May 1939, *RR/SZ* II, pp. 704-5.

175. ibid., 15 July 1939, *RR/SZ* II, p. 706.

176. Zweig to Paul Frischauer, 11 July 1939 (Atrium Verlag).

177. Max Herrmann-Neiße to Hermann Hesse, end June 1939, quoted in Völker, op. cit., p. 225.

178. Herrmann-Neiße to Friedrich Grieger, 10 July 1939, Völker, op. cit., p. 226.

179. *Gedichte II*, p. 585.

180. 'Gebet um ein Wunder' ('Prayer for a Miracle'), *Gedichte II*, p. 588.
181. Kerr, *Ich kam nach England*, p. 153.
182. Kerr to Albert Einstein, 21 November 1938; cf. Kerr's earlier letter to Einstein, 15 May 1934 (SAdK).
183. Otten to Claude Sykes, 11 June 1939 (Otten Estate).
184. Biographical notes written by Otten for the American Guild for German Cultural Freedom, dated April 1939 (Otten Estate).
185. Otten to BBC, 30 October 1939; Val Gielgud to Otten, 14 December 1939 (Otten Estate).
186. 'Distinguished Germans in Exile', Readers' Letter, *Manchester Guardian*, 24 August 1939.

NOTES TO PART FOUR

1. Booklet: 'Helpful Information and Guidance for every Refugee', dated 10 December 38, cf. *Second Chance. German-speaking Jews in the United Kingdom*, Cambridge 1991, p. 527.
2. Angus Calder, *The People's War*, London 1992, pp. 150–3.
3. Neumann to Rennie Smith, 21 September 1939 (DÖW 11.548/5).
4. Neumann to D. N. Pritt, 6 September 1939 (DÖW 11.548/5).
5. Zweig, *Tagebücher*, pp. 415–32.
6. Otten to Gottfried Bermann Fischer, 16 November 1939, S. Fischer Verlag Papers, Lily Library, Indiana University.
7. Otten to 'Madame' (i.e. Margaret Holmes), undated, early 1941 (Otten Estate).
8. 'Mitteilungen an die Rheinländer', two recordings (DLA).
9. See Karl Retzlaw, *Spartakus: Aufstieg und Niedergang. Erinnerungen eines Parteiarbeiters*, Frankfurt 1985.
10. Gottfried Bermann Fischer, *Bedroht – bewahrt. Der Weg eines Verlegers*, Frankfurt 1994, pp. 254 ff.
11. *Gedichte II*, p. 668.
12. Zweig to Guido Fuchs, 29 October 1939 (St.Bib., Vienna).
13. Cf. Neumann to Aliens Tribunal Chairman, Aylesbury, 18 October 1939 (DÖW 11.548/5).
14. Cf. correspondence between Neumann and Wolfe (DWÖ.11.548/5).
15. See Neumann, *Vielleicht das Heitere*, Vienna/Munich/Basel 1968, pp. 571–2.
16. See Neumann, *Ein leichtes Leben*, Vienna/Munich/Basel 1963.
17. The diary is part of Neumann's Estate in the Österreichische National-bibliothek (ÖNB, Ser. n. 21.608.) I should particularly thank Michael Neumann for permission to quote from his father's diary. The manuscript consists of 123 hand-written pages.
18. For a review of work on alien internment in Britain, see David Cesarani and Tony Kushner, *The Internment of Aliens in Twentieth Century Britain*, London 1993, pp. 1–11. Historians of internment have routinely complained of the tend-

ency of government departments, particularly the Home Office, to withhold relevant documents, cf. Peter and Leni Gillman, *Collar the Lot!*, London 1980, pp. xi–xiv. Though the situation has much improved since then, particularly with the release of further documents in 1986, there are still substantial gaps. Documents available in the Public Record Office are held under HO (= Home Office) 45, HO 144, HO 213, 214 and 215.

19. Rolly Becker-Neumann to Mrs Gomme, 31 May 1940 (ÖNB, Ser. n. 22.475).

20. See Michael Seyfert, *Im Niemandsland. Deutsche Exilliteratur in britischer Internierung*, Berlin 1984, subtitled 'An Unknown Chapter of Second World War Cultural History'.

21. Jesse Thoor (real name Peter Karl Höfler) (1905–1952). See Thoor, *Das Werk. Sonette, Lieder, Erzählungen*, ed. and with an introduction by Michael Hamburger, Frankfurt 1966.

22. *Scene in Passing*, London 1942, see pp. 217–20 below.

23. François Lafitte, *The Internment of Aliens*, London 1940; reprint London 1988, p. 119.

24. See ÖNB, Ser. n. 22.475.

25. Quoted in Seyfert, op. cit., p. 49.

26. *Ein leichtes Leben*, p. 80.

27. ibid., p. 82.

28. ibid., p. 80.

29. Zweig, *Tagebuch*, *Gesammelte Werke*, Frankfurt 1984, entry for 1 September 1939.

30. Zweig to Felix Braun, undated (autumn 1939) (St.Bib.)

31. Zweig to Sigmund Freud, 14 September 1939, *Briefe an Freunde*, pp. 226-7.

32. Zweig to Felix Braun, 16 October 1939 (St.Bib.).

33. Zweig to Fleischer, January 1940 and 19 June 1940 (DLA).

34. Zweig to Felix Braun, 16 December 1939 (St.Bib.).

35. ibid., undated (March 1940) (St.B.), also in *Briefe an Freunde*, p. 311.

36. Prater, *European of Yesterday*, p. 280, German edition, p. 289.

37. Zweig to Max Herrmann-Neiße, 18 May 1940, *Briefe an Freunde*, p. 311.

38. Zweig to Hermann Kesten, 24 January 1940, *Deutsche Literatur im Exil*, ed. Hermann Kesten, Frankfurt 1973, p. 101.

39. Hermann Kesten, *Meine Freunde die Poeten*, Frankfurt/Berlin/Vienna 1980, p. 99.

40. Zweig to Emil Ludwig, 30-31 May 1940 (DLA).

41. Desmond Flower, *Fellows in Foolscap*, London 1991, p. 173.

42. Zweig to Victor Fleischer, 19 June 1940 (DLA).

43. Zweig to Max Herrmann-Neiße, end June 1940, *Briefe an Freunde*, p. 313.

44. 'Verlorene Heimat' ('Lost Home'), *Gedichte II*, p. 604.

45. 'Litanei der Bitternis', ('Litany of Bitterness'), *Gedichte II*, p. 637.

46. Herrmann-Neiße to Paul Zech, 24 April 1940 (DLA).

47. Stefan Zweig to Herrmann-Neiße, 25 September 1939, *Briefe an Freunde*, p. 302.

48. ibid., 29 September 1939, p. 303.

49. 'Rechtfertigung des Dichters' ('Poet's Justification'), *Gedichte II*, p. 591.

50. 'Stadt ohne Kinder' ('City without Children'), ibid., p. 590.

51. 'Tödliche Wandlung' ('Deadly Transformation'), ibid., p. 592.

52. 'Spiele der Erinnerung' ('Games of Memory'), ibid., p. 608.

53. 'Magische Beschwörung für 1940' ('Magic Incantation for 1940'), ibid., p. 617.

54. Introduction to *An Anthology of German Poetry 1880–1940*, ed. Jethro Bithell, London 1941.

55. 'Verfehlte Freundschaft' ('Mistaken Friendship'), *Gedichte* II, p. 700.

56. Herrmann-Neiße to Jethro Bithell, August 1941 (DLA).

57. 'Wie lange noch?' ('How Much Longer?'), *Gedichte II*, p. 668.

58. Herrmann-Neiße to Home Office, 24 July 1940 (DLA).

59. 'Der teuflische Sirenenton' ('The Diabolical Sound of the Sirens'), *Gedichte II*, p. 695.

60. Note from Dr R. Hale-White, dated 24 June 1940, quoted in Völker, op. cit., p. 230. (Dr Reginald Hale-White was the grandson of the writer William Hale White, alias Mark Rutherford.)

61. 'Im Bann des Todes' ('Under the Spell of Death'), *Gedichte II*, p. 721.

62. 'Trügerisches Vielleicht' ('False Perhaps'), ibid., p. 730.

63. 'Vor dem Ende' ('Before the End'), ibid., p. 733.

64. 'Der Spiegel' ('The Mirror'), ibid., p. 737. The poem was published a month after his death in *Die Zeitung*, 7 May 1941.

65. 'Aufzeichnungen über die letzten Tage von Max Herrmann-Neiße' (DLA).

66. 'Still und unauffällig' – Zweig's obituary, reprinted in *Erinnerung und Exil. Gedichte*. Afterword by Stefan Zweig, Zurich 1946.

67. 'An Epitaph on Max Herrmann-Neiße', *PEN News*, April 1941, pp. 4–5.

68. 'Fremder Tod' ('Death Abroad'), *Gedichte II*, p. 561.

69. Robert Lucas, 'The German Service of the BBC', *PEN Symposium Report. Half a Century Writing in German abroad*', London 1983, pp. 35–43.

70. Otten to Lindley Fraser, 30 December 1940 (Otten Estate).

71. Copies of these scripts are among Otten's unpublished papers (DLA).

72. Robert Lucas, *PEN Symposium Report* (see note 69).

73. A selection of these lyrics has been published in *Between Two Languages*, ed. William Abbey et al., London 1995, pp. 205–14.

74. The original recordings, dated 25 June 1941, still survive (Otten Estate).

75. Martin Esslin to the author, 27 July 1995.

76. W. E. Williams, 'The Spoken Word', *Listener*, 21 May 1942.

77. Cf. the list of his BBC contributions which Otten compiled in support of his application for naturalisation. His Estate contains only 26 items expressly written for the series; some may have been lost.

78. D. Brown, C. Serpell, *If Hitler Comes*, London 1941, originally published under the title *Lost Eden*, London 1940.

79. *Observer*, 10 May 1942. Harrisson was best-known as co-author (with Charles Madge) of *Britain by Mass Observation*, London: Penguin Special, 1939.

80. Ministry of Information to Karl Otten, 23 September 1942 (Otten Estate).

81. Arthur Calder-Marshall to Otten, 8 February 1943 (Otten Estate).

82. Kerr to V. Duckworth Barker, European Services, 13 October 1940 (BBC WAC).

83. Duckworth Barker to Kerr, 29 October 1940 (BBC WAC).

84. Cf. Kevin Gough-Yates, 'The BBC as a Source of Employment for Film Workers and Composers during the War', *Zwischenwelt. Exil in Großbritannien*, ed. Siglinde Bolbecher et al., Vienna 1995, pp. 215–40.

85. Rilla to Kerr, 20 January 1941 (BBC WAC).

86. Kerr to Rilla, 4 February 1941 (BBC WAC).

87. Rilla to Kerr, 10 February 1941 (BBC WAC).

88. Quoted in Ilse Newberry, 'Alfred Kerr und die BBC', *German Life and Letters*, 38/3 (April 1985), pp. 260–72.

89. Kerr to Rilla, 1 March 1941 (BBC WAC).

90. ibid., 6 April 1941 (BBC WAC).

91. ibid., 24 April 1941 (BBC WAC).

92. 'das Zugbrückerl zu senken', ibid., 28 May 1941 (BBC WAC).

93. ibid., 22 May 1941 (BBC WAC).

94. Rilla to Kerr, 4 March 1941 (BBC WAC).

95. ibid., 23 May 1941 (BBC WAC).

96. Ilse Newberry, op. cit., pp. 262-3.

97. Kerr to Leonard Miall, 13 July 1942 (BBC WAC).

98. Kerr to George Bernard Shaw, 1 January 1945 (SAdK).

99. W. S. Stirling, internal memo, 26 June 1945 (BBC WAC).

100. Kerr to Latin American Service, 18 December 1946 (BBC WAC).

NOTES TO PART FIVE

1. See *Writers in Freedom. A Symposium*. ed. Hermon Ould, London/New York/Melbourne 1942. Speeches given at the congress were grouped under the headings: 'Germany Today and Tomorrow', 'Writers without Language', and 'Literature after the War.'

2. Zweig to Thomas Mann, 29 July 1940, *Briefe an Freunde*, p. 318.

3. Zweig to Desmond Flower, undated (1940) (ÖNB, Ser. n. 1183/40).

4. Stefan to Friderike Zweig, 9 November 1940, *SZ/FZ: Briefwechsel*, p. 328.

5. Zweig to Paul Zech, 12 December 1940, *Zweig/Zech: Briefe 1910–1942*, Frankfurt 1986, p. 136.

6. Zweig to Victor Fleischer, 22 February 1941 (DLA).

7. ibid., 7 August 1941 (DLA).

8. Zweig to Felix Braun, 8 July 1941 (St.Bib).

9. Stefan to Friderike Zweig, 17 September 1941, *SZ/FZ: Briefwechsel*, p. 341.

10. ibid., 10 September 1941, *SZ/FZ: Briefwechsel*, p. 339.

11. ibid., 10 September 1941, *SZ/FZ: Briefwechsel*, p. 339.

12. ibid., 10 September 1941, *SZ/FZ: Briefwechsel*, p. 340.

13. ibid., 27 October 1941, *SZ/FZ: Briefwechsel*, pp. 343–44.

14. Zweig to Felix Braun, 21 November 1941 (St.Bib).

15. Zweig to Richard Friedenthal, 19 September 1941, *Briefe an Freunde*, p. 333.

16. Zweig to Alfredo Cahn, 19 September 1941, quoted in Prater, op. cit., p. 320.

17. Zweig to Victor Wittkowski, 13 December 1941 (DLA).

18. Stefan to Friderike Zweig, 29 November 1941, *SZ/FZ: Briefwechsel*, p. 347.

19. ibid., 20 January 1942, *SZ/FZ: Briefwechsel*, p. 351.

20. ibid., 18 February 1942, *SZ/FZ: Briefwechsel*, p. 356.

21. ibid., *SZ/FZ: Briefwechsel*, p. 357.

22. Prater, op. cit., p. 349.

23. Zweig to Max Herrmann-Neiße, *Briefe an Freunde*, op. cit., p. 314.

24. Neumann, 'Goodbye Stefan Zweig', *Tribune*, 18 December 1942.

25. Neumann to Arnold Zweig, 4 February 1942 (ÖNB, Ser. n. 22.525).

26. *Ein leichtes Leben*, p. 186.

27. Neumann to Arnold Zweig, 4 February 1942, see note 25 above.

28. *Ein leichtes Leben*, p. 125.

29. *Scene in Passing*, London 1942.

30. Storm Jameson to Rolly Becker and Robert Neumann, 21 December 1939 (ÖNB, Ser. n. 21.801).

31. Cf. Neumann to Arnold Zweig, 4 February 1942: 'I have been working now for two years on an English novel.'

32. *Vielleicht das Heitere*, Munich/Vienna/Basel 1968, p. 186.

33. *Ein leichtes Leben*, p. 157.

34. Philip Toynbee, *New Statesman*, 11 July 1942, p. 28.

35. *Observer*, quoted in *Stimmen der Freunde*, Munich/Vienna/Basel 1957, p. 139.

36. Cf. Hilde Spiel, 'Exil und Rückkehr. Hilde Spiel im Gespräch', *Kunst im Exil in Großbritannien 1933–1945*, Berlin 1986, p. 290.

37. *Ein leichtes Leben*, pp. 153–4.

38. James Pope-Hennessey, *New Statesman*, 4 November 1944, p. 306.

39. Quoted from autobiographical notes, undated, 1941 (SAdK).

40. 'Abnutzung des Gefühls' ('Feelings Worn Threadbare'), *Aufbau* (New York) VI/16, 19 April 1940.

41. See, for example, the correspondence in the German-language newspaper *Die Zeitung* in April 1941.

42. Kerr to Rudolf Kommer, 17 May 1940 (SAdK).

43. *Ich kam nach England*, p. 198.

44. Kerr to Rudolf Kommer, 17 February 1940 (SAdK).

45. Autobiographical notes, undated, written 1940 (SAdK).

46. Kerr to 'Mr Davies', undated, late 1943 (SAdK). There is no indication who Mr Davies might be; the letter is written on PEN Club headed paper.

47. Kerr, 'Englischer Brief', *Aufbau* (New York) VI/24, 14 June 1940. There was no evidence to support Kerr's statement: none of the spies detected by the Intelligence Services since the start of the war had been masquerading as an émigré.

48. *Sunday Dispatch*, 15 September 1940; Kerr to H. G. Wells, 15 September 1940 (SAdK).

49. Cf. Kerr to Rudolf Kommer, 31 October 1939 (SAdK).

50. Kerr to Lincolns Prager, 6 July 1941; Kerr to Kommer, 19 August 1941 (SAdK).

51. Cf. Kerr to Kommer, 19 April 1942; Prager to Kerr, 18 August 1942 (SAdK).

52. ibid., 19 April 1942 (SAdK).

53. Cf. Kerr to Nicholson and Watson, 16 November 1944 (SAdK).

54. Kerr to Lincolns Prager, 18 August 1941 and Kerr to Gollancz, 28 November 1943 (both SAdK).

55. Judith Kerr, *The Other Way Round*, London 1989, p. 242 (first published in 1975).

56. Alfred to Michael Kerr, 17 December 1941 (SAdK).

57. ibid., 24 February 1945 (SAdK).

58. *Der Dichter und die Meerschweinchen*, typescript 244pp. (SAdK). There are two different versions of the manuscript, both typed, the first containing numerous handwritten corrections and revisions, which are incorporated in the second revised version.

59. Mollie Panter-Downes, *London War Notes*, ed. William Shawn, London 1972 – quoted in Robert Hewison, *Under Siege*, London 1977, p. 61.

60. See Robert Hewison, *Under Siege*, pp. 87–95.

61. Heinrich Fraenckel, *The German People versus Hitler*, London 1940.

62. *New Statesman*, 23 March 1940, p. 404.

63. Willi Frischauer, *The Nazis at War*, London 1940.

64. Robert Vansittart, *Black Record. Germans Past and Present*, London 1941.

65. Heinrich Fraenkel, *Vansittart's Gift to Goebbels. A German Exile's Answer to Black Record*, London 1941.

66. Julius Braunthal, *Need Germany Survive?*, with an introduction by Harold Laski, London 1943.

67. *In Tyrannos: Four Centuries of Struggle against Tyranny in Germany*, ed. Hans J. Rehfisch, London 1944.

68. Emil Müller-Sturmheim, *What to do about Austria?*, London 1943.

69. Otto Zarek, *German Kultur. The Proper Perspective*, London 1942.

70. Fred Uhlman, op. cit., p. 215. A short history of the FDKB is contained in Ulla Hahn, 'Der freie deutsche Kulturbund in Großbritannien', *Antifaschistische Literatur*, Vol. II, ed. Lutz Winkler, Kronberg 1977, pp. 131–95.

71. See Kurt Hiller, *Köpfe und Tröpfe*, Hamburg/Stuttgart 1950, pp. 12–13, also Harald Lützenkirchen, *Logokratie. Herrschaft der Vernunft in der Gesellschaft aus der Sicht Kurt Hillers*, Essen 1989.

72. The most significant publication to come out of the discussions of GUDA was *After Nazism – Democracy? A Symposium by Four Germans*, edited by Kurt Hiller, London: Lindsay Drummond, 1945.

73. PRO: Foreign Office 371/30911: German and Austrian Organisations GB 45341.

74. Kerr to FDKB, 10 November 1939 (SAdK).

75. Friedrich Burschell to Richard Friedenthal, 23 April 1941 (DEA 77/27/2), also published in *Der deutsche PEN-Club im Exil 1933–48*, Frankfurt 1980, p. 358.

76. Richard Friedenthal to Kerr, 5 December 1941 (DEA 77/27/14).

77. Quoted in Walter Huder, 'Alfred Kerr: ein deutscher Kritiker im Exil', *Sinn und Form* 18 (1966), IV, p. 1275.

78. Kerr to Hermon Ould, 13 August 1942, quoted in William Abbey, 'Die Illusion genannt deutscher PEN-Club' in W. Abbey et al., eds, *Between Two Languages. German-speaking Exiles in Great Britain 1933–45*, London 1995, p. 150.

79. *Writers in Freedom. A Symposium*, ed. Hermon Ould, London 1942, pp. 79–84.

80. Letters to the Editor, The *Spectator*, 17 April 1942, pp. 377–8.

81. Alfred Kerr, 'How was it? And how will it be?', *Central European Observer*. A Fortnightly Review (London), XIX, 14, 10 July 1942.

82. Cf. Lord Vansittart to Kerr, 25 April and 25 July 1942 (SAdK).

83. Kerr to Lord Vansittart, 23 September 1943 (SAdK).

84. Heinrich Fraenkel to Richard Friedenthal, 18 July 1942 (DEA 77/27/161).

85. 'The Influence of German Nationalism and Militarism upon the Theatre and Film of the Weimar Republic', London 1945; reprinted in Alfred Kerr, *Essays*, ed. Hermann Haarmann and Klaus Siebenhaar, Berlin 1991, pp. 383–424.

86. Report by Kerr to Hermon Ould, undated, 1945 (DEA 77/27).

87. Judith Kerr, *The Other Way Round*, London 1989, p. 29.

88. *Der deutsche PEN-Club im Exil 1933–1948*, op. cit., p. 377.

89. Karl Retzlaw, *Spartakus: Aufstieg und Niedergang. Erinnerungen eines Parteiarbeiters*, Frankfurt 1985, pp. 384–5.

90. See correspondence in Karl Retzlaw Estate (DEA 80/169).

91. Retzlaw, op. cit, pp. 393–5.

92. Otten to L. Mohrenwitz, 23 June 1940 (Otten Estate).

93. Otten to Humanitas-Verlag, 19 October 1937 (Otten Estate).

94. Otten to Wickham Steed, 10 July 1940 (Otten Estate).

95. Cf. Mohrenwitz to Otten, 28 September and 15 October 1940 (Otten Estate).

96. Stanley Unwin to Otten, 31 January 1941 (Otten Estate).

97. Otten to Stanley Unwin, 2 September 1941 (Allen & Unwin Archive, University of Reading).

98. Eden Paul to Stanley Unwin, 15 and 23 July 1941 (Reading).

99. ibid., 20 July 1941 (Reading).

100. Otten to Stanley Unwin, 24 July 1941 (Otten Estate).

101. Eden Paul to Stanley Unwin, 4 August 1941 (Reading).

102. Stanley Unwin to Otten, 7 November 1941 (Otten Estate).

103. *Manchester Guardian*, 17 June 1942.

104. *The Times Literary Supplement*, 6 June 1942, p. 287.

105. Hans Jaeger, *No More German Nationalism*, London 1943; 'A New Form of Democracy' in *After Nazism – Democracy?*, ed. Kurt Hiller, London 1945.

106. Eugen Brehm, cited in J. M. Ritchie, 'Kurt Hiller – a "Stänkerer" in Exile 1934–1955', *German Life and Letters*, Volume LI, no. 2, April 1998.

107. Retzlaw, op. cit., p. 416.

108. Ellen Otten to the author, 2 February 1998.

109. Stanley Godman, 'Germany and the Crisis of Western Culture', *The New English Weekly* (London) 3 September 1942, pp. 161–2; cf. also W. G. Peck, 'The Substance of Hitler', *Christendom*, XII, 48, December 1942, pp. 239–45.

110. 'Londoner Elegien', unpublished typescript, p. 21 (Otten Estate).

111. Neumann to Zweig, 21 February 1942 (DÖW 11.548/16).

112. Cf. correspondence between Rudolf Spitz and Neumann (DÖW 7234/6–7).

113. *Zeitspiegel*, IV/10, 7 March 1942.

114. *Zeitspiegel* V/8, 6 March 1943.

115. '"Wir sind nicht mehr allein." Rede auf der Kundgebung des "FAM" in der Porchester Hall', *Zeitspiegel, London*, IV/5, 31 January 1942, and IV/6, 7 February 1942. Churchill's first reference to the case for an independent Austria was made on 9 November 1940.

116. See Klaus Amann, *P.E.N.: Politik. Emigration. Nationalsozialismus*, Vienna 1982.

117. Cf. Jenö Kostmann, 'Österreichische Kulturkonferenz', *Zeitspiegel* IV/36, 5 September 1942, p. 7.

118. See *PEN News*, January 1943.

119. Theodor Kramer, *Verbannt aus Österreich*, London 1943.

120. Neumann to Richard Crossman, 28 February 1941 (DÖW 7243/3).

121. The manuscripts, consisting of radio scripts and talks given in the International PEN and Austrian PEN are held in DÖW 7234/2.

122. The MS can be dated from an accompanying note from Neumann, bearing the date 8 June 1942.

123. Cf. *Vielleicht das Heitere*, p. 183; the original typescript of *Those were the Men* is held in DÖW 11.548/9 and carries the names of Neumann and Thomas.

124. Broadcast on 28 January 1943 – see DÖW 7234/2.

125. A typescript of this speech, with Neumann's handwritten corrections, is contained in DÖW 7234/2.

126. *Ein leichtes Leben*, pp. 561–2.

127. The diary, covering the period March–May 1944 is held in ÖNB, Ser. n. 21.601.

NOTES TO PART SIX

1. Hilde Spiel, *Die hellen und die finsteren Zeiten*, Munich 1989, p. 206.

2. Cf. Kerr's correspondence with Gottfried Bermann Fischer in 1946–7 (SAdK).

3. Thomas Mann, Frank Thieß and Walter von Molo, *Ein Streitgespräch über die innere und die äußere Emigration*, Dortmund 1946.

4. Robert Neumann, readers' letter, *Die Zeit*, 17 November 1967.

5. In the last few years of his life, Otten edited several anthologies of Expressionist writing, including *Ahnung und Aufbruch. Expressionistische Prosa*, Darmstadt/

Berlin/Neuwied 1957; *Das leere Haus. Prosa jüdischer Dichter*, Stuttgart 1959; *Schrei und Bekenntnis. Expressionistisches Theater*, Darmstadt/Berlin/Neuwied 1959; *Ego und Eros. Meistererzählungen des Expressionismus*, Stuttgart 1963. For an overview of this work, see Hermann Ruch, 'Karl Otten und die Wiederbelebung des literarischen Expressionismus' in *Schiller-Gesellschaft Jahrbuch* 33 (1989), pp. 75–114.

6. Hans-Albert Walter in an interview with Heinz Ludwig Arnold, *Akzente*, XX (1973), p. 483.

7. Hans Sahl, *Das Exil im Exil*, Frankfurt 1991. See also 'Das Exil nach dem Exil. Zum Tode Hans Sahls', *Exil* 1993/1, pp. 63–4.

8. Judith Kerr, *A Small Person Far Away*, London 1989, p. 10.

9. Cf. Certificate of Naturalisation, dated 17 May 1947 (SAdK).

10. Kerr, 'Fünf Tage Deutschland', *Sätze meines Lebens*, ed. by Helga Bemmann, Berlin 1980, pp. 435–51. The report was written for the *Neue Zeitung*, a newspaper published by the Americans in Munich, but apparently did not appear. Cf. Kerr's correspondence with *Neue Zeitung*, particularly letter dated 28 April 1948 (SAdK).

11. Kerr, *Lesebuch*, op. cit., p. 11.

12. Trauerfeier für Alfred Kerr, 11 November 1948. Cf. *Der deutsche PEN-Club im Exil 1933–1948*, Frankfurt 1980, pp. 396–7.

13. Alfred Kerr, *Werke in Einzelbänden*, ed. Hermann Haarmann and Günther Rühle, 1988ff; Alfred Kerr, *Wo liegt Berlin? Briefe aus der Reichshauptstadt 1895–1900*, ed. Günther Rühle, Berlin 1997. At the time of writing, Rühle has plans to complete publication of the Kerr edition abandoned almost a decade ago; Deborah Vietor-Engländer is preparing a Kerr biography.

14. Robert Neumann, *Children of Vienna*, London 1946.

15. Neumann in interview with Horst Bienek, *Werkstattgespräche mit Schriftstellern*, Munich 1965, p. 74.

16. Robert Neumann, 'Unbekannt – im Lande das mich entdeckte. Ein Selbstporträt', *Welt und Wort*, 16, 3 (1961), pp. 77–8.

17. Otten, *Die Botschaft*, Darmstadt/Berlin/Neuwied 1957.

18. Otten, *Herbstgesang*, Neuwied/Berlin 1961; *Wurzeln*, Neuwied/Berlin 1963.

19. See note 5 above.

20. Cf. Manfred Brauneck, *Autorenlexikon deutchsprachiger Literatur des 20. Jahrhunderts*, Reinbek 1984: 'More significant than Otten's own literary production is his work on the legacy of his expressionist contemporaries.'

21. Max Herrmann-Neiße, *Gesammelte Werke*, ed. Klaus Völker, Frankfurt 1986–8.

Bibliography

General Works of Reference

Liselotte Maas, *Handbuch der deutschen Exilpresse 1933–45*, edited by Eberhard Lämmert, Vols 1-4, Munich 1976–90.

Wilhelm Sternfeld and Eva Tiedemann, *Deutsche Exilliteratur 1933–45. Eine Bio-Bibliographie*, Heidelberg/Darmstadt 1962.

Biographisches Handbuch der deutschsprachigen Emigration nach 1933, edited by Institut für Zeitgeschichte, Munich and Research Foundation for Jewish Immigration, New York, Vols. 1-3, Munich 1980-83.

Deutsches Exilarchiv 1933–45: Katalog der Bücher und Broschüren, Stuttgart 1989.

Kunst im Exil in Großbritannien 1933–1945, edited by Neue Gesellschaft für Bildende Kunst Berlin, Berlin 1986.

General Historical Studies/Studies of German-speaking Exile

William Abbey, Charmian Brinson, Richard Dove, Marian Malet and Jennifer Taylor (eds), *Between Two Languages. German-speaking Exiles in Great Britain 1933–1945*, London/Stuttgart 1994.

Klaus Amann, *P.E.N.: Politik. Emigration. Nationalsozialismus*, Vienna 1982.

Marion Berghahn, *Continental Britons. German-Jewish Refugees from Nazi Germany*, Oxford/New York/Hamburg 1988.

Günter Berghaus: *Theatre and Film in Exile*, Oxford/New York/Munich 1989.

Manfred Briegel, Wolfgang Frühwald (eds), *Die Erfahrung der Fremde*, Weinheim/Basel 1988.

Charmian Brinson, *The Strange Case of Dora Fabian and Mathilde Wurm*, Berne 1997.

Charmian Brinson, Richard Dove, Marian Malet, Jennifer Taylor (eds), *England? Aber wo liegt es? Deutsche und österreichische Emigranten in Großbritannien 1933–1945*, Munich/London 1996.

Charmian Brinson, Richard Dove, Anthony Grenville, Marian Malet, Jennifer Taylor (eds), *Keine Klage über England. Deutsche und österreichische Exilerfahrungen in Großbritannien 1933–1945*, Munich/London 1998.

Angus Calder, *The People's War*, London 1969.

Dokumentationsarchiv des österreichischen Widerstandes (ed.), *Österreicher im Exil. Großbritannien 1938–1945. Eine Dokumentation*, Vienna 1992.

Deutsche Bibliothek (ed.), *Der deutsche PEN-Klub im Exil 1933–48*, Frankfurt 1980.

Richard Dove, *He was a German. A Biography of Ernst Toller*, London 1990

Manfred Durzak (ed.), *Die deutsche Exilliteratur 1933–45*, Stuttgart 1973.

Anthony Glees, *Exile Politics during the Second World War. The German Social Democrats in Britain*, Oxford 1982.

Gerhard Hirschfeld (ed.), *Exile in Great Britain. Refugees from Hitler's Germany*, London 1984.

Helene Maimann, *Politik im Wartesaal. Österreichische Exilpolitik in Großbritannien 1938–45*, Vienna/Cologne/Graz 1975.

Franz Norbert Mennemeier, Frithjof Trapp (eds), *Deutsche Exildramatik 1933–50*, Munich 1980.

Benny Morris, *The Roots of Appeasement. The British Weekly Press and Nazi Germany during the 1930s*, London 1991.

Werner E. Mosse (ed.), *Second Chance. German-speaking Jews in the United Kingdom*, Cambridge 1991.

Sylvia Patsch, *Österreichische Schriftsteller im Exil in Großbritannien: ein Kapitel vergessene österreichische Literatur*, Vienna/Munich 1985.

J. M. Ritchie, *German Exiles. British Perspectives*, New York 1997.

Jürgen Serke, *Die verbrannten Dichter*, Weinheim 1977.

A. J. Sherman, *Island Refuge. Britain and Refugees from the Third Reich 1933–1939*, London 1973.

John M. Spalek, Joseph P. Strelka (eds), *Deutschsprachige Exilliteratur seit 1933*, Vol. 1: Kalifornien, Teil 1 u. 2, Berne 1976.

John M. Spalek, *Deutschsprachige Exilliteratur seit 1933*, Vol. 2: New York, Parts 1 and 2, Berne 1989.

Austin Stevens, *The Dispossessed. German Refugees in Britain*, London 1975.

Hans-Albert Walter, *Deutsche Exilliteratur 1933–50 in sieben Bändern*, Stuttgart 1978ff. (Vols 1–4 have so far appeared).

Bernard Wasserstein, *Britain and the Jews of Europe 1933–1945*, Oxford/New York 1988.

Matthias Wegner, *Exil und Literatur. Deutsche Schriftsteller im Ausland 1933–1950*, 2nd edition, Frankfurt/Bonn 1968.

Dirk Wiemann, *Exilliteratur in Großbritannien 1933–1945*, Opladen/Wiesbaden 1998.

Lutz Winckler (ed.) *Antifaschistische Literatur*, 3 vols., Konigstein 1977 and 1979.

Kunst und Literatur im antifaschistischen Exil, 7 vols., Leipzig 1978-81, particularly Vol. 5, *Exil in der Tschechoslowakei, Großbritannien, Skandinavien und Palästina*, Leipzig 1980.

Articles

James J. Barnes and Patience P. Barnes, 'London's German Community in the Early Thirties', *German Life and Letters*, XLVI, 4, October 1993, pp. 331-45.

Franz Bönsch, 'Das Österreichische Exiltheater 'Laterndl' in London' in *Österreicher im Exil 1939-45. Protokoll des Internationalen Symposiums*, edited by H. Maimann and H. Lunzer, pp. 441-50.

Charmian Brinson, 'The Gestapo and the Political Exiles in Britain During the 1930s: the Case of Hans Wesemann – and Others', *German Life and Letters*, LI, 1, January 1998, pp. 43-64.

Erich Fried, 'Nicht verdrängen, nicht gewöhnen', in *Texte zum Thema Österreich*, edited by Michael Lewin, Vienna 1987.

Erich Fried, 'Der Flüchtling und die Furcht vor der Heimkehr', in Fried, *Gedanken in und an Deutschland*, edited by Michael Lewin, Vienna and Zurich 1988.

Ulla Hahn, 'Der Freie Deutsche Kulturbund in Grossbritannien: eine Skizze seiner Geschichte', in *Antifaschistische Literatur*, edited by Lutz Winckler, vol II, pp. 131-95.

Eva Kolmer, *Das Austrian Centre. Sieben Jahre österreichische Gemeinschafts- arbeit*. Erinnerungsbroschüre des Austrian Centre, London 1945.

Dieter Lamping, 'Linguistische Metamorphosen. Aspekte des Sprach- wechsels in der Exilliteratur', *Germanistik und Komparatistik*, edited by Hendrik Birus, Stuttgart/Weimar 1995.

Birgid Leske, Marion Reinisch and Mathias Hansen, 'Exil in Großbritannien', in *Exil in der Tschechoslowakei, Großbritannien, Skandinavien und Palästina*, Leipzig 1980, pp. 147-305.

Ernst G. Loewenthal, 'Bloomsbury House. Flüchtlingsarbeit in London 1939 bis 1946. Aus persönlichen Erinnerungen', in *Das Unrechtsregime*, Vol. II, edited by Ursula Büttner, Hamburg 1986.

Waltraud Strickhausen, 'Schreiben in der Sprache des Anderen', in: *Die Resonanz des Exils. Gelungene und mißlungene Rezeption deutschsprachiger Exilautoren*, edited by Dieter Sevin, Amsterdam/Atlanta 1992.

Gabriele Tergit, 'How they resettled', in *Britain's New Citizens. The story of the Refugees from Germany and Austria*, edited by Association of Jewish Refugees in Great Britain, London 1951, pp. 61-70.

Internment

David Cesarani and Tony Kushner (eds), *The Internment of Aliens in Twentieth Century Britain*, London 1993.

Peter and Leni Gillman, *'Collar the Lot' – How Britain Interned and Expelled its Wartime Refugees*, London 1980.

Yvonne Kapp and Margaret Mynatt, *British Policy and the Refugees 1933–1941*, London/Portland 1997.

Miriam Kochan, *Britain's Internees in the Second World War*, London and Basingstoke 1983.

François Lafitte, *The Internment of Aliens*, London 1940; reprinted with an introduction by the author and an index, London 1988.

Michael Seyfert, *Im Niemandsland. Deutsche Exilliteratur in britischer Internierung*, Berlin 1984.

British Publishing

Desmond Flower, *Fellows in Foolscap*, London 1991.

Newman Flower, *Just as it Happened*, London 1950.

Ariela Halkin, *The Enemy Reviewed. German Popular Literature through British Eyes between the Two World Wars*, London 1995.

Robert Hewison, *Under Siege*, London 1977.

Sheila Hodges, *Gollancz. Story of a Publishing House*, London 1978.

J. W. Lambert, *The Bodley Head*, London 1960.

Stanley Unwin, *The Truth About Publishing*, London 1960.

Stanley Unwin, *Publishing in Peace and War*, London 1944.

Fredric Warburg, *An Occupation for Gentlemen*, London 1959.

The BBC

Asa Briggs, *The History of Broadcasting in the United Kingdom* (revised edition) Oxford/New York 1995.

Carl Brinitzer, *Hier spricht London. Von einem, der dabei war*, Hamburg 1969.

Gunda Cannon (ed.), *'Hier ist England' – 'Live aus London' – Das deutsche*

Programm der British Broadcasting Corporation 1938–1988, BBC, London 1988.

Robert Lucas, 'The German Service of the BBC', in *PEN Symposium Report. Half a Century Writing in German Abroad*, London 1983, pp. 35-43.

Gerald Mansell, *Let Truth be told. 50 Years of BBC External Broadcasting*, London 1982.

Memoirs

Elisabeth Castonier: *Stürmisch bis heiter. Memoiren einer Außenseiterin*, Munich 1964.

Ruth Feiner, *Young Woman of Europe*, London 1942.

Hans Flesch-Brunningen, *Die verführte Zeit. Lebens-Erinnerungen*, Vienna/ Munich 1988.

Michael Hamburger, *String of Beginnings. Intermittent Memoirs 1924–1954*, London 1991.

Storm Jameson, *Journey from the North*, 2 vols., London 1969, 1970.

Arthur Koestler, *Scum of the Earth*, London 1941 (reprinted London 1991).

Lilo Linke, *Tale without End*, London 1934.

Lilli Palmer, *Change Lobsters and Dance*, London 1977.

Hilde Spiel, *Die hellen und die finsteren Zeiten. Erinnerungen 1911–1946*, Munich 1990.

Gabriele Tergit, *Etwas Seltenes überhaupt. Erinnerungen*, Frankfurt/Berlin 1983.

Fred Uhlman, *The Making of an Englishman*, London 1960.

Otto Zarek, *German Odyssey*, London 1941.

Publications by and about individual authors

In order to give a more complete picture, the references to books published in exile include the names of publishers.

Max Herrmann-Neiße

Um uns die Fremde, Zurich: Oprecht 1936.

Letzte Gedichte, edited by Leni Herrmann, London: Barmerlea and New York: Fles 1941.

Mir bleibt mein Lied, edited by Leni Herrmann, London: Barmerlea and New York: Fles 1942.

Erinnerung und Exil. Gedichte. Mit einem Nachwort von Stefan Zweig, Zurich: Oprecht 1946.

Gesammelte Werke, edited by Klaus Völker, 10 volumes, Frankfurt, 1986–88.

Unpublished Papers

Letters and manuscripts in Deutsches Literaturarchiv, Marbach am Neckar.

Secondary Literature

Richard Dove, '"Monolog auf fremder Bühne": Max Herrmann-Neißes Exiljahre in London', in *Der Dichter und seine Stadt. Max Herrmann-Neiße zum 50. Todestag*, edited by Yvonne-Patricia Alefeld, Dusseldorf 1991.

Jörg Thunecke, '"Weh mir, daß ich ein Lyriker bin und noch dazu ein deutscher"', in *Deutschsprachige Exillyrik von 1933 bis zur Nachkriegszeit*, edited by Jörg Thunecke, Amsterdam/Atlanta GA 1998.

Klaus Völker, *Max Herrmann-Neiße. Künstler, Kneipen, Kabaretts – Schlesien, Berlin, im Exil*, Berlin 1992.

Alfred Kerr

Die Welt im Licht, 2 vols., Berlin 1920 (vol. 2 contains impressions of a visit to England in 1913).

New York und London. Stätten des Geschicks, Berlin 1923 (includes impressions of a visit to England in 1922).

Die Diktatur des Hausknechts, Brussels: Les Associés 1934.

Walther Rathenau. Erinnerungen eines Freundes, Amsterdam: Querido 1935.

Melodien, Paris: Éditions Nouvelles Internationales 1938.

The Influence of German Nationalism and Militarism upon the Theatre and Film in the Weimar Republic, London: Fight for Freedom 1945.

Ich kam nach England, edited by Walter Huder and Thomas Koebner, Bonn 1979.

Unpublished Papers

Unpublished letters and manuscripts in the Alfred-Kerr-Archiv, Akademie der Künste, Berlin.

Secondary Literature

Joachim Biener, '"Kämpfer sein und Melodie"': der Kritiker Alfred Kerr', *Die Weltbühne*, 26/5 (1980), pp. 158–66.

Walter Huder, 'Alfred Kerr: ein deutscher Kritiker im Exil', *Sinn und Form* (1966), pp. 1262–79.

Ilse Newberry, 'Alfred Kerr und die BBC', *German Life and Letters*, 38/3 April 1985, pp. 260–72.

Traute Schoelmann, *Ein Weg zur literarischen Selbstverwirklichung*, Munich 1977.

Deborah Vietor-Engländer, 'Alfred Kerr im Exil. Einige Bemerkungen zu seinem Englandbild', in Michel Grunewald, Frithjof Trapp (eds), *Autour du Front Populaire allemand*, Bern/Frankfurt/New York 1990, pp. 327–38.

— 'Alfred Kerr und das Judentum', *Exil*, 2/1991, pp. 41-8.

— '"I cannot prophesy. I cannot assert. But I can guess. And I can warn." Alfred Kerr in London', in: *Between two Languages*, ed. by William Abbey et al., Stuttgart/London 1995.

Karlheinz Wendler, *Alfred Kerr im Exil*, Berlin 1981 (Ph.D. diss.).

Robert Neumann

Sir Basil Zaharoff. Der König der Waffen, Zurich: Bibliothek zeitgenössische Werke 1934 (English: *Zaharoff, the Armaments King*, translated by R. T. Clark, London: Allen & Unwin 1935).

Struensee: Doktor, Diktator, Favorit und armer Sünder, Amsterdam: Querido 1935 (*The Queen's Doctor*, translated by Edwin and Willa Muir, London: Gollancz 1936).

Eine Frau hat geschrien, Zurich: Humanitas 1938 (*A Woman Screamed*, translated by Willa and Edwin Muir, London: Cassell 1938).

By the Waters of Babylon, London: Dent 1939 (*An den Wassern von Babylon*, Oxford: East and West Library 1945).

Scene in Passing, London: Dent 1942 (*Tibbs*, Konstanz: Curt Weller 1948).

The Inquest, London: Hutchinson 1944 (*Bibiana Santis. Der Weg einer Frau*, translated by Melanie Steinmetz, Munich/Vienna/Basel: Desch 1950).

Children of Vienna, London: Dent 1946 (*Kinder von Wien*, translated by Franziska Becker, Amsterdam: Querido 1948).

Mein altes Haus in Kent. Erinnerungen an Menschen und Gespenster, Munich/Vienna/Basel: Desch 1957 (*The Plague House Papers*, translated by R. Neumann, London: Hutchinson 1959).

Ein leichtes Leben. Bericht über mich selbst und Zeitgenossen, Munich/Vienna/ Basel 1963 (no English edition).

Vielleicht das Heitere, Munich/Vienna/Basel 1968 (no English edition).

Published Letters

'Arnold Zweig – Robert Neumann: Correspondence', selected and annotated by Geoffrey V. Davis, *GDR Monitor*, Summer 1987, pp. 1–20.

Unpublished Papers

Unpublished papers in Österreichische Nationalbibliothek, Vienna, and Dokumentationsstelle des Österreichischen Widerstandes, Vienna.

Secondary Literature

Richard Dove, 'Almost an English Author: Robert Neumann's English-language Novels', *German Life and Letters*, LI, 1, January 1998, pp. 93–105.

Robert Neumann: Stimmen der Freunde, Munich/Vienna/Basel 1957.

Ulrich Scheck, *Die Prosa Robert Neumanns*, New York 1985.

Karl Otten

Torquemadas Schatten, Stockholm: Bermann Fischer 1938.

A Combine of Aggression, translated by Eden Paul and F. M. Field, London: Allen & Unwin 1942 (*Geplante Illusionen. Eine Analyse des Faschismus*, Frankfurt 1989).

Die Reise nach Deutschland. edited with an Afterword by Richard Dove, Bern/ Frankfurt 2000.

Unpublished Papers

Unpublished papers and manuscripts held by Ellen Otten Estate, Minusio/ Locarno and Deutsches Literaturarchiv, Marbach.

Secondary Literature

Gregor Ackermann/Hermann Ruch, 'Die Ohnmacht des Geistigen. Karl Otten und *Der neue Tag*', in *Juni. Magazin für Kultur und Politik am Niederrhein*, 1991, nos. 2–3, pp. 270-3.

Richard Dove, 'A Casualty of Exile. Karl Otten's Unpublished Novel *Die Reise nach Deutschland*', *Modern Language Review*, Vol. 92, 1, pp. 124–39.

Werner Jung, 'Karl Otten. Ein Porträt' in *Juni. Magazin für Kultur und Politik am Niederrhein*, 1987, no. 4, pp. 19-33.

Karl Otten. Leben und Werk, edited by Berhard Zeller and Ellen Otten, Mainz 1982.

Hermann Ruch, 'Karl Otten und die Wiederbelebung des literarischen Expressionismus' in *Schiller-Gesellschaft Jahrbuch* 33, (1989), pp. 75–114.

Heribert Seifert, 'Exil Mallorca', *Neue Zürcher Zeitung*, 7 December 1995, p. 48.

Stefan Zweig

Marie Antoinette. Bildnis eines mittleren Charakters, Leipzig: Insel 1932 (*Marie Antoinette: the Portrait of an Average Woman* [no translator given], London: Cassell 1933).

Triumph und Tragik des Erasmus von Rotterdam, Vienna/Leipzig/ Zurich: Reichner 1934 (*Erasmus*, translated by Eden and Cedar Paul, London: Cassell 1934).

Maria Stuart, Vienna/Leipzig/Zurich: Reichner 1935 (*The Queen of Scots*, translated by Eden and Cedar Paul, London: Cassell 1935).

Castellio gegen Calvin oder Ein Gewissen gegen die Gewalt, Vienna/Leipzig/ Zurich: Reichner 1936 (*The Right to Heresy. Castellio against Calvin*, translated by Eden and Cedar Paul, London: Cassell 1936).

Der begrabene Leuchter, Vienna/Leipzig/Zurich: Reichner 1937 (*The Buried Candelabrum*, translated by Eden and Cedar Paul, London: Cassell 1937).

Begegnungen mit Menschen, Büchern, Städten, Vienna/Leipzig/Zurich: Reichner 1937

Three Masters: Balzac, Dickens, Dostoyevsky, translated by Eden and Cedar Paul, London: Cassell 1938 (*Drei Meister: Balzac, Dickens, Dostojewski*, Leipzig: Insel 1920).

Magellan. Der Mann und seine Tat, Vienna/Leipzig/Zurich: Reichner 1937 (*Magellan. Pioneer of the Pacific*, translated by Eden and Cedar Paul, London: Cassell 1938).

Ungeduld des Herzens, Stockholm: Bermann Fischer 1939 (*Beware of Pity*, translated by Phyllis and Trevor Blewitt, London: Cassell 1939).

The Tide of Fortune, translated by Eden and Cedar Paul, London: Cassell 1940 (partial translation of *Sternstunden der Menschheit*, Leipzig: Insel and Vienna/Leipzig/Zurich: Reichner 1927).

Brasilien. Ein Land der Zukunft, Stockholm 1941 (*Brazil. Land of the Future*, translated by Andrew St James, London: Cassell 1942).

Schachnovelle, Buenos Aires 1942 (*The Royal Game*, translated by B. W.

Huebsch, with *Letter from an Unknown Woman* and *Amok*, translated by Eden and Cedar Paul, London: Cassell 1944).

The World of Yesterday. An Autobiography (translated by Benjamin W. Huebsch and Helmut Ripperger), London: Cassell 1943, New York: Viking 1943; reprinted with introduction by Harry Zohn, Lincoln/London: University of Nebraska Press 1964 (*Die Welt von gestern. Erinnerungen eines Europäers*, Stockholm: Bermann Fischer 1944).

Published letters

Stefan Zweig/Friderike Zweig. Briefwechsel 1912–42, edited by Friderike Zweig, Bern 1951.

Stefan Zweig: Briefe an Freunde, edited by Richard Friedenthal, Frankfurt 1984.

Stefan Zweig/ Paul Zech, Briefe 1910–42, edited by Donald G. Daviau, Frankfurt 1986.

Joseph Roth, Briefe 1911–1939, edited by Hermann Kesten, Cologne/Berlin 1970.

Romain Rolland/Stefan Zweig. Briefwechsel 1910–1940, Berlin 1987.

Richard Strauss/Stefan Zweig, Briefwechsel, edited by Willi Schuh, Frankfurt 1957.

Stefan Zweig, Unbekannte Briefe aus der Emigration an eine Freundin, edited by Gisella Selden-Goth, Vienna/Stuttgart/Basel 1964.

Stefan Zweig, Briefwechsel mit Hermann Broch, Sigmund Freud, Rainer Maria Rilke und Arthur Schnitzler, edited by Jeffrey B. Berlin, Hans-Ulrich Lindken and Donald A. Prater, Frankfurt 1987.

Sigmund Freud/Arnold Zweig. Briefwechsel, Frankfurt 1968.

Erich Ebermayer, *Denn heute gehört uns Deutschland*, Hamburg 1959.

Erich Ebermeyer. Buch der Freunde, edited by Peer Baedecker und Karl Lemke, Munich 1960.

Stefan Zweig, Spiegelungen einer schöpferischen Persönlichkeit, edited by Erich Fitzbauer, Vienna 1959.

Stefan Zweig. Bilder, Texte, Dokumente, edited by Klemens Renoldner et al., Salzburg: Residenz-Verlag 1994.

Unpublished Material

Manuscripts in Theatermuseum, Vienna.

Musical manuscripts in British Library (Department of Manuscripts).

Correspondence in Stadtbibliothek, Vienna.

Correspondence in Österreichische Nationalbibliothek, Vienna.

Correspondence in Deutsches Literaturarchiv, Marbach/Neckar.

Secondary Literature

Joseph Leftwich, 'Stefan Zweig and the World of Yesterday', *Year Book III*, Leo Baeck Institute, London (1958), pp. 81-100.

Emil Ludwig, 'Stefan Zweig zum Gedächtnis. Zwei Briefe des Abschieds', *Aufbau* VIII/9, 27 Feb. 1942, p. 15.

Hartmut Müller, *Stefan Zweig. Mit Selbstzeugnissen und Bilddokumenten*, Reinbek 1988.

Donald Prater, 'Stefan Zweig in England', *German Life and Letters*, October 1962, pp. 1-16.

Donald Prater, *European of Yesterday. A Biography of Stefan Zweig*, Oxford 1972 (revised and expanded German edition: *Stefan Zweig. Das Leben eines Ungeduldigen*, Frankfurt 1984).

Joseph Strelka, *Stefan Zweig. Freier Geist der Menschlichkeit*, Vienna 1981.

Friderike Zweig, *Stefan Zweig*, translated by Erna McArthur, London 1946.

Index

Agate, James 42
Alexander, Elias 29, 107, 109
Allen & Unwin (publisher) 40, 65–6, 71, 233, 242
Allert de Lange (publisher) 61, 86, 111
Altmann, Lotte 53, 58, 146, 162–3, 184–7, 189, 209, 211, 214, 215
Anderson, Sir John 172
Apfel, Alfred 41
Ardrey, Robert 249
Asch, Schalom 32
Asquith, H. H. 101
Auden, W. H. 9, 12–13
Auernheimer, Raoul 140, 150

Bachmair, Heinrich (publisher) 112
Badt, Kurt 244
Baer, Max 125
Bahr, Hermann 31
Balzac, Honoré de 186, 209–11, 215
Baratieri, Oreste 108
Barbusse, Henri 31
Barker, Duckworth 203
Barr, Robert 201
Barthel, Kurt (KuBa) 258
Bartlett, Vernon 41
Bartok, Béla 32
Baruch, Hugo 103–04
Bassermann, Albert 83
Baudelaire, Charles 31–2
Becher, Johannes R. 8, 258
Becker, Franziska (Rolly, later Neumann) 71, 155, 167, 173–7, 181–2, 184, 216–17, 248, 261
Beecham, Sir Thomas 125
Beethoven, Ludwig van 44
Bell, George, Bishop of Chichester 233
Bell, Julian 9, 12
Berg, Alban 32
Bergner, Elizabeth 95
Bermann Fischer, Gottfried (publisher) 60, 110–11, 116, 142, 148, 170–1, 213, 256

Bermann, Richard A. 159
Bernal, J. D. 231
Bertelsmann (publisher) 266
Bilbo, Jack (see Baruch, Hugo)
Bithell, Jethro 192
Blake, William 45, 149
Blei, Franz 102–3
Bloch, Martin 88, 128
Bodley Head (publisher) 41
Bonham-Carter, Lady 225
Bonn, Moritz 98, 100
Borkenau, Franz 106, 221
Borne, Ludwig 7
Borneman, Ernest (Ernst Bornemann alias Cameron McCabe) 222
Boshell, Gordon 200–1
Boswell, Ronald 41
Brandes, Georg 32
Braun, Felix 146, 148, 150, 157, 186, 209, 211, 213–14, 216
Braunthal, Julius 232
Brecht, Arnold 258
Brecht, Bertolt 2, 7–10, 35–6, 155, 165, 191
Bredel, Willi 16
Bridie, J. M. 6
Brinitzer, Carl 196
Broch, Hermann 150, 154, 157
Brockway, Fenner 101
Brown, Douglas 201
Bruckner, Ferdinand 62, 71
Büchner, Georg 7
Budberg, Moura 85
Burschell, Friedrich 235–6
Busch, Fritz 264
Byron, Lord 92

Cahn, Alfredo 209, 213
Calder, Angus 169
Calder-Marshall, Arthur 8
Canetti, Elias 157, 250, 264
Cape, Jonathan (publisher) 40, 242, 266
Carleton Greene, Hugh 196
Carlow, Viscount 149

Carossa, Hans 46
Cassell (publisher) 40, 43, 52, 57, 59, 143,
    147, 152, 154, 210
Castonier, Elisabeth 222
Caudwell, Christopher 12
Chamberlain, Neville 100, 168, 196
Christie, Agatha 10
Churchill, Winston 98, 182–3, 242, 250
Connolly, Cyril 42
Conrad, Joseph 219
Corinth, Lovis 18
Cornford, John 9, 12
Crankshaw, Edward 66
Creswell, Peter 108
Croce, Benedetto 31
Cronin, A. J. 10
Crossman, Richard 199–200, 251
Cunningham, Valentine 9
Curtis Brown 152
Czinner, Paul 95

Davies, Peter 64
Davringhausen, Heinrich Maria 103
Dawson, Geoffrey 99
Dawson Scott, Catharine 73
Day Lewis, Cecil 9
de Maistre, Roy 128
de Mendelssohn, Peter 3, 208, 222–3, 255
Defoe, Daniel 7
Dent, Anthony 159, 219
Dent (publishers) 159, 220
Desch, Kurt, Verlag (publisher) 262
Dietrich, Marlene 39, 85, 206
Disraeli, Benjamin 121, 122
Döblin, Alfred 181
Dollfuß, Engelbert 29, 46, 72, 139
Dos Passos, John 208
Drinkwater, John 49, 58
Drummond, Lindsay (publisher) 227
du Maurier, Daphne 10
Duhamel, Georges 34
Dukes, Ashley 70

Ebbutt, Norman 99
Ebermayer, Erich 34, 56
Ebert, Carl 264
Edward VIII, King (later Duke of
    Windsor) 98

Ehrenstein, Albert 162
Einstein, Albert 89, 206
Eisenstein, Sergei 25
Eliot, T. S. 42, 124
Emil Oprecht (publisher) 87, 111, 136,
    256
Engelhorn (publisher) 151
Erasmus, Desiderius 212
Ernst, Max 24
Esslin, Martin 199
European Books (publisher) 110

Fabian, Dora 62
Farr, Tommy 125
Feiner, Ruth 3, 37, 42
Feuchtwanger, Lion 16, 17, 39–40, 52,
    73, 81, 155, 207
Field (translator) 243
Fischer, Heinrich 205
Fischer, S. (publisher) 21
Fleischer, Victor 55, 58, 147, 186, 189,
    209–11, 214
Flesch-Brunningen, Hans 1, 28, 37
Flower, Desmond 57, 63, 144, 184, 188,
    209
Flower, Newman 40, 57, 149
Folio Society 42
Forster, E. M. 208
Fraenkel, Heinrich 221, 232–3, 237
Franckenstein, Baron Georg 141
Frank, Bruno 6, 71, 81, 85, 133, 181
Frank, Leonhard 83, 85, 181
Fraser, Lindley 197
Freiligrath, Ferdinand 7, 266
Freud, Sigmund 31, 185, 214
Freyhahn, Max 179
Fried, Erich 2, 266
Friedell, Egon 146
Friedenthal, Richard 180–1, 209, 213,
    236, 238–9
Friedmann, Marie (Mitzi) 25
Friedmann, Professor Hermann 234
Frischauer, Paul 2
Frischauer, Willi 6, 85, 163, 221, 232
Fuchs, Guido 149
Furth, Charles 66

Garbo, Greta 69

Gardner, Captain 225
Gebek, Helene (Leni) *see* Herrmann-
    Neiße, Leni
Gellner, Julius 197
Gerlach, Helmuth von 20
Gide, André 34
Gielgud, Val 107, 167
Gilbert, Martin 99
Glyn-Jones, John 200, 201
Godman, Stanley 245–6
Goebbels, Josef 19–20, 29, 48
Goering, Hermann 201
Goetz, Walter 196
Golding, Louis 10, 149
Gollancz, Victor (publisher) 39, 40, 41,
    66–7, 110, 152, 174, 227, 261, 266
Goring, Marius 200, 205
Gould, Gerald 42
Graetz, Paul 21, 81, 127, 130
Grautoff, Christiane 101–2
Greene, Graham 11, 196
Greenwood, Walter 10, 11
Grenfell, Colonel A. M., and Mrs 226
Grieger, Friedrich 78–9, 264
Grieger, Fritz 163
Gröhl (later Retzlaw), Karl 103, 171, 234,
    239–40
Gross, Fritz 127, 244
Gross, Otto 241
Grosz, George 20, 22, 79
Grünbaum, Fritz 179
Grune, Karl 70

Haffner, Sebastian 6, 221
Haldane, J. B. S. 231
Hall, Admiral 225
Hall, Radclyffe 8
Hamburger, Michael 266
Hamilton, Hamish 40–1
Hamish Hamilton (publisher) 121, 266
Hamlyn, Paul (publisher) 264
Hammerschlag, Margarete 59
Hardy, Lo 68
Harrisson, Tom 201
Hartl, Franz 249
Hartung, Gustav 83
Hauptmann, Gerhart 18
Haworth, Louise 244

Hay, Julius 19
Heiden, Konrad 109
Heilig, Bruno 180, 249
Heine, Heinrich 7, 21
Henseler, Franz 24
Herrmann-Neiße, Leni 21, 74–5, 78, 84,
    127, 129–33, 135–6, 170, 190, 194
Herrmann-Neiße, Max 20–3, 74–88;
    arrival in London 3, 37, 74–5; and
    Kerr 3, 18, 131; in Berlin 21–3, 81;
    and Zweig 58, 87, 131–2, 135, 138,
    187, 190, 192, 193, 216; and Neumann
    69, 85; and German PEN group 73;
    and English language 75–6, 137;
    poems 76–7, 79–80, 82, 83, 99, 127–8,
    129, 130, 134–9, 164, 189–95;
    published on his 50th birthday 87–8;
    and Grieger 78–9; unhappiness in
    London 76–7, 80–3, 85–6, 88, 128–9,
    136; on Nazi Germany 98–9, 193; in
    Zurich 74, 83, 132–3; fear of war,
    death and internment 163–4, 170, 173,
    191, 194; death 195; posthumous
    reputation 263–4
    see also Herrmann-Neiße, Leni; Kerr,
    Alfred, and Herrmann-Neiße
Herzl, Theodor 31, 58, 214
Hesse, Hermann 39, 133, 163
Hiller, Kurt 234, 236, 245
Hindenburg, Paul von 62
Hitler, Adolf, accession to power 15, 26,
    27, 29, 41, 72; reoccupation of
    Rhineland 100–1, 139; and take-over
    of Austria 139–40; Zweig on 150; and
    Czechoslovakia 159; satirised 198;
    Kerr on 206, 237; Otten on 241; Fight
    for Freedom Group and 244
Hofmann, Gerd 266
Hofmann, Michael 266
Hofmannsthal, Hugo von 49
Horvath, Ödön von 7, 72
Huebsch, Ben 45, 53–4, 57, 214, 265
Hugo, Victor 4
Hulse, Michael 266
Humanitas Verlag (publisher) 153–5
Hutchinson (publisher) 110, 220, 227,
    253, 266
Hutchinson, Walter 220, 261

Huxley, Aldous 10
Huxley, Julian 231
Hynes, Samuel 9

Ibsen, Henrik 18
Ihle, Peter 195
Insel Verlag (publisher) 46, 54
Isherwood, Christopher 9, 12, 13, 95

Jacob, Berthold 62
Jacobs, Monty 195, 238
Jaeger, Hans 234, 244–5
Jameson, Storm 10, 155–8, 174, 181, 184, 217–18
Jaspers, Karl 241
Jerome, Jerome K. 3
Jessner, Leopold 81, 128
Johannsen, Ernst 40
Johnston, Denis 6
Jonson, Ben 31, 49
Joyce, James 32
Jung, Franz 24
Jünger, Ernst 40

Kafka, Franz 39
Kaiser, Georg 15
Kalmus, Joseph 180
Kerr, Alfred 17–20, 88–96, 118–26, 223–9, 234–9; and Herrmann-Neiße 3, 18, 131, 136, 192, 195; as critic 18–19; and PEN 73, 208, 235–9; film projects 91–2, 95–6; arrives in London 93–5; and English language 119, 223, 228–9; publishes verse anthology 120–1; Jewishness as theme 121–2; on England 123–5, 226; on Germany 125–6, 134, 233, 236–7; longing for war 164–5, 168; and BBC 203–6; and Thomas Mann 205; son's internment 226; and Free German League of Culture 234–5; after the war 256, 258–60; return to Germany 259–60; death 260
Kerr, Judith 88–9, 92, 94, 122, 124, 224, 227, 238, 258–9
Kerr, Julia 88, 91–4, 224–6, 259
Kerr, Michael 88–9, 94, 96, 124, 224–6, 228, 259, 260
Kesten, Hermann 155, 187, 193

Kippenberg, Anton 46, 53
Klabund (Alfred Henschke) 18
Klein, Robert 62
Knopf (publisher) 110
Koestler, Arthur 201, 222, 264
Kokoschka, Oskar 234, 249, 250
Kolbenheyer, Erwin 127
Kommer, Rudolf 90–2, 118, 120–1, 126, 224, 225–6
Korda, Alexander 69, 93–5
Körmendi, Ferenc 147
Korrodi, Eduard 86
Kortner, Fritz 70, 81, 95
Kossuth, Lajos 152
Kramer, Theodor 7, 251
Kraus, Karl 28, 205
Kroner, Ellen see Otten, Ellen

Lafitte, François 180
Lampel, Peter Martin 26
Landauer, Walter 111
Landshoff, Fritz 61, 86, 133
Lane, Allen 41
Lane, John 41
Langer, Frantisek 208
Laski, Harold 231, 232
Laski, Neville 169
Leavis, F. R. 8, 42
Left Book Club (publisher) 41–2, 152
Leftwich, Joseph 50, 57, 59
Lehmann, John 8
Lehmann-Russbüldt, Otto 16, 98, 101, 234
Leslie, Henrietta 155, 219
Lessing, Theodor 62
Levy, Rudolf 103
Library of Contemporary Books (publisher) 151–2
Liepmann, Hans 62
Liliencron, Detlev 21
Lincolns Prager (publisher) 226, 227
Linke, Lilo 3
Little, Brown & Co. (publisher) 117
Lochner, Stefan 246
Loeb, Walter 237
Londonderry, Lord 101
Lorant, Stefan 6, 68
Lorre, Peter 95

Lothar, Hans 117, 118
Lothian, Lord 101
L'Ouverture, Toussaint 25
Löwenstein, Hubertus, Prinz zu 117
Lucas, Robert 196, 197, 198
Ludwig, Emil 32, 57, 188, 215

McCabe, Cameron *see* Borneman, Ernest
Macke, August 24
Macmillans (publisher) 226
MacNeice, Louis 9, 201
Magellan, Ferdinand 144
Mahler, Anna 174, 181, 250
Mahler, Gustav 250
Mairet, Philip 246
Mann, Heinrich 7, 15–17, 19–20, 39, 51,
    97, 136, 138, 181, 205
Mann, Klaus 47–8, 91, 130
Mann, Thomas 15–16, 28, 32, 39, 51, 60,
    109, 127, 193, 205, 207, 209, 215–16,
    256–7
Marc, Franz 24
Marchand, Captain 107–8
Marchwitza, Hans 8
Marcuse, Ludwig 48, 155
Maritain, Jacques 208
Marley, Lord 101
Marston, Jeffrey 167
Martin du Gard, Roger 34
Martin, Kingsley 101, 256
Marx, Karl 121–2
Masereel, Frans 31, 33, 56, 187, 214
Mehring, Walter 130, 181, 198
Meidner, Ludwig 20
Menne, Bernhard 234, 244–5
Menzel, Simon 155
Methuen (publisher) 110
Meusel, Alfred 235
Miall, Leonard 205
Mitchison, Naomi 41
Mohrenwitz, L. 240, 242
Molo, Walter von 256
Montaigne, Michel de 212
Mortimer, Raymond 42
Mosley, Sir Oswald 209
Mosse, Rudolf 89
Mozart, W. A. 44, 51
Mühlen, Hermynia zur 1–3

Mühsam, Erich 24
Muir, Edwin 39, 42, 67–8, 153
Muir, Willa 42, 153
Müller-Sturmheim, Emil 233
Murray, Gilbert 233
Musil, Robert 18, 158
Mussolini, Benito 139, 140

Neale, J. E. 55
Neukranz, Klaus 8
Neumann, Heinrich 71, 167, 253–4
Neumann, Heinz 73
Neumann, Michael 261
Neumann, Robert 27–30, 63–73, 151–9,
    247–54; studies of 1; arrival in London
    3, 27, 29–30, 37, 63, 107; and Otten 3–
    4; in Vienna 27–9, 72–3; work pub-
    lished in translation 64–8, 152–4, 158–
    9; film writing 69–71; and Herrmann-
    Neiße 69, 85; and refugees of 1938
    141; and German-speaking market 2,
    151–2, 154–5, 158, 261–2; in Sanary-
    sur-Mer 155; and PEN 155–8, 167,
    250–1, 260; naturalisation 167; rebuffs
    to 169–70; classified as 'enemy alien'
    173; internment 174–84; and exile
    theme 208–9; marriage 216; as writer
    in English 26, 217–23, 247, 260;
    political activity 248–53; and BBC
    251–3; death of son 253–4; and
    Gruppe 47 257; death 262; post-
    humous reputation 265
    see also Zweig, Stefan, and Neumann
Neumann, Samuel 28
Neumann, Stefanie 28, 30, 69, 71, 167,
    253
Nevinson, Henry W. 156
Newman, Edward 9
Nicholson and Watson (publisher) 227
Nietzsche, Friedrich 253
Nikolaus, Paul 21, 79
Nobel, Alfred 70

Olden, Ika 216
Olden, Rudolf 37, 42, 69, 73, 81, 98, 100,
    105, 109, 167, 216, 235
Orwell, George 10–11
Ossietzky, Carl von 16, 98, 100

Otten, Ellen (earlier Kroner) 26, 102–6, 108, 110–14, 165–6, 200, 240, 246–7, 262–3
Otten, Hugo Julian 25, 165–6
Otten, Karl 102–18, 239–47; and Neumann 3–4; in Germany 23–7; in Majorca 27, 102–4; arrival in London 3, 104–7; and BBC 107–9, 167, 197–202; expatriation 109; attempts to publish in English 111–18, 158, 166–7, 265; marriage 165; work for British Intelligence 170–2; on Nazism 233, 240–3; social circle 244; and Germany 246–7; blindness 247; anthologies 257; after the war 262–3; death 263
Otten, Mizi 165–6
Ottwalt, Ernst 7–8
Ould, Hermon 73, 85, 136, 156–7, 167, 207–8, 235, 237–8
Ovid 4
Owen, Wilfred 8
Oxford, Lady 101

Pabst, G. W. 25–6
Palmer, Lilli 68
Panter-Downes, Mollie 230
Parker, Gibson 205
Patsch, Sylvia 1
Paul, Cedar 42, 54–5, 242
Paul, Eden 42, 54–5, 242–3, 246
Pearson 266
Penguin Books (publisher) 41
Petersen, Jan 258
Pfemfert, Franz (publisher) 25, 112
Phaidon (publisher) 264
Pinkus, Klaus 76, 81
Pirandello, Luigi 31
Plath, Sylvia 266
Plievier, Theodor 8
Polgar, Alfred 5, 121, 181
Pollatschek, Walter 103
Postgate, Raymond 66
Prager, Eugen 226–7
Prater, Donald 55
Preiss, Hans 87, 131, 195
Pressburger, Emeric 264
Priestley, J. B. 10–11, 156, 208, 233, 248
Pritt, D. N. 65–6, 167, 169

Querido Verlag (publisher) 61, 67, 86, 90, 142

Rathenau, Walter 90, 120
Ravel, Maurice 32
Readers Union 42
Reed (publisher) 266
Reger, Erik 8
Reich-Ranicki, Marcel 257
Reichner, Herbert 46, 142–3, 148, 153
Reinhardt, Max 206
Remarque, Erich Maria 8, 39
Renn, Ludwig 16, 40, 164
Reprint Society (publisher) 42
Retzlaw, Karl see Gröhl (later Retzlaw), Karl
Rich & Cowan (publisher) 29, 65
Richardson, Dorothy 64, 68–9
Rickman, Alfred 171
Rilke, Rainer Maria 28, 186, 210
Rilla, Walter 197, 199–205, 244
Ringelnatz, Joachim 21–2, 82
Rolland, Romain 31–3, 35, 46, 53, 55–6, 58, 144–6, 148, 162
Romains, Jules 31, 34, 56
Rose, Professor William 131, 136–7, 149, 167
Rosenblüth, Anni 105, 106, 112
Roth, Joseph 14, 144–5, 162, 185
Rothermere, Lord 99
Rowse, A. L. 54–5
Russell, Archibald G. 149

Sahl, Hans 257–8
Savoir, Alfred 92
Schach, Max 69
Schaeffers, Willi 21
Scheffauer, Ethel Talbot 111–12
Schickele, René 145, 147
Schiele, Egon 24–5
Schmoller, Hans 264
Schnitzler, Arthur 18, 31–2
Schuschnigg, Kurt 140, 155
Schwarzschild, Leopold 41
Sebald, W. G. 266
Secker & Warburg (publisher) 117, 121
Secker, Martin 39
Seehof, Arthur 103

Segal, Arthur 103, 104, 244
Seger, Gerhart 101
Seghers, Anna 258
Serpell, Christopher 201
Servaes, Franz 33
Shakespeare, William 75–6
Shaw, George Bernard 10, 18, 92, 93–4, 123, 206, 259
Sherriff, R. C. 8
Sievers, Max 103–4, 112, 171
Simpson, Wallis (later Duchess of Windsor) 98
Sinclair, Upton 3
Smith, Rennie 169
Sondheimer, Alphonse 74–5, 79, 83, 84, 86–7, 127, 132, 190, 193–4
Spender, Stephen 9
Spiel, Hilde 3, 72, 219, 221–2, 255–6
Spoliansky, Mischa 199
Spring, Howard 10
Steed, Henry Wickham 101, 113, 162, 171, 233, 241
Sternfeld, Wilhelm 234
Sternheim, Carl 28
Stirner, Max 241
Stokes, Donald 201
Strauss, Richard 32, 49
Strindberg, August 18
Sutton, Eric 42–3
Swift, Jonathan 7
Swinnerton, Frank 219
Sykes, Claud 117, 166

Tawney, Richard 231
Taylor, A. J. P. 243
Tergit, Gabriele 238
Thames and Hudson (publisher) 264
Thieß, Frank 257
Thomas, Dylan 252, 266
Thompson, Dorothy 17
Thor, Jesse 179
Thorndike, Sybil 233
Toller, Ernst 3, 6–7, 12, 16–17, 37, 63, 71, 73, 81, 87, 101–2, 128, 130, 155, 162, 164–5
Toscanini, Arturo 32, 49
Toynbee, Philip 218–19
Tucholsky, Kurt 17, 198

Turteltaub, 'Mitzi' 179

Uhlman, Fred 97–8, 101
Unwin, Stanley (publisher) 40–1, 65–6, 174, 242

Valéry, Paul 32, 34, 187
Vansittart, Sir Robert 232–3, 237, 242, 244
Verhaeren, Emile 31
Verlaine, Paul 31–2
Vespucci, Amerigo 210
Viertel, Berthold 13, 81, 95, 127–8, 135, 234–5
Völker, Klaus 77–8
Voltaire 144

Wajda, Ladislaus 25–6
Walbrook, Anton (Adolf Wohlbrück) 95, 197
Walden, Herwarth 73
Walpole, Hugh 58
Walter, Bruno 32, 49, 205–6
Walter, Hans–Albert 1, 257
Warburg, Fredric 40, 117–18
Wassermann, Jakob 32
Wedekind, Frank 198
Weidenfeld & Nicolson (publisher) 264
Weill, Kurt 9
Weismann, Gert 224
Weller, Curt, Weller Verlag (publisher) 261
Wells, H. G. 10, 32, 85, 136, 155–6, 159, 174, 184, 226, 248
Werfel, Franz 32, 44, 72, 135, 149, 157, 215
Wesemann, Hans 62
West, Rebecca 208
Wheen, A. W. 43
Wilder, Thornton 208
Williams-Ellis, Amabel 101
Wimborn, Lady 226
Winternitz, Friderike von 32–5, 45–6, 53, 55–6, 144, 189, 209–15
Wittkowski, Victor 213
Wodehouse, P. G. 10
Wolf, Friedrich 62, 155
Wolfe, Humbert 173

Wolfenstein, Alfred 80
Wolfsohn, Hans 105, 106
Wolpe, Berthold 264
Woodman, Dorothy 66
Woolf, Virginia 10, 208
Wurm, Mathilde 62

Yeats, W. B. 31

Zaharoff, Sir Basil 29, 64–5, 151, 173
Zarek, Otto 233
Zech, Paul 80, 128, 136, 190, 210
Zille, Heinrich 22, 192
Zimmering, Max 258
Zsolnay, Paul (publisher) 29, 151–2
Zuckmayer, Carl 72
Zweig, Alfred 150
Zweig, Arnold 19–20, 39–40, 216, 258
Zweig, Stefan 31–5, 43–60, 142–51, 184–
9, 208–16; literary reputation 2, 31,
39, 44–5, 52; arrival in London 3, 32,
37, 43; and Neumann 4, 30, 58, 63, 67,
69, 70, 153–4, 174, 248; marriage to
Friderike 32; in Austria 31–2, 35; on
Nazism 33, 47–8; changing views on

London and England 34, 44, 46, 53,
55, 57, 76, 98, 148, 161; voluntary
exile 43–4; and German-speaking
market 46, 60, 72, 147–8; and Richard
Strauss 49–51; work published in
translation 54–5, 207, 242; and
English language 56–8, 216; and
Jewishness 58–60, 186; francophilia
31, 33–4, 89; productiveness 142–3;
and PEN 143; in Brazil 143, 188–9,
208–9, 211–12; separation from wife
144; growing depression and fear 145,
149, 170, 188–9, 209, 211–12, 215;
stateless 150; naturalisation 150, 184,
190; and Roth 162; leaves London for
Bath 162–3, 186–7, 190; classified as
'enemy alien' 173; and death of Freud
185; quotes Rilke 186, 210; and Kerr
206; autobiography 208, 210, 213–14;
suicide 215–16; and native language
213, 216; and Free German League of
Culture 234; posthumous reputation
264–6
see also Herrmann-Neiße, Max, and
Zweig

AEA-5565